INTRO

MASSEY TEXTS

An imprint of Massey University Press
First published in 2014 by the New Zealand Journalists Training Organisation
This revised edition published in 2018 by Massey University Press

Massey University Press, Private Bag 102904, North Shore Mail Centre
Auckland 0745, New Zealand
www.masseypress.ac.nz

Design by Sarah Elworthy
Cover photographs: Stuff

A catalogue record for this book is available from the National Library of New Zealand

Printed and bound in China by 1010 Printing International Limited

ISBN: 978-0-9941473-1-8

Edited by Grant Hannis

INTRO

A PRACTICAL GUIDE TO JOURNALISM
IN AOTEAROA NEW ZEALAND

MASSEY TEXTS

EXERCISES

There are practical exercises with model answers for all the chapters in this book. These exercises can be found online at www.jeanz.org.nz

"Journalism is more than a job – it's a lifestyle. You get to meet the most amazing people and do just about anything you want through the contacts you make. It's a huge, changing, exciting environment to live in. I often think how incredible it is that I get paid every week for doing something so cool."

DEBBIE GREGORY
NEW ZEALAND JOURNALIST

Contents

Introduction

We live in revolutionary times.

The world of communication has undergone numerous revolutions in the past. Perhaps the first were the development of drawing and speech, although exactly when these occurred is unknown. The next was the invention of writing, which seems to have occurred about 5000 years ago. The next was the development of printing, which occurred in Europe in the 15th century, although printing had been invented in Asia long before that.

As technology developed, so the revolutions in communication accelerated. The 19th century saw the development of the telegraph and the industrialisation of printing. The 20th century saw radio and television. The most recent revolution – the one we're living through now – is the digital one. This revolution has presented exciting new opportunities for journalists in finding and telling news. But it has also thrown down the gauntlet to the conventional business model for journalism by eroding its traditional markets, making it all the more important that journalists become multimedia experts.

This book reflects this revolution. It includes chapters on the new digital world, including web-based reporting, digital photography and using social media. But there is also much in this book about the fundamentals of journalism, including news writing, newsgathering and covering specialist rounds. Radio and television journalism are also discussed. All these topics remain as vital as ever. As fake news floods the internet, the basic journalism skills practised by professional, well-trained journalists are more valuable than ever.

The book also reflects the unique place of Māori in Aotearoa New Zealand and the country's multicultural society, with chapters on reporting Māori affairs and reporting on diversity.

For all of the chapters there are exercises with model answers available online. Go to www.jeanz.org.nz

Journalism education is a partnership between educators and practitioners. That is why this book contains chapters written by educators and journalists, and why the chapters include contributions from working journalists.

As the editor of this book, I am profoundly grateful to all the educators and journalists who contributed to *Intro*. I am also grateful to Massey University Press for publishing this new edition.

As you embark on your career in journalism, I invite you to re-read the quote from Debbie Gregory at the front of this book. Journalism is a wonderful career. Enjoy it!

Grant Hannis
Editor

PART A

Finding the news

1

Understanding journalism

First things first

Grant Hannis, Massey University; Allan Lee, AUT University; Charles Riddle, Waikato Institute of Technology; Catherine Strong, Massey University; Greg Treadwell, AUT University

Journalism is an exciting, challenging, busy and rewarding career. As a journalist, you will get the opportunity to inform, influence and entertain your audience. You may write for a news website or local community newspaper, you may anchor the national television news, you may be the court reporter, or you may manage a chain of newspapers. Whatever your role, you will meet people, learn about their lives, and interpret their world for your audience. You may even provoke radical change.

This book considers the main skills that the novice journalist needs to know. But before we get into the details, we need to understand the bigger picture. In this chapter we'll discuss the history of journalism in New Zealand, how modern newsrooms operate, the challenges the industry faces and its likely future.

> We can define journalism as words and/or images on matters of current interest, published for a wide audience.

The history of journalism in New Zealand

Today's media scene is a far cry from the time when there were only two television stations producing New Zealand news, a handful of radio stations, and no internet news. People mostly had to rely on daily newspapers to find out what was going on in their community.

The desire to learn the news has always been in our blood. In the pre-colonial period Māori would have relied on oral news, as preliterate societies everywhere did. The early New Zealand colonists were very keen to have newspapers. So keen, in fact, that the first issue of the first paper, *The New Zealand Gazette,* was actually published in London in 1839. Issue number 2 was printed by Samuel Revans in Wellington's Hutt Valley in 1840 (Scholefield, 1958).

Also in 1840, Barzillai Quaife published the *New Zealand Advertiser and Bay of Islands Gazette* in Kororāreka (later renamed Russell). The paper was needed by Governor Hobson to make official decrees, but when Quaife questioned the government policy of undertaking inquiries before Māori land could be sold to settlers, Hobson closed the paper down. Later papers met a similar fate. The first paper to have a stable run was the *Southern Cross*, which began publishing in Auckland in 1843. It was followed by *The New Zealander* in 1845. *The New Zealander* eventually closed. *The New Zealand Herald*, started in 1863 by W.C. Wilson, was far more successful. The *Southern Cross*, run by A.G. Horton, merged with the *Herald* in 1876. The *Herald* was a morning paper, and an evening competitor, the *Auckland Star*, commenced publication in 1870 (Hastings, 2013).

The colonial government also began publishing in Māori, including *Te Karere o Nui Tireni* ("The Messenger of New Zealand"). With the outbreak of the colonial wars, Māori began publishing their own papers, including Waikato's *Te Hokioi E rere atu-na* ("The warbird soaring above").

Other papers sprang up around the country, including Wellington's *Evening Post* (1865), and the country's first daily newspaper and first to be produced using industrial-age printing technology, the *Otago Daily Times* (1861). *The Press* in Christchurch also began in 1861. New Zealand's oldest surviving paper, the *Wanganui Chronicle*, commenced publication in 1856.

One of the very few dailies established in the 20th century was *The Dominion*, first published in Wellington in 1907, the same year New Zealand became a dominion. Much later, the paper became part of the stable of newspapers owned by INL, which also included *The Evening Post*, Christchurch's *The Press*, the *Sunday Star-Times* and the *Nelson Mail*. INL sold its publishing assets to Australian company Fairfax in 2003. Fairfax's New Zealand operations are now called Stuff.

The other major newspaper chain to emerge and survive was Wilson and Horton, which owned *The New Zealand Herald*, and later bought the *Bay of Plenty Times* and the *Wanganui Chronicle*. Wilson and Horton was eventually sold to Australian company APN. In 2016, the New Zealand operations were spun off and floated on the New Zealand sharemarket as NZME.

Evening papers slowly began to lose popularity to television. This resulted, for instance, in the closure of the *Auckland Star,* and the 2002 merger of *The Evening Post* with *The Dominion* to become *The Dominion Post*.

Both Stuff and NZME supply news copy online, via such sites as www.stuff.co.nz and www.nzherald.co.nz. Each company also shares copy between its stable of newspapers, in a form of internal news agencies.

Sunday papers emerged in the 1960s, with a range publishing today, including the

Journalists have freed the wrongly convicted, helped bring the guilty to justice and even helped bring down a corrupt US president. Those stories will be found elsewhere in this book.

New Zealand journalists are among the most free in the world.

Sunday Star-Times and the *Herald on Sunday*. Along with specialist business newspaper *National Business Review*, the "Sundays" are the country's only national newspapers.

Magazines have also proven popular in New Zealand. The *New Zealand Woman's Weekly* began publishing in 1932, and the *New Zealand Listener* in 1939. *Metro* was launched in 1981, and its sister publication, *North & South*, in 1986. There are now a host of specialist magazines for myriad tastes.

Radio broadcasting began in New Zealand in the 1920s, but for many years was state-owned. Setting up a radio station in New Zealand was also tightly controlled, leading to pirate Auckland radio station Radio Hauraki broadcasting in the 1960s. Radio New Zealand (now known as RNZ) was established as an independent government-owned agency with its own news service in 1975 (Day, 2000).

Gradually controls were relaxed, and RNZ's commercial stations were sold to the private sector. There is now a proliferation of private stations, including the Newstalk ZB and Radio Live stations. There has also been enormous growth in the number of Māori radio stations.

Television broadcasting started in New Zealand in 1960. For many years, New Zealand was serviced by one television network, the government-owned New Zealand Broadcasting Corporation (NZBC). The NZBC covered both radio and television, and NZBC journalists prepared news reports for both media. In 1975, the government split NZBC into three organisations: RNZ, Television One and Channel 2.

The two television stations originally both ran news programmes, but this eventually ended. In the mid-1980s, the government opened up the television market, initially with the arrival of TV3 (whose news service is now called Newshub), and latterly with various regional stations and pay TV stations such as Sky. Three competing news

Some newspapers continue to be owned independently, such as the *Otago Daily Times* and the *Gisborne Herald.*

For details on the history and development of Māori radio broadcasting in New Zealand go to www.irirangi.net

RICK NEVILLE

Rick is editorial director of the Newspaper Publishers' Association, which represents the country's newspapers. He has had a 45-year career in newspaper and magazine publishing, including editorships of daily newspapers and senior roles at APN (now NZME) and INL (now Stuff). He says the role of journalism is "to tell people the truth of what's going on around them, so they know, and understand, what's happening and how it might affect them".

He is proud that "New Zealand journalism has largely held to principles of truth and independence. Our media outlets are mostly free from partisan influences, which has meant journalists have been able to go about their work unconstrained by the political or business interests of their owners."

There are some elements of New Zealand journalism he is uncomfortable with. One is "an increasing 'pack attack' approach evidenced by the new shock-jock style of some television political reporters. They appear to think they are bigger than the story." He also says "quite a lot of our sports journalism is still lifeless and dull".

He describes the future of journalism as "clouded, because of the fragmentation of media outlets caused by the internet and the inability of the new media to generate profits". At the moment, he says, "most serious journalism in this country is written by journalists on newspapers and magazines, which are under strong attack from the new media, including publishers' own websites. Paywalls, in whatever form, cannot come quick enough."

systems can now be found on Television One, Prime and Newshub. There has also been a Māori presence on television, especially with the news programme *Te Karere*. The Māori Television station began broadcasting in 2004. There are also now a range of online-only news outlets, like newsroom.co.nz and scoop.co.nz.

New Zealand journalists have a huge advantage over journalists in many other countries in the freedom to report and write the news. New Zealand media is one of the most free in the world – rating in the top 20 (Reporters Without Borders, 2017). Even journalism students have the freedom to cover local government proceedings, court cases, and political media conferences.

The newsroom

The pressure of unrelenting deadlines means life in the modern newsroom is never dull. In fact, most newsrooms work at only two speeds: busy and feverish. Journalists and editors live by the clock. There are the continuous deadlines of the news websites, the hourly deadlines of radio news, the daily deadlines of the newspapers and main TV news. Newsrooms can be intimidating to young recruits who are often expected to write stories without much supervision or feedback.

Journalists' roles are broadly similar across print, broadcast and online newsrooms, yet their job descriptions and job titles differ between the platforms. In a print newsroom like *The Dominion Post* in Wellington, reporters and photographers work under the direction of editors who assign them to stories and who make the tough calls about story ranking and placement. While the overall boss at a newspaper is called *the* editor, there are other editors, too, including the business editor, the sports editor and the features editor.

Broadcast newsrooms are no less hectic. Radio journalists at news-based stations RNZ National, Newstalk ZB and Radio Live focus on gathering audio grabs from newsmakers for the next bulletin, never more than 30 minutes away at peak times. A senior staffer known as the news director or chief reporter assigns stories, helps with scripts and organises news bulletins. Another ranks stories and compiles the final bulletin. Radio reporters are either out at news events, interviewing sources over the phone, or writing and editing stories. Reporters and on-air producers often work together to contact and secure interviews with newsmakers.

More than any other platform, television news production is all about teamwork. Stories get to air thanks to a partnership between the reporter, the camera operator, and the video editor. Senior newsroom staff at TVNZ, Newshub, Prime and Māori Television have a variety of titles, including news producers (mid-range journalists who don't appear on camera but help the reporting team to research, write and package a story), assignment editors (senior journalists who decide what stories are covered and direct reporters and technical staff) and executive editors (who take overall responsibility for news and current affairs programmes).

Television and print newsrooms have always run like factory assembly lines where journalists work towards a daily deadline, be it the evening news bulletin or the 11pm press run. At key stages in the production cycle, senior editors hold news conferences to direct reporting resources to the top stories and to determine what goes on the front page or leads the bulletin.

Once, all journalists worked in single-platform newsrooms, but most news organisations today operate across two or three platforms in what are known as converged or digital newsrooms. It's called converged journalism because all the old media technologies – written words, photography, audio and video – have converged on internet news sites. Although a newspaper is very different from a TV news show, a newspaper's website is very similar to a TV news show's website.

In learning multi-platform storytelling skills, journalists have had to adapt to new technologies, new audiences, new demands from those audiences, and a transformation in the routines and culture of their workplaces. Radio stations like RNZ may include visual items that are broadcast online and even on pay TV. A Stuff reporter at a regional newspaper can expect in one shift to be filing several text stories, still photographs, a blog, slideshows, audio, video and possibly a piece to camera as she meets the needs of the Stuff website, its mobile app and one or more newspaper titles. Similarly, a Newshub reporter is no longer filing just for broadcast: she too is filing text, still images and perhaps a blog post for newshub. co.nz and mobile platforms. Online-only news organisations like scoop.co.nz, with

Producing quality journalism to deadline is no solo effort. It requires high levels of teamwork coupled with clear lines of responsibility and authority.

no antecedents in traditional media, have always been multimedia publishers.

There is no single definition or model for convergence in the newsroom, but media companies worldwide have opted for what Deuze has called "at least some form of cross-media cooperation or synergy between formerly separated staffers, newsrooms and departments" (Deuze, 2008, p. 8). In practice, digital newsrooms are located somewhere on a continuum: at one end is minimal convergence with little more than cross-promotion happening between, say, a newspaper and its website; the mid-point is regular content sharing between platforms; while complete convergence is where editors routinely use the strengths of each platform to best tell each story. Convergence has also involved developing cross-media cooperation.

Physically, newsrooms have tended to be open-plan offices with reporters at one end and editors at the other. The overall look is slightly dishevelled, with newspapers, media releases and reports strewn everywhere. Journalists are not known for being tidy. There is a constant hum of activity and ringing of phones. In larger newsrooms, reporters are seated within departments such as general news, sports and business. The move to multi-platform publishing has brought with it new ideas on newsroom layout, wth one recent trend being work stations lined up like spokes on a wheel leading out from the central editors' hub. The theory is this layout improves communication between team members.

One of the spokes is the online team. Deuze says an ongoing debate since news websites were introduced in the 1990s has been "whether to integrate the online journalists into the main radio, television or print newsroom, or to set up separate office space for them" (Deuze, 2008, p. 13). In New Zealand, online teams were initially set up as separate operations, but the model now has them integrated into the heart of the main newsroom. A trend some digital newsroom researchers are reporting is a gradual flattening of strict hierarchies and a devolution of decision-making to mid-level editors (Robinson, 2011).

Journalism is generally a competitive industry, with each news outlet and each journalist striving to be the first with the news and to break big stories. But there is also a cooperative aspect to journalism. Within a newsroom, journalists may work together on big stories, especially stories across different media. News outlets may also cooperate, such as when journalists from different organisations worked together on the Panama Papers, a vast cache of leaked documents detailing global tax avoidance (Obermaier & Obermayer, 2017).

Journalists may also act collectively on points of principle. For instance, accounting firm EY used to sponsor business journalism awards in New Zealand, but in 2017 disqualified an article that criticised one of EY's clients. Believing EY's actions were prompted by a conflict of interest, other journalism organisations withdrew their entries and declined to attend the awards dinner. EY had no option but to abandon the awards, which were replaced by new business journalism awards with no commercial sponsorship (Smellie, 2017; Hawkins, 2017).

Converged journalism

Today's journalism means your stories have a potentially huge audience, right from

There used to be teams of sub-editors in newsrooms, who would check reporters' articles for grammar, structure, etc. prior to publication. But these days reporters are increasingly expected to sub their own work. This reduces costs and means material can be quickly uploaded. For details on grammar and structuring news stories, see Chapter 14 and Appendix 1.

Journalists haven't always backed each other. In 1982, then Prime Minister Rob Muldoon, unhappy about journalist Tom Scott's criticisms of him, made Scott leave a Beehive media conference. The other journalists present did nothing (Te Ara, 2017).

PAUL THOMPSON

Paul is the chief executive of RNZ. He has been a journalist since he was 17.

"Journalism improves people's lives by making them think and giving them pleasure and knowledge," he says. "It also has a powerful positive effect on wider society. People of influence and organisations behave better, and make better decisions, when they are under independent – and at times irreverent – scrutiny."

He is most proud of journalism's scoops, which are when a journalistic investigation breaks a story. "Every journalist feels immense pride when they realise that their endeavour has revealed information that would otherwise have remained hidden."

One thing that disappoints him in journalism is "inaccuracies". He is also concerned with the way journalists sometimes use their power. "The media wield immense power that, if misused, has a dramatic effect on individuals."

He says the future of journalism is "bright but it will be different. The advertising subsidy that has nourished newsrooms in commercial media for decades is weakening, so we have to look at ways to be leaner, more efficient and intensely focused on the content that is truly valued by audiences."

the start of your career. Even if you produce stories for a tiny community newspaper with a small circulation, it is probably also loaded online and viewed throughout the world. Every story you produce may have an impact much wider than what you originally intended.

Your audience may be reading, viewing or listening to your story. And they may be doing this on their smartphone, home computer, a standard newspaper, or whatever. Converged journalism means the journalist needs to produce stories for all of these media. This requires the ability to visualise a story, and also to know the sound opportunities to make it into an audio story.

On top of this, you have direct contact with your audience in the form of online comments, internet polls, tweet conversations, etc. Being a journalist is now a two-way conversation with your readers/listeners/viewers. Previously, journalists didn't really know what their readers thought about a topic or the way a story was written unless they received a letter to the editor. Today's massive (and sometimes frank) audience feedback can be daunting, but it makes for better reporting to know immediately if something is wrong or right.

Being a journalist in the era of new media is breaking new ground. Many older journalists have not dealt with multi-platform reporting nor with social media interaction with their audience. This is unique to 21st-century journalism. Students who gain new technology skills are empowered for a solid career in the future. They have the flexibility to shift in whatever direction the media happens to go. A survey

Even if you plan to concentrate on online video or audio stories, these will be uploaded online with text. That means you'll still need strong grammar skills.

Female, white, young and paid the average

New Zealand newsrooms were once a male domain, but that has changed. A 2013 survey of the full-time journalism workforce by Massey University and Waikato University found women comprised 57 per cent of newsroom staff. By contrast, across all New Zealand industries, women comprised 41 per cent of the full-time workforce (Hannis, Hollings, Pajo & Lealand, 2014).

And it was a disproportionately white workforce. A hefty 83 per cent of the journalism workforce was New Zealand European, 5 per cent Māori, 2 per cent Pasifika and 1 per cent Asian. Across the New Zealand population generally it was a different story, with New Zealand Europeans comprising 74 per cent of the population, Māori 15 per cent, Pasifika 7 per cent and Asians 12 per cent.

And it was a young workforce. A third of the journalism workforce was aged 30 years or younger, and almost 60 per cent of the journalism workforce was aged 40 years or younger. Across the entire New Zealand full-time workforce, only about 25 per cent of workers were aged 30 years or younger and about 45 per cent aged 40 years or younger.

The journalists' average annual before-tax income was estimated at $60,000. This was basically the same as the average income of $59,000 for the entire full-time workforce. Nearly 60 per cent of journalists earned the average or less.

All figures are from Hannis, Hollings, Pajo and Lealand (2014).

Crowdsourcing is when a news outlet makes a database available online and asks the online community to trawl through the material for newsworthy items. The news outlet then publishes the results.

of working journalists who had learned converged skills said they had a greater confidence in their future career (Strong, 2008). They felt that multimedia skills gave them another dimension to their employability. Sure, it's hard work, with continuous deadlines and myriad skills required, but it's exciting and new.

In addition to being posted on your own news organisation's website, your online stories can easily be passed around through social media. An example of the impact was the prolific tweeter Sultan Al-Qassemi during the Middle East democratic uprisings, called the Arab Spring. @SultanAlQassemi was considered one of the most reliable sources of news on the Arab Spring (Fastenberg, 2011), and yet he wasn't a journalist, and didn't originate any news stories. He simply retweeted breaking news stories. Al-Qassemi monitored dozens of television, radio and online news programmes during the time of the uprising, both in English and in Arabic (Al-Meiri, 2011). He quickly learned which ones were accurate and which ones weren't. He would retweet the most accurate accounts, giving credit to the originating news agency, such as Al-Arabiya or Reuters. Other news media learned to depend on him.

In essence, Al-Qassemi took over the role of the editor or programme producer in a large newsroom. He determined the news value and validity of the information, then retweeted it to his 200,000 followers, who in turn retweeted to all their followers. He told followers that they helped save people's lives with the retweets of accurate Arab Spring information (Al-Meiri, 2011). Protesters in Egypt told him that his accurate and up-to-the-minute tweets helped them avoid certain streets when there were bloody attacks occurring.

The rapid dissemination through social media can be a problem, especially when

ACCURACY

In journalism, you are expected to be as accurate as possible, often under tight time constraints. If you get it wrong, you and/or your publication can look foolish, be forced to publicly apologise, be taken to a complaints body or even sued.

We all make mistakes, so if you do make the occasional error, most editors will understand. But if you make persistent or negligent errors, you could be dismissed. So before sending any story to your editor or chief reporter, use the following checklist to ensure your story is as accurate as possible.

Check your facts: Visualise the story in your mind. A car accident 10 kilometres south of Wellington would be somewhere in Cook Strait. Perhaps the factual errors aren't yours – they're in the source material you are using. Never take anything at face value.

Check names: Check people's names, even common ones. "McLean" can also be spelt Maclean, MacLean, Mclean, McLain, etc. A name like John could be spelled without the "h". Make sure you've spelt the name correctly every time it appears in the story.

Check for assumptions: Have you filled any gaps in the story with what you suspect or imagine happened, rather than finding out what did happen?

Check for balance: Have you run critical comments past the person/organisation being criticised? You'll be surprised at how this will reveal mistakes.

Check your sources: Can statements made in the story be attributed to reliable sources? Wherever possible, speak directly to the people you're writing about. Don't rely on second-hand information.

Don't misquote: Have you correctly transcribed the quotes in your story from your notes or recording?

Don't editorialise: Stick to reporting the news, don't comment on it in your stories. A newspaper will do that separately in its leader on the op-ed (opinion-editorial) pages.

Check your spelling and grammar: If you don't know how to spell a word, check. We all read what we think we've written rather than what is actually written, so use any electronic grammar and spelling checker on your computer – it'll often pick up something.

Check the house style: Does your story conform to your publication's house style? These kinds of errors are bound to annoy the subbies (sub-editors), as it gives them extra, needless work to do fixing your copy.

Always make sure you have enough time to properly check your story after you have written it. If you feel unhappy about any aspect of a story, discuss it with your chief reporter or editor.

Work hard to make your news reports as accurate and well written as possible. You'll soon develop a reputation in the newsroom as a reliable journalist who produces clean copy. Not a bad reputation to have!

you make a mistake. An example was the reporter on a small US newspaper who reported that the 2013 Seddon earthquakes that hit Wellington had occurred in Australia. Although the newspaper had a circulation of only about 22,000 among small suburbs in Nevada, the story was seen by many New Zealanders when it was passed around via social media. Within a few hours the newspaper received almost 500 complaining comments. The reporter had to quickly post an apology (Ukinski, 2013). So check your facts!

A changing business

Among the most fundamental issues journalism faces is the increasing failure of the news business model that generated large profits for media companies through much of the 20th century. Essentially, both advertisers and readers/viewers are heading online where the action is, leaving traditional media behind. With a consequent decline in advertising revenue, the number of journalists employed by traditional news organisations is shrinking significantly. This relatively sudden decline in the fortunes of these old media markets across the world, after decades of strong growth, is threatening democratically significant journalism (Ellis, 2010). While today large newspapers remain profitable – and some very profitable indeed – the ongoing restructuring of the newsroom in response to the related pressures of the commercial bottom-line and technological change is disrupting established professional practice in significant ways.

In June 2013, shockwaves went through global media when, without warning, one of the largest newspapers in the United States, *The Chicago Sun-News*, fired its entire photographic staff. The newspaper, editorial managers announced, would now rely on its reporters to also take pictures and footage for its digitally savvy audience who were increasingly clamouring for video stories. Pulitzer-winning photojournalist John H. White, who had worked there for three decades, told Radio New Zealand it was like cutting the eyes from the body of journalism: "One cannot go out there and capture the intimacy of life with a snapshot" (White, 2013).

But in spite of the changing fortunes of the news business and regular academic discourse about the death of newspapers, newspaper editors in New Zealand – and elsewhere – argue they will be around for a long time yet.

Public faith in the news media

In the United Kingdom, the public went through an apparent crisis of trust with journalism. Lord Justice Leveson was appointed in 2011 to head a powerful inquiry into the culture, ethics and practice of the British press, and to examine, along the way, the extent of the apparent cosiness in its relationship with the police and politicians (Leveson, 2012).

The Leveson inquiry was sparked by public revulsion that reporters from British tabloid newspaper the *News of the World* had hacked into the mobile phone messages of murder victim Milly Dowler. This and similar outrages led to criminal charges and the newspaper closed ignominiously in July 2011.

While championing the role of the press in democracies, Lord Justice Leveson made two things clear – there was a need for the British press to clean up its act, and there was a need for stronger regulation to help it do that.

In New Zealand the Law Commission, an independent government agency, has undertaken its own inquiry into the state of the news media (Law Commission, 2013). The review was not sparked by concerns over the quality of New Zealand journalism. Indeed, a recent survey of New Zealanders found nearly three-quarters said the news media mostly or always provides adequate coverage of the most important issues of the day (Law Commission, 2012). Instead, the commission's review was sparked by

BERNADETTE COURTNEY

Bernadette is the editor-in-chief of *The Dominion Post* newspaper in Wellington. She has worked in print journalism for 30 years, both in New Zealand and Britain.

She sees the role of journalism as "independently informing, sparking debate and holding organisations and people to account … Being relevant and connected to people and their lives is more important than ever, given the phenomenal amount of noise created by social media and how connected people are now through new technology. Journalism in its truest form is about investing in great storytelling with integrity."

She proudly proclaims that Kiwi journalists "are among the best in the world. Journalists here have a strong connection to their communities and readers and operate with absolute integrity and professionalism."

As to the journalistic scandals, like those that engulfed the *News of the World,* she says: "I am disappointed that many great journalists and their reputations have been tarnished by the illegal activities of a few. Only a small number of journalists operate with no personal moral compass, but their activities smear the good name of journalism."

She is optimistic about journalism's future. "More than ever people are connected, via smartphones and computers. These people – our readers – might be on the move but they now have 24/7 access to information, which means they are even more hungry for news and information, which can only be good for journalism.

"It means we need to be more relevant to their lives than ever, and move with them in the types of content we offer them. There will always be journalism, but the change will be in how readers access it. I am firmly of the view that good newspapers that have a connection with their community will survive, only the bad ones won't.

"I feel privileged to be an editor in this great period of change. The industry is changing with speed and no one has a crystal ball to predict what it will look like, but isn't that what excites us all?"

Advice from journalism graduates

The Massey Journalism School celebrated its 50th anniversary in 2016. The photo opposite shows two graduates from 1966 cutting the celebratory cake with two graduates from 2016. As part of the programme of events, the school's graduates were surveyed (Hannis, 2017). One of the questions was what advice they'd offer journalism students.

Most graduates were positive about the industry. "Go for it!" one exclaimed. Another said the job "offers great opportunities and a lifelong career". Some respondents gave specific advice. "Specialise – for example, technology or business offers better long-term career opportunities." Another said, "Work really hard to get an awesome portfolio, make connections with people in class and in the industry." Other advice included: "Be curious and seek hands-on experience." "Know spelling and grammar, develop fortitude, be curious and never give up." Several advised young people to embrace multimedia. "Acquire as many skills as you can – video, digital, etc.," said one. "Train in social media!!" said another. "It's where all the jobs seem to be developing. Make sure you're capable of shooting and editing short-form videos, even if you're wanting to work in print." Students were advised to be flexible. "Be not just willing, but enthusiastic, about relocating to chase employment, including to regional areas." Some respondents highlighted that journalism teaches

From left: Robin Ormerod, Fran Wilde, Julie Iles and Miri Schroeter.

skills helpful for those who wish to move into other careers. "Great job, but doesn't pay very well. Have a go before going into PR."

However, some respondents were more ambivalent or even negative in their comments. "You realise you will struggle financially for the rest of your life, don't you? But you'll have a great career, meet extraordinary people and mostly love it," said one. Another commented: "It's a poorly paid cynical industry, becoming much less about the story and much more about the bottom dollar."

the rise of the digital media world. The commission wanted to see if new media was adequately covered by the authorities that at the time oversaw standards in the news media: the Press Council (now the Media Council), the Broadcasting Standards Authority and the Online Media Standards Authority. The Law Commission concluded there were gaps in the current system and recommended a single news media standards authority, which would absorb the existing watchdogs. The government decided no changes should be made to the current regime, however ("Nats reject need," 2013).

Another recent challenge is the rise of what's called fake news. With news so easily available online it is quite easy for unscrupulous non-journalists to peddle fabricated news online. Fake news can be reposted or retweeted far faster than journalists or others can publish information setting the record straight. It is incumbent on journalists and others to keep a sceptical eye on the information published online (Brown, 2017). And it is all too easy for those with an agenda to discredit journalists to use epithets like "fake news" in an attempt to undermine the legitimate news media.

The future

Few industries have been altered by the internet so quickly and profoundly as journalism. The current model of journalism that served so well since the late 19th

THE INDUSTRY'S ADVICE TO NOVICE JOURNALISTS

Here's what our industry experts say you need to do to have a great career in journalism.

"Learn as many different skills as you can, work harder than your colleagues, and prove you're better than the rest," **Rick Neville** says.

"We're in a transitional phase between old media and new – no one's quite sure where it will go.

"The only thing certain is that the number of media positions will decrease, and competition for good journalism jobs will increase.

"As quickly as possible, you want to get yourself into a position where you're attractive to a range of potential employers.

"If you're really keen on journalism, and believe you'll be good, then ignore all the doomsayers and go for it. Journalism's a great career – far more interesting than most occupations.

"It will give you opportunities to travel to amazing places, meet all sorts of people, and gain a deep understanding of how societies work. And writing – along with subbing and taking photos – isn't really work. It's therapy. But if it's quick and big money you're after, then try something else."

Bernadette Courtney agrees you need to keep learning on the job.

"Enter the industry with an openness to change and an appetite to learn new skills as you go.

"To be good you need to have passion – a passion for people, a passion for stories and a passion for getting those stories to readers.

"Be inquisitive and don't rely on handouts. Get in there boots-and-all and challenge. Journalism is an amazing career. It brings you into contact with all sorts of people and aspects of life."

Paul Thompson says you should "work hard on developing your core skills – news judgement, emotional intelligence, accurate note-taking, clear and active writing, cultivating sources and analytical thinking.

"These are rare and highly prized qualities that will be a foundation for a successful career and life.

"Journalists who lack expertise, intellect and enterprise are going to struggle. Those who have those qualities will thrive and will have a large degree of control over their working lives."

century is struggling to meet the challenge of the internet. The huge advertising revenue newspapers earned from classified advertising has melted away as people advertise online. Also, in the enthusiasm to go online, many news outlets made their news content available free of charge, a decision they now rue.

Various experiments to charge readers for online news content have been tried, but it is unclear to what extent a surge in "paywalls" will generate a viable solution for the wider news industry. Currently seen as having the most potential, it seems, is the idea of a metered paywall system under which website readers can access a number of stories of their choice before they start paying for their news (Indvik, 2013).

British magazine *The Economist* has said the biggest shift in journalism in recent years is that journalists now have to share the stage with others. "Ordinary people are playing a more active role in the news system, along with a host of technology firms, news start-ups and not-for-profit groups. Social media are certainly not a fad, and their impact is only just beginning to be felt" ("Coming full circle," 2011). Journalists generally have welcomed social media, even if it has meant that more than ever they no longer have an exclusive access to the news.

But there is plenty that only journalists can do. They are the ones trained in media law, shorthand, news reporting, court reporting, etc. They are independent of the events they cover (unlike, say, protesters who post video of their activities online). They filter the vast amount of news and other content, producing a digestible package for their audience. Indeed, when they want the real story, your average consumer seeks out reputable, mainstream news outlets.

Portuguese multimedia content producer Alexandre Gamela says the modern journalist faces 10 changes to their job description (Gamela, 2008). Today's journalist should expect to work:

- for different media platforms (eg, print and online, broadcast and online)
- as their own editor in order to meet immediate deadlines
- on their personal brand by developing blogs, slideshows, podcasts, etc.
- on their networks of sources, both online and off
- on developing skills as a designer and producer of video, audio and photography
- on databases, as an information archaeologist
- as a moderator filtering the dialogue between journalists and audience
- as an authenticator verifying and validating "facts" and "truths" bandied about freely by others
- as a traffic cop guiding people in the search for information, and
- as a DJ remixing the news flow.

Gamela's list is daunting, but indicates a career filled with challenges and opportunities. Many still see journalists primarily as writers. Writing will always remain as the solid core of the craft – only now journalists are expected to produce illustrated content across media platforms, in short time spans, while blogging the bits that are of personal interest, all the time sending tweets.

Among all this change, one element has remained constant – few journalists have ever been sure what their working day will hold in store. And that's where the fun lies.

Further reading

Cartwright, M. (2009). *Teeline gold standard for journalists*. Harlow: Heinemann. New Zealand journalists are often expected to know shorthand. Shorthand requires its own textbook, such as this one.

Hastings, D. (2013). *Extra! Extra! How the people made the news*. Auckland: Auckland University Press. The fascinating story of Auckland's newspaper wars in the 19th century.

http://paperspast.natlib.govt.nz A superb digital archive of New Zealand newspapers from the 19th and 20th centuries.

Hollings, J. (Ed.) (2017). *A moral truth: 150 years of investigative journalism in New Zealand*. Auckland: Massey University Press. A great collection of the best of New Zealand's journalism. It includes introductions with comments from the journalists about how they did their stories.

Law Commission. (2013). *The news media meets new media*. Wellington: Law Commission.

Myllylahti, M. (2017). *JMAD New Zealand media ownership report 2017*. Auckland: AUT Centre for Journalism, Media and Democracy. Available at www.aut.ac.nz/study-at-aut/study-areas/communications/research/journalism,-media-and-democracy-research-centre/journalists-and-projects/new-zealand-media-ownership-report. A very helpful guide to the ownership of the New Zealand media industry.

www.codecademy.com If you wish to learn how to design and build your own webpages from scratch, a useful skill for the modern multimedia journalist, you can teach yourself for free on this site.

www.irirangi.net A resource covering the history of Māori radio broadcasting.

Yska, R. (2010). *Truth: The rise and fall of the people's newspaper*. Nelson: Craig Potton. The history of New Zealand's most salacious newspaper, *NZ Truth*, which closed in 2013.

References

Al-Meiri, M. (Producer). (2011, May 5). *Current affairs*. [Radio broadcast]. Dubai, United Arab Emirates: Zayed Radio.

Brown, L. (2017, April 19). *My close shave with fake news*. Retrieved from http://www.radionz.co.nz/news/on-the-inside/329096/my-close-shave-with-fake-news

Coming full circle. (2011, July 9). *The Economist* [special report], p. 16.

Day, P. (2000). *A history of broadcasting in New Zealand*. Auckland: Auckland University Press.

Deuze, M. (2008). Understanding journalism as newswork: How it changes, and how it remains the same. *Westminster Papers in Communication and Culture*, 5(2), 4–23.

Ellis, G. (2010, August). *Paying the piper*. Paper presented as part of the seminar series "The end(s) of journalism?" at the University of Auckland.

Fastenberg, D. (2011, March 28). 140 best Twitter feeds. *Time*, p. 28.

Gamela, A. (2008). *10 changes in journalist's role (and 5 things that remain the same)*. Retrieved from http://olago.wordpress.com/2008/11/18/10-changes-in-journalists-role-and-5-things-that-remain-the-same/

Hannis, G. (2017). Journalism education in New Zealand: Its history, current challenges and future opportunities. *Asia Pacific Media Educator*, 27(2), 233–248.

Hannis, G., Hollings, J., Pajo, K., & Lealand, G. (2014). Survey of New Zealand journalists: They enjoy the job despite everything. *Ejournalist*, 14(2), 1–20.

Hastings, D. (2013). *Extra! Extra! How the people made the news.* Auckland: Auckland University Press.

Hawkins, J. (2017). *NZSA launches new business journalist awards.* Retrieved from www.nzshareholders.co.nz/pdf/correspondence/Media%20Release%20-%20NZSA%20Journalist%20Awards.pdf

Indvik, L. (2013). *Washington Post to go behind metered paywall this summer.* Retrieved from http://mashable.com/2013/03/18/washington-post-paywall/

Law Commission. (2012). *Public perception of news media standards and accountability in New Zealand.* Wellington: Law Commission.

Law Commission. (2013). *The news media meets new media.* Wellington: Law Commission.

Leveson, L. (2012). *An inquiry into the culture, practices and ethics of the press.* London: The Stationery Office.

Nats reject need for single media watchdog. (2013, September 13). *The Dominion Post,* p. A2.

Obermaier, F., & Obermayer, B. (2017). *The Panama Papers: Breaking the story of how the rich and powerful hide their money.* London: Oneworld.

Reporters Without Borders. (2017). *World press freedom index 2017.* Paris: Reporters Without Borders.

Robinson, S. (2011). Convergence crises: News work and news space in the digitally transforming newsroom. *Journal of Communication,* 61(6), 1122–1141.

Scholefield, G. (1958). *Newspapers in New Zealand.* Wellington: Reed.

Smellie, P. (2017). *Ethics clash sinks business journalism awards.* Retrieved from www.nbr.co.nz/article/ethics-clash-sinks-ey-business-journalism-awards-b-205853

Strong, C. (2008). *Nailing convergence journalism: A case study of Massey's multi-platform reporting course.* Paper presented at the Journalism Education Association of New Zealand Conference, Christchurch, New Zealand.

Te Ara. (2017). *Controlling the media.* Retrieved from https://teara.govt.nz/en/video/33199/controlling-the-media

Ukinski, T. (2013, July 21). *Update: Severe earthquake strikes Australia/correction – New Zealand.* Guardian Express. Retrieved from http://guardianlv.com/2013/07/severe-earthquake-strikes-australia/

White, J. (2013, June). *The Chicago Sun-Times lays off its entire photography staff.* Retrieved from www.radionz.co.nz/national/programmes/ninetonoon/audio/2557807/the-chicago-sun-times-lays-off-its-entire-photography-staff.asx

2

Newsgathering

Understanding what news is and how to find it

Margie Comrie, Massey University

The most fundamental – and perhaps most daunting – task when you start out in journalism is working out where to find news and how to recognise that it is indeed news. Oceans of ink have been used attempting to penetrate the mystery of what is news, while reporters themselves are generally happier seeking out and producing news rather than spending time defining it.

You'll come across a number of well-known sayings about news. These bear repeating because they reflect the ongoing paradox of the low and high purposes of journalism – hot gossip versus citizen-empowering information.

Occupying the high ground is *Washington Post* editor Philip Graham describing news as "a first rough draft of history" (quoted in Keyes, 2006, p. 107). Or there's the saying: "News is what somebody somewhere wants to suppress. Everything else is advertising." In various forms, this saying is linked to so many illustrious names that it's best described as anonymous (quoted in O'Toole, 2013, para. 29).

Conversely, other maxims tout news as novelty, excitement and surprise. News is what makes people talk, or, using American editor Arthur MacEwan's now quaint description, "News is anything that makes a reader say 'Gee Whiz!'" (Franklin, Hamer, Hanna, Kinsey & Richardson, 2005, p. 97). Perhaps the most quoted definition also goes back at least a century, "When a dog bites a man that is not news, but when a man bites a dog that is news" (quoted in Keyes, 2006, p. 14).

Journalists walk a tightrope between the important and the entertaining. Much of what we read or click on therefore bears little resemblance to the high ideals of news. There's actually a regular diet of dog-bite stories, and far more on rate rises, local vandals, healthcare woes or the latest tearful sports celebrity confession than on history in the making. News organisations have to pay their way and, even if they are publicly funded, they still have to justify their existence. In short, news needs an audience.

What stories hook the audience?

So what do audience preferences tell us about news? The internet allows media organisations to track the favourite stories of online readers. Most days you will see crime and human-interest stories topping the readers' choice list, while major accidents and exceptional weather events are also popular, along with Hollywood and local celebrity news adding light relief. True audience interest is, however, harder to judge because the very fact that stories are listed in a top five increases the likelihood of further clicks.

Research company UMR surveys New Zealanders regularly, asking them how closely they followed key stories of the previous month (UMR, 2017). Top stories across 10-year periods from 2000 onwards show the dominance of local/national news: the February 2011 Christchurch earthquake has topped the billing ever since, followed by the 2010 Christchurch earthquake and the Pike River mining disaster. Half the top 20 stories are regularly about the weather or natural disasters; also high up are stories about missing children and crimes involving children. In the latest available results (2003–2015) only three of the top-10 stories were international (the 2005 London bombings, the 2004 Boxing Day tsunami and the 2009 Samoan tsunami). The top-ranking sports story was the All Blacks winning the 2015 World Cup. Major crimes and criminal trials featured, but political stories never made the top 20.

All this reinforces the point made by British *Guardian* editor-turned-academic Alistair Hetherington: "Anything which threatens people's peace, prosperity and well-being is news and likely to make headlines" (1985, p. 40). However, while there are clear trends in what stories appeal to mass audiences, they are only part of the picture of what is news.

News values

Academics take the analysis of what's been broadcast or published as their starting point for identifying what's news. Below, we've adapted a list of 10 contemporary news values compiled by two overseas researchers (Harcup & O'Neill, 2001). They say news stories that generally have one or more of the following values are likely to be published:

The power elite: These are stories concerning powerful individuals, organisations or institutions. That's why we have news featuring the Prime Minister, Shell Oil, Fonterra, government departments, major research institutes and so on. Locally, it might be the mayor and council, or a major local employer, such as the hospital.

Celebrity: These are stories about famous people. Don't just think of film stars and rugby heroes here, there are also local celebrities who make good story material too.

Entertaining: These are stories concerning sex, show business, human interest, animals, an unfolding drama, or offering opportunities for humorous treatment, eye-catching photographs or witty headlines.

Surprise/unusual: These are stories that have an element of the extraordinary. New Zealand shark-attack stories, for instance, are both unusual and, of course, bad news (see below).

Bad news: These are stories with particularly negative overtones, such as conflict or tragedy. We get pulled into negative stories, especially when they are related to people. So, political journalists often report the hostility between Members of Parliament rather than the policy issues that underpin their differences.

Good news: These are stories with particularly positive overtones, such as rescues and cures. As well, items about people who turn their lives around are popular, and New Zealanders love stories of national successes (*The Hobbit* movies or Kiwi entrepreneurs making good in the United States). The same success story formula, on a local scale, also applies to many regional papers, while community papers frequently specialise in good news.

Magnitude: These are stories that are perceived as particularly significant either in the numbers of people involved or in the potential impact. This applies not only to stories like massive tsunamis but also to complex stories like the global economic crisis. It's why stories about policy changes or local council spending plans take up media space – they impact on many of us.

Relevance: These are stories about issues, groups and nations perceived to be relevant to the audience. A big earthquake in New Zealand will have far greater prominence in our media than one in China with many more casualties. British and US stories get more prominence in New Zealand news than those from Asia. Rugby stories are seen as more nationally relevant than, say, hockey stories. Importantly, journalists also try to make their stories relevant/interesting to the audience. Banks make it tougher to get housing loans, so reporters find people who can no longer afford to buy a house. Reporters look at how funding decisions have affected local schools or how inflation has impacted on the typical cost of a week's groceries.

Follow-up: These are stories about subjects already in the news. We'll have more on this later.

News agenda: These are stories that set or fit the news organisation's agenda. For instance, TV programme *Campbell Live* ran campaigns on issues like milk prices and Christchurch homeowners' dealings with the Earthquake Commission. John Campbell has carried his 'people' agenda to RNZ's *Checkpoint*. At the time of writing, the *Manawatu Standard* is barracking for viable alternatives to the shattered Manawatu Gorge highway.

As you follow the news, you'll see these news values appearing time and again. When writing news, journalists choose an angle to highlight and intensify news values, making stories more interesting and newsworthy. When you start reporting, though, plenty of questions still remain. How do you know what makes a story relevant to the audience? How big or important does the story have to be before

Remember: the news is about what's new – what happened yesterday, today, five minutes ago. But past events can become newsworthy again – such as the 10th anniversary of a natural disaster.

Journalists don't consciously use lists of news values as a yardstick for what stories to chase. Instead, they develop a "nose for news" or "news sense" on the job.

FINDING COMMUNITY NEWS

Many new reporters start their careers writing for community newspapers. **Simon Edwards** began editing community newspapers in the 1980s. Here's his advice on finding great community stories.

"People and their successes, concerns and problems are news.

"In a smaller community where folk tend to know each other better, readers love to learn more about local characters and personalities, people who have unusual interests, kids who achieve something special at school or on the sports fields, businesses which have expanded or been able to hire more staff.

"Community newspapers often have more space to explore these topics."

Many events can be news, he says, including golden and diamond wedding anniversaries, someone turning 100, a person getting a civic award, or a teenager making a representative team.

And don't rush your interviews. "Seemingly mundane assignments can turn into real gems of stories when a community news journalist spends a bit of extra time getting to know the interview subject, gaining their trust and getting them to open up.

"The recollections and early memories of long-time residents can make very interesting reading for newer generations and arrivals in a district."

The longer deadlines of community newspapers (weekly or twice-weekly) mean there is more time to find fresh local angles on existing national stories, he says. These stories are called "local matchers", in which you can explore the direct impacts of national events on your publication's community.

"No one has a better opportunity to describe what is going on down at the local council or community board, the school, the neighbourhood shopping area, than the community newspaper serving that patch," he says.

"It brings an immediacy and intimacy to the community news reports that daily media can't match."

the editor or chief of staff accepts it? How can you write a follow-up to provide new interest? News sense is difficult to explain and is often a hard-won skill. There's little substitute for intensive training and practice on the job.

Where do you find news?

If you're a novice reporter, you'll quickly find your local community is full of stories. Contact schools, sports clubs, voluntary groups, community organisations, charities, local and regional councils, businesses, tourism and promotion groups, churches, museums, art galleries and libraries. They all provide plenty of news stories. Visit local community websites, go to meetings and ensure you are on their email lists for upcoming events.

When you start out in a larger newsroom, the chief of staff or chief reporter is likely to assign you the story you will cover that day. Most journalists, though, gain the greatest satisfaction in finding their own stories, and you'll win respect when you put forward good ideas at newsroom meetings. If you are given a news release, report, research paper or set of new statistics, use it as a springboard. Check the facts. Confirm the figures. Think about who's affected and interview them.

In the newsroom you will be given a specialised field about which to write stories, called a "round" or "beat". This could be transport, health, science, police, etc. Your own interests might encourage you to concentrate on something like music, the computer games scene or a particular sport. These areas provide starting points for news stories.

Essentially, news is about people: people involved in events, relevant authorities, eyewitnesses, pressure groups, government ministers, Members of Parliament, chief executives, public information officers, academics and members of the public. Some of these people – like eyewitnesses, or victims and their families – you may talk to just once when you go to report an event or its aftermath. Others, however, become contacts you will work with over many years to help you come up with a regular supply of new news stories. The newsroom round system is a way of structuring newsgathering, of finding out what is happening in certain places and sectors of society, and of helping journalists gain access to newsmakers.

Developing and maintaining contacts

For most journalists, contacts provide the bread and butter of their news stories. Your sources are generally developed as part of your round. When you are given a round, don't be afraid to ask for help and suggestions from colleagues. Most will be happy to guide your first steps.

You will need to do your research. So read up on previous stories run by your news organisation: the earthquake-susceptible parish church scheduled for demolition; the new council-supported recording studio; the fracas following last year's school ball. Get familiar with searching your newsroom's databases of stories and contacts, as that will put you in the picture and alert you to new developments and potential stories.

Ultimately, though, a round is all about building relationships and trust. Find out who the movers and shakers in your area are. Meet with them in person and regularly. They might not always have a story for you, but when a story does come up they may think of you. Also, the next time you call one of them up for a comment on a story, you'll be more than just an anonymous voice at the other end of a phone.

It's easy enough to locate people in official positions, and you will gradually get to know those who may not front in the media but can provide background material and potential stories. When building your round, remember any community is made up of diverse groups and interests. So think beyond the usual suspects and develop relevant contacts among different ethnic groups, or those representing alternative views in your area of interest.

Being a journalist gives you every excuse to meet interesting people. Keep

Journalists are only as good as their contacts. Cultivate a large number of contacts, stay in touch with them, and keep your list of their addresses up to date and easily accessible.

Getting news from leaks

Occasionally a source will offer you a leak or anonymous insider tip. We're not talking WikiLeaks or exposés of illegal spying here. More likely the leak will be about a fight between community board members, a discipline problem at the local school, or a draft report on selling off local council parkland.

It's gratifying to be approached, but these confidential story hints should give rise to a number of questions. First, is it really news, or am I just excited by the possibility of a scoop or because I've heard a secret? How reliable is the source and how can I check the story out? What motivates the person giving me the leak, and does that make a difference? Finally, what are the consequences – personal, social, financial and so on – to the players if the story is run? Conversely, what are the consequences if it isn't run?

Good contacts can give you an edge over other reporters. As Stuff's Manawatu regional editor Jonathon Howe recalls: "A good example of a round contact coming through for me was when I was working the police round at the *Standard*. I was at a job where police were chasing a gunman who had killed a man and shot another. We were trailing police around all the checkpoints for hours,

and at one of them I noticed a constable from Palmerston North who I was quite friendly with. He came up to me and told me they'd caught the guy just down the road, well before any official announcements were made. His tip allowed me to phone it in to Stuff and we got it online first, which was a great result."

For political journalists who develop trust with contacts, being given a leak as part of the strategy of politics is normal. Newshub's political editor Patrick Gower talks of one typical instance where an expected announcement by the Prime Minister was delayed so it could be presented by another minister the following day. As Patrick well knew, this typically happens when the announcement is a back-down that the PM does not want to be associated with. "Now, through a source I basically got a leak of what the announcement was going to be the next day, and was able to go on the news that night and tell people that it was a total back-down and that it was going to be perceived as humiliating. Through what I would call basic source work, I was able to get in ahead of them. I didn't have to play their game."

it professional, though. Remember you are dealing with busy people who don't always welcome journalists' questions. That's why following up a media release with a personal call may open doors. But again make it clear you can never promise coverage – you are not a public relations person for those on your round. In the end, trust is established with your contacts by being consistent in your approach and demonstrating your integrity by accurate and balanced reporting.

Good contacts, then, will give you story ideas and background material. Ideally they'll be prepared to talk to you when a story breaks, even though they are busy and their organisation may be under pressure or facing criticism. Also, contacts can put you in touch with others. It is easier when phoning a stranger during a breaking story to have an endorsement from someone they know or work with.

Observation

Once you begin thinking as a journalist you'll be open to a simple yet under-rated source of stories – observation. Many stories are simply spotted. Why is the rubbish not being collected? Who decided to redevelop that park and why? Look for changes in your area, unusual events, problem areas such as unfinished buildings, or delays. Ask why things are happening (traffic bottlenecks) or why they are not (why is that hole in the road still there?).

Good journalists are curious, almost nosy. They have a hunger to find out more about the people they meet, events they observe, or simply what makes the world tick. Thinking like a journalist means thinking of consequences of events. For instance, what will happen to a neighbouring school if a planned new supermarket goes ahead? What do parents, teachers and the kids think?

You must be interested in people and in listening to people from all different walks of life. So, when you are out and about, listen to what people are talking about. Taxi drivers have long been regarded as legendary sources of news. You can pick up news ideas on the bus, or at the mall and in the supermarket queue, as well as at various functions you might attend.

Just as becoming more open and observant can help you pick up ideas for news stories, so can becoming alert to the significance of your own experiences. If you are having problems finding a flat, probably a lot of others are too. If you run into difficulties finding a job, getting through to a help service, getting insurance replacement after a burglary, look into it. It may well provide a news story in itself or lead to finding out about a wider problem, development or trend.

Intelligent curiosity, backed up by broad general knowledge, can turn any outing into a newsgathering opportunity. Jonathon Howe, Stuff's regional editor for Manawatu, tells this story: "During one news meeting, a reporter told us she went into a dairy to buy something, only to see a shop owner selling banned legal highs. Instant story. All it involved was her being observant in her everyday life, and having knowledge of the legal high issue."

Secondary sources

The internet has opened up a huge range of official records, reference works, earlier news stories, recordings and video or film files, statistics, reports, advertisements, newsletters, news statements, computer sites and electronic records. These can add enormously to a news story. A car crash might warrant a news brief; but if your research shows it's one of a series at the same corner during the past six months, you have a much bigger story.

Research can provide background and show up comparisons and trends, all of which might be news. It can answer questions like: Are burglaries really increasing? Is the closure of a local factory reflected in other centres? How does this region compare in the latest health, education, or crime statistics?

You can check official reports for local impact. A quick scan of the Ministry of Health website (www.health.govt.nz) reveals the latest New Zealand health survey (with details on amphetamine use, obesity problems etc.), publications on gambling harm, annual drinking water quality reports, along with a bank of health statistics and data sets on 38 topics, ranging from alcohol use, through infectious diseases and prisoner health to urban–rural health.

Being alert to story possibilities

RNZ political reporter Craig McCulloch says the best stories come from leg work and observation: "There's no off switch for journalism."

"I still remember a story RNZ ran several years ago about New Zealand Post quietly removing hundreds of suburban post boxes around the country. One of our reporters had ducked out to post a letter one day and discovered his local post box had disappeared. Some might have just left it at that, but this reporter hopped in his car and drove to the next nearest post box. Also gone. He went home and started making phone calls to New Zealand Post. Sure enough, he discovered those boxes weren't the only ones that had been removed – and he wasn't the only one a bit put out about it either."

Getting out and meeting people is essential. "One day, during the aftermath of the 2010 earthquake in Canterbury, I drove out to one of the most affected suburbs. I walked up and down the streets and talked to every person I bumped into. I returned to the office with the beginnings of at least five different stories."

Often, you'll be interviewing someone on one story and they'll say something that sparks a completely different line of inquiry.

"About a week after the Christchurch earthquake in February 2011, I arranged an interview with a Chinese embassy official, Cheng Lei, to discuss how the families of those who'd died in the disaster were coping. Nearing the end of our conversation, Mr Cheng mentioned that some families felt uncomfortable at the level of compensation being offered. I pressed further and he explained they wanted more money because of China's one-child policy."

The resulting *Morning Report* interview was picked up by all the major national and international news organisations.

A typical local body council website can spark story ideas with agendas and minutes of all meetings, reports on current projects and official hearings, the council's media releases, and public notices. Or click happily through the user-friendly Statistics New Zealand website (www.stats.govt.nz) for a wealth of information with the homepage organised by major topics or locations, along with the population clock, latest news releases and a number of useful links. The 'Browse for stats' section takes you much deeper and online tools allow you to create tables and comparisons.

Most government departments are rich sources, whether it is the Department of Conservation's studies of endangered species or the Ministry of Justice report on victims' rights. The Ministry of Business, Innovation and Employment site is loaded with publications and provides access to open data sets under various headings. The Parliamentary website also includes research papers. The list goes on. Similarly, university websites have interesting publications and reports rarely sent to the news media, and their latest news sections can be worth following up.

Of course, you cannot simply browse the internet aimlessly hoping for inspiration. If you have a round you'll become familiar with websites, or sections of websites, relating to your area. For instance, those on the transport round need to know and check the sites of the NZ Transport Agency, the Ministry of Transport, the Rail and Maritime Transport Union, police, airlines, railways, Automobile Association, relevant sections on the local council website, and you can look for associated blogs on sites like kiwiology or blogdirectory. You'll also use internet sources to add to stories sparked by news releases, when following up from earlier stories and events, or localising (matching) a national or international story.

When investigating a story you might need confirmation of something only available from the minutes of a government meeting, or you want a report or cost–benefit analysis never publicly issued. This is when you can use the Official Information Act.

Newsletters and websites

Newsletters from government departments, councils, pressure groups and industries can be a great source of stories. Many paper-based newsletters and specialist magazines of smaller organisations have been replaced by websites. You can easily find newsletters and briefs from a huge range of causes: the SPCA, Forest and Bird, the Salvation Army, Rainbow Wellington, the Tenants Protection Association, the Alcohol Drug Association, the Council for Civil Liberties and many, many more. Most organisations also have a Facebook page, and it pays to become familiar with the social media activities of key groups in your area.

Specialist publications for industries are also available on the internet for instant browsing (for example, *New Zealand Construction News; Dairy News; Food NZ; Computerworld;* and *Tourism Business*). Similarly, almost every organisation connected with the arts and culture has a lively online presence with plenty of detail of events, activities and so on.

If religion is your beat, there are, to name just a few resources, the national *NZ Catholic* newspaper online with local stories, various Anglican parish newsletters and the Methodist newsletter on Facebook. Publications and news releases are on the Federation of Islamic Associations of New Zealand website, while Secular Buddhism NZ and the Humanist Society have newsletters. Scores of sports and hobbies are also represented online.

Again, while you can dip casually into these resources, just as you can with New Zealand hard-copy subscription magazines, it's most effective to browse with a purpose, concentrating on ideas for your news round.

Advertisements

Public notices and advertisements – such as product recalls – are a good source of news. Ideally the advertising department on a paper should tip off the newsroom about an interesting ad coming up. Sometimes a major company apologises for a mistake or an event that has inconvenienced or harmed customers. A public figure might take out an ad championing a cause. The robust nature of political advertisements at local body and national election time might be newsworthy.

It is worthwhile remembering, however, that some companies – like HELL Pizza, whose campaigns have been labelled sexist, racist and blasphemous, and have included such gimmicks as sending out condoms and pens mimicking blood-filled syringes (Easton, 2012) – court public controversy by the nature of their advertisements. To what extent does a consequent news story merely serve as additional advertising for them?

You'll find more about using the Official Information Act in Chapter 12.

In Chapter 4, you'll find more on using social media to find newsmakers and stories.

Public functioning, meetings and talks

Many news stories come from the public functioning of official organisations and corporate bodies in the exercise of their duties, like the courts, Parliament, government departments, local bodies, residents' associations, community boards, the stock exchange, annual meetings of sports bodies and companies. Check out the other chapters in this book for details on covering these.

As well, any community has meetings, talks, lectures, book readings, etc., all with story potential. To find out about the many groups in your area and their activities, look at community group directories, which are online for most cities. Here, you can find contact details and reports about upcoming events. For instance, Whangarei's community directory lets you find the politically active Ngunguru Coast Action Group and details of its next meeting, while the Visit Waimakariri site details future events in Rangiora, Kaiapoi and seven other local towns offering possible picture stories.

Following up and localising

While breaking news may be the most satisfying for journalists, follow-ups are perhaps the greatest source of news stories. Essentially you are creating stories

A PASSION FOR FINDING GREAT STORIES

Bernadette Courtney says PR has become far more powerful these days, and it is all too easy for reporters to become passive, when they should be passionate about finding stories. "Don't sit in the corner waiting for a press release to come in. Go out there and find stories. A great reporter is one who brings their own great stories in."

Build up your contacts book, she advises. "Draw up a list of people and talk to them. There are the usual contacts – council, police, court staff – but you also need to speak to people in the community."

Stories are everywhere, she says. "Pound the pavements. You've got to get out there. When you're walking along the street you'll probably pass five stories." And don't be a slave to the newsroom's conventional wisdom. "Sometimes I hear, 'Oh, he won't talk to us. He hasn't for five years.' I say, 'Well, get on the phone and see if he'll talk to you now.'"

Monitor what your competitors are doing, she says. "See what's on the TV news and the websites." Think of ways you can develop a story or give it a fresh angle. She tells the story of a keen new recruit in *The Dominion Post* newsroom. "The week before she started, she rang the head of news with six story ideas." That's the kind of passion Bernadette is talking about.

And it doesn't matter how high up the ladder you get, you never lose that passion. "I'll be at a party listening to someone tell me something they probably shouldn't. I'll rush outside and make a few notes. When I'm back in the office I'll say, 'This is something we should follow up on.'"

from stories. The discussion of follow-ups and localisation has been left until last because the process of following up and matching or localising a story incorporates the techniques and news sources discussed above.

Many news stories are not isolated events, they unfold over time. For instance, you might write a number of stories describing a major crime. This is later followed by details of the ongoing police investigation. An arrest may follow, and eventually details of the trial, which again can be spread over a number of days or weeks. Or an event may draw attention to underlying issues and a series of stories may flow from this.

A major example of a long-running series of stories is the Christchurch earthquakes exposing the issue of building safety standards in New Zealand. This spawned a number of reports, regulations and resulting impacts for communities around the country. Additionally, ongoing issues, in themselves not particularly newsworthy, often precipitate news events. So being aware of issues – whether nationwide, like farmers' disquiet over new financing arrangements, or more micro, like neighbourhood concern about the presence of gang members – means you are first when people speak out or action is taken.

Follow-up stories satisfy the basic natural curiosity of audiences and journalists: What happened next? Who else is affected? They allow us to fill in the details that may be missing from the initial breaking story, and in the same way they can also add balance to initial reports. So you need to look back over earlier stories you've covered and ask yourself whether an update is needed.

Looking for the local angle will also provide news stories. In fact localising national and international stories is staple news fodder, especially in regional and local newsrooms. Olympic team announcements – which athletes are from our area? Budget announcements – how do they affect local schools and hospitals, and what do local union representatives have to say? National crime figures on the rise – what's happened in our area? Internet addiction rampant among young teens – how do local experts react to the report?

When big events happen overseas, there's almost a mania for localising. Our media scramble for the New Zealand angle when a Kiwi survives an overseas cruise ship sinking, tsunami, earthquake, pirate attack, major storm or terrorist bombing. While the emphasis can be overdone, these human-interest stories add to the coverage of the event. They're also more likely to be effective for audiences of local and regional media, and local reporters with their community and social media links may well be the ones to locate Kiwis in hot spots overseas.

Remember, a single news story does not have to be the definitive statement of an event. Instead, complete coverage can roll out over time, across a series of stories and backgrounders.

Developing professionalism

By now you should be getting the message that you develop your news sense by reading widely in the news media and beyond. Start looking at the world as a newshound and feed your curiosity. News is all around. Journalists find it by getting out and developing contacts with potential newsmakers in their area, by becoming immersed in the media and following up stories. When you first hear about something happening, get an idea or a tip, you need to research, find out more, get in touch with people and verify it.

FINDING THE NEWS ANGLE

Much has been written on news *values*, but less on news *angles*.

The interesting part of this dichotomy is that in newsrooms across the globe it is the term "news angle" that is used constantly by journalists. The term "news value" is more of an academic term used when you step back and analyse a collection of news items.

Journalists are always looking for the news angle. The difficulty for journalism students is to understand the news angle for a single article, and particularly to avoid confusing it with news value of a topic.

The news value is whether the story is a newsworthy topic. The news angle is what is most newsworthy about it. The news angle usually appears in the first sentence of the story, known as the intro. One way to think of a news angle is to ask yourself whether the first sentence of your story is Relevant, Unexpected, Today (think RUT):

Relevant. A national TV news items has to be relevant to the whole country, whereas a city newspaper's news items have to be relevant to people in that city.

Unexpected. This means it is information the audience doesn't already know. Heavy traffic in the city centre at 8am happens every day, so isn't big news. The traffic report will instead say "traffic is unusually heavy today" or give details of accidents.

Today. News is fleeting. If most people already know about it, then it's old. People don't read the newspaper or watch TV news to find out what happened last year. Radio and online news is even faster. This doesn't mean you can't put some historical information into a story (to give context, say), but it isn't the news angle or main reason for running the story.

The main task of your article's news angle is to tell the audience immediately that this is something they need to take notice of. It gives them a reason to stop and read this particular news item. Most people are bombarded by information every day and constantly have to decide what to read. The headline helps grab their attention, but the angle lets them know if the story is relevant to them.

To help find the news angle, court reporter Fran Tyler would think about how she would tell news stories to her mother, who had English as a second language.

"I had to simplify the information and explain the most important and interesting aspect of the story in a short and simple way," she says.

Once, Fran was covering the latest conviction of a habitual shoplifter. It looked like it was the same old story, except when she learnt he tried to steal a weedeater by stuffing it down the front of his pants. He was stopped by the security guard who'd noticed the bulge. That was the story she told her mother. "My introductory paragraph was not much different!"

There's more on news angles and intros in Chapter 14.

You'll need to develop professional systems too. Keep an organised list of your contacts. Keep it up to date and accurate. You'll want to greet people correctly when you meet, phone or email them, and you'll certainly lose credibility if you get sources' names or positions wrong. When researching a story, or trying to find people to comment, note down the names of those who helped you along the way. You may want to come back to them for another story.

You have plenty of computer support, so make your calendar or diary work for you. With every story, diarise anything you can follow up next week, next month or next year. Make sure your calendar notes are clear – who you are to contact and what you are checking up on.

Look for follow-ups on stories from other media too, and enter into your diary to check when a report might be due, a new building started and so on. Also note down your less time-sensitive story ideas as they occur and revise them regularly so you can fit them into a story researching and writing schedule. This could be making sure to ring retailers in October to find out what toys are going to be big this Christmas.

Professionalism is also about attitude. Good journalists are curious, observant and interested in people. They are also sceptical (rather than cynical) and think critically about themselves and their stories, seeking for the right sources and information to provide balance and fairness. Most of all – they have fun!

Read overseas news websites, newspapers and magazines. Watch overseas TV news. These will all give you ideas for similar stories you can do in New Zealand.

Further reading

Bugeja, M. (n.d.). *Think like a journalist.* Available at http://newstrust.net/guides

Buttry, S. (2012, August 27). *The Buttry diary: 10 ways Twitter is valuable to journalists.* Available at http://stevebuttry.wordpress.com/2012/08/27/10-ways-twitter-is-valuable-to-journalists/#more-9360

Galtung, G., & Ruge, M. (1973). Structuring and selecting news. In S. Cohen & J. Young (Eds.), *The manufacture of news* (pp. 62–71). London: Constable.

Ingram, D. (2012). Journalism and media glossary. *The news manual: Online edition.* Available at www.thenewsmanual.net/Resources/glossary.html

McGregor, J. (2002). *Restating news values: Contemporary criteria for selecting the news.* Paper presented at 2002 ANZCA conference, Queensland, Australia. Available at www.anzca.net/component/docman/cat_view/27-anzca-02/28-refereed-proceedings.html

References

Easton, P. (2012, January 30). *Parents shocked at Hell Pizza's syringe promo.* Retrieved from www.stuff.co.nz/business/6332782/Parents-shocked-at-Hell-Pizza-syringe-promo

Franklin, B., Hamer, M., Hanna, M., Kinsey, M., & Richardson, J.E. (2005). *Key concepts in journalism studies.* London: Sage.

Harcup, T., & O'Neill, D. (2001). What is news? Galtung and Ruge revisited. *Journalism Studies, 2*(2), 261–280.

Hetherington, A. (1985). *News, newspapers and television.* London: Macmillan.

Keyes, R. (2006). *The quote verifier: Who said what, when and where.* New York: St Martin's Press, Macmillan.

O'Toole, G. (2013, January 30). *News is what somebody does not want you to print. All the rest is advertising.* Retrieved from: http://quoteinvestigator.com/2013/01/20/news-suppress

UMR. (2017). *The mood of the nation.* Retrieved from http://umr.co.nz/updates/mood-nation-2016

3

Interviewing

Interviewing comes down to getting the jewel quote

Catherine Strong, Massey University

The art of interviewing can look effortless, appearing to be a casual discussion where the journalist deftly directs the focus back and forth and then extracts an unexpected piece of information or opinion. But interviewing is more than an art; it is a skill that requires lots of practice to get it right. The more you interview, the better you become.

Being able to conduct good interviews is the tool that separates a professional journalist from others. Any member of the public can take a video or a photograph of a news event and send it into a media outlet, or post it themselves somewhere online. Trained journalists, however, go further. They obtain in-depth information, from difficult-to-access newsmakers, to put the event into context, and to get both sides of the issue. This extra information is often only attainable through interviewing a newsmaker, or a witness or affected victim. In a competitive media market where several reporters are covering the same story, the crucial difference can be the story with the most unexpected quote from a key person. This is the jewel in your story.

Consider interviewing as one of the valuable tools for your search for truth to share with your audience.

You are not usually lucky enough for the newsmaker to simply *give* you the best quote. Usually it relies on your asking the right question. Remember that many newsmakers are suddenly thrust into the spotlight, such as disaster victims, sports winners, or witnesses. They aren't media experts. They don't know the journalist's job, so they don't know exactly what words or what information you are looking for. Your questions help direct them to the angle you need for your story.

There are many types of interviews, from a few quick questions of the attending police officer, to opinions from random people on the street, to long, intense studio interviews with a global leader. Each interview is quite different from another, but the guidelines below can be used for all types of news interview. Always remember that the news interview is to gain information on behalf of your audience, not simply to have the opportunity to chat to someone famous.

Entrance to another world

One of the joyous privileges of being a reporter is being able to integrate into someone else's life, even for just a short time. They let you into their environment, their family, their culture, so you can do your job. These stories may be dramatic, horrific, jubilant or sorrowful, but they are often pivotal parts of a newsmaker's life. The person being interviewed may reveal deep-seated emotions, unpopular opinions, or gruesome experiences. They trust that you, the reporter, will capture the information accurately. This doesn't mean you need to empathise with them, nor agree with their viewpoint, but you must be accurate.

You may also be called on to interview people with rather different backgrounds to yourself. This can be people from different socio-economic groups, or people from countries or religions you've never heard of before. One way to prevent being distracted and overawed when dealing with diversity is to experience it beforehand. Take every opportunity to meet and mingle with a wide range of people. This can be accomplished by volunteering in a soup kitchen or new immigrants centre, attending public cultural events, or accepting every opportunity to get out of your own comfortable world.

Know your motivation

The first step is to determine who is to be interviewed, and why. Start with what information or opinions you need for a balanced story, then decide who is the best person to provide it. The worst thing for both you and your interviewee is to talk around in aimless circles.

A robust news story requires more than one voice, meaning it should include information and quotes from two or more people. But the second and third person shouldn't be used simply to pad it out. They should provide an opposing view or supporting evidence. In other words, they play a part in telling the story.

Ask why you are doing the interview. If it is simple facts or statistics you want, perhaps they are quicker to find on the ministry's website or from an email request that someone in the ministry or department can provide. However, if you want an expert opinion, a witness's description, a victim's feelings, or a politician's rationale, you need to identify a specific person for an interview.

Once you decide who the best source of the information is, double-check the appropriateness of the person. For example, a local doctor may be easy to interview,

The newsmaker needs to trust you, to know you will handle their information appropriately.

Many seasoned interviewers say their careers have been enriched by constantly sharing other people's stories.

One way to prepare for diversity is to read about it, even in novels. Vicarious experiences can be as valuable as tangible exposure for new journalists. For more, see Chapters 5 and 6.

Many meandering interviews are caused by reporters unsure what they wanted in the first place.

TIPS FOR LIVE RADIO INTERVIEWS

Kim Hill has won numerous awards and has been a high-profile current affairs interviewer for more than 20 years. She has been called the queen of the broadcasters (Vaughan, 2012). You can hear her on RNZ National, Saturdays 8am to noon.

One of her characteristics is that she is well researched for an interview, and has an eclectic collection of interests, which is why she recommends new journalists read as widely as possible. Here are other interviewing tips she gives to new journalists.

"Listen to the answers, instead of concentrating entirely on the next question you had in mind. The most interesting interviews go off in unexpected directions because you react to things you didn't know. And having a love affair with your own questions is a hollow experience for everyone! Don't be afraid to repeat a question if you don't understand the answer or think you didn't really get one.

"Don't call politicians by their first names.

"Be interested, because if you're not, the listener won't be either.

"In fact, there aren't really any more 'rules' I can think of, because every interview is different, and because I still make terrible mistakes and forget to ask The Most Important Question, but it's all a work in progress."

but may not know very much about the rheumatic fever epidemic you are investigating.

To get the story first, there is a temptation to take shortcuts in selecting the person to interview. An example in the United States was when Congresswoman Gabby Giffords was shot at a shopping centre, and first reports were that the shooting was fatal. Some media interviewed other media for their stories, which resulted in incorrect information being reported. Other media pursued normal channels of trying to interview hospital, family and police, and finally discovered she was alive (Tenore, 2011).

In New Zealand there are numerous instances of newsrooms making mistakes by relying on social media as a source. One example was the first radio report I heard of the Boston Marathon bombing, which said 12 were killed, based on tweet messages. In fact it was confirmed that three were dead once the media relied on first-hand sources. The lesson for young journalists is to interview accurate sources.

A link to a re-enactment of this case is in Further Reading at the end of this chapter.

Slice through the filter

The first hurdle in conducting a good interview is to actually get to the person you want to interview. It is your responsibility to determine who is the best person to talk on the topic. Some people are shy, or afraid of journalists. Get alongside them by explaining why their story is worth publicising, and why they are the best one to talk.

Try to interview the person who actually has the first-hand information. If

TIPS ON PREPARING QUESTION LINES

Kathryn Ryan conducts several live interviews every weekday for RNZ National's *Nine to Noon* programme. She says every interview needs to collect the 5Ws and H (see page 51), but longer interviews require more.

"This tip is about preparation, especially for set-piece or longer-form interviews. They are a different beast from your standard news interview. You are looking to open up, and to reveal something new from your subject, to get to an underlying truth or revelation about them. Whether this is someone who has never been interviewed before who has a significant story to tell, or someone who has done a thousand interviews, this is an interview you plan. Here is how and why I plan.

"Read everything that is relevant about your subject that is available to you. While researching, jot down the questions you as a reader (or listener to online sources) find yourself asking. These are the questions your audience will want asked.

"I structure this kind of interview, generally, in three parts, three different broad areas I want to explore. You will know which the three most relevant areas of your interview should be. It might be your subject's current event of 'newsworthiness'; their background and what it is that formed or shaped them; any other significant dimension that you believe reveals a truth about them, or reveals a truth about 'us', your audience.

"Within the three broad areas I've chosen to explore, I script question lines that anticipate responses, and provide key facts to the audience along the way. I am endeavouring, first, to establish rapport with my guest, and then to guide him or her along a path of being able to tell his or her story. I never direct the story. It is theirs. I simply want to be prepared to help prompt with facts, anecdotes, that assist them along the way of telling it, and, where appropriate, challenge them.

"Having prepared an interview structure and question line I know will at least be adequate, I throw it out. It sits in front of me, as a reference point if things are not going well, or if I have become absorbed in the interview but have reached the end of a thread, and need a prompt for where to go next. Otherwise, the interview, the best interview, follows its own course, with barely a reference to my question line.

"By structuring and preparing a question line, I have prepared myself for an interview that ideally may make little reference to it. The act of preparing a structure has prepared me."

And she says difficult or sensitive interviews "require detailed strategic planning, and often the following of the plan, if you are to reach the revelation of information you seek. The more sensitive and complicated the subject, the more strategic and detailed your preparation should be. Anticipate answers, anticipate diversions, anticipate reactions, and have strategies (and facts at your fingertips) to deal with them."

your story is about the zoo's sick elephant, talk to the person who is caring for the elephant, not the accountant in the office. Definitely don't settle for the media officer. Although the public relations people will want to be involved, if they are doing their job correctly they won't hamper you. They will, in fact, help you get contact with the elephant keeper – and maybe even suggest photo opportunities or sound effects.

Getting access to the correct person may be difficult at times, as other people will try to filter out any media contact with the person. Very often an officious staff member will protect the person from reporters and try to fob you off. They may insist he is too busy or unavailable. They may urge you to send an email instead. They may simply be evasive. You need to be persistent.

Sometimes a crime victim is willing to talk, but the family automatically turns away reporters on the telephone. At times the victims don't even know reporters are trying to contact them. In these cases, respect the family, but be persistent to find out if the victim is willing to be interviewed. Sometimes use another person as a go-between, such as a family member, police officer, or funeral director. The word "interview" can sound daunting to someone not used to the media. It might be better to ask them to "chat" or just "talk" with you. Of course, make it quite clear this is on the record and for publication.

In summary, be tenacious and resolute when trying to convince someone to be interviewed. Try different avenues. There are lots of ways to slice through the filters, use them all before giving up.

> Filters set up to block journalists often exist if the newsmakers are high-profile and sought after by many reporters.

Select the medium

The best way to conduct an interview is in person, face-to-face. You can gauge the meaning behind the words better than on the telephone, Skype, Twitter or email. The newsmaker often appreciates the effort it takes to actually travel to their home or office. Being able to look around their environment, viewing photos on the wall or souvenir decorations, helps you learn more about them.

Unfortunately, it is not always possible to conduct an interview in person, because of timing or distance. Previously, most interviews were by telephone, because it is quicker and easier than travelling to the newsmaker in person. In more recent times more interviews are even more impersonal, simply being by email or social media. Even the newsmaker may prefer telephone or email because they can correspond while doing other things. Once you get to know someone, there is less need for rapport-building and a phone call is acceptable. But face-to-face should be your first choice, especially for sensitive issues. It would be crass to ask someone about a recent bereavement without first trying to see them personally.

But there is also a stronger reason to avoid internet-based interviews. That reason is that you don't really know who is answering your question. The newsmaker could be handing it over to an office assistant or a friend. Someone else may have simply logged onto the newsmaker's computer and decided to respond. If it is a contentious issue, the newsmaker may have turned it over to someone else to answer. If you are gaining information from an email, tweet, or via Facebook, you should acknowledge this fact in your story, such as: "In a Twitter message Smith said he was shocked at the outcome." Another way is: "'I am shocked at the outcome,' Smith tweeted."

The overarching goal is to be accurate and open about the source of the information, so the audience can decide the veracity of the story. If a person refuses to be interviewed, put this in the story. Be sure, however, that they really did refuse, and not that you were unable to access them at a time convenient to you. Often a newsmaker is available when you are busy with other things. This is not a case of refusing to comment.

Step through the interview

All interviews are different, and they often unexpectedly take a turn in the middle. This is actually the fun and challenge of interviewing. My beginning university journalism students say that when facing their first interview the biggest fear was forgetting to ask an important question, or having a question ridiculed. One student said she got so nervous on her first interview that she almost vomited, another said her hand shook so much she could hardly read her own writing. These are the extremes, but it is common to have apprehensions before interviewing someone for the first time. It helps to have a checklist and a list of questions.

After conducting several interviews, the process will become automatic and you won't have to check off each step on the list. At the beginning, however, be sure to get all the information needed by following these steps.

Step 1: Prepare

Before any interview it is important to prepare by researching. Find out as much as possible about the topic, the interviewee, and past controversies. One reason for this is to avoid embarrassing yourself by misunderstanding the issues or the nuances of the controversy. A second reason is that the person may be put off having to provide basic background information to you if it has been widely published before. Student journalists sometimes get the phone slammed in their ear with someone growling, "Don't waste my time when you can get this information on our website."

Find out what has already been published about the person and topic in the news

---

TIPS TO LISTEN, *REALLY* LISTEN

Geoff Robinson was the voice of *Morning Report* on RNZ for three decades. He says the most important thing he was taught about interviewing is to *listen*.

"Listen to the answers, they'll help you formulate your next question. Listen to the tone of voice, it will give you a hint of whether they're telling the whole story, telling porkies, or just trying to avoid the question.

"And listen to yourself to make sure you have the right tone of voice to go with the question (and sometimes lull the interviewee into a false sense of security)."

TIPS FOR TELEVISION INTERVIEWS

Mike McRoberts is a Newshub prime-time news presenter and has conducted interviews in many of the world's war regions. He says the hardest thing about television interviewing is often making the talent (the interviewee) feel comfortable in an unnatural and often uncomfortable environment.

"As a rule I never use notes when I'm interviewing someone, not even for lengthy current affairs interviews. I think it's important to maintain eye contact with the person you're talking to and try as much as you can to make them forget that they are sitting in a studio or studio-like situation with a camera pointing at them.

"If you have notes and keep referring to them, then every time you disengage eye contact you are reminding them that this is not a conversation but a television interview.

"Not having notes also forces you to know your subject-matter very well, and to listen when the interviewee is speaking. You also get the chance to see their face and their body language as they react to various questions."

Photo: Catherine Strong

media. Be sure to know what has been produced by your own news outlet already, as there is nothing as time-wasting as going back with an angle that someone in your own newsroom has already done. Search separately on the major news sites, but remember their archives go back only a year or two. A quicker and more thorough way is to use Newztext Plus, which searches most New Zealand news outlets, and goes back several decades. This is by subscription only, but many university and polytechnic libraries have a direct link to this for their students.

Less formal research includes simply asking other journalists in your newsroom. They may have done a similar story previously and can give you some tips. Of course don't overlook traditional library resources that may help.

Step 2: Set up the interview

Once you contact the newsmaker, introduce yourself, but this is more than simply telling them your name. Let the person know you are a reporter and who you work for. If you are freelance, explain where the story may be published. If you are a student, make it clear if this is in fact only a student assignment, or otherwise be clear that it might end up being published or uploaded online. Make it clear that this is on the record. Also give the person an approximation of the time the interview will take, and try to stick to it.

The most important part of setting up an interview is developing a rapport. No one is obliged to talk to you, so take the effort to settle them into your interview. One way to break the ice is to find something in common – perhaps you had met before or went to the same college. Show you have done some research and mention their hobby, or a recent award. This shows respect, no matter what their background.

Be accurate, so take notes carefully and use a recorder. Digital recorders aren't too intrusive to the conversation, as they are fairly small and often double as a mobile phone. Showing them the recorder, however, is a good way to remind them that this is a media interview and is on the record.

Don't rely solely on the recorder, however, as many technical problems can occur. Take notes in addition to digital recording. This way you have the basic information for a quick story, but can use the recorder to find precise quotes and information for the fuller story.

Take responsibility to set up the physical environment for the interview. Don't leave it to chance. Find someplace quiet, and without interruptions. If it is in their office you may have to suggest closing the door, or moving to a quieter corner. Set the chairs so you are sitting next to each other, not across a wide desk, as it gives a stiff feeling, as well as sometimes doesn't pick up good sound on the recorder.

Step 3: Ask identity questions

Find out the person's name and how to spell and pronounce it. If your news organisation uses honorifics (rare these days), ask the person what honorific they prefer, such as Mrs, Ms, Miss, Dr, Mr, etc. Do not assume you know the honorific, as both single and married women often prefer to be Ms So-and-so. Also, some people have doctorates and qualify to be "Dr" even though they are not medical doctors. Some people with doctorates do not want to use the "Dr" honorific. The important thing is to ask them what they prefer. Get their title in relation to the topic of the interview, and at the same time find out their authority to speak on this topic. For instance, the person may own a plumbing business, but also is a city councillor. Use the identity that relates to the topic, such as the councillor if it is on

---

Generally speaking, it is against journalism's ethical codes to misrepresent yourself, so don't pretend to be someone you're not. For details, see Chapter 21.

Develop rapport by talking to interviewees person-to-person, not simply note-taker to newsmaker.

TIPS TO RESEARCH IN A HURRY

Sometimes five minutes' preparation is all you have before conducting an interview, especially when you are assigned to rush out to catch someone currently in a breaking news story. In these cases your best friend is your mobile internet device. It only takes five minutes to fully brief yourself on both the topic and the interviewee. The first step is to use a search engine such as Google, Bing, or Yahoo and select "news" to find your story topic. This will give the latest news, so you are not asking old questions at the interview.

Another trick to be prepared for last-minute interviews is to keep up regularly with news and current affairs. Follow daily news in any way you prefer, such as newspaper, online, radio, television. In addition, keep an eye on your Twitter or other social media account to see what events are trending. Take a note of anyone important visiting the country. Yes, you can just tweet out a request for help to prepare your questions, but your reputation as a journalist may suffer.

Some reporters think they can get through any media conference with a set of formula questions. Catching a group coming out of a political meeting they simply ask: How did the meeting go? What are the unresolved issues? What progress was made? Where to now? Any final comments? If it is a dramatic event they ask: What happened? Who is to blame? How much will it cost? But interviewing cannot be boiled down to a formula.

Yes, formula questions may help you squeak through an interview you are totally unprepared for, but why risk it? Without knowing the issues you may easily miss the major feature of the person or event, and may come back without the best news angle. This looks amateurish for the reporter who didn't ask the burning question of the day. The secret to avoid this embarrassment is to research beforehand.

---

the district plan vote, but a plumber if it is on how to fix drains.

If you are interviewing a witness to a crime, be sure to get them to describe exactly where they were and when. Too often a well-intentioned neighbour will give you wonderful quotes: "There were shots and screaming", but then it turns out that they weren't even at the scene; they'd heard the details from another neighbour.

If the interview relies on something the person has already said or done, be sure to check the validity of your prior information. "You have been quoted as saying 'xxxx'. Is this true?" may prevent conducting an entire interview about wrong information.

Step 4: Ask the basic questions

No story is complete without the 5Ws and H, so make sure you know the *who, what, when, where, why* and, also, the *how* of the story. Much of this basic information is often already available from a media release, website, police media line, or ministry handout. Nonetheless, double-check with your interviewee that the information hasn't progressed or changed. And always double-check the spelling of names.

The basic questions, and the identifying questions, can be asked at any time during the interview. They can also be asked before you turn on your recorder, when you are jotting notes on a notepad, settling into a seat, or finding a quiet corner for the interview. They can be asked at the end. The important thing is to ensure you have this information before leaving your interviewee.

Step 5: Ask angle questions

Keep looking for what is different about this event or issue. Keep asking questions to find out what is newsworthy about this response. This is the key to a good interview, but can be very difficult. The news angle quote is the gem in the middle of all the other spoken words and phrases from your interviewee. At first you may not recognise the best quote until you go back and listen to the interview again.

With practice you will instantly know when someone has told you something newsworthy. Once you can recognise the jewel while still in the middle of the interview, you can ask more about it, or ask the question in a different way in order to get an even better quote.

One of the best ways to recognise the jewel of the interview when you hear it is to have done enough prior research. Being well-briefed means you know when the interviewee is saying something that hasn't been published before, or that they are contradicting themselves, or that their words perfectly describe the atmosphere.

One tip for getting the angle is to not take anything for granted. Don't assume that this has been said before, or that the monotone voice means it is boring information. Don't assume that it isn't newsworthy simply because your interviewee said it wasn't newsworthy. It is a favourite politician's trick to tell a young reporter, "This isn't news" when they want something played down. Conversely, someone who really wants publicity may not know what an angle is. You have to dig.

Step 6: Ask the tough question

Don't avoid asking a question you think will get you kicked out of the room. However, ask the question without judgement or sarcasm, and don't apologise or seek permission to ask the question, such as: "Do you mind if I ask ..." Just act interested in their response, as though you are genuinely curious about their side of the story, "Why *did* you take $2 million from your clients?"

Don't shy away from asking a question simply because, if the roles were reversed, you wouldn't want to answer it.

Soften the blow if the question is emotional, or the interviewee needs a hint that you are changing direction. Say, "There is no easy way to ask this, but it needs to be cleared up." Or else, "I know this is a difficult time, but please tell me how you ..." Never be afraid of silence. Sometimes this is a reporter's best friend, as a pause is when the newsmaker will blurt out something unexpected or newsworthy. In normal conversations we verbally rush to fill gaps in the conversation, as a way of being polite, but this prevents the other person completing their thought. However, in an interview let the person mull over a question, or quietly consider their response. The silence is for them to fill, not you. Of course in a live-broadcast interview this is not possible as the audience doesn't tolerate dead air, but in all other interviews if the interviewee seems to have more to say, just stay silent and let them tell you in their own time.

If the tough question is a potentially explosive topic, where the interviewee may walk out or stop the interview, leave the question until towards the end. Get all the other information and quotes first, so you don't leave completely empty-handed. Once you have asked the tense question, move on to other less-contentious questions. Keep the conversation going and end on a neutral topic.

Step 7: Clarify and wrap up

Recap by making sure you understand the newsmaker's points. Clarify everything you've heard that may be included in the completed story. It's okay to seem dumb and ask basic questions. If you don't understand, probably your audience won't either. Check facts and figures and anything you may have missed. Often it is useful to let them know what angle is planned for the lead. This prevents them being surprised. However, until you are experienced, you may be unsure of the lead until you have gone over your notes back at the office.

If there has been any discussion about what is on the record, clarify at the end what you have agreed to publish (see the box on page 54). While you still have your notepad out, double-check you have their contact details and tell them you may need to get back if there are any other questions.

Another good idea is to ask the interviewee if there is anything else they'd like to add, anything you haven't covered in the interview. Usually, the interviewee will think and say, "No, I think we've covered everything." Occasionally, though, they may add some excellent additional information.

Once you are finished, don't linger too long, especially if they are busy officials. If you said it would take 20 minutes, try to stick somewhat to that time frame. And don't forget to thank them. Even if it was a spirited interview and they were annoyed at having to answer some sensitive questions, thank them for their time. Remember that in most instances they did not have to meet with you in the first place. Before saying goodbye, give them your business card so they can contact you if they have any further thoughts for your story.

Often it is at the door, while saying goodbye, after you have put away your recorder, that the newsmaker gives you the best quotes or anecdotes. Try to remember accurately what they said, or whip out your notebook and pen to capture it.

Problem questions

Often a young journalist will return to the newsroom from an interview crestfallen because they didn't get very much information, and don't know why. When they listen to the recording of the interview it usually becomes very clear that the newsmaker didn't tell them much because the questions were poor.

What makes a poor question? Well the first thing is closed questions. They encourage closed answers. A closed question is one that only asks for a one-word answer, such as "Was the car blue?" (Answer: "No") or "Was the gunman tall?" (Answer: "Yes"). There

Another good question to ask is: What's going to happen next?

After the interview, if you feel you need to contact the interviewee to clarify something or ask some follow-up questions, do it.

On and off the record

The presumption with any standard interview is that it is on the record. That means you can use all the information from the interview, including the quotes, the person's name, their job title, where they work, etc.

If an interviewee says they want to go off the record, be careful. Start by asking them why. It could be you can allay any fears they have and so stay on the record.

If they continue to say they want to go off the record, the safest response is to say no, you don't take anything off the record because you are gathering information to be made public. This is the best policy because often you can get the same information somewhere else, but may be bound to keep it confidential if you had previously agreed to take it off the record from one of your sources. The other reason for using a blanket "no" response is that the interviewee may have a personal agenda for wanting the information to be made public anonymously. This agenda may compromise your quest for total accuracy.

If they insist on going off the record, clarify exactly what they mean by that. Do they mean that you can use nothing from the interview, that you can use general information from the interview but not attribute it to them, that you can attribute the information to "informed sources" or say "we understand that …", or what? Once you've clarified this, you will need to decide whether you want to go off the record.

If you do go off the record, get back on the record as soon as possible. Politely but repeatedly tell them, "I want to go back on the record now" until they agree. Make it clear when you are back on the record.

Make sure your notes state what information was on and off the record.

Ask your interviewee if there are any ways to obtain the off-the-record information some way that is on the record, such as through an Official Information Act request (see Chapter 12).

For a discussion about off-the-record briefings with politicians, see Chapter 7.

Whether you are reporting for radio, television, online or print, a one-word quote is usually not very useful.

are better ways to ask the question, ways that allow the newsmaker to tell you more.

In the examples above you could have asked open questions, such as "What did the gunman look like?" or "Can you describe the car?" The answers to these open questions give the newsmaker the opportunity to talk more, to give further answers, to give you good quotes for your story. That is the difference between a closed question and an open question.

Another problem with questions is sticking too closely to your list of questions, and not listening to what your newsmaker has just told you. Listening is the best skill you can perfect to become a professional interviewer. The newsmaker may have given an answer that was incomplete, or hinted at other information. You need to ask follow-up questions, which clarify or expand on the previous answer. You may get the jewel quote you need for your story simply by asking "Why?" or "What did you mean?"

Here are six types of questions that often create problems and allow the newsmaker to avoid giving explanatory answers. Practise asking questions without using these problem questions. In reality you will hear many of these problem questions on spirited television interviews. Remember that there are no absolute rules in interviewing, only guidelines, so you may use any type of question if it helps gain the facts. These problem questions are used sometimes to be provocative. They are entertaining. But if you are trying to elicit information, they are not the tools to use. They have their place, but know why you are using them.

Six problem questions

Leading questions give the phrase that the journalist wants for their story, and guides the newsmaker into agreeing. It may not be how the newsmaker would actually describe the event. An example is: "Don't you think the referee's decision was shocking?" Of course she is going to say yes it was shocking, even though she may actually think it was "unexpected" or "suspicious". It would be better to ask: "What is your opinion of the referee's decision?"

Rhetorical questions are self-answering, and don't give the newsmakers a chance to give their own opinion. An example is my mother's favourite question: "Do you really want that extra slice of chocolate cake with all the calories?" These types of questions don't need an answer, as the question is couched in such a way that it is the message already.

Don't be intimidated by other journalists who are looking for angles different from what you're interested in. Trust your instincts.

Presumptive questions focus on the journalist's personal opinion and almost force the newsmaker to take this point of view. An example is: "You don't agree with the idiots on that side of the council, do you?" Note how difficult it would be to disagree with the tenor of the question. This isn't fair to the newsmaker.

Double questions roll two questions into a single sentence. It confuses the newsmaker, or allows them to answer one and not the other. An example is: "Do you think snorkelling is more fun than diving, or at least safer?" It should actually be asked as two separate questions if the journalist really wants this particular information.

Ego questions show off the reporter's knowledge, but don't elicit a good quote from the respondent. Often it is very long, and refers to famous people or places the journalist has experienced. Newsmakers are able to avoid answering such questions by listening patiently to the long, convoluted question then simply saying they didn't understand what the actual question was.

Statement questions express a position, but don't actually ask anything. An example is: "The public won't like that policy." These types of questions sound provocative, but they allow the newsmakers to remain silent if they want, as there is no question to answer. In reality people often will give a response, because they are polite.

> ### TIPS TO CHANGE DIRECTION IF NECESSARY
>
> Kathryn Ryan of RNZ explains that despite all your preparation, you may have to change the question line mid-interview. She says the better prepared you are, the more attentive a listener and better judge of direction you will be.
>
> "Be patient when you hear responses that may take you down another path from that which you are pursuing. When someone throws you an interesting diversion in a response, you do not have to pursue it immediately. Note it down, and return to it. Resist jumping all over the place in interviews. Pursue your line of questioning for as long as it deserves, and return to the 'diversion' you were thrown later (unless it is of immediate and startling priority).
>
> "Be savvy about when you 'go with' your interview subject down the more interesting and revealing path they are taking you. And when you must, bring them back to the issues and the questions you know your audience wants answered. All going well, you can achieve both objectives.
>
> "Don't be afraid to yield an interview to your guest. Often their path is the more interesting and revealing. Your preparation is largely an act of being prepared to discern that."

Every interviewer's nightmare is to miss asking an obvious follow-up question when the newsmaker has said something that requires further exploration.

The media conference

Organisations that face many journalists wanting the same information sometimes call a media conference, so the newsmaker can answer all the questions at one time. Conferences can be proactive, when they have news they want to announce, or reactive, when they are defending something that has gained media interest. Whatever the reason, it puts the journalist in a complex position. Every answer from the newsmaker is being recorded by all other journalists, which means there are no scoops. On the other hand, it means you can use information from another journalist's question, perhaps questions you hadn't thought of.

Some conferences are called media scrums, because many journalists are crowded around the newsmaker trying to get the best photo and the best information. Don't hold back. Ask your questions as soon as possible, before the newsmaker ends the conference and walks out.

On the other hand, however, don't ask questions that show you have done little or no research. Often you will be given a fact sheet at the conference, so you can rely on this information to start the interview. But this may not be enough, so do your preparation like any other interview.

Keep alert

You dig for the angle by asking follow-up questions, which are the ones that spring from the responses from the interviewee. Ask them to explain more, or to clarify something that sounded interesting to you. Sometimes a single word will draw your attention to ask another question about it: "What did you mean when you said your accountant acted 'out of character' before he disappeared?" Another sign that you should ask a follow-up question is to read their body language. Don't draw attention to the fact that their face turned red, or that they had a nervous twitch, but simply ask, "How did you feel when that happened?" or perhaps more directly, "Did that irritate you?"

It is interesting that even one of the top interviewers in New Zealand, Kim Hill, says she is still working on her interviewing skills (see breakout box on page 45). And this is the key to good interviewing: always assess your work and try to improve. No matter what level you are at, you can improve.

To ask the right follow-up question means listening very carefully to your interviewee. Don't just hear the words, but *listen* to what is being said with words, tones, body language – and what isn't said. Some of the best quotes were when asked, "Why didn't you mention person/place/time?" Active listening takes a lot of effort. Concentrate on the person and the topic.

You know full well that in class, while the lecturer is talking, your mind can wander off to such things as your plans for the evening, problems with your mobile phone, undone tasks at home, etc. Don't let this happen while at an interview. Train yourself to put 100 per cent of your concentration on the interview. This can be facilitated by sitting forward on the edge of your seat, taking notes, anticipating what they will say next. Obviously it is difficult to listen actively if you had a bad night's sleep, or you are hungover, so be physically ready for the interview too.

The advice I've given to myself throughout thousands of interviews is to expect the unexpected. Before an interview, or an event where I might score a valuable interview, I would mentally visualise everything that could possibly occur, both good and bad. It's important to visualise potential problems, so you can have a solution or an alternative plan ready to go. Imagine several versions of how the answers to the interview might go. This means that if the interview takes an unexpected turn you are ready for it.

Further reading

http://journalism.about.com/od/reporting/tp/interviewingbasics.htm and **http://journalism.about.com/od/reporting/a/interviewing.htm** Interviewing tips from US professor Tony Rogers, who has worked as a journalist in New Zealand and the United States.

King, L. (1994). *How to talk to anyone, anytime, anywhere.* New York: Three Rivers Press.

www.knowledge-basket.co.nz/newztext/welcome.html Newztext segment of Knowledge Basket, accessed by payment.

www.youtube.com/watch?v=qkjdOEj6xGY&feature=endscreen A re-enactment of the media mistakes in reporting a US congresswoman dead after a shooting, by relying on the wrong interviewees.

www.youtube.com/watch?v=4eOynrl2eTM Interviewing tips from Katie Couric, a top US network news presenter.

References

Tenore, M. (2011). *Conflicting reports of Giffords' death were understandable, but not excusable.* Poynter Institute, St Petersburg. Retrieved from www.poynter.org/latest-news/top-stories/113876/conflicting-reports-of-giffords-death-were-understandable-but-not-excusable/

Vaughan, R. (2012, November 8). *Kim Hill crowned Queen of the world's broadcasters. National Business Review.* Retrieved from www.nbr.co.nz/article/kim-hill-crowned-queen-worlds-broadcasters-rv-132049

4

Using social media

How the online community can help you break stories

Helen Sissons, AUT University

Social media have revolutionised how journalists gather news. Journalists can obtain information faster than ever before and interact with a variety of sources across multiple platforms at the click of a mouse. This chapter examines the way social media have redefined what it is to be a 21st-century journalist. It will show how journalists build relationships and find sources on social media platforms. It will also illustrate how material from users is incorporated into the day's news.

The internet journalist

To be an effective journalist today, you need to be multi-skilled. That means gathering and producing news stories across a variety of different platforms. The written word captures the story. However, contemporary journalists also use video, audio and photos.

The internet has enabled readers to become "users" who use the internet for a range of experiences, such as buying online, interacting socially and finding information as they go about their daily lives. So it is not surprising that their taste for fast and easily accessible news has become more complex too. Users now expect to see breaking stories appear instantly online and, where appropriate, click on a video clip or sound track of the interview or see the event in photos. They also expect to be able to share the story through online social networking sites such as Facebook or Twitter, and post their comments about an event.

When we consider some of the important news events of the past few years, we can see that social media have proved a rich resource in the production of news. During the Arab Spring in the early months of 2011, the Arabic news broadcaster Al Jazeera aggregated social media content, including YouTube videos and material from Facebook and Twitter, and delivered it to its television viewers, as many did not have access to the internet (Selb, 2011).

During the Christchurch earthquakes of 2010 and 2011, people turned to Twitter to discover what was going on and to share experiences. By using the keyword or hashtag #eqnz as part of the tweet, search engines could find the constant stream of comments, advice and warnings being posted on Twitter (Seitzinger, 2010).

Organisations were among those posting reports. For example, GNS Science put updates about the aftershocks on Twitter, which enabled people to stay informed as the crisis unfolded (Dann, 2011). Crowdsourcing was also used (Macnamara, 2011) to help people identify which shops had survived earthquake damage and were open to sell food and where Cantabrians could go to buy petrol. It was the first time New Zealand had seen social media, particularly Twitter, used on this scale for these purposes.

The importance (and limitations) of user-generated content

Paul Harper, social content producer at Stuff, explains how news organisations interact online with their audiences.

"During breaking news events, user-generated material is vital. Newsroom resources are stretched at the best of times, so when an unexpected event occurs, such as the Christchurch earthquakes, content from readers is particularly important.

"Often readers email us eyewitness reports/video/images without us asking, sometimes they respond to requests online, while other times we ask for it from people on Facebook and Twitter. Putting a post on Facebook or Twitter, and keeping an eye on the relevant hashtags, is a great way of finding leads, eyewitness reports or photos and video. Of course user-generated content should be verified when necessary."

Paul is also a fan of following readers' comments on online news stories, as these can lead to new angles and stories. But he warns that those working online have to become accustomed to receiving negative comments.

"People are more likely to be negative online than complimentary, so valid criticism can be lost in the sea of hate which is the internet."

All this communication offered a wealth of material for journalists to use for news reports. However, not all information that is gathered from social media sources is reliable. A case in point is the coverage of the bombings during the Boston Marathon in America in April 2013. Mainstream media organisations drew on social media content as they raced to be first to deliver the news. But in their haste, misinformation was reported, factual errors were made and reputations tarnished. Several news organisations reported the wrong number of people dead, accused innocent people of being suspects, and falsely reported that arrests had been made (Beaujon, 2013). As journalists, accuracy is at the forefront of all that you do and it is imperative that you check everything, every time. This is especially so if you want to avoid being beguiled by the unchecked comments and misinformation available on social media, which do not become more true the more they are repeated.

A hashtag is a label put on a particular topic or conversation on Twitter. It is a simple way for people to search for tweets relevant to that conversation.

A new relationship with the audience

Arguably, it is the journalists' relationship with their audience that has undergone the biggest change in recent years. Traditionally, the audience only had limited access to the journalists who reported the news (Sissons, 2006), and it was very much a one-way process with little chance for interaction. Consumers were restricted to writing letters to the editor, phoning in with tip-offs and whistleblowing when they felt injustice had taken place.

However, new technologies have afforded many more opportunities for interaction, and for the first time given news organisations a wealth of information about what audience members want in their news. By looking at the way users interact with news sites, journalists are able to understand users' tastes and preferences through "likes", "shares", "comments" and "feedback".

Social shares, the number of times an article is shared on social media, are an important way of judging the popularity of an article. They are significant because they demand a conscious action by a user to tell the people they are connected to that they value a particular article and so are sharing it. Facebook "likes" also demand an action from a user. However, writing a comment on an article requires the most effort, as the user has to have a strong enough reaction to wish to record their thoughts.

When a journalist uses crowdsourcing, they go to their audience to collect or verify information for a story.

All these user actions increase the engagement with the audience and spread the journalists' work more widely.

User-generated material

User-generated content is material uploaded to the internet and social media sites by the user. It includes comments, tweets, audio, video, photos and blog posts. Thanks to new technology including "smart" or web-enabled mobile phones, users can now contribute directly to the reporting process. In fact, in a breaking news situation, it is often users who bring the story to the public first. But rather than feeling threatened by this, journalists should see it as an opportunity to produce better, richer and more exciting news.

Nieman Visiting Fellow Hong Qu analysed the role social media played in breaking the news of the Boston Marathon terrorist attack in 2013 (Qu, 2013). He compiled

A smart device is an electronic device small enough to be carried and can connect to the internet via WiFi, 3G, 4G, etc. It includes smartphones and tablets.

GLOSSARY OF SOCIAL MEDIA PLATFORMS

Facebook (www.facebook.com)

Facebook is a social networking website that allows users to create profiles, upload photos and video, send messages and keep in touch with friends, family and colleagues. Search facilities help members locate other members and "friend" them by sending them an invitation.

There are three main types of users on Facebook. First, individuals who create a Facebook profile to interact with friends. Second, businesses that create a page to promote products and brands where fans can post comments. Facebook provides demographic statistics on usage. Third, there is the Facebook "group" where any community of people with a common interest can come together. Group administrators accept or reject member requests. Facebook's search engine allows journalists to find the Facebook pages of newsmakers and their friends, search for employees of particular companies and search for people with particular jobs or interests.

Flickr (www.flickr.com)

An image-sharing and social networking site where users upload photos and video and can also access images for use elsewhere. Users can add an identifying tag to the images by using the tagging feature.

Journalists can use Flickr to help with newsgathering. For example, you can set up a group or photo pool where users submit photos on a particular subject. In 2016, Wellington City Council set up a Flickr photo set to illustrate to Wellingtonians how the Wellington Region Emergency Management Office was reacting to the earthquake and damage around the city. A news organisation could ask users to contribute to a similar group. You can see it on http://bit.ly/15fgQ1L.

Journalists can also crowdsource information by asked users to identify individuals in photos. There is also a way of locating where a photo has been taken by importing the Flickr photos into a Google Map. For how to do this, see http://bit.ly/15fgDvt.

Flipboard (www.flipboard.com)

Flipboard is a social network aggregation tool that presents material in a magazine format so that you can browse your content by "flipping" the pages. It collects the content of social media and other websites, and presents it in a chequerboard format of small items with the source. You can then choose where you go from there.

Hootsuite (www.hootsuite.com)

Hootsuite is a social media management tool that uses a dashboard interface. It allows you to display feeds from several streams or feeds at once. To set up, you sign up for Hootsuite.com and then you choose the social networks and streams you wish to feature. With the free version you can have five social media platforms feeding your display. It is particularly useful for journalists to manage their social media feeds.

Instagram (www.instagram.com)
Instagram is an online photo-sharing and social network platform that allows users to upload, edit and share photos through the Instagram website and other social media sites. The "Explore" table allows users to search for others to follow or find photos by following hashtags. Instagram is used by journalists to engage with users about the story behind the pictures. Journalists can share photos, solicit photos from users on breaking stories, and actively build a community.

Storify (www.storify.com)
Storify enables users to embed material from social networks in their own stories. Journalists use it to tell multimedia narratives that bring together the latest information from across the web.

Tumblr (www.tumblr.com)
Tumblr allows users to post multimedia and other content to a short-form blog. Users can embed photos, audio, video and other media (like tweets) in text posts. Users can follow the blogs of others and add short comments or mark an entry with a "like".

Twitter (www.twitter.com)
Twitter enables users to send and read text-based messages of up to 280 characters, known as "tweets".

The default settings on Twitter are public, and unlike Facebook you don't need to be an approved social connection to follow another member. In addition, tweets are permanently posted on the Twitter website and so are searchable. Journalists can search and follow users, and build up a following by posting their own tweets.

WordPress (www.wordpress.com)
WordPress allows users to run their own blogs. Posts can be drafts, pending review, scheduled or posted.

The blogging software offers some added extras or "plugins" that provide additional functionality which are useful for journalists. These include a "post revision display" where the writer can add text to the bottom of a post that has been updated or corrected since it was first published and "Edit Flow" that adds a writing workflow into WordPress. In Edit Flow, the "editorial comment" component allows you to have private discussions about a post. Notifications let selected authors know when a post has been commented on or needs another revision.

Dan Lampariello (@Boston_to_a_T) uploaded this photo to his Twitter account a minute after the bomb exploded.

A blog, short for web-log, is an online diary, where the blogger records their views and activities for followers to read and comment on.

26 tweets that went out in the minutes after the two explosions. What he considers the first of these was at 2.50pm, when an eyewitness took a photo of fire and smoke in the distance.

But Qu does not believe this has made the journalist redundant. Far from it. He thinks journalists play three vitally important roles in the news cycle: checking the credibility of the sources, creating a narrative from the information, and communicating the information to a mass audience.

To fulfil the three roles effectively, journalists draw on their traditional skills. They must first sift through all the available information being uploaded to social media sites and identify the most reliable sources, and check facts to ensure they are accurate. They must then use the information gathered from the sources to compile a news story that is accurate, contains enough background information and is clearly understood and engaging for the audience. Finally, they must broadcast or publish the story to a mass audience.

This journalistic process is much more rigorous and time-consuming than clicking the retweet button. But it is a role the public needs its news organisations to perform in order to maintain a professional end-product, something which sets it apart from citizen journalism: "As citizen journalists inadvertently gather and (attempt to) distribute news, they lack the ability to broadcast to millions of people. In theory, their posts in social media can reach anyone who has internet access. However, in practice, few can find them among all the noise and, even when found, few will have reason to trust them" (Qu, 2013, para. 30).

What Qu is saying is that news organisations and journalists who remain trustworthy and accurate know people turn to them for the truth. Further, those who are good storytellers, as well as being trustworthy ones, will always be in demand.

The Guardian in the United Kingdom is among several news organisations that believe journalism should not compete with social media, but harness it for the greater good. These organisations claim that, if used properly, interacting with social media and receiving feedback from readers can improve the accuracy and relevance of news coverage. For example, *The Guardian's* Reality Check Blog looks at the "big issues" of the moment, and calls on readers to help with the fact-checking process. In one case it asked readers to test broadband speeds and got 5000 responses (McAthy, 2012).

The New Zealand Herald's former social media editor, Troy Rawhiti-Forbes, used a similar form of newsgathering and storytelling when he live-blogged from Christchurch's eastern suburbs after the 2010/2011 earthquakes. Not only did he file reports on the paper's website, nzherald.co.nz, but also on Tumblr, Twitter and Storify. The public responded by retweeting *Herald* tweets, sending in information and telling their stories. His work was awarded a Canon Media Award for best website community interaction.

Journalists who want to take full advantage of user-generated material will gather it in one of two ways:

- You will be approached by a user or users with images, sound or information about an event.
- You will search for or solicit information from users who are involved in an event. Sometimes that will supplement the material you already have.

If you take the second route, then you are most likely to find information and contributors through a range of sites, including blogs, discussions, Facebook and Twitter.

Where to find social media material

Social media allow for discussion and debate among users who share online their thoughts and feelings about current events and issues. All this interaction is perfect for journalists looking for a good story. But the key is to harness it and use it wisely.

Google

You are very likely to begin with a search in Google. However, many people don't know how to take full advantage of this powerful search engine. Note the list of words along the top of the window – you can search for images, news and YouTube videos, among other things. If you click on the "News" button, for example, you can also choose which geographical edition you wish to receive. So you can set it to New Zealand, or somewhere else if you wish to see news from another region.

Let's say you decide to search the New Zealand region for material about Auckland house prices. First you click "News" in the top bar and set it to the New Zealand edition.

Next, type in your search term "Auckland house prices" and hit the return key to see a selection of material Google believes is relevant to this search.

If you click the "More" button under the Google logo you can search blogs. There are some excellent ones, but remember they are not necessarily objective. You can also find discussion groups that may be talking about topics or events you are interested in. Other areas to search under the "More" or "Even More" buttons are

Live-blogging is taking notes, sounds and pictures of an event as it happens and posting them to social media sites as short entries.

Google set to the New Zealand edition.

Google Scholar, if you want experts on a given subject and academic journal articles, and Google Alert, to obtain email updates on topics you are interested in.

In the middle of the bar, to the right of the "More" button, there is the "Search Tools" function. If you click on this, it gives you the opportunity to search within a particular time frame. This can be very useful when you want the latest on an event, rather than background or archival information. If your search so far has proved fruitless, there is a circular indicator on the far right of the screen. When you click on it you will see an advanced search function revealed.

This will help you to narrow your search. For example, you can look for exact words. A particularly useful function here is the search within a site or domain, such as when you have heard something is on Facebook but you can't find it.

The other useful thing, which will save you lots of time, is to use the "file type" function, as this allows you to search for PDFs, spreadsheets or jpeg images, among others.

Facebook

Facebook is one of the largest of the social media sites and potentially a rich source of stories. It allows you to keep an eye on communities that are talking about topics of interest, and to find possible interviewees on these topics.

Facebook can be particularly useful if you are new to an area or have just been assigned a beat or patch. You can familiarise yourself with your new patch by signing up to the Facebook pages of local groups and keeping an eye out for events. Many groups prefer to set up a page on Facebook to publicise an event rather than send out a press release or phone the media.

Digital journalist Greer Berry says Facebook is the biggest social media point of contact for most media companies and their readers, including her own. She uses it to post links to stories, take polls, share images and video, crowdsource information and ask for feedback from readers. "We often ask our fans and followers if they have witnessed an event occurring in the community. For example, following the Seddon earthquake we – *Manawatu Standard* – used Facebook to update readers on what we knew as fact, and to quickly let them know that there didn't appear to be damage in the Manawatu region."

Sometimes Berry and her team use Facebook to follow up stories from other news outlets. This post prompted 13 comments and lots of debate among local people: "Stuff ran a story today about a family that had 15 children. It got us thinking – what's Manawatu's biggest family?"

Facebook can be used for stories from the hyper-local to the international. Community news reporter Rhiannon McConnell writes for the *Wainuiomata News*. "I'm part of about four Wainui Facebook groups," she says. "After the big storm we had recently, people were putting on stories about local heroes who had come to their rescue – helped with their roofs, that sort of thing. I would not have found that

USING FACEBOOK TO GENERATE STORY MATERIAL

Palmerston North's *Manawatu Standard* newspaper posted a question on its Facebook page, asking if anyone had experienced problems with ATM machines in the city. It is a good example of using Facebook to find people affected by an event, who you can interview for a story.

There are reports this morning of ATM and eftpos outages in Palmerston North. Have you been affected?

Danny Jones Na cause i›m still in bed lol
Like · Reply · 1 ·
9 August at 08:22 via mobile

Shona Cudby Yes couldn›t pay my parking meter with my Eftpos card like usual and had no coins so had to wait for someone to come along that could give me some coins.

information if it hadn't of been for that Facebook page. I was able to write a full page that week on heroes of the storm." To see the stories, go to page 3 of the June 26, 2013 edition of *Wainuiomata News*: www.wsn.co.nz

BBC World Affairs producer Stuart Hughes used Facebook to find interviewees for a story he was writing on the Paralympics. He went to the page of an interest group for amputees interested in sport. He put out a message saying he was working on the story and asking anyone who had a view to get in touch. One person who responded was an amputee athlete who lived in a remote part of Montana. He emailed her, and arranged an interview over Skype. Her quotes were used in the final story (see http://bbc.in/17tvB39).

Twitter

Twitter is undoubtedly one of the most useful tools for a journalist. It has real-time breaking news, and if you are following the right people, you will get some very valuable information. More and more comments and events recorded on Twitter are becoming news. A typical example is the coverage generated by Christchurch rapper Scribe's comment on Twitter that "Cantabrians don't beat people up for no reason" after cricketer Jesse Ryder was attacked outside a bar in the city (see "Rapper riles with Ryder tweets," 2013).

To take advantage of what Twitter has to offer, you first have to set up a profile, including a photo and some brief information about who you are. Then you choose

Once you've set up a Twitter account, follow a variety of news sources, such as government agencies, to catch breaking news they tweet. For instance, the MetService may tweet a major storm warning.

a few people who you think may be useful to follow. Watch their conversations and get used to the language and the sorts of things people are talking about. For example, that they use # (hashtags) to indicate the topic they are referring to, such as #americascup or #EmiratesTeamNZ for stories about New Zealand's most popular yacht-racing team.

Rhiannon McConnell from *Wainuiomata News* is a fan of Twitter. "You can put in a keyword, like 'Wainui', and it will search anyone who's tweeted about that in the last 10 or 15 days, or as far back as you want to go." If you identify a story or topic you are interested in investigating, Twitter can enable you to find key people to follow. Simply identify one or more important hashtags referring to that topic, then key them into Twitterfall.com where you can see everything being posted on social media sites using those hashtags, including photos, audio reports and written reports.

Although news organisations often republish material from social media sites, this could be breaching copyright. See Chapter 20 for details.

Managing your interactions

To manage your interactions, you need a clear idea of what you want to achieve through engagement on social media.

It is likely your aim is to reach new audiences, and find interviewees and contributors. Also, you probably want to increase your newsgathering capability by collaborating with your audience on stories, crowdsourcing knowledge and information, and getting real-time feedback.

You need to choose which platforms will be the most useful to you from among the many, including Facebook, Twitter, Tumblr, Storify, Instagram and WordPress. Then you have to determine what content you will post – news, comment, images, perhaps a blog diary – and what tone of "voice" to use. You will need to post some content in order to attract a following.

Once you start to engage on social media, there are several applications that can help you manage all the information coming in. We are going to look at one: Hootsuite. It allows you to display feeds from your social media platforms in a dashboard-style

Keeping your private and public lives separate

You can separate your private Facebook persona from your public profile. You do this by using the "subscribe" button, which allows you to have people subscribe to your page who are not your friends. These subscribers will only see the posts you set for public viewing. Subscribing also allows you to read the public posts of interesting people; for example, bloggers who cover a topic you are interested in. At the same time you should set the privacy settings on your Facebook page to maximum.

In addition, you can set up a separate Facebook page for your brand. This may be useful if you are a freelance journalist as it allows you to build a community around the topics you specialise in. But to maintain it, you would need plenty of content and a willingness to promote engagement and join the conversations on your page.

GETTING THE MOST OUT OF TWITTER

Highly experienced digital journalist **Greer Berry** explains how journalists can use Twitter.

"When I began a Twitter account in 2007, I was one of the first New Zealand journalists on there. Because of that, I used the medium to break news to my followers, to find contacts, to promote stories I'd written and to create a relationship with my readers. It's that relationship that has proved to be the most productive part of social media for me.

"Journalists who only use Twitter, for example, to constantly crowdsource for story tip-offs will quickly find it an uphill battle where the relationship between the reader and writer matters.

"When you're asking them to open up to you, they expect you to open up in return. What readers have really responded to is getting to know the person behind the byline.

"Where once print journalists were never expected to step out from behind their typewriter, now there is an expectation that they manage, control and promote their 'brand' – ie their name – across various mediums, which include social media.

"Readers respond well to journalists who they think they know personally – that's where being a 'real' person, by interchanging tweets about their personal lives and professional lives, works well, when it's done well.

"Not a lot has really changed in the years since I began using social media; only the audience has got bigger and more journalists have seen the advantage of having and controlling their own online presence.

"Where it was once seen as narcissistic, sites like Twitter are instead being seen as a compulsory tool for all journalists. Media employers will frequently ask in interviews how many people a potential employee follows on Twitter, who they think is doing it well/not so well, what news agencies they follow online, etc."

display so that you can see four or five streams or feeds at once. To set up, you sign up for Hootsuite.com and then you choose the social networks and streams you wish to feature. With the free version you can have five social media platforms feeding your display.

Another useful tool is Flipboard (www.flipboard.com). This allows you to bring together the content of social media and other websites of your choice and present it in a magazine format. This makes browsing it for ideas and sources easy. Even if a story has already been covered, seeing other people's comments on it can give you an idea for a follow-up. Often an event will affect people in a certain way, and you can see them on Flipboard expressing their views. You can then contact them and turn what they have to say into a story.

Use Twitterfall to find interviewees

A BBC broadcast assistant at Radio Kent, Selina Williams, used Twitterfall to find all the people in the county of Kent in the UK tweeting about the Christchurch earthquake.

Among those she found was a mother tweeting about her son, who was working in Christchurch. Williams contacted the mother through Twitter and was able to get the son's name. She turned to Google advanced search, putting in the son's full name, Keith Hake, and two keywords, Christchurch and Marden (which is in Kent). She searched within the domain Facebook. This gave Williams three results, one of which was Keith Hake's Facebook account.

She was able to message him directly saying who she was and asking him for his mobile number. He responded within five minutes. Consequently, just 20 minutes after finding the original tweet, Keith Hake was interviewed live on BBC Radio Kent and was able to describe his experience of the Christchurch earthquake to his home county (Williams, n.d.).

Building an audience

All journalists know that one of their most important assets is their personal contacts list. Often these contacts have been nurtured over years, and their names are jealously guarded. This hasn't changed in the age of the internet and social media. It is still important to have a set of contacts that you go to regularly for comment on stories or tip-offs. However, journalists today need to know how to interact, influence and maintain relationships with the online community via social media.

Some journalists believe that interacting with the public on social media is too time-consuming. However, if you become adept you will find it saves time by connecting you with suitable sources or interviewees more quickly than traditional journalism techniques (as we saw with the journalist at BBC Radio Kent). But no one is going to answer your call for eyewitnesses or approach you with sensitive information until you have built a credible online reputation and large number of connections.

One simple way to build an audience is to ensure your website easily allows users to receive your RSS feeds. These are updates on chosen topics in summary form sent to users who have signed up with the news organisation. These feeds are a form of advertising, building user loyalty.

You should also monitor users' comments on your online news stories. The more comments a story attracts, the more interesting it is to users and therefore worthy of further coverage. These comments can also give you tips and ideas for follow-up stories. Users who comment with potentially "newsworthy" information can become valuable sources for a news story, helping to develop it and/or enhance its accuracy.

You can encourage further comments by interacting with those who read and comment on your stories. This may lead to new topics of interest. To stimulate discussion and provoke users to comment, you can ask a question at the end of your article.

To build up a following of people listening to you, who will eventually trust you with their valuable information, you must interact with your followers, whether they are on Twitter, following your blog, etc. And you mustn't just tweet headlines or self-promotional snippets, but respond to comments or questions from your followers and readers.

Should we be right or first?

In the era of instant news, there's constant tension between being first and being right.

"We simply can't be the eyes and ears of everything happening in the community anymore," says Greer Berry. "We have to accept that news events will be caught and captured on the likes of smartphones and disseminated immediately, without the careful eye of an editor or journalist to act as an intermediary."

Digital media trainer Steve Buttry advises publishing a story, either online or over social media, incrementally as you discover the facts. This is the way of working pioneered on the news website *Talking Points Memo* in the United States.

Your followers and readers should see you working hard to cover a story and break new information. They are more likely to help if they admire your work.

Once you have verified the main or a pivotal fact of a story, it allows you to publish that fact and carry on chasing the story. Buttry adds that you can also crowdsource, or ask the audience to help with some of the details, and report each development as it happens. This is termed "iterative journalism". You can report what the source said, but you should note that you have not yet verified it.

Unfortunately, just stating that you have been unable to independently verify something doesn't always prevent the audience being very critical, and your journalistic credibility being compromised if that fact turns out to be wrong. Therefore, to keep your reputation safe always make a serious attempt to verify any user-generated material you receive via social media, before publishing it. That's because, although it's tempting to assume that the pictures and video you find on social media sites are what they are claimed to be, get it wrong and the audience will soon lose faith in the accuracy of your journalism.

When deciding whether to use material posted by a user, the rule of thumb is to try to speak to the person who has posted the material either face-to-face or on the phone (not by email). Usually, people who are genuine witnesses to events are eager to talk and you have an opportunity to learn more than was posted. If they are reluctant, you should be suspicious. Anyone who has taken photos or video needs to be contacted as they are the copyright holder, and you will need to gain their permission to use it.

There are continuous deadlines in online news, but there's no point being first with wrong information. Check your facts.

The BBC in the United Kingdom have staff verifying the huge amounts of material coming from social media. They use the following techniques to check the authenticity of material (Murray, n.d.). Some of these you can adapt for your own use:

- Reference locations against maps and existing images from, in particular, geo-located ones.
- Search for the original source of the upload/sequences and check its properties – the file metadata will provide source location and date of original recording (right-click on the file and open the properties option to view this).

- Examine weather reports and shadows to confirm that the conditions shown fit with the claimed date and time.
- Maintain lists of previously verified material to act as a reference for colleagues covering the stories.

Remember, it takes the professional skills of a journalist to turn raw information into a well-crafted news story. The audience relies on you to mine the social media noise for the nuggets of information gold. They need their journalists to have checked the veracity of the information and placed it in context to craft a readable, engaging news narrative. Finally, they expect you to let them know about it by publishing to them on whatever platform they are using. It's these steps that differentiate a professional journalist from a user. It's these steps that help a journalist to stand out as a voice that can be listened to and trusted.

I would like to express my appreciation to two of my colleagues at AUT for their help with this chapter: Danni Mulrennan, for her patient reading of an early draft and the sage advice to "loosen up", and Lyn Barnes, who took time to approach her students to ask if they would recount their experiences with social media. My sincere thanks to both.

Further reading

http://bit.ly/1duAtXT An interesting discussion on live-blogging.

Kiwi Journalists Association on Facebook, **Steph@LazyMediaFeed** and **journalism.co.uk** on Twitter. Online resources used by journalists to discuss current issues.

References

Beaujon, A. (2013, April 18). *NY Post runs pictures of men it says feds are looking for.* [Weblog message]. Retrieved from http://www.poynter.org/latest-news/mediawire/210708/ny-post-runs-pictures-of-men-it-says-feds-are-looking-for/

Buttery, S. (2011, July 29). *A false choice – and an excuse – for journalists: Better to be right than first.* [Weblog message]. Retrieved from http://stevebuttry.wordpress.com/2011/07/29/a-false-choice-and-an-excuse-for-journalists-better-to-be-first-or-right/

Dann, C. (Reporter). (2011, November 25). *Social website networks critical to response. One News.* Retrieved from http://tvnz.co.nz/national-news/social-network-websites-critical-response-video-4041971

Hughes, S. (n.d.). *Social media newsgathering. BBC College of Journalism.* Retrieved from http://bbcjournalism.oup.com

Murray, A. (n.d.). *Social media: Verification. BBC College of Journalism.* Retrieved from http://bbcjournalism.oup.com

Macnamara, T. (2011, May 18). *Eq.org.nz – The power of Ushahidi. NZCS Online.* Retrieved from http://www.iitp.org.nz/newsletter/article/94

McAthy, R. (2012, July 9). *Lessons from the Guardian's open newslist trial.* Retrieved from http://www.journalism.co.uk/news/open-journalism-guardiw

Rapper riles with Ryder tweets. (2013, April 1). Stuff. Retrieved from http://www.stuff.co.nz/the-press/news/8493025/Rapper-riles-with-Ryder-tweets

Qu, H. (2013). *Social media and the Boston bombings: When citizens and journalists cover the same story.* [Weblog message]. Retrieved from http://www.niemanlab.org/2013/04/social-media-and-the-boston-bombing-when-citizens-and-journalists-cover-the-same-story

Seitzinger, J. (2010, September 4). *Social media use in a crisis – #eqnz – which hashtag prevails?* [Weblog message]. Retrieved from http://www.cats-pyjamas.net/2010/09/social-media-use-in-a-crisis-eqnz-which-hashtag-prevails/

Selb, P. (2011, September 27). *Why the Arab Spring was the best and worst thing to happen to Al Jazeera.* [Weblog message]. Retrieved from http://globalpublicsquare.blogs.cnn.com/2011/09/27/why-the-arab-spring-was-the-best-and-worst-thing-to-happen-to-al-jazeera/

Sissons, H. (2006). *Practical journalism: How to write news.* London: Sage.

Williams, S. (n.d.). *An introduction to social media. BBC College of Journalism.* Retrieved from http://bbcjournalism.oup.com

5

Inclusive journalism
Being a journalist in New Zealand's diverse society

Tara Ross, University of Canterbury

Accurate and responsible journalism reflects the society it serves, in all its diversity. To report on one group or view but not others is fundamentally flawed. For example, research published some time ago showed that Europeans then comprised 67 per cent of the population but apparently accounted for more than 80 per cent of news voices (Comrie & Fountaine, 2005). That painted a skewed picture of New Zealand's society, its peoples and their interests.

> As journalists, we enjoy an authority that has become so firmly established that news often has the status of "common sense". We have a responsibility to wield this authority carefully.

Accurate journalism demands that reporters make an effort to become more familiar with and reflect the full range of communities and perspectives within Aotearoa New Zealand. That is not about pandering to certain groups; it is about recognising the distorted nature of much news coverage, which overemphasises the interests and perspectives of certain groups, usually white, middle-class, heterosexual men.

It matters that journalists get this right. For one, the news media play a key role in how a society sees itself. Journalists claim to know what is "really" happening in society, and audiences believe that journalists communicate that factually, truthfully and objectively (Zelizer, 2004).

New Zealanders cannot possibly know all of their fellow citizens directly. Instead, we rely on what we are told in the media, and so the manner in which journalists report different groups can have a real effect. Good diversity reporting can help communities to be seen, heard and accepted; poor reporting can fuel misunderstanding, racism and division.

The health and survival of your news organisation also depends on your ability to capture the fullest range of voices. If people do not see or hear themselves in your stories, they will not view you as a credible source of information and they will look elsewhere for news that is relevant to their lives. That has implications for your newsroom's bottom-line – and its ability to call on a digitally connected audience to help report the news. The commercial drive to reach the largest audience has meant news media often pitch to the dominant group in society and not minority groups. But just as the business of news is changing, so is its audience. It will not be long before there is a majority of none, and who will be the dominant group then?

New Zealand population projections (www.stats.govt.nz) hold that by 2026 two-thirds of New Zealand children will identify as Māori, Pacific and/or Asian. You owe it to your news organisations – and to those future readers, listeners and viewers – to include these groups in your reporting, and to include them in ways that are ordinary and routine. People are made different often because we treat them as different, as the exotic "other" or "them" segregated from "us". Our aim as journalists should be to pull together so many voices in our storytelling that diversity becomes the unremarkable norm and chapters like this become redundant.

Diversity in the newsroom

News coverage routinely reflects Pākehā interests. That's partly because mainstream newsrooms remain, by and large, white and middle-class. A recent survey found that 83 per cent of the journalism workforce was New Zealand European, 5 per cent Māori, 2 per cent Pasifika and 1 per cent Asian. By contrast, across the New Zealand population generally it was a different story, with New Zealand Europeans comprising 74 per cent of the population, Māori 15 per cent, Pasifika 7 per cent and Asians 12 per cent (Hannis, Hollings, Pajo & Lealand, 2014). It should be no surprise then that news stories are often constructed in ways that reflect the experiences and assumptions of dominant groups.

Mainstream media are part of the power establishment, and there are plenty of examples of how they are biased in favour of powerful, often Pākehā, institutions and interests (Nairn et al., 2012; Walker, 2002). Partly, that is the result of a reliance on news values that tend to advance dominant views, and news routines that make it easier to cover council meetings than Pacific fono (Abel, 2004). It is also the result of a reliance on Pākehā sources, even in stories about other ethnic groups.

For more on reporting Māori issues, see Chapter 6.

A 2007 study (Rankine et al., 2008) of newspaper and television news about Māori issues and Te Tiriti o Waitangi found that even when Māori sources outnumbered Pākehā sources, stories were invariably framed within a Pākehā perspective. Māori were represented as a problem or source of conflict and their rights were silenced. Clearly, the perspective of the journalist writing the story is crucial – and can distort how we report.

PEOPLE ARE PEOPLE

Katy Gosset, RNZ journalist and former producer of *One in Five* (www.radionz. co.nz), a programme about the issues and experience of disability, says it is easy for euphemisms and stereotypes to sneak into stories. When you write about the achievements of a person with a disability, for instance, do you cover their achievement on its own merits or as a cliché of the heroic individual? Is it, "It's amazing that you've managed to get out of bed to do the washing!"?

Effusive admiration for a person's "courage" and determination assumes that life with a disability is awful and unsatisfying. That is not only a gross assumption, but also a stereotype.

"That still has the potential to be isolating and single people out, rather than looking at the person as just a person in the community," Gosset warns. In other words, always take care with the messages you convey in your stories. "People have all sorts of issues and quirks and characteristics. They're not a certain way because they happen to have a disability."

Be aware of your own biases

As journalists we must recognise how our own histories and biases can affect our storytelling. Writer and blogger Sarah Milstein (http://dogsandshoes.com/) says if you are among the majority group – white, middle-class, heterosexual – you have an obligation to scrutinise systems of inequality, not only because you are probably a beneficiary of them, but also because you are less likely to be aware of the role that prejudice plays on a daily basis.

We all have some type of bias. To report fairly and accurately, we must be aware of it and work to overcome it. Start by being open to difference and the worldviews of other cultures. Avoid making incorrect assumptions about other communities by reading up on issues and people's histories. Examine your stories closely for bias. Are you reporting on all aspects of communities, positive and negative? Are you looking for different perspectives?

Part of mitigating bias is about listening – really listening – to others. Expose yourself to communities and people who are different from you, ask them questions and listen. Try to understand where they are coming from. The more questions you ask, the more inclusive your stories are likely to be. This goes for reporters working in mainstream media and alternative media.

Robert Khan, founder and managing director of Indian station Radio Tarana (www.tarana.co.nz/), says you need to get into the community to understand it. He requires every new reporter to learn about different communities by visiting places of worship and spending time with leaders to build deeper knowledge and meaningful relationships. "Just as you have to be able to interview the Prime Minister and report court, you've got to have some element of diversity reporting," he says. "You have to remember, we need the story. They don't have to tell us the story, so we need to be respectful."

It is not that hard, a Pacific journalist says. "It's the same as any other job. You just make your contacts, people need to trust you and you've got to feel comfortable in that community. I'm not Samoan, but I feel totally comfortable in that community."

Broaden your sources

At its most basic, inclusive reporting starts with your contacts and Twitter, Facebook and other social media lists. How diverse are they? Who do you follow? If you sorted your sources roughly by age, gender, ethnicity and so on, where would you fall short? Make the effort to cast your net widely and develop a range of sources that reflects the broader community. Ask your contacts for other sources – who do they seek out for community news?

Strive for a diverse range of voices from within each community. The Pacific population, for instance, comprises significant linguistic and cultural differences, and people may align themselves variously with their village, island, church or family identities. Avoid treating ethnic and other groups – including your own – as if they were homogeneous. How closely do you share the views of your family or your classmates? Why would you assume that ethnic groups all share the same view or perspective? Try to get the names of everyday people and do not assume that leaders speak for everyone. Many Pacific leaders are island-born elders who may not be expert on the issues facing New Zealand-born youth who now make up the majority of Pacific peoples in Aotearoa New Zealand.

In her guide to Māori news and current affairs, *Pou Kōrero* (2007), Carol Archie says you need to aim for a cross-section of sources. Look for Māori, as well as Pākehā, sources, and look for credible Māori sources, not just the "Pākehā-sanctioned" dial-a-Māori, who may not be held in high regard in the Māori community.

Follow community newspapers, radio stations and websites, and note who speaks in their stories. Follow the growing media from New Zealand's many ethnic communities. Paying attention to what, who and how they report will pay dividends. Join online communities and know where different communities meet. For example, many Pacific peoples are on Facebook and YouTube, but few are on Twitter.

Be aware, too, that many communities lack access to digital technology. It is vital that you also get out of the office and meet people face-to-face. You should:

- attend cultural events and community meetings
- visit different places of worship: temples, mosques, Pacific churches
- talk to people with disabilities, not their service providers
- talk to women and young people, not just male leaders
- try to find activities that take you into a new community.

Tagata Pasifika (http://tvnz.co.nz/tagata-pasifika) journalist John Utanga urges journalists to make the effort to meet people *before* they need to interview them. "I'll make contact first day, go back another day and then schedule a filming day once

It is not easy to find good sources on demand. Put in the groundwork early so that you have a pool of reliable sources when a story breaks on deadline.

we've got everybody on board. You don't bowl up with your cameras straight away, especially where you need people to be more open about the issues that affect them.

"The ethnic communities are often involved in a lot of cutting-edge social issues, so any young journalist should have solid contacts across the board, particularly in Auckland."

Good reporting requires good relationships, and those must be earned. Didien Malifa, a manager of the *Samoa Observer*'s New Zealand operation, says his reporters work continually to build and maintain their relationships with different Pacific and Māori communities. "We thought it was going to be easy, but we've had to earn that respect," he says. "It doesn't come overnight." His advice: "If you really want to focus on the Pacific or Māori communities, learn about the culture. If you know a little bit more about them, then doors will slowly open."

Giving voice to a broader range of

Tagata Pasifika journalist John Pulu crosses live to TVNZ's Auckland studio from the state funeral of King George Tupou V of Tonga, 2012.

people in your reporting is also about more than just covering the occasional cultural festival. You need to cover minority affairs all year long, and bring minority voices to all your stories. Include minority voices in the everyday stories that affect us all. Find a Pacific businesswoman for your story on tax changes, look for a Māori scientist for your story on science funding, and interview Chinese parents for your story on childrearing.

Including people in this way not only helps you to avoid ghettoising minority voices and news, but also helps you to avoid assuming Pākehā mainstream values are the norm. Mark Revington, former editor of Ngāi Tahu magazine *Te Karaka* (www.tekaraka.co.nz/Blog/), points to environmental journalism as one area where different values emerge, with a tension between the conservation focus on locking away resources and protecting them from use, and the view of many iwi who place an emphasis on sustainable use within the framework of kaitiakitanga or stewardship. "That Māori viewpoint is hardly ever reported properly, if reported at all," Revington says. Always ask yourself: does your story angle reflect *your* culture or the culture you are writing about?

Be careful not to overlook the largest minority group, which, in New Zealand, accounts for about 17 per cent of the population: people with disabilities. The US-based Society of Professional Journalists (www.spj.org) says whether you are writing about education, unemployment or the economics of ageing, there is always a disability angle to uncover. When a new school is built, ask if the buildings comply with the law. Are they accessible to people with disabilities?

Pay attention to cultural norms

Inclusive reporting requires more than seeking out a range of sources or ensuring a range of perspectives are in your stories. It also demands a degree of cultural competence, and that starts with an awareness of your own beliefs, values and cultural practices. You must understand your own identity to understand how it may differ from others, and how it may frame your storytelling. Your attitudes and approach to the job do not come from an innocent nowhere.

To interact effectively with people across different communities, you need a sound knowledge of different cultural practices and worldviews. In Māori and Pacific communities, for instance, it is important to identify a person's hapū/iwi or island/village affiliation. *Te Karaka* magazine requires all writers to report hapū and iwi affiliation. "They are incredibly important," Revington says. "Hapū more than iwi, quite often." If that information is missing, he makes the writer rework the article. In Muslim communities, it is important to be aware of gender protocols. Female reporters must cover their heads and wear a garment that covers most of their legs when visiting a mosque. Male reporters should take care approaching Muslim women, and do so through an intermediary. Both men and women should avoid shaking hands with the opposite sex.

Brush up on appropriate customs. Check protocols with a key contact or advocacy organisation if you are not sure. It is important to get first impressions right. If you cannot get in the door, you are not doing your job. Some suggestions:

> Look for stories on larger societal and structural issues. People with disabilities often struggle on low incomes. These bigger stories need telling too.

EXPECT BEHAVIOURAL DIFFERENCES

A Pacific journalist says one of the biggest problems journalists face when reporting Pacific communities is people's feeling of inferiority or shame, known in Māori as whakamā.

"There's a word for it in every single language across the Pacific. They just don't want to talk and there's several reasons for that. One is, for example, in the Kiribati culture, to talk means that you are standing out. You're a person who is trying to show off. Look at that person, look at her, why is she saying that?

"If it's someone in authority, that's okay, or someone who is perceived to be in authority then that's fine, but just your average family member, it's very hard to get people to talk."

When you make connections in a new community, stay in contact. After Lynda Chanwai-Earle's documentary series aired, she returned to the Wellington Masjid to follow up on more stories. "That to me was affirmation," she says. "If they had been offended they wouldn't have allowed me back."

Taking things slowly

Lynda Chanwai-Earle, producer and presenter of RNZ's *Voices* and former reporter for TVNZ's *Asia Down Under*, took a slow and measured approach to her four-part documentary on New Zealand's Muslim communities in the lead-up to the 10th anniversary of 9/11.

For an episode on Muslim women, she first contacted the Office of Ethnic Affairs to get the right introductions, then the president of the Federation of Islamic Associations of New Zealand (FIANZ) (www.fianz.co.nz/) to get the names of women in different communities.

Chanwai-Earle started with Reihana Ali, a spokeswoman for the Wellington Masjid in Kilbirnie. She visited Ali to ask about the appropriate protocols when visiting Muslim families and mosques, and took time to introduce herself and her story ideas. She was sensitive to the fact that the community was wary about talking to media.

"Since 2001, the Muslim community have been dealt to by mainstream media and they've lost their trust," she says. "I was very conscious that this was going to be broadcast at the time of the 10th anniversary and I didn't want to create a programme that was sensationalist."

Lynda Chanwai-Earle interviews Verpal Singh at the Auckland Sikh community's Gurdwara Sri Guru Singh Sabha. She wears a chunni (scarf) out of respect for Sikh customs.

Ali, a respected figure in the community, took Chanwai-Earle to the mosque to introduce her to other Muslim women. Chanwai-Earle then returned for another meeting at the mosque, this time with her recording gear, and it was only then that she began her interviews.

"Even if you're not taking your recording device, to initially meet and say this is where I'm coming from – putting that face to a name – is so important. It breaks down so many barriers."

Chanwai-Earle took several key steps to ensure she included voices that may not have been reached before. She:

- learned who to approach first
- learned appropriate protocols and a little of what she was walking into
- sought out a key respected contact who could introduce her to the community
- took time to meet face-to-face before conducting interviews.

- Know when to adopt a formal or informal form of address. Informality can be seen as forward in some cultures.
- Know whether to make direct eye contact or shake hands. Both can be seen as disrespectful in some communities.
- Know whether to use first names or titles and surnames. Using first names can be seen as rude or disrespectful.
- Know how to greet people. In some cultures, physical touch is okay, in others it is not. You might be expected to shake hands, using one or both hands; to hongi; to kiss on the cheek or both cheeks; to Namaste, pressing your hands together in a prayer position and bowing slightly; or to perform a deep bow.

To report society in all its diversity you need to know something about your country and its peoples. At the very least, that means having a grasp of tikanga and te reo Māori, as well as a good understanding of New Zealand history and Te Tiriti o Waitangi. Make sure you are familiar with the structure and tikanga of pōwhiri. Know how to perform a basic mihi, preferably in Māori.

Make yourself familiar with and observe marae etiquette. On many marae, for instance, it is not appropriate for women to speak on the paepae. Seek permission to use microphones and to film or take photographs. Ask someone to explain where camera crew and photographers can and cannot go. Observing these protocols is more likely to earn you goodwill and cooperation. It is about respect, Utanga says. "If you respect people, you'll be fine."

Pay attention to language

Your words matter, so be accurate. The terms you use can reinforce stereotypes or help to correct them. For people with disabilities, commonly used terms often do not represent their experience. Wheelchair-users, for instance, generally do not consider themselves "confined". When considering what terminology to use, Gosset offers the following advice:

- Put people first, not their disability.
- Emphasise abilities; for example, people *use* a wheelchair; they are not "confined to a wheelchair".
- Avoid generic labels, such as "the deaf".
- Avoid emotive language; for example, a person *has* multiple sclerosis, they are not "afflicted with", "crippled with", or "a victim of" it.
- Keep your language simple, accurate and neutral.

If you use certain labels, make sure you are clear about your reasons for doing so. Beware of letting place names like Ōtara or Aranui stand in as code words for negative news. Be specific. Muslim, Arab and Middle Eastern identities are not the same. Arabs come from Arabic-speaking nations in the Middle East, but not everybody in that region is Arabic. Islam is the dominant religion in 49 countries, including Ethiopia, Indonesia, Bangladesh, Turkey and Kosovo, and there are as many Muslims living in Nigeria as in Iran. The Middle East-North Africa region accounts for only a fifth of the world's Muslims; the majority, six-in-ten, are concentrated in the Asia-Pacific (The Pew Forum, 2011).

Always check terms with your sources, particularly when referring to someone's identity. For transgender subjects, for instance, you should use the name and personal pronouns that are consistent with how they live publicly. If possible, ask which pronoun or term they prefer. Check with Pacific peoples which identity they prefer. More often than not, they are lumped under the broad umbrella "Pacific", when they would rather be referred to as "Samoan" or "Tongan" or "Niuean". Never assume how someone will self-identify; many Pacific peoples have mixed ethnicity and their answer may surprise you.

Think about why you or your audience would want to know. Does that information add to the story? Would it seem out of place if you left it out? The Association of LGBTQ Journalists (www.nlgja.org/) provides a checklist of reasons for asking (and not asking) about a subject's sexual orientation (LGBTQ is lesbian, gay, bisexual, transgender and queer).

As a rule of thumb, refer to someone's difference only if it is central to the story you are writing.

Take care with names. When people tell you their names, repeat them back to them to make sure you can say them correctly. When Utanga is in the field, he asks people to say and spell their names to camera, so that he gets a pronunciation guide and a spelling guide on tape. In Japan, China and Korea, the first name follows the family name, so a man called Zhang Wei is Mr Zhang. If you are not sure which is the first name and which is the last, ask. As with words, take care with images, including your own, Utanga says. "In terms of your demeanour and your dress sense, try not to clash. You want to be sensitive to what's in front of you, because the goal is to get in the door and get people to talk."

When photographing or filming people with disabilities, show them in everyday social situations or in their work environment. Avoid focusing on a medical set-up or a dependent relationship. Likewise, do not let assumptions about ethnicity determine your news selection. If you are reporting on poverty, ask yourself: Do I illustrate my story with footage of a Māori family? Poverty is often equated with Māori and Pacific peoples, but the New Zealand Household Economic Survey shows they make up only 23 per cent of the lowest-earning fifth of the adult population,

KEEPING AN OPEN MIND

As a longstanding reporter in Pacific communities, John Utanga is knowledgeable about Pacific customs, but had to go back to basics when chasing a story on a Muslim community in central Auckland.

"All those things that I'd learned and have taken for granted in the past 20 years came back to me, and you just click into it. You're in a completely foreign environment, but when in Rome do as the Romans do," he says. "I had to go to a mosque prayer, take food afterwards, wash the feet and all that stuff. That was all new to me, but I just kept an open mind."

SEXUAL ORIENTATION

Reasons to ask about sexual orientation

- It adds context to the story. You are interviewing them because they are members of the LGBTQ community.
- It is central to the story. You are interviewing them as someone directly affected by same-sex marriage laws, for instance.
- You are trying to add diversity to your story or to highlight how different populations might be affected differently.

Reasons to avoid asking – or reporting – sexual orientation

- It would harm your subject.
- It is to sensationalise the story or pander to lurid curiosity.
- It is not relevant. Would you include the information if the subject were heterosexual? If not, think about why you want to include it. It needs to be relevant.

Source: The Association of LGBTQ Journalists (2013). Reprinted with permission.

whereas NZ Europeans comprise 62 per cent (Statistics New Zealand, 2017). In that case, it would be more representative to film a NZ European family.

Use statistics to cross-check your assumptions – and use them carefully. You need to know when the data is more or less representative. Look for selection bias in survey sampling, especially phone and email surveys. Have all population groups been adequately represented? One-parent families with dependent children are less likely to have access to phones or the internet than two-parent families with dependent children, and Māori and Pacific peoples are less likely than Pākehā to have access to phones or the internet (http://socialreport.msd.govt.nz).

Interviewing

Learn from ethnic news media and take your time. In the first instance, take time to find the right person to talk to. "If you went to a government department or a business they'd fob you off onto their spin doctors. If it's the local rūnanga or marae, they don't have a spin doctor," Revington says. "You've got to make a whole lot of calls to find the right people."

Take the time, too, to deal with sources in person. In a time-pressured newsroom that can be difficult, but kanohi ki te kanohi, or face-to-face, discussion is crucial in Māori and Pacific communities. You will earn trust and respect if you develop your relationships face-to-face, and once your sources know you it will be easier to phone them for comment when necessary. "Make sure you learn some reo. Make sure you pronounce people's names properly and get the spelling right. And make sure you get out there and talk to people to develop the relationship," Revington says. "One of

If the community you are reporting on is primarily immigrant and speaks English as a second language, develop a relationship with an advocacy organisation that can help with translation.

the best things you can do is say, 'I don't know much about this; I want to know.' As a journalist, that's the best way to uncover any story."

If you do use an interpreter, be careful about how you choose and use them, especially when reporting a controversial issue. Many ethnic minority communities are small, and your interpreter may have a stake in the story. If you are using a NZ Sign Language interpreter, allow for regular breaks – five to 10 minutes for every 30 to 45 minutes of interpreting.

Think about your subjects' needs and what will help them to feel comfortable. If your subject is in a wheelchair, sit. If your subject has a guide dog, avoid patting it. Like you, it is working. Always try to deal with your subject directly rather than through an intermediary. Gosset describes interviewing a subject who needed a support person to translate their words. She was mindful of needing to engage her subject as well as the interpreter who was providing the audio. So she used two microphones to capture both sources, and was careful to maintain eye contact with her interview subject throughout their meeting.

Diversity as accuracy

Inclusive journalism is really about nothing more than covering our society in all its guises. It is about including in your stories those who have been frequently left out of the news. It is about reporting deeply – providing context and explaining why things happen, not just what happens. It is about paying attention to the point of view that frames a story. Is it white? Is it middle-class?

It is also about finding stories that help your audience understand the people and the world around them. For ethnic media, that can mean taking extra steps to ensure they report the bad with the good. Self-censorship is a risk for small community news media. Journalists can be under huge pressure to protect their communities from negative stories, but those stories cannot be swept under the carpet. *Tagata Pasifika* journalist John Pulu says it is tricky when you have to report on your own community.

He should know. He reported on his own church, the Free Wesleyan Church of Tonga, when a new church it built in Sydney with big donations from the Tongan community folded, owing NZ$27 million. "I had to put on my reporter hat," he says. "The thing with our people, most of the time we encourage the positive stories, but we have to do these stories to show that some things have to change." Another Pacific journalist says reporters cannot ignore issues and events that need to be discussed just because they make their community uncomfortable. "Once you let yourself be swayed, you're not a journalist, you're a commentator … if you want to be a journalist you cannot cross that line."

Regularly audit your portfolio: over time, what issues are you reporting and from which viewpoint? Whose voices are you regularly including or excluding, and whose interests are you amplifying? As a Pacific journalist says, if you stop questioning how you're covering things, it's danger time:

"I always question: 'What are the important issues facing the community?' I also ask, 'Why is this interesting to my audience?' And generally it is that

To ensure your reporting is inclusive and accurate, check each story for balance, point of view, voice, context and framing.

people love stories. I get so many people coming up to me – quite middle-class, white New Zealand if you want to term them in such ways – but I get all sorts of people coming up to me saying, 'I love your stories'. They find them interesting. I think that the news bosses across the spectrum need to wake up and realise that New Zealand is actually interested in other people's stories."

Further reading

Archie, C. (2007). *Pou kōrero: A journalists' guide to Māori and current affairs.* Wellington: New Zealand Journalists Training Organisation.

http://nzpacific.nz *New Zealand Pacific.*

http://tvnz.co.nz/shows/tagata-pasifika *Tagata Pasifika.*

www.asianz.org.nz Asia New Zealand Foundation.

www.dpa.org.nz Disabled Persons Assembly NZ.

www.fianz.co.nz The Federation of Islamic Associations in New Zealand.

www.homevoice.co.nz One example of the many Chinese-language newspapers operating in New Zealand.

www.journaliststoolbox.org/category/diversity-issues Journalist's Toolbox.

www.tetaurawhiri.govt.nz Māori Language Commission.

www.mpp.govt.nz/pacific-people-in-nz Ministry of Pacific Island Affairs' guide to Pacific peoples in New Zealand.

www.newsu.org/resources/covering-islam Poynter resources for covering Islam and Muslim communities.

www.nlgja.org The Association of Lesbian, Gay, Bisexual, Transgender and Queer Journalists.

www.radionz.co.nz RNZ.

www.spj.org/dtb.asp The Society of Professional Journalists' diversity resources.

www.stats.govt.nz Statistics New Zealand.

www.tarana.co.nz/index.php Radio Tarana.

www.ngaitahu.iwi.nz/te-karaka *Te Karaka.*

References

Abel, S. (2004). All the news you need to know? In Goode, L., Zuberi, N. (Eds). *Media Studies in Aotearoa New Zealand* (pp.183–196). Auckland: Pearson.

Archie, C. (2007). *Pou kōrero: A journalists' guide to Māori and current affairs.* Wellington: New Zealand Journalists Training Organisation.

Comrie, M., & Fountaine, S. (2005, July 4-7). *Who is making the news?* Paper presented at the Australian and New Zealand Communication Association Conference, Christchurch, New Zealand.

Hannis, G., Hollings, J., Pajo, K., & Lealand, G. (2014). Survey of New Zealand journalists: They enjoy the job despite everything. *Ejournalist,* 14(2), 1–20.

Milstein, S. (2013). *Can Twitter make white people less racist?* Retrieved from http://www.dogsandshoes.com/2013/02/can-twitter-make-white-people-less-racist.html

Ministry of Social Development. (2010). *The social report 2010.* Retrieved from http://socialreport.msd.govt.nz/social-connectedness/telephone-internet-access.html

Nairn, R., Moewaka Barnes, A., Borell, B., Rankine, J., Gregory, A., & McCreanor, T. (2012). Māori news is bad news. *MAI Journal.* 1(1), 38–49. Retrieved from http://www.journal.mai.ac.nz/content/Māori-news-bad-news

Rankine, J., Nairn, R., Barnes, A. M., Gregory, M., Kaiwai, H., Borell, B., & McCreanor, T. (2008). *NZ: Media and Te Tiriti o Waitangi 2007.* Auckland: Kupu Taea Media and Te Tiriti Project.

Statistics New Zealand. (2017). *New Zealand household economic survey: Year ended June 2016.* Wellington: Statistics New Zealand.

The Association of LGBTQ Journalists. (2013). *Tip sheets on LGBTQ coverage – are you gay?* Retrieved from http://www.nlgja.org/tips/are-you-gay

The Pew Forum on Religion and Public Life. (2011). *The future of the global Muslim population: Projections for 2010–2030.* Retrieved from http://www.pewforum.org/future-of-the-global-muslim-population-muslim-majority.aspx

Walker, R. (2002). Māori news is bad news. In McGregor, J., & Comrie, M. (Eds.) *What's news? Reclaiming journalism in New Zealand* (pp. 215–231). Palmerston North: Dunmore Press.

Zelizer, B. (2004). *Taking journalism seriously: News and the academy.* Thousand Oaks: Sage Publications.

6

Māori affairs reporting

A field of journalism unique to Aotearoa

Carol Archie, Television New Zealand

It's a pleasure to read or listen to the work of professional journalists who understand Māori – or those who know how to use the meanings of Māori words and concepts in their writing. Such stories stand out as informed, richer and more intrinsically rooted in the New Zealand media landscape. Competent pronunciation of the Māori language and a basic knowledge of taha Māori are essential skills for those who want to reflect our society accurately and practise inclusive journalism. Reporters with these skills are confident and relaxed in Māori settings. They are also likely to make good contacts and get the scoops.

The mainstream media in New Zealand is largely Pākehā-owned and dominated. It can also be argued that most stories are written from a Pākehā viewpoint with the assumption this is what readers and listeners see as "normal". Our challenge as journalists is to include Māori perspectives and not depict them as an "other", to demonstrate through our stories that Māori are part of the mainstream too.

This chapter assumes you've done the background research and study required to understand common terms, organisations, concepts and history of Māoridom. Some guides to get you started can be found in Further Reading.

Māori language, culture, history and the Treaty

Te reo Māori

At the very least, journalists covering Māori stories should be able to recognise Māori greetings and return them, and be able to introduce themselves in Māori. They should

This chapter offers advice to Pākehā and Māori reporters reporting Māori issues for the mainstream media. For information on Māori media, see the "News outlets" box on page 100.

also understand key concepts such as tangata whenua, whakapapa, whanaungatanga, manaakitanga, kaitiakitanga, tino rangatiratanga and mana.

Journalists talk about the pleasure they receive from knowing a little (and especially a lot) of Māori language and getting their pronunciation right. Those with knowledge of te reo Māori not only reap insights into the experiences and stories of the marae but also feel comfortable greeting people in Māori. They know what to say in their phone calls and emails. These reporters are able to pass on, in their stories, an enthusiasm for the language, and a sense of belonging in Aotearoa New Zealand that comes with it.

On the website that accompanies this textbook is material to assist you with the Māori language. You'll find advice on pronunciation, use of te reo Māori in English-language stories, terms for emails, and handy words for songs and prayers.

More help with the meanings and use of Māori words is available online at www.learningmedia.co.nz/ngata.

History

Knowledge of New Zealand history and the Treaty of Waitangi will help you understand how historical and current disadvantage for Māori in this country (and most cross-cultural tensions) stem from the failure of the Crown to honour its Treaty promises.

The pattern of the past is that Māori nearly always came off second best in their dealings with the Crown. The facts show a legacy of broken promises and injustices for Māori despite the guarantee of continuing tino rangatiratanga in the Treaty of Waitangi. The injustices include the land wars, land taken by confiscation and legislation, political and cultural domination, and numerous policies and laws that discriminated against Māori. The disadvantage suffered by Māori at the hands of successive New Zealand governments continues into the present day. Most attempts at reparation have been made on the Crown's own terms and are small gestures compared to what was lost.

The Treaty of Waitangi

The Treaty of Waitangi was a solemn commitment based on principles as relevant today as they were in 1840. Journalists "honour" the Treaty of Waitangi by ensuring that Māori voices are heard and fairly represented in our media.

Another duty is to inform people about the circumstances that have led to Māori disadvantage. For example, it's deceptive and unreasonable to trivialise the settlement of historical Treaty breaches by referring to "lucrative Treaty settlements" for hapū and iwi. So often the elders who took the original claim have died along the way. It's been a painful journey for people to tell their story to the public at last and to have all that has happened to them heard and acknowledged.

While it is commendable that the Crown is making a gesture towards redress for major spiritual, social, cultural and economic losses, it should be clear that most iwi are offered a tiny percentage of the value of what was taken.

It's also insensitive to report settlements as though they're just about money. Loss

MICHAEL KING

The famous New Zealand historian and journalist wrote in his 1995 guide for journalists covering Māori activities that current affairs are always the outcome of history – especially for Māori. This is still true today.

"The present is the complex outcome of acculturation, military defeat, land confiscations, contradictory legislation, population displacement, racism, personality conflicts and continuing cross-cultural misunderstandings. In addition, the past is always potently present in Māori life" (King, 1995, p. 47).

of language and culture along with the destruction of whānau and tribal structures were a bitter price to pay for these not so "lucrative Treaty settlements". News stories seldom mention that it's usually the Crown that chooses monetary rather than other forms of redress.

It's unfair to suggest that "race-based policies" have somehow given Māori privileges in society. Race-based policies in the past denied Māori equal rights. Māori were not on a level playing field. Even in the 21st century injustices continue. For instance, the foreshore and seabed legislation overrode Māori rights as citizens and treated them differently from other New Zealanders.

Since colonial times Māori have to a large degree been prevented from controlling their own affairs and their own resources. Often it is a struggle simply to "be Māori". Politicians and others belittle whakapapa and deny the basic human rights of Māori to define themselves, for example, by making provocative statements about there being "no full-blooded Māori left" in the country. Calls for "one law for all" are actually "one Pākehā law for all" or "do it our way".

Journalists must look with a critical eye at every topic – including those about the Treaty and the settlement process. But it must be informed criticism. This means digging behind the easy headlines and common clichés to try to understand some of the complexities. If you are aware of the underlying dynamics you'll be in a better position to explain Treaty stories more clearly to your audience.

Until 1945, Māori widows, invalids and older people were denied the full state social welfare benefits available to Pākehā. That contributed to poverty in Māori families in the first half of the last century. And it's just one of countless policies that discriminated against Māori (Dally & Tennant, 2004).

Researching Treaty and other claims

Most Treaty claims go first to the Waitangi Tribunal, although some are made directly to the Office of Treaty Settlements for negotiation with the Crown, sidestepping formal hearings with the Tribunal. Find out if a claim has a "WAI" number, ask for a copy of the statement of claim from the Tribunal and the timetable for researching and hearing the matter.

Explore other claims and legal cases initiated by your local whānau, hapū and iwi – for example, to the Māori Land Court, Land Commissions, the High Court, the Māori Appellate Court, a local authority or the Environment Court.

Settlements

When the Crown has made a settlement with an iwi or hapū you'll find copies of the Deed of Settlement on the iwi's website or on the website for the Office of Treaty Settlements. An agreed public announcement is made at the time of the settlement, where the Crown acknowledges the need for redress of historical Treaty breaches and outlines how the redress will be made. Each settlement is different. Over the years it will be important to report how the settlement is being used for iwi members.

Start in your local area

After learning something about New Zealand history overall, the next step to prepare yourself for reporting Māori affairs is to research the history of the hapū and iwi in your local area. If you become familiar with local events then you'll find it easier to tackle stories in other tribal areas, even though they have different histories, personalities and so on. It's an inherent part of Māori culture to acknowledge and respect tangata whenua first, so you'll be following a well-trodden and effective cultural path.

Local authorities usually have lists of local iwi and hapū contacts. Te Puni Kōkiri has a directory online called Te Kāhui Māngai. Most iwi have websites. Make an appointment to visit your local iwi trust board or rūnanga office. Some questions you'll need to ask are:

- Who are the local hapū and iwi?
- What is their history?
- What are the places (for example, maunga) of significance in the area?
- Who were their ancestral figures and who are the leaders today?
- Where are the local marae?
- What was the impact of colonisation?
- What is the nature of Treaty claims, other claims and settlements in your area?

A sense of place

It can be like the missing piece of a puzzle if you know the location of old pā sites, wāhi tapu, the identity of sacred mountains, rivers and rocks, where the great personalities once lived, where great battles of the past took place, and the significance of local proverbs. Referring to these adds interest and depth to local stories.

Māori place names

In your area, it's good practice to provide Māori names for local towns and cities when the opportunity presents itself. Knowledge of the meanings of place names, and the stories behind them, will add another dimension to your report. It may also help your pronunciation.

For instance, Whakatāne was named when the *Mataatua* waka arrived in the Bay of Plenty. Traditionally, men went ashore first and left the women in the waka. On this occasion the women saw that the waka was taking them out to sea, but for reasons of tapu they were not able to use the paddles to bring it back to shore. Finally, in desperation, the captain's daughter, Wairaka, seized a paddle and cried

"Kia whakatāne au i ahau." (I will act as a man). The other women joined her and took the waka to safety. Whakatāne means "to be manly".

Some place names suffered from faulty spelling and misunderstandings by colonial settlers. For example, Te Tihi a Maru became Timaru. Te Oha a Maru became Oamaru. Pito-one became Petone. Whanganui became Wanganui.

Māori names for towns and cities can be found on the Māori Language Commission website, and the New Zealand History website has a guide to the origin and pronunciation of 1000 Māori place names (see Further Reading).

Local marae

Once you've made local contacts you are likely to be invited to their marae. The marae is the hub of Māori life and culture, so it will always be a place to meet the people who make news.

At a marae, you are likely to hear debate between local Māori groups about their mana in connection with the land in your local area. The people are discussing issues of control and authority, influence and prestige – as it was in the past and how they see it in the present and future.

Some make distinctions between those who are tangata whenua, those who have maintained ahi kā and those who exercise manawhenua or rangatiratanga.

Traditionally in most tribal areas whānau, hapū and iwi had overlapping and changing interests in lands, forests, bird-hunting sites, waterways, fisheries, marine areas and other resources. Tribal boundaries were not like fixed lines on a map. They would alter depending on matters such as conquests, whakapapa, occupation, alliances, gifts of land and reciprocal arrangements.

These rules were overlaid (and distorted) by new laws, based on Western concepts of property ownership, following the establishment of the colonial government. The Crown recognised some tribes before others and often made questionable deals when buying customary land and awarding titles to Māori groups or individuals.

Those are just a few reasons why relationships between Māori groups and their status on the land are still hotly argued today on marae and in forums such as the Waitangi Tribunal. Of course, raupatu or confiscation undermined tribal mana and created dispossession of a different sort in some regions.

The dispossession of Māori land is a major source of grief and loss in most parts of the country, but social, cultural and economic losses are as much a part of the story.

Understanding the wider impacts of colonisation will explain the priorities and goals of the legal entities representing iwi and hapū in your area, whether it be a trust board or rūnanga or other body. You'll find them intent on improving the health and well-being of their members, supporting educational achievement and cultural revival, and developing an economic base so they can be self-sustaining, as a group, for future generations.

Other local marae

Nowadays, as a response to migration and other modern needs, marae are established for a number of different purposes. For example, Auckland has dozens

CHANGING TIMES

Michael King also spoke about a change in the way Māori leadership operates.

"In pre-European times, leadership of hapū was hereditary and the mana of past rangatira was generally passed from oldest son to oldest son.

"In contemporary times, mana is still a vital ingredient in Māori leadership – though it tends often to be interpreted as social and political standing as well as spiritual power.

"Increasingly, it is the people with acquired rather than hereditary mana – organisational ability, communication skills, successful careers – who are emerging as the media spokespeople most acceptable to Māori committees and groups. These are not necessarily the same people who will be spokespeople on ceremonial occasions, which are regarded as taha Māori rather than taha Pākehā" (King, 1995, p. 44).

of marae that are not tangata whenua-based. They have been established to serve a range of Māori communities: taura here, multi-tribal, churches, schools and universities.

Tangata whenua initiatives

It's likely hapū and iwi in your area are involved in a wide range of activities, from health and education provision to language and cultural revival or resource management and business. You'll find a variety of structures to govern these affairs from trusts to corporate bodies.

Taura here and pan-tribal groups

In urban areas in particular, there's a spectrum of Māori organisations with multiple and sometimes competing interests.

In Auckland, where a quarter of all Māori live, the tangata whenua are vastly outnumbered by people from other tribes. This pattern is common in other cities and parts of the country. Most Māori people live the majority of their lives away from their tribal areas.

www.maorimaps.com has photos, addresses, contacts and information about marae around the country.

Taura here are Māori individuals or groups with kinship ties who join together for a common purpose and who either live outside their tribal territories or are urban-based.

For example, Auckland's biggest taura here group is from Ngāpuhi, followed by Waikato and Ngāti Porou. Many families have been in Auckland for three or more generations. Some urban Māori see themselves as belonging in Auckland and do not relate to their home tribes. To serve such groups the city has marae that are not tangata whenua-based.

Organisations based on multi-tribal groups include the New Zealand Māori Council, the Māori Wardens Association, the Kōhanga Reo and Kura Kaupapa Māori

FACE-TO-FACE CONTACT

Journalist **Debra Reweti** (Ngāti Ranginui, Ngāi Te Rangi, Te Arawa) runs a film-production company called Fantail Media. She emphasises the cultural element of covering Māori.

"When you choose to cover issues of particular interest to Māori or when you decide to pursue the Māori angle on any newsworthy issue you need to be both self-aware and aware of the fact that you are dealing with a dynamic, challenging and multi-layered culture," she says.

For instance, Māori appreciate face-to-face contact. "My grandfather told me that when you speak to a person for the first time, you must not only acknowledge him or her but also the people 'standing behind them' – meaning their whānau and ancestors. It illustrates the belief that we are all part of a larger, interconnected whole.

"This attitude also predicates the often-asked question 'No whea koe?' meaning, 'Where are you from?' If you are asked this question it's safe to assume that the person is not asking what news organisation you are from but rather where you were born and bred."

She encourages journalists to get involved. "It's a new age, one which invites all journalists to tell the entire range of stories that make Aotearoa New Zealand what it is. Embrace it and enjoy the stories that the Māori cultural feast can provide."

movements and the Māori Women's Welfare League. Many Māori professionals are represented by local and national organisations such as those for Māori lawyers, artists, businesspeople and doctors. The Federation of Māori Authorities represents most Māori authorities, with an asset base of billions of dollars.

Establishing contacts

In all areas of journalism, establishing contacts takes time and commitment and good "relationship management".

Sometimes the spokespeople for Māori groups are the same as they would be in any other organisation – the chair, vice-chair or chief executive, or they may have Māori titles such as kaihautū, kaiwhakahaere, kaumātua, kuia and kaiāwhina.

At times the most productive relationships you can build are with people who are not yet leaders themselves but who know the local kaumātua and kuia and others in authority. They may be willing to act as a bridge until you have established your own credentials by introducing you to new contacts, particularly elders. Helpful "go-betweens" will also assess who is the appropriate person with the expertise to answer a particular question.

> Whether or not you are Māori will be less important to most contacts than whether you have integrity and the skills to produce a fair report on Māori issues.

DIARISE UPCOMING MEETINGS

When journalist Adam Gifford was a radio news editor, he encouraged his reporters to diarise the annual meetings of local iwi, rūnanga and similar corporations, and ask for copies of their annual accounts.

"Like any organisation, annual meetings are when they should review where they have come from and say where they are going: always useful for stories and profiles," he says.

"Look for growth in revenue, profit or loss, return on assets, and also look at how any benefits are being expressed – grants to marae, education or sports scholarships. As settlements come on stream, the tribal corporates are important parts of regional economies."

Building relationships

In time, reporters will automatically remember (or take note of) the primary tribal background of their Māori contacts because this is at the essence of who their contacts are and where they belong. Adam Gifford, a Pākehā who is the English news editor at *Waatea News*, says that in te ao Māori having a rudimentary grasp of someone's whakapapa is common courtesy, as well as useful when looking for the correct source of information.

"If I am talking to someone in Whangārei who says they're from Tainui, I am aware they are not from there, and therefore are unlikely to be a quotable source on a local tribal issue – unless they've been designated as such by some specific relationship."

The reporter/contact relationship is often personal as well as professional – you take an interest in each other's families for instance. Gifford says this connection is apparent at a hui. "You make physical contact, through the hongi and handshake. So when you meet someone later you are more comfortable in their presence. You respect the mana of each person."

Become familiar with the major institutions affecting Māori life apart from the purely Māori organisations. For instance, the Waitangi Tribunal, the Māori Land Court, the Crown Forestry Rental Trust, the Māori Trustee and Te Ohu Kaimoana each have their own rules and procedures, which will be relevant to hapū and iwi at some time.

Read, watch and listen to see how other journalists handle Māori perspectives on television, radio, in print or online (for instance, E-Tangata). The Māori media in particular will provide useful background.

Māori leadership

It is said that the kūmara does not talk about its own sweetness. This means you'll find respected older men and women who would never profess to be kaumātua. But the mana of kaumātua will be apparent in the wisdom and integrity of what they say and do. You'll be looking for respected elders with knowledge of tikanga, history and Māori language – often with a desire to share, teach and guide future generations.

Ngāti Tūwharetoa have an ariki and Tainui the Kāhui Ariki. But they'll seldom be available for media interviews and tend to communicate through nominated spokespeople, avoiding the day-to-day controversy of current affairs.

Recently, it's become common for media spokespeople to be younger. Younger people may also play what used to be senior roles in their whānau because of their proficiency in the Māori language and knowledge of tikanga.

The current generation of older people were educated at a time when Māori language learning was discouraged, so some young ones are more qualified even to speak on the marae.

Respecting people's names and affiliations

Sometimes reporters avoid identifying people with Māori names and affiliations because the words are unfamiliar and seen as hard to pronounce or spell. These are poor excuses. The more you use Māori words and terminology, the easier it will become to get them right.

Where you have permission to take photographs on a marae, every effort should be made to use correct names, rather than print captions such as "a group of tribal elders" or "a member of the welcoming party".

Māori are usually identified by their tribal affiliation, and often their place of residence ("Haimona Taihau, a Ngāi Tahu elder, from Wellington").

Try to use iwi or hapū names to describe people, things and ideas rather than the label "Māori", ie "Ngāpuhi lands" or "Ngāi Tūhoe tikanga". Often a story has little to do with the fact that the person is "Māori". But care is needed if you are using iwi identity as an adjective to describe people – for example, "Ngāi Tahu artist". This may not be how the artist wishes to be portrayed. "Artist Hōne Bloggs, of Ngāi Tahu" or "Artist Hōne Bloggs, who has Ngāi Tahu ancestry" is likely to be more accurate.

Some people you interview may not know their whakapapa. Examples are Māori who have been adopted or whose family have been disconnected from their tribal area for so long that they cannot answer this question. In such cases it's appropriate to use the word "Māori" (if that is how the people choose to identify).

Appropriate spokespeople

Using inappropriate spokespeople or giving certain "celebrities" far more credence than they command in te ao Māori is a common mistake for journalists who are new to this field.

Experience helps, but so does logic. As an example, a hapū member may have the expertise to speak with authority about the tikanga of the foreshore and seabed but not about the management of fisheries assets. A kaumātua at a local marae may not be the person to discuss an iwi business venture or the legal structure of a new tribal trust. A rūnanga executive may not be your best informant about matters of history or whakapapa. Marae or rūnanga often have a policy on who is appropriate to speak on which subject. Ask people directly if they are speaking as an individual or on behalf of others.

Often journalists use a tribal label such as "Ngāti Whātua", which is insufficient

The Māori voice in the media

Dr Sue Abel of Auckland University has researched extensively on Māori in the media. Here are her thoughts (Abel, 2010).

"[W]hen Māori do speak as sources, they do not necessarily get the chance to articulate a distinctively indigenous worldview. By this I mean two things:

"Firstly, a Māori voice which is informed by a distinctively Māori worldview – a different way of knowing things, with different cultural values and priorities to those of the Western world.

"I am also using the term 'indigenous voice' to refer to a Māori voice informed by the processes of colonisation and their aftermath, including the relevant history which is important to an understanding of the issue at stake" (Abel, 2010, paras. 7–9).

to identify the group they represent. The person may be speaking for a hapū of that iwi – for example, Ngāti Whātua o Ōrākei or Ngāti Whātua ki Kaipara – and not on behalf of the whole tribe. Sometimes hapū and iwi spend months or years finding a consensus view, only to find a few dissidents taking a large and undeserved share of space in the media. It may be difficult, at first, for you to assess how representative the dissident views are, so it's best to be cautious rather than fuelling unnecessary divisions in a kinship group.

Covering Māori occasions

Many Māori public functions that journalists cover take place on a marae. They include hui such as conferences, tangihanga, perhaps even birthday parties. In all these instances, visitors go through a welcoming ceremony. To be confident and know how to respond at such events, journalists need to be familiar with the pōwhiri structure and understand it.

> The object is to get your story, and you are more likely to earn the goodwill and cooperation of your Māori contacts if you respect protocol.

A detailed explanation of marae etiquette for journalists is available in Chapter Two of *Pou Kōrero: A journalists' guide to Māori and current affairs* (Archie, 2007). Many kaumātua and Māori journalists helped write this chapter, so you are strongly advised to read it if you want to be well prepared to do your job.

The marae is private property; in most circumstances visitors do not arrive at a marae unannounced. On the marae you are operating in an environment where tikanga Māori sets the rules. It may, initially, seem time-consuming and unnecessary but ultimately it's speedier to follow marae protocols from the outset. It's not unusual for journalists and TV crews to be asked to leave marae simply because they didn't follow correct procedures. That's a poor excuse for missing a story.

There are professional benefits from behaving courteously and acknowledging Māori ways of doing things. Sensitivity and good manners are not barriers to rigorous, fair and accurate reporting. They are the pathway.

A PĀKEHĀ JOURNALIST COVERING MĀORI

Lois Williams is a journalist for RNZ in the Northland region. She is one of many Pākehā journalists who have derived personal, as well as professional, satisfaction from reporting on Māori activities.

"Having grown up in Invercargill in the 1960s, I'd encountered about three Māori people in my entire life, and like most New Zealanders of the era, had left school with my ignorance of Māori/Pākehā history largely intact."

Her introduction to reporting Māori stories was the first Waitangi Tribunal hearing of Ngāi Tahu's land claim in 1987, as RNZ's junior Greymouth reporter.

"The Waitangi Tribunal hearing was a revelation. For the first time I was hearing Māori stories of New Zealand's history – told by Māori. I remember feeling outrage at the things that had been done to these people, and the way they'd been sidelined from the economic and social developments the settlers brought.

"When I began working for RNZ in Northland in 1989, I was plunged into covering Ngāpuhi stories. This was a more complex proposition: Ngāpuhi are a third of the population, and have a long history of seeking justice from the Crown. Their leaders – people like Sir Graham Latimer, Erima Henare, Haami Piripi, the late Matiu Rata and Hone Harawira – have been at the forefront of the major gains for Māori in the past three decades.

"I had a great deal of help from people like Matiu, in particular, who managed to slip lengthy background lessons into every interview, and I read everything I could get my hands on about the history of the place, the people, and Te Tiriti.

"I would recommend to any reporter starting out that they do the same. Sit through a Waitangi Tribunal hearing. Read the evidence. Talk to the people, face-to-face. Get to know the kaumātua, the kuia. Never make the mistake of assuming that any one person speaks for Māori, or even for a particular group. Develop a working knowledge of the language; learn a mihi, learn some waiata. It is worth signing up for language classes at your local wānanga. You'll learn heaps, and make valuable new contacts, even friends.

"It's another world, another culture, but it is a rich and warm and generous one, and if you have a genuine interest, and approach your reportage in a spirit of fairness, respect, honesty and goodwill, you will find people will go out of their way to help you. You'll be closely watched, and judged by your work. And if you do a good job, they'll go on talking to you.

"There's still a big divide between Māori and Pākehā in this country, and while Māori are well-served these days by Māori media, it's important for the sake of our democracy and our social cohesion that Pākehā listeners and readers are helped to understand te ao Māori. It can only enrich us all – and for me it feels like a privilege to be able to do this work."

As can be seen in this 2006 cartoon by Chris Slane, Māori are frequently blamed for dependence on the state and negative social statistics.

Reproduced with permission

Journalists who work in te ao Māori

Many Pākehā journalists have discovered that an open mind and respect for people will get you a long way, even if you're still coming to grips with taha Māori.

Pattrick Smellie is a Wellington journalist and content wholesaler who calls himself "semi-competent" in reporting Māori matters. "I've never been formally welcomed onto a marae in my 21 years as a journalist. I was prepared to take part in a formal welcome once, but it proved unnecessary. Maybe the expectations of media were so low to start with there were no expectations!"

He's reported Māori economic issues, politics and business for years, but never as a specific round. "I do try to take a careful and sympathetic view. Given the adversarial way some major resource claims have had to be handled, with all parties willing to use the courts and political process, it can be difficult not to write in a way that seems to be critical of Māori interests going down those routes too. In those circumstances, I try to concentrate on the issues. The Māori issues reporting I'm proudest of has exposed such differences of opinion in a way I hope has been helpful.

"Of course, there's never a single Māori view on an issue, any more than there is ever a single Pākehā view."

Smellie has here stressed a fundamental point that anyone working in this field must understand. Māori opinions are as diverse as any other group in our society. It may be inconvenient to have to include a variety of different "Māori" views in your stories, but it's only fair and accurate to do so.

Checklist

As journalists, you are frequently in a position to shape the public mood on a topic, so it's well to pause and reflect on what message you're conveying. Some reporters consider themselves trained to be "objective" – forgetting that even their training was developed from a particular cultural starting point. Your attitudes and approach on the job will not come from a neutral nowhere.

If you are committed to being fair in your approach to covering Māori stories, this summary may help you develop a kind of antenna to avoid some of the pitfalls:

A MĀORI ON THE MĀORI ROUND

Yvonne Tahana (Ngāpuhi, Te Rarawa), a former Māori affairs reporter at *The New Zealand Herald* who's now working for TVNZ's *One News*, believes the mainstream's coverage of Māori stories is improving.

"At the *Herald*, reporters from other rounds, and those who are not Māori, are writing more about Māori and doing a good job of it."

As the Māori affairs reporter, Yvonne decided that she was not into what she calls "advocacy journalism". She was there just to ask questions. Like all those on the Māori round, she had to build trust with Māori leaders. "But it isn't a one-way street, as reporters can't be expected to 'go soft' on them. I think managing contacts is one of the most challenging aspects of journalism.

"The *Herald* offers a window on the Māori world without patronising Māori. I wrote from a mainstream perspective, but it didn't stop me having Māori contacts and writing fair and balanced stories."

She enjoyed doing the round but was very clear that as a senior journalist she wanted to be recognised as having the skills to write across a range of rounds, not just Māori affairs.

- Try not to judge Māori stories by your own cultural values. Ask yourself: Is my story from my culture or from the cultural perspective of those I am writing about?
- Be inclusive. Ensure your stories advance, rather than impede, cross-cultural understanding. Avoid terms like "they", "them", "we" and "us" or ideas that imply that Māori are an "other". Referring to "*our* nursery rhymes" assumes a Pākehā heritage. Remember: all cultures have so-called "myths and legends".
- Ensure your stories do not perpetuate unhelpful stereotypes of Māori. For example, do they portray Māori as disruptive elements in our society (radicals, activists, criminals) or failures (education, poverty, poor health)? Think carefully about adding to the plethora of depressing negative messages about Māori which reinforce stereotypes (sicker, poorer, academic failure), especially when you have not included any historical or socio-economic context. Explore alternative, less divisive ways to report debate that don't create or inflame conflict. Where feasible, look for more positive aspects to these stories, without romanticising or sacrificing rigorous inquiry.
- When using Māori as sources, cite iwi and hapū affiliations where possible and appropriate. Widen your pool of Māori spokespeople to show the spectrum of Māori viewpoints. Don't choose Māori spokepeople just because they conform to your values. Look for female Māori commentators – they are poorly represented in the media.
- Avoid using Pākehā to comment or "balance" stories about Māori issues and events.

News outlets that cover Māori issues

TV current affairs

Native Affairs on Māori TV: www.maoritelevision.com/tv/shows/native-affairs

Marae on TV One: http://tvnz.co.nz/marae

Māori-language news

Te Karere on TV One: http://tvnz.co.nz/shows/te-karere

Te Kāea on Māori TV: www.maoritelevision.com/tv/shows/te-kaea

Radio

Te Manu Korihi on RNZ: www.radionz.co.nz/news/te-manu-korihi

Iwi radio stations: www.irirangi.net/listen-online.aspx

Waatea News at www.waateanews.com

Print

Kōkiri magazine, published by Te Puni Kōkiri: tpk.govt.nz

Te Karaka, Ngāi Tahu's magazine: www.tekaraka.co.nz

Rotorua Daily Post: www.nzherald.co.nz/rotorua-daily-post Click on "Trending Topics" and then "Te Maori"

Online news

E-Tangata: https://e-tangata.co.nz

Spasifik magazine: www.spasifikmag.com

- Look closely at the terms you use. Avoid the term "part-Māori suspect" (we don't say "part-Pākehā") and the thoughtless use of the very word "Māori", which homogenises Māori as being all the same, with one Māori voice.
- Be wary of stories that claim or imply Māori are privileged – the facts don't support this. Speak up if your story is distorted, for example, by provocative headlines or TV news teases.

Crime is the bread and butter of news coverage, but the stories rarely touch on the systemic, social and economic factors that have led to Māori being over-represented in a monocultural justice system.

Your antenna may not be sensitive enough to pick up on all these matters every time you write a story about Māori matters. But now you know some of the ways your work might be assessed by Māori readers and listeners and by media experts in the field. This is an invitation to make considered decisions about your approach and to be open to change. Ultimately the best advice for journalists covering Māori affairs for the first time is simply to relax and be open to this new opportunity. It's rewarding, stimulating and worthwhile. You'll meet wonderful people and reach fresh understandings. What's more, you'll write some stunning stories of interest and significance to us all. Have fun!

Further reading

Archie, C. (2007). *Pou kōrero: A journalists' guide to Māori and current affairs.* Wellington: New Zealand Journalists Training Organisation.

Calman, R. (2003). *The Treaty of Waitangi.* Auckland: Reed Books.

Consedine R., & Consedine, J. (2012 update). *Healing our history: The challenge of the Treaty of Waitangi.* Auckland: Penguin. Also available as an e-book at www.waitangi.co.nz

https://nzhistory.govt.nz/culture/maori-language-week/1000-maori-place-names Origin and pronunciation of 1000 Māori place names.

Iwi websites. Most iwi have websites recording their own narratives. Examples are: www.waikatotainui.com, www.ngapuhi.iwi.nz, www.ngatiporou.com, www.kahungunu.iwi.nz, www.ngaitahu.iwi.nz

Māori organisations. Here are websites of the key organisations you are likely to contact: New Zealand Māori Council: www.maoricouncil.com, Māori Wardens Association: www.nzmwa.co.nz, the Kōhanga Reo movement: www.kohanga.ac.nz and Te Runanga Nui o ngā Kura Kaupapa Māori: www.runanga.co.nz. Research information about Māori business at the Federation of Māori Authorities: www.foma.org.nz

Network Waitangi. (2016). *The Treaty of Waitangi: Questions and answers.* Whangārei: Network Waitangi. Excellent questions and answers about the Treaty, available as a free download at www.nwwhangarei.wordpress.com

Peace Movement Aotearoa. (2011). *"Race", "Privilege", and the Treaty.* Available at www.converge.org.nz/pma/priv.htm. A collection of useful articles and reports.

Reed, A. (1996). *The Reed dictionary of Māori place names.* (3rd ed.). Auckland: Reed.

Slack, D. (2004). *Bullshit, backlash and bleeding hearts: A confused person's guide to the great race row.* Auckland: Penguin.

Walker, R. (2004). *Ka whawhai tonu matou: Struggle without end.* Auckland: Penguin.

www.learningmedia.co.nz/ngata A useful Māori–English dictionary.

www.maorimaps.com This site can be used to find marae around the country. It has maps, photos, addresses, contacts and other information. Also see www.takoa.co.nz

www.maoridictionary.co.nz Another excellent Māori–English dictionary.

www.ots.govt.nz This site has reports on the Crown's position on Treaty issues.

www.teara.govt.nz *Te Ara - The encyclopedia of New Zealand*, an excellent historical guide.

www.tetaurawhiri.govt.nz Website of Te Taura Whiri I Te Reo Māori (The Māori Language Commission). Plenty of information on learning Māori, Māori names for towns and cities, etc.

www.tkm.govt.nz Te Kāhui Māngai is a directory of iwi and Māori organisations.

www.trc.org.nz/resources/media.htm An analysis of anti-Māori themes in the media.

www.waitangi-tribunal.govt.nz Waitangi Tribunal reports and Treaty claims are available on this site.

References

Abel, S. (2010). *A question of balance.* Retrieved from www.nzherald.co.nz/journalism/news/article.cfm?c_id=63&objectid=10663343

Dalley, B., & Tennant, M. (2004). *Past judgement: Social policy in New Zealand history.* Dunedin: University of Otago Press.

King, M. (1995). *Kawe korero: A guide to reporting Maori activities.* Wellington: New Zealand Journalists Training Board.

7

Political reporting

Covering Parliament and local councils

Colin Espiner

If you're lucky enough to be offered the politics round for your news organisation, then congratulations, you've hit the jackpot! There's no other beat for a journalist that offers the variety, the intrigue, the complexity, the workload, or – let's be honest – the number of lead stories, than politics.

Whether it's central or local government reporting, politics puts you at the centre of decision-making in your country or community. And for a journalist eager to tell stories that matter to readers, viewers or listeners, finding news in this environment is like shooting fish in a barrel. But before you get out the shotgun, it pays to get your ducks (or politicians) in a row.

It's often claimed that politics is a specialist subject, but the reality is that it's quite the reverse. Although the political editors you see on the evening news give the impression of being experts, in practice covering politics requires you to be a Jack or Jill of all trades, and not necessarily a complete master of any of them.

Government reporting will test your personal skills. There are few other rounds in which your ability to forge good contacts who can help you get the jump on the competition is so important. Because politics involves the clash of wills and ideas as well as simple policy debates, you will also often feel like you are reporting on a game of chess (or sometimes a boxing match) rather than a dry piece of legislation.

HOW PARLIAMENT IS STRUCTURED

New Zealand has what is known as a Westminster style of government, which means we follow the basic rules and traditions of the British system.

Parliament consists of the Queen, represented in New Zealand by the Governor-General, and the House of Representatives, the elected Members of Parliament (MPs). The party – or coalition of parties – with the most votes at the end of a general election forms the government. The most senior MPs in the government form the Cabinet, and are called ministers with specific portfolios, such as Finance or Health. The Cabinet is the most powerful group of MPs in Parliament and is chaired by the Prime Minister (PM). It meets every Monday.

The term "Parliament" is also often used to refer to Parliament Buildings, where MPs work. Next to Parliament is the Beehive, an office complex for senior MPs.

MPs debate in Parliament's debating chamber, and the written record of the debates is called *Hansard*. When MPs are at work to debate, Parliament is said to be sitting or in session. Sitting days are Tuesdays to Thursdays. The debates are run by the Speaker of the House. The Speaker is chosen by a vote of all MPs, and is usually from the main ruling party. The Speaker has very wide powers and their word is final.

The Speaker is also in charge of Parliament and its grounds and must authorise any event held there. There are also officials who assist with the running of Parliament, including the Clerk of the House.

Laws are made in Parliament through the passage of Bills. A Bill is simply a draft piece of legislation. Bills are introduced to the House either by the ruling party or through the weekly ballot of MPs' Bills. Each Bill is debated, or read, in Parliament. To become law a Bill needs to pass three readings: if it gets past the first it goes to a select committee, made up of MPs, for further refinement and alteration. The Bill is then reported back for its second reading, when MPs argue over the fine points of each clause. If it gets through this, it goes to a third reading, at which point MPs make speeches for or against the Bill before a final vote. If it passes, the Bill is then signed off by the Governor-General on behalf of the Queen, New Zealand's head of state, and becomes an Act of Parliament. Sometimes a Bill is passed under urgency, which means its passage into law is fast-tracked. Acts are also called statutes and legislation.

For more information on Parliament, see www.parliament.govt.nz

As you get more confident in reporting politics, you will also likely be called upon to give your own opinion of what's going on. Commentary – whether on television, in blogs, on the radio, or in newspaper columns – is an essential part of good political reporting. It's what separates political editors from mere political reporters, and it is what you should aim for if you want to make your mark in covering Parliament or your council.

There are a number of things you need to know before you apply for accreditation for membership of the New Zealand press gallery (see below), or turn up at your local council meeting. We'll go through them in this chapter, starting out with the basics of how you go about your daily round, people you should cultivate, what you ought to read, where you should go and even what you must wear.

How the system works – or, where's the bathroom?

Parliament can be a bewildering place for newcomers – and not only for journalists. Newbie MPs can also be found wandering the labyrinthine corridors looking for the bathroom ... or the press gallery! The entire complex runs to its own strange rhythms: caucus meetings, Post-Cab, the bridge run, select committees, and the biggie of the Parliamentary day – question time.

All the MPs of one party are called its caucus.

What is the press gallery?

Okay, so it can be a bit confusing. The press gallery actually refers to three different things – the offices where the reporters accredited to Parliament are based, the area in the debating chamber where reporters sit and record the proceedings of Parliament, and the Parliamentary reporters themselves.

Everyone who reports Parliament must be accredited. This means the head of your news organisation must write a letter to the Speaker, stating that you are going to cover Parliament full-time, from Parliament. A copy of the letter must also go to the chair of the press gallery (elected by the members of the gallery). You will be issued with a photo ID on your first day by Parliament's security. If you don't already have office space in the gallery you'll need to contact the gallery chair to discuss whether any more space can be found – office space is always at a premium, and smaller organisations usually share.

Although reporters are naturally competitive, there is a very collegial atmosphere in the press gallery. It is common for reporters to share notes or recordings of press conferences or even to pool resources to ensure things are covered. Obviously this doesn't apply to exclusive stories!

A question of privilege

One of the good things about Parliamentary reporting is that, as long as you fairly and accurately report the business of the House, without malice, you and your media organisation are protected from being sued for defamation.

For more on privilege and other legal issues, see Chapter 20.

That means that as long as you're careful to provide a fair and accurate report of proceedings (and this can be a subjective judgement!) you can report the most outrageous and clearly libellous statements made by MPs.

This only applies to remarks made by MPs in the House's debating chamber or its committees. It does not apply to anything they say elsewhere, such as in the lobbies or chatting over a coffee at Bellamy's, Parliament's cafe and restaurant. Defamation is a real risk when reporting politics, so if in any doubt at all, make sure it is checked by the lawyers.

Reporting restrictions

It's not all open slather when reporting Parliament. There are a few restrictions you need to be aware of. The most obvious is the need for accreditation. Without your ID card you won't make it past the front door, let alone into the press gallery or debating chamber. It doesn't matter if the security guards have seen you every day for 10 years, if you ever leave your pass at home you won't get inside.

The second thing is only some select committee meetings are open to media. The deliberations of the privileges committee, for example, which deals with the behaviour and conduct of MPs, are usually out of bounds unless specifically stated otherwise.

Likewise, other committees can go "in committee" at any time, and you'll be asked to leave.

Television journalists are subject to stricter restrictions than radio, print and online reporters. TV crews can only film in set places – the lobby, the Beehive Theatrette (where the PM holds Post-Cabinet media conferences), the corridors outside party caucus rooms, and of course in the debating chamber itself.

For any other event the networks need to get special permission *every time*. It is up to the Speaker whether or not the request is granted – usually it is, but not always.

TV crews are also subject to arcane rules around what can be filmed in the House. Technically, only an MP who is on their feet and speaking may be filmed. This is supposedly to stop the filming of MPs picking their nose or having a snooze. The TV networks generally abide by these rules, although not always – if an MP's behaviour is outrageous enough or the story big enough they will break them, and wear the inevitable penalty – which is usually being banned from the chamber for anything from a day to a week.

Since the advent of Parliament TV, a government service that provides a continuous feed from the debating chamber while Parliament is sitting, the networks can take much of what they need without having to be in attendance. However, they often still attend question time or contentious debates, just to make sure they get the shots they want.

Print and radio reporters can pretty much go and record anywhere they like, without any further permission – even up on the ninth floor of the Beehive, where the PM's offices are. There are some exceptions, like secured areas and the debating chamber itself.

Radio networks can also take Parliament's feed from the chamber, although all broadcast journalists still attend question time. Sometimes there's no substitute for being there!

Journalists without accreditation are allowed to attend open select committee meetings, but will be subject to security checks and may not get a seat if the meeting is well attended.

Dress code

Men complain about this, but Parliament isn't an equal place when it comes to what you can wear. The boys must wear a jacket and tie when sitting up in the press gallery of the debating chamber (as opposed to the press gallery offices where you can wear whatever you like) watching the proceedings of Parliament. Don't think you can get away without the tie, either – Parliament pays sticky beaks whose sole job is to monitor this sort of thing, and they'll drag you out by your ear if you try it on. Women can wear what they like, within reason, although most female journalists wear a business suit when in the press gallery.

Outside of sitting days (ie, Mondays and Fridays, and when the House is in recess) the code is a little more casual. However, as a general rule of thumb, it's always best to err on the side of caution and put on the suit and tie. Because journalists covering Parliament are always on call for a media conference or unexpected door-step of an MP, you're going to spend a lot of time getting caught on camera. Your boss (and your mum) doesn't want to see you in your track-suit pants.

The PM's Post-Cabinet press conference

You've probably seen clips from this on television. Every Monday at about 4pm the PM descends from their offices on the ninth floor of the Beehive to the bowels of the Beehive Theatrette, where "Post-Cab" is held. The PM starts by listing anything Cabinet signed off or spoke about that morning – at least, anything that they want to make public!

After this the PM takes questions, which are shouted out by journalists. Don't be shy. Unlike many other press galleries around the world, Kiwi press gallery journalists don't take it in turns to ask questions or put their hands up and politely wait to be asked to speak. It's a bun fight, and you have to be brave enough and loud enough to shout above the crowd. The whole thing normally lasts about an hour, although it can sometimes run longer.

The Post-Cab is an essential diary item for all press gallery journalists. Most accredited journalists, including those who do not actually have offices at Parliament, attend.

The caucus run

Tuesday morning is when most out-of-town MPs fly into Wellington for the week, and all parties hold their weekly caucus meetings that morning. Press gallery journalists camp outside each of the party meetings to interview the party leader and anyone else they want to talk to on their way in. The PM and the Finance Minister are usually the most sought after, along with the Leader of the Opposition. Parliament's smaller parties are usually covered on merit, depending on what the issue *du jour* is.

Your news organisation will expect you to file pieces from caucus runs, with short snaps commonly filed from your smartphone going straight to its news website.

The caucus run is a bit of a jostle – stake your position in advance and be prepared for camera operators and television reporters to push their way to the front of the huddle. Sometimes MPs refuse to stop, so you have to get used to walking backwards while holding a tape recorder.

Question time

The most important days of the Parliamentary week are Tuesdays through Thursdays, which is when the House sits, starting at 2pm with the major theatrical event, question time. Most press gallery journalists attend question time, watching and recording proceedings from ringside seats above the debating chamber. The senior

A day in the life of a press gallery journalist

Tracy Watkins is the bureau chief of Stuff's political office in the press gallery. She got into political reporting the way many journalists do, via community newspapers and then as a daily rounds reporter on a metropolitan daily. In today's 24/7 news environment most days are hectic, she says. "For a print reporter, the day usually involves a fairly fast-moving news file to the web then turning your attention to the newspapers later in the day, where you're hoping to either break a story, or at least dig up new angles on the main stories.

"For a typical day you would come in anywhere between 7am and 9am, and the mornings are often taken up with media stand-ups with the PM or other ministers, select committees, press conferences, new reports, etc. In the afternoon there are usually more stand-ups, and Parliamentary question time. In between you try to squeeze in one-on-one interviews with ministers or MPs, or reaction outside Parliament. If someone is working on a good scoop I'll try to keep them free to work exclusively on that.

"Depending on what stories are big, we will often work on commentary and analysis pieces later in the day for the next day's newspapers, and we also try to work on features for the weekend papers. We also have to try and generate exclusives for the Sunday papers.

"Depending on the story, or what legislation is up before the House, you might keep filing to the web till late, as well as work on the newspaper file.

"A standard day usually finishes about 7.30pm though it's not unusual to get home about 9pm. The big downside is the unpredictability. Stories can blow up at any time and often do, so it's difficult to organise social events midweek."

Her advice to young journalists seeking to get into political reporting is to "know your stuff", by reading everything. "You need a huge amount of institutional knowledge to be able to cover and report on politics in today's fast-breaking news environment.

"You just can't come into it cold. You need to be across the issues before you even attempt to take it on. I've hired a number of young reporters for the Stuff political office over the years and this is the one thing that sets them apart from the rest."

Although political reporting is challenging, the rewards are huge, she says. "There are days when it feels like the best job in the world. No day is ever the same and you are at the heart of many of the big news stories. I've reported on some amazing stories and events over the years. When people drag out the history books in years to come I'll be able to say 'I was there.'"

journalists get the best spots – some even have their names carved in the old wooden bench they write upon.

Each day an order paper is prepared, listing the business of the day in the House, starting with a list of usually 12 questions to the PM. You can pick this up from the Bills Office (see below) from around midday, and choose which questions you're most interested in. The major opposition party and the government get the most questions.

Question time is when most MPs play up to the television cameras, and is usually where you will find the best quotes and the most entertaining stories.

It's also a very useful place to observe the body language of the various MPs and their parties, and to see who is confident and who is not. Although the wider public don't often see it, question time is a real test for ministers in particular, and their chances of promotion rest at least partially on how well they perform in Parliament's bear pit. Like the Post-Cab, question time cannot be missed by dedicated political journalists.

> Government questions – known as "patsies" – are usually used to allow ministers to boast about their latest achievements. Backbench government MPs are made to ask patsies, and they loathe it!

Select committees

These are often derided as boring and dull, and it's true a journalist can spend many wasted hours at Parliament's regulations review committee listening to MPs debating whether to set up a subcommittee to debate whether a subcommittee is needed to form a subcommittee! The trick, therefore, is choosing well.

Committee hearings normally take place between Tuesday morning and Thursday afternoon, and are held throughout the day but not during question time. The most glamorous is probably finance and expenditure, as this committee gets to carpet all the state's chief executives and ministers – ostensibly to quiz them on their departments' accounts, but in reality to grill them on whatever is the most pressing issue of the day. Select committees are broken down by subject, and include finance and expenditure, health and commerce. All parties are represented on most committees, which normally have a government chair.

Accredited media are allowed into any select committee unless there is an "in committee" sign on the door, meaning the meeting has moved into private session. These are usually kept to a minimum, since opposition parties would much rather the media were present! If a big issue or a big name is coming up, expect to see television cameras in attendance – and MPs playing up for them. They usually settle down once the cameras have left. That is often the best time to get a story the television news has missed. Be patient, and you will often grab an exclusive from a throwaway comment made in a select committee. You can also request reports referred to in committee meetings, but only if they have been tabled during open session.

A word of warning: never publish the report of a select committee before it has been tabled in the House, or the contents of any select committee discussion held behind closed doors (even if a member of the committee gives it to you). Otherwise you could find yourself in contempt of Parliament, and having an unpleasant meeting with the Speaker, who has the power to revoke your press gallery accreditation.

The bridge run

Another opportunity to grab MPs, particularly the PM and ministers, is on what is known as the bridge. The bridge is a small walkway that connects the Beehive to Parliament Buildings, where the debating chamber is housed. Every afternoon at around 1.50pm, ministers walk from their Beehive offices to question time, and most expect to get stopped by media on the way.

Actually, the media stand-ups with ministers no longer take place on the bridge itself because of congestion, but immediately on the other side in Parliament's foyer. Everyone still calls it the bridge run, though. It can be a little chaotic, with reporters darting between huddles around ministers, and other MPs trying to run the gauntlet without being stopped.

The reality is that while some politicians love to look too busy to stop and talk, they still walk past because of the presence of the television cameras. If they really wanted to avoid the bridge run there are alternative routes, which an under-fire minister will sometimes take.

The bridge run is a good chance to grab the PM or other ministers on issues that have cropped up during the morning, ahead of question time and the sitting of the House, which might tie them up for hours. It's therefore often your last chance to get audio or pictures, in particular.

The importance of contacts

Contact-building is a crucial part of the job for any journalist, but in political reporting it is even more essential. It is contacts that will separate you from a mere reporter of facts and allow you to interpret the events around you for your readers, viewers and listeners. It is also your contacts who – hopefully – will tip you off to a good story and help you stay ahead of the pack.

Contact-building is an essential part of building your network as a political reporter.

Friends or enemies?

Obviously MPs themselves make crucial contacts, particularly backbench MPs and minor party leaders. Why bother, you ask? Well, because Parliament's minnows have more time on their hands to talk to reporters, and are more likely to be flattered by your attention. And while they may be small fry, it doesn't mean they don't know anything. All MPs attend caucus meetings, most are on select committees, and, next to journalists themselves, MPs are the biggest gossips. So get chatting. It's amazing what a bit of time invested and a couple of cups of coffee will lead you to.

A change of government is another very good time to make contacts. Newly minted government MPs take a while to learn the discipline that comes with good governments and can be a mine of information. They will also be euphoric at their victory and keen to share it with you. That said, never forget that MPs are not your friends. You might get on better with some than others, and even enjoy their company immensely. But when push comes to shove, they will put themselves and their party ahead of you – and you should do the same. Always remember that your news organisation and its customers come first.

To socialise or not to socialise?

One of the perks of the job – or one of its downsides, depending on the sort of person you are – is the vast number of social opportunities Parliament affords. There's barely an evening during sitting weeks where there isn't some soirée, and a chirpy journalist with a wine glass in hand is almost always welcome. You don't have to join in (and let's face it, some of these events are awful – "The New Zealand Deerstalkers Association Annual Fund Raising Event, Hosted By The Hon Dull Ard") – but it's worth going to a few if you can bear it. It's amazing how chatty MPs get with a couple of drinks on board, and while these events are generally Chatham House Rules (ie, you can't report what's said), there's nothing stopping you dropping the MP a quick text the next day to see how much they remember telling you – and whether they'd like to go on the record now they've got a clear head!

Most parties also have functions – usually a Christmas knees-up and a mid-winter do – and press gallery journalists are always invited. Most of the public relations firms in Wellington also hold Christmas parties, and these range from the ordinary to the truly memorable.

The press gallery holds its own Christmas function. Almost all MPs show up, from the PM down, and leading PR people. This is one party you can't afford to miss.

Other places to build contacts

It isn't just MPs and PR flacks you should cultivate. Often, a well-placed official source can work wonders when another confirmation of a story is needed. This will take time and effort, since most government department employees are either terrified of or loathe reporters. The worst are former journalists themselves, some of whom are so embittered with their former profession they will go out of their way to make life as difficult as possible for you.

It isn't worth getting angry or snarky with these people. As gatekeepers to the information you need, try to get on their good side. Sometimes a cup of coffee and a scone is all that's needed. And take pains to report them fairly and accurately. Many public servants feel they have been burned by reporters who took what they said out of context. Become one of the reporters they know and trust.

MPs' press secretaries are another source of good contacts. Often a press secretary feels the need to give some information to a reliable reporter without going through the normal channels of a press release. Sometimes they're just bored and want to cause a bit of mischief. Get onside with them and make sure you're the one they call first.

Don't ignore the little people either. Security guards, cleaners, messengers, and the ladies in the service area at Bellamy's usually know more than you do about what's going on. A smile and a friendly word each day might mean you get a nod or a wink about which way an MP fleeing the press pack went when you're trying to chase them down.

On or off the record?

One of the first questions any political journalist must ask at the start of any interview – or even just a chat – is whether the conversation is on or off the record. You should also be clear that your subject or source knows what this means. Although the phrase can be used to mean "not for quoting", it is usually meant as "not for attribution"; in other words, you can use the information, as long as you do not source it. Also known as "background briefings", off-the-record information is crucial for political journalists, both when cross-checking news stories and for formulating commentary pieces. Off-the-record briefings also prevent embarrassing errors – for example, where a source can explain the background to a story the journalist may have been unaware of.

Such briefings can range from a chat with the Speaker in their office or a Ministry of Foreign Affairs and Trade sit-down before an overseas trip, to a chat with the Leader of the Opposition on upcoming policy releases or, as was her wont, a personal phone call late of a Sunday evening from then PM Helen Clark.

Bear in mind that in all such briefings, the person giving it will have an axe to grind – even if it's a genuine desire to see the "truth", as they see it, come out. That doesn't mean you shouldn't report it, but always ask yourself: Why is this person telling me this?

Whatever you decide to do with information provided in confidence, make sure both parties understand what is going to happen next and make sure you stick to your end of the bargain. The easiest way to a brief career as a political journalist is to routinely burn off a source. People risk their careers talking to you, and if you carelessly or deliberately mislead them, you'll find future phone calls and text messages go unanswered.

Information overload

Because politics is a subject on which everyone has an opinion, you'll never be short of resource material. Quite the contrary. The weight of information a political journalist is expected to read through on any given day is inhumane, verging on impossible. You'll need to become a very fast skim-reader and very familiar with the executive summaries of major reports. Here are some of the major sources.

Press releases

Much maligned but still useful. Make sure you're on the distribution list for all the major political parties and the Office of the Clerk. It also pays to make sure major lobby groups have your email address and fax number. Use press releases as a starting point for a story – don't copy and paste them into your stories.

Official reports

Parliament churns these things out on a daily basis. Get on the mailing list for anything that interests you, particularly in the areas of environment and public transport, which tend to be contentious. If time is short, go to the executive summary first – that will give you a few pars for an internet deadline, and you can flesh it out once you have more time. Put some time aside to wade through these. You'll get the stories other journalists couldn't be bothered to find.

Official Information Act (OIA)

Most of Parliament is subject to the OIA, and this enlightened piece of legislation is your best friend. You can request most things under the OIA – all you need to do is fire off an email to the relevant minister's office or council making it clear your request is an OIA one.

Be as specific as possible about what you want. For example, don't say: "I request any correspondence about the Budget." This is far too general, and will almost certainly be declined. Instead say: "I request any correspondence, including emails, phone logs, reports, or notes regarding Budget decisions on the housing policy released on May 20, 2018." Officials have 20 working days to respond. If you're unhappy with the result, write or phone the Ombudsman's Office. They can often help prise a document from an official's grasp.

For more on the Official Information Act, see Chapter 12.

Parliament's Bills and Table Offices

If you're working at Parliament, learn where these offices are and visit them frequently. Any piece of legislation, and most reports from select committees, will turn up at the Bills Office first. You can get the jump on your colleagues if you make a habit of dropping by each day to see what's new.

The Table Office is where any document tabled by an MP in the House ends up. If you see an MP waving a document during question time and want a copy, this is where you will find it.

The General Assembly Library

Just because everything's online now doesn't mean you shouldn't stop by this grand old building on a frequent basis. Helpful staff can find you articles, quotes from *Hansard*, and virtually every newspaper, magazine, reference book and periodical ever published.

Blogs

Blogs on politics have provided a wealth of new material for journalists, but be careful how you use them. There's a list of some of the better ones in this chapter.

The explosion of internet blogs on politics has provided a wealth of new material for journalists, and some of it is even accurate. In the United States, blogs like *The Drudge Report* have set the political agenda and scooped the mainstream media. That happens occasionally here too, but be warned: much of what you read on the blogosphere is either misinformed or plain wrong.

Never use information or a tip from a blogger without thoroughly checking it, and always get a proper, conventional source to confirm the information. Trolls, or political bloggers with a specific axe to grind, are ready and waiting to catch you out. For them, scoring a victory over a MSM (Mainstream Media) outlet is a badge of honour. Nevertheless, you should have some political blogs bookmarked, if you don't already.

Policy reporting versus political reporting

In the past, the focus of political reporting was on policy, and this was driven by the agenda of the House of Representatives. Before websites, Sky Television and Parliament TV, Twitter and Facebook, when consumers still got most of their daily news from the mainstream media, this was the daily diet of the political journalist.

Parliamentary debates were thoroughly (some might say exhaustingly) covered by

THE NITTY-GRITTY OF POLICY REPORTING

So you want to report on the policy detail? Excellent. In doing your research, here are the questions Jacqueline Cumming, Professor of Health Policy at Victoria University of Wellington, suggests you ask yourself:

- What is the problem this policy is trying to solve?
- What do we know about the problem – what data/research is available?
- What are the goals of the policy (are they clear)?
- What are the details of the policy?
- How will the policy be implemented, and over what time frame?
- How will the policy be monitored and evaluated?
- Which groups is the policy aimed at?
- Does the policy seem logical (do we believe the goals will be achieved by the policy and is it clear how the policy's activities will lead to the achievement of the goals)?
- How much will the policy cost and who will pay for it?
- What evidence is there that the policy will work?
- What alternatives were considered and why were they not chosen?
- What are the potential downsides – which groups might be disadvantaged by the policy?
- Who is responsible for driving the policy forward?

You can always ask for background papers, Cabinet documents, recent academic articles or book chapters or blogs, etc., on the topic, or seek advice from respected independent experts (such as academics).

reporters, particularly in newspapers, which also ran diaries of the House, including Bills debated in Parliament and what select committee reports were available.

How things have changed. Most newspapers no longer bother even trying to cover everything Parliament does, television never did and even RNZ does not have the time or the space. And nor is it strictly necessary that they do so, given the wealth of information now at the fingertips of every member of the public.

Any Bill before Parliament can quickly be accessed online, and every sentence uttered in Parliament is available through *Hansard* transcripts uploaded to the web every evening. Parliament TV provides coverage of the House while in session, and the Office of the Clerk also has a very good website providing constant updates of everything happening that day.

The changes wrought by the digital age have led to a change in the media's focus on politics. Reporters pick and choose subjects based on what interests them, and, hopefully, their audience. Rolling deadlines for all media and a tightening of belts amongst all media owners mean reporters must do more with less time, and that

A big annual political story is the Budget. See Chapter 10 for details.

inevitably leads to making some hard calls about what to cover. You'll need to quickly learn what topics push buttons for your readers, listeners or viewers, which sessions of Parliament are most likely to generate interest, and what to leave to other media or Parliament TV.

Because politics inevitably involves winners and losers, some reporters have a tendency to reduce everything to a match report. It's possible to frame almost any story in terms of who won and who lost, to describe various plays and counter-plays, tackles and rearguard actions as if they were reporting on a sports event. Sometimes this makes sense and can make for good copy. For example, most political reporters produce what are known as Year Enders – commentaries scoring the exchanges in Parliament over the year, winners, losers, chumps, charlatans, etc.

But be careful not to reduce everything to such a simplistic level. Politics, like most things in life, is rarely black and white, and your audience may not thank you for treating them like idiots. Try to remain aware that your job is to explain to your audience what is happening, and why. Sometimes there are no winners or losers – only different sides of an argument.

Reporting on polls

One of the most obvious examples of match-report politics is the coverage of political polls. Journalists love numbers because they make a story sound more solid and balanced, even though the reverse can sometimes be the case. It's very easy to report that the Monster Raving Loony Party is making a run up the back straight or is pipping the Truly Awful Party at the post. It's much harder, and more time-consuming, to explain to your audience why this may be the case.

Polls make good copy but watch for the pitfalls when reading the numbers.

There is also a danger that in over-reporting polling figures your news organisation can actually influence the story. If you constantly report that the Down in the Dumps Party is on the way out, chances are your readers will vote that way and your reportage can become a self-fulfilling prophecy. But not always. Voters in recent years have delighted in upending media and pollster consensus. Britain's shock vote to leave the European Union – "Brexit" – and the remarkable victory of Donald Trump in the 2016 US Presidential election left political pundits deeply embarrassed and scrambling to explain why they had not predicted either event.

The reasons are not simple or easily solved. Much political polling still revolves around calling landline telephones, which are rapidly becoming extinct, particularly among younger generations. Fewer people agree to answer the pollsters who do manage to get hold of them – perhaps due to a combination of time pressure and increased cynicism.

Polls are particularly prone to failure around support for minor parties, where the margin for error is much greater. This is because most polling companies use sample sizes of around 1000 people, taken at random around the country and then adjusted for ethnicity, location, age and gender.

But that means the sample size of those plumping for, say, the Monster Raving Loony Party might be very small indeed – fewer than 10 people – and their vote when expressed as a percentage could change dramatically if just a few supporters didn't answer the phone. When reporting on polls, pay more attention to the big, established polling companies used by the major outlets – Newshub, TVNZ, Stuff and *The New Zealand Herald*. Disregard free polls, those done by special interest groups, and internet-only polling, which tends to be extremely self-selecting.

What to look for

Check the sample size (it should be at least 1000 respondents), the method (it should be random, not self-selecting), and the margin of error (anything over about 4 per cent is too high to be meaningful). Be careful with interpreting the results of parties polling under the 5 per cent threshold, as they tend to swing wildly (see above). Ask yourself whether the questions posed are valid. For example, if a voter is asked "Should firefighters be allowed to strike and risk having your house burn down just so they can get a pay rise?" the answer is likely to be "No". If, however, the question is "Should hard-working firefighters be allowed to strike to ensure they are properly rewarded for their dangerous job?" most people are going to vote "Yes".

For more on opinion polls and statistics generally, see Chapter 13.

The best advice for reporting on polls is not to pay too much attention to any one poll; rather, look at the rolling average of a poll over time. The trend – whether a party is going up or down – is always more important than the headline number.

Covering elections

Election time is often seen as the glamorous part of the triennial political cycle, and it's true that your stories will get no greater prominence on news bulletins and on the front pages than during election season. It's also a wild ride – most political reporters travel with the leaders of the major political parties for the campaign proper, usually

---

POLITICAL BLOGS

Here are some worth bookmarking:

http://blog.greens.org.nz – Green-aligned Frogblog

http://dimpost.wordpress.com – Danyl McLauchlan's Dimpost

http://norightturn.blogspot.co.nz – Idiot/Savant's No Right Turn

http://publicaddress.net/hardnews – Russell Brown on Public Address

http://thestandard.org.nz – Labour-aligned The Standard

www.kiwiblog.co.nz – David Farrar's Kiwiblog

www.politik.co.nz – Richard Harman's take on politics

www.pundit.co.nz – Journalist-penned Pundit

www.thecivilian.co.nz – The satirical Civilian

www.thedailyblog.co.nz – Left-wing commentary from former political staffer Martyn "Bomber" Bradbury

www.whaleoil.co.nz – Cameron Slater's Whaleoil

about six weeks – and it's an intense, exhilarating (and exhausting!) time. Covering elections is also a time to have all your wits about you. Stories, rumours, accusations and counter-accusations fly thick and fast and you must be able to sort fact from fiction, quickly and succinctly.

What is good election coverage?

This is largely in the eye of the beholder and depends on who your audience is, how deep the pockets of your media organisation are (covering elections is very expensive, particularly if you are on the road) and what style of coverage you are aiming for. Some newspapers devote pages to long, often dull articles listing every policy of every party, which make the media organisation feel as if they have done their civic duty but are not widely read. Others take a much more light-hearted approach, and look for personality conflicts, human-interest stories and easily digestible poll results.

The best-read and watched pieces are probably those that seek to compare and contrast the main parties' policies in an easily digestible way. Good profile pieces of the main party leaders are also popular. Campaign diary-style pieces can be brilliant, if done well, but require a little flair. Have a look at the work of Jane Clifton in the *New Zealand Listener* or Steve Braunias in *The New Zealand Herald* to see how the masters do it.

Blogs come into their own during an election campaign. If you don't have one already, get your media organisation to set you up with one before an election. They're a great place for anecdotes you can't squeeze into a news report, and for behind-the-scenes commentary on the campaign trail. They also give your audience somewhere to place feedback and comments on the goings-on during the mad few weeks that constitute the campaign.

Local government reporting

Local Government New Zealand represents councils across New Zealand, and may also be able to help if you have a query or a complaint.

Much of the advice contained above holds equally true for local government reporting. Most regional, district and city councils are also divided along political lines, although these are usually not the same as the national parties'. The largest political grouping tends to dominate the council chamber in much the same way as it does Parliament. The main difference is that the mayor is elected directly by voters. This can mean that the mayor can often have difficulty getting bylaws and regulations through a hostile council. By the same token, councillors tend to be less rigidly aligned politically, which means less discipline and often better and more interesting stories for the journalist.

New Zealand's local government landscape is primarily divided up into regional councils, district councils and city councils. Regional councils are usually the largest bodies, since they cover the biggest areas – but that does not necessarily make them the most powerful. In practice they often lock horns with the district and city councils in their areas, especially where responsibilities overlap. Regional councils generally concern themselves with matters that impact upon the environment – fresh and salt water, soil, pollution, air quality, forestry and transport.

Smaller towns have district councils, while larger towns and cities have city

LIFE ON THE COUNCIL BEAT

Glenn Conway is a former local government reporter at Christchurch's *Press* newspaper. He began his career reporting on council as a cadet journalist in Gore: "I have always had an interest in politics, so this was a great way to see elected politicians at work every day."

One of the appeals of the council round is its variety. "One day, you can be sitting at a meeting where ideas are being raised, the next you could be interviewing people in communities affected by those decisions and the following day you could be in the middle of a major political argument."

Every week usually involves at least a couple of days of attending committees and full council meetings, talking (on and off the record) with councillors, mayors and council staff and then having conversations with residents who bear the brunt of the decisions these people make.

"The challenge is ensuring you get to the heart of the stories while achieving balance – both sides of the story, because in council/politics there are always two if not three views!"

His advice to young journalists seeking to get into council reporting is to go for it. "It is such a fun, exciting round – the best round, I reckon. Be prepared to be swamped with figures, viewpoints and debate. But that's why it is so much fun."

He says the rewards of covering councils are breaking important stories for your audience "and being in the thick of it as these decisions and debates are happening".

Photo: Stuff

councils. These typically are responsible for local roading, sewerage and rubbish collection, libraries, parks, town planning, etc. Because of local body amalgamation, some, such as Auckland's super city, have become very large indeed and very powerful.

Most councils also have committees and subcommittees, which are usually broken down by topic (much like select committees at Parliament – transport, waste water, finance, environment, etc.). Often these are worth attending, as they will provide the first inkling of what a council is up to and the direction it is headed. They will discuss policy proposals, hear public submissions and make recommendations. Meetings of the full council will often simply rubber-stamp policies recommended by the committees.

Councils generally must hold monthly meetings of the whole council in public. Most also hold ward, or local, meetings in various towns or suburbs, which are usually also open to the public.

You have the right to attend and report on these meetings, and your coverage of these meetings attracts much the same qualified privilege as reports from Parliament

– as long as they are a fair and accurate summary of proceedings. Unlike Parliamentary debates, however, where everything is in the public domain, councils can go "in committee", and at these times the public and reporters are asked to leave. Councils must inform you of the reasons for going in committee, and these are laid down in the Local Government Official Information and Meetings Act. Broadly, councils can only enter private session to discuss commercially sensitive information, or where there is a compelling need to protect someone's privacy. You can challenge a council's excessive use of private sessions by contacting the Ombudsman.

Covering council meetings

Notice that the spelling is "councillor". It is not "councilor" or "counsellor"!

Councils deal with the bread and butter of our daily lives: roading, rubbish, rates, building permits, zoning, commercial activities, tourism, public events, even prostitution and gambling. Sure, some of it is deadly dull and loaded down with jargon and long-winded explanation. But any journalist willing to put in the hours and to form relationships with their local councillors will uncover a treasure trove of stories of high interest to your audience.

Each council meeting will have an agenda, beginning with apologies and minutes from the previous meeting, and then moving on through each item of business before usually going into committee at the end to deal with any confidential issues. It often pays to wait until after the in-committee stage is over, just in case the council tries to slip through any last-minute order of business without the media present (it has happened!).

You may also wish to talk to any councillors who may have objected to a particular item or who may have more to say on an issue you're interested in. Just remember that any privilege attached to their remarks only applies to those made in the meeting itself – not outside.

Get council meeting agendas sent to you in advance under embargo to ensure a head start. Most councils will agree to send legitimate news organisations their meeting papers in advance, so long as you don't breach the embargo. They are often also available online on the council's website. At the very least, most councils will provide some outline of what will be discussed and where and what time the meeting will be held. That way you can prioritise ahead of time what topics are likely to be of the most interest, and let your editor know in advance.

Councillors and officials often drop the word "the" when referring to their council: "Council decided to defer its decision." Don't follow suit. Make sure you use the word "the", as it's how your readers speak: "The council decided to defer its decision."

Since council meetings are often held in the evenings, when deadlines are tight, it pays to have at least some of your stories partly pre-written and your research already completed. Most councils are happy to allow you to use your laptop on the press bench provided in the council chamber, so you can file your stories direct from the meeting.

Of course, the meetings themselves are only a starting point. As with reporting on central government, it is essential you make good contacts. Many councillors have ambitions to be in Parliament one day, and therefore will be extremely keen to make their mark. Seek out the ambitious ones, and let them know they should contact you first with any scoops they may have!

You should also use the meeting agendas as a basis for finding out what the council

TWITTER

Twitter (and, to a lesser extent, Facebook) has had a huge impact on the coverage of politics. Politicians, journalists, commentators, party hacks and just about everyone else use Twitter to berate, enrage, entertain, and even occasionally inform!

Tweets from politicians and political parties often make excellent news. Sometimes someone may even say something they shouldn't have. So build a list of the Twitter accounts of people whose views you value, and make sure you follow a range of politicians from all parties.

Never accept at face value anything you read on social media. Parody and fake news abound. And remember those on Twitter represent only a small segment of the population. Don't assume that just because the Twittersphere is boiling over the rest of the country is similarly consumed!

Many political journalists post on Twitter, and it can be a good tool for reaching a wider audience and publicising your stories. Posting pictures can also be very effective. But be wary of being seen as partisan. With few characters to play with in Twitter posts, nuances get lost and you may polarise your readers. And remember the Twittersphere talks back, so avoid being dragged into Twitter feuds.

is up to and for making your own inquiries. Become familiar with the council staff in your area, and contact them regularly to see what's up. There is probably also some form of citizens and ratepayers' association in your area, and they are a good place to find out what the hot-button issues in your community are, and whether there is any general unhappiness with the performance of the council.

Community boards

At the lower end of the pecking order are community boards. These usually contain some elected councillors and other members of the local community, such as representatives of local community groups and organisations. They also issue agendas, and meet at least monthly. These are a very good source of hyper-local news, which is particularly attractive to community newspapers, but can also be useful to larger news organisations, especially when there is a stoush brewing in a community. Don't just file stories based on reports of community board meetings – use them as the basis for informing you about what is going on in your local area.

Money, money, money

Of all the contentious issues councils deal with, it is the annual rates-setting that causes the most angst – and the best chance of a front-page story. Councils raise money from rates, which are levied on anyone who owns property in the district,

Be careful how you interpret rates rises when reporting on local government.

plus charges for services and borrowing. Rates rises also affect anyone paying rent, since hefty increases will probably lead landlords to charge more for their properties. Councils generally increase rates each year, and normally by at least 2 per cent, depending on whether there are any major infrastructure developments planned, or plans to pay down debt. Larger rates increases may be a signal that all is not well with the council's finances, and this is a signal for you to start digging!

In general, ratepayer organisations want a zero rates increase, while community groups might hope for a bigger rise, as it could mean more money for the council to spend on their pet projects. Make sure you get a balanced range of opinions before writing your story, and consider whether the rates rise is actually justified.

So filing a story with an introduction such as: "XYZ Council has outraged ratepayers by hiking up annual rates 3.5 per cent despite promising last year to hold cost increases to a minimum" might be completely unfair if the council is operating in a high-inflation environment where the average rates rise around the country is in fact 4 per cent. There could also be other factors at play. For example, XYZ Council might be using the extra rates money to fund public transport, in which case a more appropriate intro might be: "Public transport is the winner in XYZ Council's new annual plan, but ratepayers are upset it is being funded by a 3.5 per cent rates rise."

Further reading

www.beehive.govt.nz The homepage of the New Zealand government. The place to find ministerial press releases, biographies, government policy statements and speeches.

www.elections.org.nz Everything you want to know and more about how our triennial general elections are run; party lists, electorate breakdowns, voting patterns, electoral donation returns and much more.

www.labour.org.nz The Labour Party's homepage, with the same sort of material as National's – only much more Left-leaning!

www.legislation.govt.nz Gives you online access to Acts and Bills.

www.lgnz.co.nz Official website of Local Government New Zealand, which represents all the councils in the country.

www.localgovt.co.nz Online portal and central repository for information on all local councils in New Zealand, including council district plans, policies, mapping and statistics.

www.national.org.nz National's website, including party campaign material, policy statements, candidates and videos featuring the leader.

www.parliament.nz/en-nz The homepage for Parliament, including live TV feeds, select committee reports, Bills, the business of the House and much more.

www.parliament.nz/en-nz/pb/debates/debates The online home of *Hansard*. If you need a quote from a speech made during a debate, *Hansard* will probably have it.

8

Police and court reporting

From reporting the discovery of a murder victim's body to covering the sentencing of the killer

Deborah Morris, Stuff; Fran Tyler, Massey University

Police and court stories have been a mainstay for media organisations for years, allowing the equivalent of watching the dirty dealings of neighbours through twitching curtains. But the news media also has a social responsibility to report police and court stories. Justice must be seen to be done, and society's condemnation of the acts of criminals through having their names published is often seen as part of the punishment.

The police round

Police generally have a policy that the media must go through official channels and deal with the force's communications people. But some of the best information comes from the police on the ground.

While the police media centres are available, it is important to invest time and effort in getting to know local officers, from the area commander to the traffic patrol officers. Make sure you learn their ranks and how to spell their names. By taking time to chat with your local police, you are more likely to hear about the many police stories that would otherwise go unreported.

Police should be treated like any other contact: make regular phone calls to them

Police encourage media to go through the police media centres. For details, visit www.police.govt.nz/news/police-media-contacts

and occasionally take them for a coffee. Email should be your last resort, as it's all too easy for the recipient just to hit delete!

Some officers will want to keep their identity confidential, as they may be disciplined for leaking information to the media. You must respect this wish. A breach of this trust will quickly damage your reputation and end the flow of information.

You may find, especially at media conferences or in press releases, that officers use a unique jargon or police-speak to describe events or people. For example, you might be told, "The offender decamped the scene in an easterly direction." Instead of reporting this, you should say something like: "The man ran towards the shopping centre." Make sure when you recast words in this way that your reporting remains accurate.

If you are ever unsure what the police are trying to tell you, ask them to clarify.

Reporting a police story

The structure of a police story is no different from any other news story, and should be written in the usual inverted-pyramid style (see page 213). You need to include the basic who, what, when, where, how and why. Lead with the most relevant and interesting information – especially any information exclusive to your news organisation – before fleshing the story out with other information you have gathered, including what happens next.

You need to make the story as balanced as possible, even if you do not have information from the victim or suspect/accused. While it can be tempting to take sides, remember you are there to report the facts as they are presented, not give your opinion. For example, it may turn out later that the "victim" in an assault case was actually a mugger who got the worse end of the deal when his intended victim fought back. Wild unsupported accusations, no matter how salacious, should be avoided. Never assume that someone is blameless or that someone is guilty.

Dealing with the police

Mark Stevens was police reporter for *The Evening Post* and now is editorial director at Stuff. He warns about getting too friendly with your police sources.

"In my time covering the police beat, I went to the police bar only once and even then only after I'd been on the round for several years.

"The toughest and most important task for any young police reporter is making good solid contacts, without becoming friends. Once you're friendly, you risk making concessions for the wrong reasons – only to keep them onside. Those concessions in the early days of your career can be damaging."

The kinds of concessions he is talking about include times when police ask you not to publish things. It's true there are times you shouldn't publish information – for instance, the name of a murder victim may be withheld until the family is informed – but you should be very clear as to what can be released and when. You should keep your chief reporter or editor aware of any proposed deals.

Photo: *The Dominion Post*

Always keep your eyes open for good ways to illustrate your story. Perhaps police can provide you with security video or stills that show the event in progress. Sometimes they may want to appeal for information about weapons they have found and could provide you with photographs. Drug busts can provide great images of police pulling out huge cannabis crops. While murders and other serious crimes are the most obvious news stories, smaller and insignificant offences can make good stories too. Whatever the scale of the offence, police stories must meet the news values of being unusual, unexpected, relevant and timely.

Police reporters use a scanner to monitor police radios. While it's not an offence to do this, it is an offence to act on the information. Reporters therefore try to find alternative sources of information, such as social media.

The story breaks

The first reports of a police call-out are likely to come through official police channels, for example, from police website incident reports (see www.police.govt.nz/news) or from a media release. Anything that comes through official channels, such as police or emergency services, can be immediately written up and published on your news organisation's website, before any follow-up work is done. If a story is posted, it is acceptable to ask the public to make contact via a news-tip line or other means if they have more information, saw events taking place or have photographs. At other times you might be alerted to a police story by a member of the public, who may phone with a tip-off, or you may get an alert through social media.

Police stories are human stories. While telling of a robbery at a corner store will interest readers, the experiences of the shop assistant who was confronted with an armed robber will be more engaging, as most people will not have experienced this.

Going to the scene

Police reporters usually write about events that have already happened. This means that often information comes from interviewing others.

REPORTING DEATH

Blair Ensor is a former police reporter for *The Dominion Post* and now Stuff's chief news director for Canterbury-Otago. He shares his experiences of covering human loss.

"The visits we make to [bereaved] people are known inside the newsroom as 'death knocks'. This blunt terminology implies no disrespect, but simply acknowledges they are a necessary part of newsgathering.

"Police and justice reporters cover more death knocks than any other staff and they are often enormously touched by their encounters with grief.

"Since starting out as a reporter in 2008 I've witnessed tragic scenes at some of New Zealand's biggest news events, including the Christchurch earthquakes and the Carterton balloon crash. I've covered homicide cases extensively and reported on the aftermath of countless fatal crashes.

"Death knocks never get any easier, but I've always made a point of doing them in person rather than hiding behind a telephone, simply because I think people trust a reporter more if they see who they're talking to.

"There's no way of knowing how a grieving family will respond to a reporter who turns up unannounced at their front door, but my first words will always explain who I am and that I'm sorry for their loss. I then tell them that we're writing a story and that we'd like to offer them the chance to contribute details about their loved one and reaction to their death.

"Some have welcomed me into their home, others have given me a few words at their doorstep and others have slammed the door shut in my face.

"Whenever I'm invited inside I'm always incredibly humbled, but if I'm told to leave I respect their decision. If they don't want to talk then, I always leave a phone number because they often change their mind and call back a few hours later. If they don't, I'll try to make other approaches through a family friend or another relative.

"Some people criticise journalists for invading a grieving family's privacy in a time of incredible suffering, but it is a necessary part of our job.

"Police have often told me grieving families don't want to talk, but that is rarely the case and it is important we approach them directly.

"News is about gathering the most reliable and detailed facts, and more often than not the people who know the most about an incident and the person involved are their family. Talking to a grieving family also allows them to pay tribute to the loved one they've lost and warn people of any potential dangers associated with the incident.

"While death knocks are a daunting task, there have been moments that have made it all worthwhile.

"When Amanda Taufale was killed in her home in Tawa (November 2012) her father was very upset and apprehensive about talking, but he did. The next day I was touched when he thanked me for the story almost immediately after he had placed his daughter's casket in the back of a hearse.

▶

"There have also been moments I'd rather I hadn't been the police reporter. "The morning a police officer told me that the father of a very good friend [of mine] had accidentally shot himself while out hunting will always stick with me. It made me realise how small New Zealand is and how incidents can impact on anyone. I'm always nervous the next death I have to cover will be someone else I know."

Photo: *The Dominion Post*

If the event is still in progress or has recently happened, make contact with police, neighbours, witnesses, the victims and their families and anyone else who can fit together the events. You may be expected to report from the scene, especially if you're working for television, radio and online news sites.

When you arrive, you may be confronted with a line of white and red emergency tape. Make yourself known to the scene guard and ask to be directed to the officer in charge. Do not cross the tape unless you are told you have permission to do so. Police do not take kindly to reporters trampling on their crime scenes – you may inadvertently destroy important evidence. That should not stop you from knocking on neighbours' doors or speaking to other potential witnesses, outside the tape.

You should always gather the names of those involved, including the victim(s), and contact details for anyone who you have spoken to. There may be some question about whether to publish the name of a victim or a suspect, especially when this information has not come from police. With the proliferation of social media it is entirely possible that you will learn the name of a victim or suspect before police are ready to tell you. You should speak to your chief reporter or editor and not release information yourself.

A note of caution: If a person is in custody, an arrest is imminent or has already been made, the media cannot report any details that may prejudice a future court case. For example, if a woman has been killed and her husband has been taken away by police, you should not report statements from the neighbour claiming that he was "always beating her", as it could make him look guilty. This is called "*sub judice*" and is discussed in more detail later in this chapter.

After filing, all information should be updated as soon as new verified details come to hand. Information could change quickly and if an arrest has been made you may need to remove any legally dangerous portions.

Police may tell you that someone has been arrested and will appear in court at a later time. This should be included in your story.

Follow-up stories

Even if the event itself is over, there may be interesting news stories in follow-ups. The police may be still looking for witnesses or want information about vehicles or a particular person.

To make sure you have recorded a person's details correctly, turn to a blank page in your notebook and ask them to write their name and phone numbers. Give them your contact details in case they want to tell you more later.

Other sources of information you could explore are social media sites, such as Facebook and Twitter. A simple internet search may reveal a victim's old school friends and more background information, such as clubs, hobbies and interests.

When writing a news story that will run later, you will have more time to re-angle and expand your story. Remember, the public will most likely already know that the incident has occurred and will have the basic facts; they will be expecting a more in-depth story and interviews. This may involve going back to the newsroom and phoning neighbours whom you haven't already spoken to, or making contact with the victim, if possible, and/or their family and friends. You should also make contact with other emergency services, such as ambulance and fire officers. If the victim has been hospitalised, you should call for an update on their condition.

For large investigations, you should be checking with the police daily for new information.

Keep a diary, so that you keep track of significant events like knowing when a person who's been charged is to appear in court or when the anniversary of an unsolved case rolls around.

Other crime stories

While police might be the usual first stop for stories, other agencies can also provide good stories. Agencies like the Commerce Commission, Customs, Internal Affairs and local councils investigate things like consumer rip-offs, border violations, gaming fraud, dog attacks, etc. It pays to subscribe electronically to these agencies' e-newsletters, which often include ongoing investigations and upcoming court cases. But nothing beats regular one-to-one contact!

Police statistics can often be a good source of information for exploring police trends. Remember, police reporting is about the people involved, so these stories can benefit from finding a human-interest angle. Interview a victim, or even an offender, and tell their story alongside the statistics.

Another source to consider is experts in the field. A criminal psychologist may be able to explain what kind of person would most likely perpetrate a series of rapes, or give their opinion on how police could capture the offender. A security specialist may be able to provide advice on how to prevent becoming a victim of a gang of burglars working in a neighbourhood.

Some police stories will come to you before a complaint has been laid with police or other agencies. For example, a board member of the local school may tell you the chairperson has been helping himself to school funds. Your first step should be to ask for proof of their claims, including any documents they may have. You must then proceed cautiously to build up an accurate picture and gather further evidence from other sources before you confront the person who has been accused. In a case such as this, you could request to be provided with correspondence between the Ministry of Education and the school board, as well as any financial returns. You should also speak to other important parties involved, like the principal of the school and other board members. Remember, sometimes your informant may have a vested interest and may not have provided you with all the facts. There may be a perfectly good explanation for where the money has gone.

In another case you may be given information on dangerous criminals. You may be told that a local gang is dealing in drugs. It is important not to put yourself into a dangerous situation. In cases such as these you should always talk to your chief reporter or editor for advice on how best to proceed.

This kind of investigative reporting can provide some very rewarding results, but remember it is not your job to catch criminals; it is to tell a story.

There needs to be a good working relationship between police and court reporters, who are often following two halves of the same story. The process from arrest until trial can be lengthy, so it is important to keep track of where the case is at in a court diary. This can be a physical book that is kept on the court reporter's desk that everyone in the newsroom has access to, or it can be done electronically on a calendar programme.

Most pre-trial hearings are held in closed court. Generally, media are allowed to attend but permission must be sought. Even if you are allowed to sit in, you cannot report what happens until after the trial or hearing is completed. While it may not seem worthwhile going to these, in some cases people will plead guilty at this stage.

For the difference between criminal and civil law, see Chapter 20.

Court

Young reporters may find court one of the most daunting and scary places to go to, and certainly it seems impenetrable on first appearance, but it is also one of the most rewarding experiences, and can provide moments of sadness and humour.

New Zealand has an adversarial justice system based on the centuries-old English system. There are four courts that hear criminal and civil cases:

- The District Court. Everyone who is charged with an offence appears for the first time in the District Court, regardless of whether they are charged with murder or parking on broken yellow lines. The court hears civil claims up to $350,000.
- The High Court presides over the more serious criminal cases. It is also the first point of appeal for cases from the District Court.
- The Court of Appeal hears appeals arising from decisions of the High Court and in some cases the more serious charges heard in the District Court.
- The Supreme Court is the final court of law, and hears appeals on points of law, but only where there is a public interest or risk of a miscarriage of justice.

Our justice system is based on the principles that justice must be seen to be done and that someone is innocent until proven guilty. Charges are laid by police or any other body able to prosecute, such as government departments or local and regional authorities.

The media are considered part of the court system, as representatives of the public. Without the media, justice will not be seen to be done. It is assumed that the media will fairly and accurately report proceedings. Reporters thus have a right to be present in court and can widely report what happens, but must follow the rules.

The court process

A judge sits on the bench at the front of the court. In front of the judge sits a court registrar, who calls the names of those to appear and records proceedings.

The prosecutors, the ones bringing the case, usually sit at the front table. Behind them sit the defence lawyers. The defendant in most cases stands in the dock. The general public sit in a gallery at the back of the court.

> **OTHER COURTS**
>
> As well as criminal courts, reporters also have the right to attend and report on several other courts. These include the Coroners Court, the Family Court, the Youth Court, the Environment Court, the Māori Land Court, Courts Martial and a variety of tribunals and hearings.
>
> There are some tribunals reporters do not have a right to attend, such as Disputes Tribunal hearings and mediation hearings for the various tribunals. Many tribunals do, however, publish decisions. They can be found at: www.nzlii.org/.

The Coroners Act includes controls on how deaths by suicide in New Zealand can be reported. For details, see Chapter 21.

Reporters are usually provided with a table to sit at in the body of the court. However, there may be times when there are too many to fit at the table and then it is acceptable for reporters to sit in the public gallery. You need to make the registrar aware and have photographic identification.

First appearance

The defendant's name is called, and they step into the dock from the back of the court (or the cells if they are in custody). They will usually be represented by a lawyer, who will stand up and introduce themselves to the judge. The lawyer will usually seek a remand, which means the defendant must appear again at a later date. The lawyer may also enter no plea, or a guilty or not-guilty plea.

If the defendant pleads guilty in the District Court, the prosecution will read out a summary of facts outlining the police case. Usually, the defence lawyer will then have the opportunity to present any facts that the judge should take into account in sentencing. For example, if the defendant has pleaded guilty to stealing bread from a supermarket, the lawyer may want to tell the judge that this was done to feed hungry children. This may then turn out to be the more interesting angle to the story, instead of "man steals bread".

Some cases are remanded to a later date, at which the judge will sentence the person (that is, say what their punishment will be). This may be so a pre-sentence report can be prepared, or other details can be made available to the judge. In your story, you should say this has happened.

Pay attention in court. The lawyers and judges speak quickly and not always clearly, and a defendant's first appearance may be over in a few minutes.

If a person enters no plea or pleads not guilty in the District Court, various avenues may be followed. The prosecutor will speak to the judge if they are seeking a remand in custody or bail (when the defendant is allowed to leave the court until their next court appearance subject to certain conditions, like where they can live). The judge will then announce what is to happen, which could be a remand in custody for two weeks or the bail conditions.

If the charge is not serious, the defendant will be remanded to a hearing or trial in the District Court; this could be before a jury or heard by the judge alone. If it is a serious charge such as murder, it will be remanded to the High Court.

Photo: *The Dominion Post*

Trial

The case begins with the charges being put to the defendant. The prosecution then makes its opening statement outlining the case, followed by the defence, who may make a short statement explaining the issues in contention.

The prosecution will then call witnesses to give evidence. The defence then has the opportunity to cross-examine the witness, and finally the prosecution can re-examine to clarify or explain the points raised.

Once the prosecution has finished its case, the defence can call its own witnesses and the process is reversed, with the prosecution having the opportunity to cross-examine. The defence is under no obligation to call their client to testify.

Both sides then give their closing arguments and the judge will present his or her summary of the case and any directions to the jury.

The jury or judge will retire to consider the verdict. In some cases, a judge may reserve their decision, which means they will give their verdict at a later date.

Some District Court judgments are available on request from the District Court at which the judgment was issued. Many court decisions are available online (see Further Reading).

Reporting court

When you arrive to cover a court case, tell the registrar who you are and that you will be writing while court is in session. You should always carry identification as a member of the media, as the public are not entitled to write in the gallery.

Your first source of information is the press sheets. These sheets are a copy of the charge that is on the police file. They contain a good basic set of details. On them is the name, date of birth, address, occupation, and country of birth of the charged person. You will also find the wording of the charge, the law and the section of law they are charged under, the date of the alleged offence, possibly a victim's name and when they are to appear.

Press sheets should be available the first time someone appears on the charge. They should not be withheld from you for any reason. The sheets are available either at the court office or on the press bench in court. After the defendant's first appearance, they are kept by the court for one month, available to you if you ask.

Each day, the court publishes a list containing the names of the people appearing, the list of charges they are facing and, often, when and where they will appear. You can look at it at the court; it is not available online.

Cameras in court

If you want to film a trial inside a courtroom, you must apply to do so ahead of time, using the approved form (available at https://www.justice.govt.nz/about/news-and-media/media-centre/media-information). The judge decides whether to grant the request. Even though you are supposed to apply in advance, for an overnight arrest it is worth asking for permission, as judges are required to consider any application.

There are a number of basic rules regarding in-court coverage. The jury or people in the public gallery cannot be filmed, there are usually restrictions on when the defendant can be filmed, and witnesses can ask not to be filmed.

The reporter must ensure all court rulings and suppression orders are complied with before their story is broadcast. This may mean blurring faces and/or "beeping" out names during editing. If someone is granted name suppression, the reporter must also ensure they don't show any close relatives or friends in case that leads to the person being identified.

In some high-profile cases judges may require media to work together and have only one camera present in court.

Judges sometimes decline in-court camera applications. But for any major case, your newsroom should have library pictures of the police scene and victim.

As well as television cameras, still photography is possible in court. The application process is the same as for television coverage.

You can film or take photographs outside the court. As these are in a public place, you do not need to ask the judge's permission to do this (although, of course, you must abide by any suppression orders). These images can include the defendant walking in and out of court, the prison van (if they are in custody), the defence team and defence witnesses, and the defendant's family. You can also take pictures of the victim or their family walking in and out of court, the police officer in charge of the investigation, the prosecution team and witnesses.

You can take shots of the court building and close-ups of any signs. You can give a piece-to-camera (see Chapter 18), with the court buildings in the background.

Some courts now have an electronic noticeboard. It is a guide only – it cannot be taken as accurate or as privileged information. Do not rely on it for things like the spellings of names, and the number and type of charges. The list must be returned to the court when you leave.

Keep a diary with all information you need for each appearance of each of the cases you are following. Make sure that when you have written your story, you diarise the date of the next appearance and any new information.

If another reporter goes to court, you need to ensure that they also have access to your diary and that they update it.

Get to know your court. Each court has sentencing at different times and on different days. Build up a relationship with the court staff, the prosecutors and the defence lawyers; they may be able to provide you with valuable tips.

Be on time. Being late will invariably result in your missing the very thing you were there for. Sit at the press bench if available. Don't drink, eat, read the paper or do anything else except pay attention.

Dress appropriately for court. There is a dress code:

- Men must wear a collared shirt, tie and business trousers, not jeans.
- Women must wear tidy business-type clothing.

Reporters have been asked to leave courtrooms because they were inappropriately attired.

You are allowed to use electronic devices such as laptops and tablets in courtrooms, but the equipment must be silent.

Mobile phones can be used for texts and emails, but this must be done as unobtrusively as possible and be silent. You cannot use a phone to call anyone.

There are about five hours of evidence every day in a trial and accurate notes are essential. It's useful to highlight the best material as you go.

It's also worth remembering that if your laptop crashes you could find yourself without notes, so handwritten notes are also a good idea.

Do not record proceedings – you have to ask permission for that. You'll need good shorthand!

Any stories sent electronically cannot be posted for 10 minutes. The 10-minute delay rule does not apply to appeals, jury verdicts, sentencing, or a judge's summing up.

Like all news stories, your court stories should lead with what is most newsworthy. You should not editorialise in court stories, giving opinions or drawing conclusions about evidence, guilt or innocence.

Be careful of the wording of the charges. Sometimes altering the wording alters the type of charge a defendant is facing. Sexual violation by rape and unlawful sexual connection are not the same thing, for instance.

A court story needs to include the correct spelling of everyone's name. This includes the judge, lawyers and the defendant. Give the defendant's full name.

Include when the offending is alleged to have taken place, where it happened, how the defendant pleaded, and what happened in court (for instance, the defendant was remanded/sentenced or the trial is continuing).

The story should also include the defendant's age, occupation, the suburb or general area they live in, the name of the court they appeared at (for example, Auckland District Court or Supreme Court) and when they appeared.

If you miss something or are not sure of what happened, check with the registrar at a convenient break when the judge is not in court. Do not approach anyone in court during the sitting.

Legal issues in court reporting

Qualified privilege

Reporters have the right to publish anything said in open court even if it is defamatory or untrue. This is called "qualified privilege". However, your report must be balanced and accurate.

As some cases run over several days or weeks, your coverage of the entire case must be balanced. It is okay if on one day you report only one side of the story, as long you later report the other side. For more on privilege, see Chapter 20.

Suppression

At any stage during a court hearing the judge may suppress certain information.

BEING A COURT REPORTER

David Clarkson is a veteran court reporter. Here's his advice on getting the most out of the round.

"Court reporting is not a passive business, especially in a big courthouse. Reporters have to be nimble to get all the places they want to be, and they have to be organised, and they have to network.

"When a pair were about to be brought into court facing charges of intentionally causing grievous bodily harm, the case might have gone unremarked if police had not quietly mentioned that the file alleged they had poured petrol over the victim and set him alight. Good contacts are as important to a reporter working at the courts as anywhere else."

David points out that a court reporter's knowledge can be used for more than just court stories.

"The public's interest in the courts goes far beyond the business of the day, and a reporter with a history can add a lot of colour to the coverage. It's even more important at court when the key figures are unlikely to give background, or even grant interviews.

"When a 65-year-old drifter with a reputation of drunkenness and aggression was found dead in a fire in an abandoned house in central Christchurch, a court reporter was able to delve into his dodgy past, simply from his knowledge of the man's regular court appearances.

"Not only did the man have 300 previous convictions, mainly for disorder, but the reporter could tell how he was bailed one day to fly to Auckland to stay with his mum, but never managed to walk past a pub on the way to the airport.

"When the death was reported of a particularly clever burglar, the court reporter could write about how he would raid bedrooms and coordinate his breathing with the sleeping victim, how he could run from the police along the tops of fences, and how he would carry stamped envelopes and mail his loot back to himself. When he was stopped he never had any stolen cash on him!"

That means you cannot report it, although you can report that information was suppressed.

A judge may make a suppression order over any part of a hearing or even the whole hearing. A suppression order can include the name, address and occupation of anyone involved in the trial, or any other detail of the case. Any argument over suppression may itself be suppressed.

Any suppression order should be clearly noted in the court file and be available for you to check. The court file is the file that is kept by the court and notes any details relating to the case, such as the charges, the judge's comments and suppression orders. The best way to check what suppression orders are recorded on the court file is to approach the court registrar and ask them to check the file for suppression orders. The quickest way to do this is to write your query down in a note and during a break ask the registrar to pass it to the judge. A judge should never refuse to tell you the details of any suppression they have made.

If you are unsure, do not use the information until you have checked, or you will likely end up in court yourself!

There are a number of automatic suppressions in every court. These include the identity of any victim in a case of sexual offence and the name of the defendant in an incest case. This is done to prevent identification of the victim. A court can permit publication of a defendant's name in incest cases if the victim understands that they could be identified and consents to it. There is also automatic suppression of the identity of all child victims (unless they are dead) and anyone under the age of 18 who is a witness in a case. This does not prevent the publication of the defendant's name (unless it is the same as the victim's).

There are also some types of court hearings that have automatic suppressions. In a bail hearing you may only publish the name of the defendant, the charges they face, the decision of the court (ie, whether they got bail) and any conditions of bail if granted.

You are also not able to publish anything about sentencing indications where a defendant asks a judge for some idea of what sentence they are likely to receive.

It is common for a judge to refer to just "name suppression". However, this extends to any information likely to lead to the person's identification.

There are two types of suppression orders:

- An interim order expires at either the defendant's next appearance or when the judge has indicated it will expire (for example, at the end of the trial).
- A permanent suppression remains in force forever. It does not expire even if the person dies.

Penalties for breaching suppression range up to six months' jail or a fine of up to $50,000 for a person or $100,000 for a company.

A court registrar also has limited powers to grant suppression. A registrar may grant interim suppression on the defendant's first appearance in court if the case is adjourned and has consent from the prosecution and defence. That order can last up to 28 days. A registrar can only grant interim suppression once, unless they are continuing a suppression already granted by a judge.

With jury trials, you are not allowed to approach or speak to the jury. You are also not allowed to report anything that happened in court when the jury was not present.

Clearing the court

At times, a judge may clear a courtroom either to hear sensitive information or if there is a disturbance. That means the public has to leave. Reporters do not have to leave unless the judge specifically directs them to do so. Security staff and court staff do not have the power to remove media from court.

Judges can interrupt hearings to hear submissions "in chambers". Reporters do not have to leave unless directed to, but nothing can be published without the judge's consent.

Contempt of court

You can criticise a judge's decision but not the judge personally.

Contempt of court is anything that has the tendency to lower the authority of the courts and so weaken their effectiveness.

The judge can find you in contempt if you comment on trials in progress, attack the character of judges or refuse to obey court orders. Contempt can include comments from people outside the court, like victims' families. If you are found in contempt, you can be fined and even imprisoned.

The most important type of contempt is *sub judice*. This prevents you from publishing anything that prejudices someone's right to a fair trial. The sub judice period runs from the time an arrest is imminent until a conviction/acquittal is entered.

The Latin term "*sub judice*" is pronounced either "sub jew da kay" or "sub jew da cee". It means "under a judge".

Sub judice most often means you cannot publish anything about a defendant's previous convictions, whether they have been acquitted of similar offending, whether they have committed an offence while on bail or if they are of bad character generally.

It can also include publishing photographs (if identity is at issue in the case), or statements from those outside court on what has happened or what the outcome may be.

You should be wary of using anything that may be in contention at a trial.

***

Further reading

Cheer, U. (2015). *Burrows and Cheer: Media law in New Zealand.* (7th ed.). Wellington: LexisNexis. All court reporters should have a copy of this book. Chapters 8 and 9 cover court reporting and contempt of court.

https://www.justice.govt.nz/about/news-and-media/media-centre/media-information/media-guide The Ministry of Justice's handbook on reporting court, which includes all the rules about the media's access to court.

www.courtsofnz.govt.nz/going-to-court/calendar/daily-lists Case lists and summaries for the Supreme Court, Court of Appeal and High Court, available online daily (these often include suppressed information, so care is needed).

www.courtsofnz.govt.nz/judgments Judgments from the Supreme Court, Court of Appeal, High Courts and District Courts.

www.districtcourts.govt.nz A number of District Court judgments are available here.

www.legislation.govt.nz All legislation can be found on this site.

www.nzlii.org Other judgments, including tribunals and sentencing notes, can be found here.

9

Science, environment and disaster reporting

From climate change to resisting fake science

Alan Samson, Massey University

Since the 2010 and 2011 earthquakes devastated Christchurch, news media have been swamped with stories ranging from deaths and heroism to housing and insurance woes in the city. Evidenced again with the destructive 2013 Seddon and 2016 Wellington quakes, as time passed some media branched out, exploring the science and the environmental impacts. But at all such events, scientists and academics complain stories insufficiently cover all the important environmental and scientific issues at play. Larger concerns aired are that the media shy away from complex science, and are quickly bored with environmental concerns.

A less-aired criticism, put by journalists themselves, is that reporters sometimes trust scientists too much, forgetting to be sceptical (Regalado, 2006; Blum, 2006; Kunzig, 2006). This chapter explores the sometimes undervalued realms of environment and science reporting, as well as disaster reporting, which, of course, encompasses both disciplines. In doing so, it examines some of the great research underpinning today's science.

Confronting science: differences and tensions

Science and journalism are not an easy mix. Science is a method of finding how things work – by figuring out which explanation *best predicts* what actually happens. The scientist:

- sees something happening and asks: Why does it happen that way?
- creates hypotheses to explain or predict what will happen
- experiments to test the hypotheses, then notes which fit the experiment's outcomes.

When a scientist announces a cancer breakthrough, it is likely to mean that, in 20 years or so, trials *might* lead to a new drug that, *if all goes to plan, could* lessen the impact of the disease. The journalist, however, wants to shout in 36-point headlines: "Cure for Cancer Found!"

Accuracy in science reporting

It is common within science and academe to hear strident criticisms of science reporting, notably that:

- journalists don't understand how science works
- whether from laziness or ignorance, most miss a wealth of good science going on in our numerous research institutions
- journalists frequently misrepresent science, mainly by oversimplifying complicated concepts
- they often forego balance, finding it easier to regurgitate the account of a single "expert"
- they stick to familiar experts as spokespeople, even when they are not appropriate, sometimes not reflecting accepted science standpoints
- television especially often resorts to airing uncritical overseas science "breakthrough" stories fed by drug companies
- appeal to fear is paramount: GIANT ASTEROID ON PATH TOWARD EARTH!

Should reporters, in the idealistic tradition of their industry, even attempt to be *objective*? Perhaps a reporter seeking to expose a criminal toxic spill *should* take sides (Tully, 2008; Frome, 1998; Hansford, 2016). Note the Media Council's principle for accuracy, fairness and balance includes: "In articles of controversy or disagreement, a fair voice must be given to the opposition view." But this was added to in a recent amendment: "Exceptions may apply for long-running issues where every side of an issue or argument cannot reasonably be repeated on every occasion" (New Zealand Media Council, 2014, para. 13), a clear out option when facing extreme minority, often social media-fuelled "fake science".

In the wake of the Leveson inquiry into the state of the press, Britain's Science Media Centre (UK, 2012) created reporting guidelines, which included:

- Always state the source of the story – with enough information for readers to look up, or a web link.
- Specify the size and nature of a study – who were the subjects, how long did

Appendix 3 gives more information on weather terms; measurement of weather, earthquakes and volcanoes; and New Zealand scientific organisations.

While the scientist deals in *probabilities*, the journalist chases *outcomes*.

If you don't know how science works, you can't judge its importance, you can't tell real scientists from fake, and you certainly can't tell real science from bogus science.

PROVIDING AUTHENTICITY

Broadcaster and science writer **Veronika Meduna** observes that most of the information reported in new research builds on previous findings, by backing up earlier results, modifying their interpretation, or even overthrowing them. For that reason she always tries to include as much *context* as possible in her reporting.

"This approach avoids overstating the significance of new findings, it allows readers/listeners to dig deeper and it adds authenticity/depth to the story," she says. "Sometimes, all it takes is a short phrase such as: 'This supports/ rejects earlier findings by ...'"

Perhaps the most important way of adding context, Meduna says, is checking the background of sources. "As a broadcaster, I often try to get an interviewee to explain his/her background on air, by asking the simple question: 'What's your interest in this?'"

Another piece of advice Meduna offers is consider your audience. Most people find it easier to imagine "one in five" than 20 per cent, or "twice the population of New Zealand" than eight million, she says. "A phrase describing the level of risk in words – 'A 26 per cent rise in breast cancer might sound alarming, but it actually means a difference of less than one case in every 1000 women per year' – makes the information more digestible, and perhaps less threatening."

Photo: Andy Reisinger

it last, what was tested? If there's space, mention its limitations.

- Give a sense of the stage of the research – eg, cells in a laboratory or trials in humans – and a realistic time frame for a new treatment or technology.
- Include the absolute risk whenever available – if "cupcakes double cancer risk", state the outright risk of that cancer, with and without cupcakes.
- Try to frame new findings in the context of other evidence. Does it reinforce or conflict with previous studies?
- Try to quote both the researchers themselves and external sources with appropriate expertise. Be wary of scientists and press releases over-claiming for studies.
- Distinguish between findings and interpretation or extrapolation: don't suggest health advice if none has been offered.
- Don't call something a "cure" that is not a cure.

Readers need to be told if a climate-change denier is a retired coal researcher, or if somebody making claims about health benefits of a substance is on the board of a relevant company.

Developing a healthy scepticism

The biggest lesson to be learned in "getting to the truth" may simply be common sense. As Consumer New Zealand is fond of saying, if something sounds too good to be true, it probably is. Reporters should investigate of a claim:

Cases for caution

GM claims

During the 2000–2001 Royal Commission on Genetic Modification, covered by *The Dominion*'s Alan Samson (print) and RNZ's Veronika Meduna (broadcast), claims were repeated that Monarch butterflies had died after eating Bt corn pollen (grown with a modified insecticide). Checking, it was noted deaths occurred only after *force-feeding* in a laboratory, and later experiments did not replicate the results. Forearmed, wrong reporting was avoided (Samson, 2001a).

There was similar caution after Oregon State University soil biologist Elaine Ingham claimed a bacterium (*Klebsiella planticola*), engineered to produce alcohol from plant debris, had killed all the wheat plants it was added to. GM opposers saw this as long-awaited proof the technology could spiral out of control. The finding turned out to be an "extrapolation" from the laboratory, not field tests (Samson, 2001b).

Claims made by Rowett Research Institute (Scotland) researcher Arpad Pusztai were less easily dismissed. Sacked from his university after going public with findings of damage to the organs of rats fed with modified potatoes, Dr Pusztai powerfully challenged others to repeat his research: either the damage he observed was statistically significant or it was not (Samson, 2001c).

Lyprinol

In August 2002, three news media outlets – *One Network News, Holmes* and *The New Zealand Herald* – went big on the news an extract from the humble green-lipped mussel offered "hope to cancer sufferers worldwide". The television promo ran: "On *Holmes* tonight, a cure for cancer." The *Herald* headline was: "The cure for cancer?". The dramatic story sparked a rush on pharmacies reminiscent of Boxing Day sales. But the Ministry of Health pointed out that the claims far outstripped evidence: promoted as a medicine, the extract was not proven to be one. The Broadcasting Standards Authority later ruled the television reports were wrong and that the channel's first coverage lacked balance. The two companies that launched the product were convicted on charges of selling the extract as a medicine (Ministry of Health and TVNZ, 2000; "Lyprinol firms admit guilt," 2000).

Never be frightened to ask "dumb" questions: reporting skill isn't about knowledge of a subject, but the ability to translate the complex into a language readily understood by your audience.

- Is it likely? Are there other explanations?
- Was the research statistically relevant, with enough subjects, and conducted with proper controls?
- Are claimants authoritative and with experience in the field of the claim?
- Has the claim been supported in a respected scientific journal? Was it peer-reviewed?
- Where was the work done – at a university, or someone's house?

FINDING BURIED GEMS

Science writer **Kiran Chug**, formerly with *The Dominion Post*, notes that covering science and environment involves the same techniques as any other round: cultivating valuable contacts, spending time getting to know the issues – and writing great yarns.

"Science and environment are two big areas where it can be hard to find the real gems, as these can be buried under scientific jargon," she says. "This is why it's important to have good contacts who can help alert you to interesting stories coming up, or point out the juicy bits in a dry research paper."

It could be hard to pitch stories when working for a general news organisation. "But if it's a great yarn and you've worked out why it's interesting to a general audience … the fact that it's a science story shouldn't put anyone off."

Chug warns against being too narrow in story choices. "Mix up the quirky, specialised pieces with the big issues. It'll be more interesting for your readers and for you." Once you get into the round, she says, the scope for great stories is endless. "There is always someone new to meet, whose research is fascinating but as yet unreported, and there's always another paper being published that, once personalised, will be of huge interest."

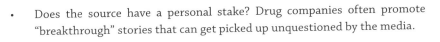

- Does the source have a personal stake? Drug companies often promote "breakthrough" stories that can get picked up unquestioned by the media.

All of New Zealand's universities do significant research, as do many local and regional councils. Put them on your contacts list.

Interview questions should at the very least include:
- Where did you get the data?
- How do you know?
- How sure can you be?
- Are your findings reproducible?
- Could your data be interpreted to say something else?

Note, claims such as that an asteroid will hit Earth on Friday are useless without further information testing their accuracy (Kunzig, 2006).

On giants' shoulders

Theory of gravity espouser Sir Isaac Newton famously said: "If I have seen further, it is by standing on the shoulders of giants." To be able to write authoritatively about science, it is necessary to have a degree of understanding of its achievements.

A good science reporter should be aware of the great science, from Aristotle (who devised a classification system for grouping animals in *genera*) to Marie Curie (who established the properties of radioactive matter). It's easy to spout Einstein's

Reporters should think hard about how much space they give to protest. At the very least, they must never sacrifice accuracy in the face of emotion.

MAJOR RECENT DEVELOPMENTS IN SCIENCE

Deoxyribonucleic acid (DNA)

Knowing the structure of DNA opened the floodgates to understanding the genetic make-up of all living things, generating great medical hopes (the possibility of screening out genetic diseases) and great ethical fears (cloning, genetic engineering). Americans James Watson and Francis Crick and New Zealander Maurice Wilkins in 1962 won Nobel Prizes for revealing that structure, a double helix resembling "a gently twisted ladder". Sadly, fourth contributor American Rosalind Franklin is largely forgotten after dying before the awards – Nobels are not given posthumously. A wealth of discovery has followed, notably the Human Genome Project that has seen the precise mapping of the about 20,000 genes making up a human.

Genetic modification (GM)

GM, the cloning of DNA molecules in foreign cells, came to fruition after a chance after-conference meeting at a Hawaiian deli by two American biochemists. Herbert Boyer had isolated an enzyme that cut DNA at specific locations; Stanley Cohen was working out methods for introducing small pieces of DNA into bacteria that would copy genes when the microbes divided. Sharing their findings, the two subsequently spliced DNA fragments from several different species of an organism, mixing the traits of each to create a previously unknown variation – the first genetically engineered organism.

Nanotechnology

Nanotechnology, working with matter at a molecular scale, was first explored in-depth by American engineer K. Eric Drexler. A nanometre is *one billionth* of a metre – there are more nanometres in a centimetre than there are centimetres in kilometres! Reporters need to be able to get their heads around the concept of research that *grows* materials from the atomic level. The ability to work at such micro levels is revolutionising research in areas ranging from new materials to robotics and medicine, not to mention breaking miniaturisation size barriers in computers.

Stem cells

Scientists have known about the self-renewing behaviour of bone marrow cells since the 1960s, but it wasn't until the 1980s that techniques were devised for targeting and altering genetic material in this manner. In 1998, University of Wisconsin researcher James Thomson successfully removed cells from spare embryos and grew them in a laboratory – the world's first embryonic stem cell line. This has been followed by evidence that such cells have the potential to generate replacement cells for body tissues and organs, including the heart, liver, pancreas and nervous system (Science Media Centre, 2012; Science Media Centre, 2008; Science Media Centre, UK 2009; Science Media Centre, UK, n.d.; Hall, 2006).

NEW ZEALAND'S NOBELS

New Zealand has had three Nobel Prize winners, all of them for chemistry.

Ernest Rutherford (1871–1937) is famous for the slightly misleading "splitting the atom" – by disintegrating the atom he for the first time artificially altered nuclear and atomic structure. But he won his Nobel in 1908 for his first great work, verifying theories of radioactive decay, how atoms change form on the emission of radiation. His experiments revealed the concentration of an atom's mass lay in a small, positively charged nucleus with electrons inhabiting that atom's farthest reaches, making him arguably the father of all nuclear physics and sub-nuclear science.

Wairarapa-born **Maurice Wilkins** (1916–2004), whose Irish parents moved back to Britain when he was six years old, was honoured – with Crick and Watson – for his part in the discovery of DNA. His identification of crystalline patterns in DNA made it possible to photograph molecules, revealing the actual shape of DNA – the characteristic double helix – allowing Crick and Watson to build their detailed model.

Alan MacDiarmid (1927–2007) won his Nobel (with American Alan Heeger and Japanese Hideki Shirakawa) in 2000 for the discovery and development of polymers that can conduct electricity. Single molecule electrical circuits connected by polymers (nanotechnology) are set to revolutionise future electronics, promising to smash the size – and speed – barrier of all existing electronics (Meduna & Priestley, 2008).

$E=mc^2$ formula, but most reporters would have little understanding of his theories explaining the laws of motion and gravity.

What about more recent "giant steps"? The box opposite gives a *flavour* of some of the most current developments requiring some understanding. Note that each, while promising great hope in areas ranging from treatment of rare diseases to abundant crop production, has also generated substantial ethical fears.

The environment: growing public awareness

If it weren't for a burgeoning environmentalism reflected in the news media, the following might never have come to be etched in the public mindset: ozone hole, fluorocarbons, rainforests, whales, Exxon Valdez, Chernobyl, *Rainbow Warrior*, greenhouse, toxic waste, acid rain, recycling.

But journalist awareness can be traced back further than any of these, with links to a few international conferences reflecting growing global concerns.

Conferences lead the way

Environmental journalism in New Zealand is usually traced back to 1960s' reporting

Some opposers of the new argue for moratoriums until 100 per cent safety can be demonstrated. What would that mean for the future of human progress?

The media has had a role in changing attitudes on fur coats, fertilisers, plastics, preservatives, tourism, petrol, vegetables, sunscreens, junk food and toilet paper.

of the furore over the raising of Manapouri lake levels for hydro-electricity. However, the first significant international discussion of issues was the ground-breaking 1972 United Nations Conference on the Human Environment in Stockholm. Called by developed countries, its agenda focused on the threat posed by economic growth and industrial pollution. Developing countries responded that poverty posed a greater threat to both human welfare and the environment. Economic growth was not the problem but the solution.

The next significant forum, the "Earth Summit", was the 1992 UN Conference on Environment and Development at Rio de Janeiro, Brazil. Rio produced a declaration on environmental rights, a climate change convention, a biodiversity convention and a focus on forestry. It also produced an action plan, Agenda 21 – see http://sustainabledevelopment.un.org/content/documents/Agenda21.pdf – (UN Sustainable Development, 1992), which affirmed that socio-economic development and environmental protection were intimately linked, and that effective policy-making must tackle them together.

The conference that sparked the biggest inter-governmental debate, however, was the UN Conference on Climate Change in Kyoto, which in 1997 produced the contentious Kyoto Protocol to restrain human-induced climate change by reducing greenhouse gas emissions by industrialised nations. Taking effect in 2005, its signatories agreed to reduce net emissions to 5 per cent below 1990 levels in a first commitment period from 2008 to 2012. The protocol was amended in 2012 to accommodate a second commitment period (2013–2020), with countries that had not signed up – such as Russia and Japan – excluded from trading emissions.

The subsequent 2015 Paris Climate Accord allows each country to determine its own contributions to mitigate warming, but each target must go beyond previously set targets. As of September 2017, 195 members of the UN Framework Convention on Climate Change had signed this agreement, and 162 of these had ratified it. Aiming to keep global average temperatures below 2°C above pre-industrial levels and to keep trying to lower this to 1.5°C, it was praised as the world's first comprehensive climate agreement. However, in June 2017, US President Donald Trump announced to widespread condemnation that the United States would withdraw from the agreement, although the earliest date he can do this is November 2020 (UN framework convention on climate change, Kyoto Protocol, n.d.; UN framework convention on climate change, Paris Agreement, n.d.)

When environment becomes news

It's hard to know why an issue becomes a *cause célèbre*. The extent of emotion surrounding Lake Manapouri took all by surprise. So did the depth of feeling surrounding New Zealand's nuclear-free stance that became law in 1987. Coverage of issues such as lingering toxic waste, weeds or litter might leave less impression on the wider public, but might be very significant to policy-makers. The environment most frequently becomes news, however, through disasters or in response to the actions or statements of environmental players, from government to lobby groups.

Critics of environmental reporting say:

- Reporters are too easily manipulated by adept green groups.
- Media portrayal of disasters is often shallow – India's 1984 Bhopal poison gas disaster, for instance, was represented as Third World incompetence, rather than multinational corner-cutting.
- Negative news prevails: there is a fine line to be drawn between honest coverage and alarmism.
- Immediate crises drive the news: long-running stories like ozone depletion and global warming quickly turn the news media off.
- At a time of fewer industry resources, complex environment stories are the ones less likely to be followed through.
- On issues like global warming, where only a handful of scientists disbelieve the phenomenon, the journalistic ethos of seeking "balance" effectively sacrifices truth.

> Most journalists argue it is not their job to censor. Most would agree, however, it would be misleading to trot out the sceptics for "balance" in every story.

Clean and green: New Zealand's environmental audit

In 1997, then Environment Minister Simon Upton launched a 650-page epic entitled *The state of New Zealand's environment*. If ever a document was to dispel a nation's "clean and green" reputation it was this. It pointed to disturbing increases in carbon dioxide emissions, poor waste disposal practices, inadequate landfill quality, possum-induced collapse of forests, overfishing, loss of species, et al. (Taylor & Smith, 1997).

The report found positives, but its most powerful message was that we risked being lulled into a false sense of security by the "pretty pictures" of coffee-table books and advertisements. Findings included:

- Since human settlement began, 85 per cent of the country's lowland forests and wetlands had gone and the related decline of species (it identified 800 threatened species, including the iconic kiwi) was severe and getting worse.
- New Zealand had more than 7000 sites contaminated by organochlorines (chemical pollutants), oil-based products, heavy metals and other chemicals.
- Waterways were under pressure from sewage and factory effluent discharges, as well as contamination in rainwater run-offs from paddocks and roads.
- About 10 per cent of our known fishery populations had fallen below levels of maximum sustainable yield.

Subsequent audits and scattered reports have highlighted persisting problems in most areas, but none have been as thorough as the original.

An ill wind: global warming, greenhouse and El Niño

Most scientists today accept the reality of human-induced global warming but, for every extreme climatic event, other variables, too, must be taken into account.

A small minority doesn't accept the phenomenon of human-induced warming at all. Nevertheless, during the past century, the atmospheric temperature has risen 0.6°C, and the sea level has risen several centimetres, a terrifying trend for low-lying Pacific states such as Kiribati, Tuvalu and Tokelau (the last a New Zealand territory). Should we be reporting minority science?

Global warming

Global warming is an increase in the average temperature of the Earth's atmosphere, sufficient to trigger climate change. It is commonly associated with a *human-induced* upsurge in greenhouse gases. Likely contributing factors are the burning of petroleum products (carbon dioxide, methane and nitrous oxide), deforestation (carbon dioxide), methane released in animal waste, and increased cattle production (deforestation, methane, and use of fossil fuels).

Over the past century, the atmospheric temperature has risen 0.6°C, and the sea level by several centimetres. If the trend continues, long-term results will include the melting of polar ice, even higher sea levels, coastal flooding, corruption of fresh water, significant changes in agriculture, species' extinction, more frequent tropical storms, and more tropical diseases.

Greenhouse effect

The greenhouse effect is the heating of the atmosphere by the presence of carbon dioxide and other gases. Without these gases, heat from the sun would return to space in the form of infrared radiation. Carbon dioxide and other gases absorb some of this radiation and prevent its release, warming the Earth – just as glass in a greenhouse traps the infrared radiation and warms the air. All that's perfectly natural.

What scientists worry about is the effect of "anthropogenic" (human-induced) greenhouse effect. Most agree that over the past 150 years human activities have released increasing quantities of harmful gases into the atmosphere and that these are responsible for much of the warming we're experiencing. The only way to absolutely eliminate harmful emissions would be to banish entirely all polluting energy sources – including the phasing out of petrol- and diesel-run cars.

El Niño and La Niña

Even when the
weather is less than
dramatic, it is still of
interest. It affects
almost everything we
do and is a major topic
of conversation.

El Niño is a warming of the ocean surface off the western coast of South America that occurs every few years, linked to a large-scale shift of atmospheric pressure. In the cycle, New Zealand tends to experience stronger or more frequent winds from the west in summer, leading to drought in east coast areas, and more rain in the west. In winter, the winds tend to be more from the south, bringing colder conditions. In spring and autumn, south-westerly winds prevail. The not-to-be-confused La Niña is a *cooling* of the ocean surface off the west coast of South America, with warmer sea-surface temperatures around New Zealand. Air temperatures also rise here, with anticyclones becoming more frequent in the south-east. North-easterly airflows are more frequent over the North Island, and easterlies over the South Island. There is also a pattern of greater monsoonal activity over Indonesia and north Australia, sometimes bringing terrible storms here, such as in 1968 when the inter-island ferry *Wahine* foundered.

Weather reporting

Obviously, the weather is the source of most act-of-God events and disaster news stories. Gale-force winds in Wellington forcing the cancellation of air traffic and ferry sailings are news, snow killing stock and blocking roads in Canterbury, floods hitting

Photo: Stuff

the Wairarapa, fog closing airports, rain causing a cricket test at Eden Park to be washed out, or slips (pictured, Kingston, Wellington, 2013).

Has this summer been better than last year's? Hasn't it been a lot windier? Has Wellington had more sunshine hours than Auckland? To cater for this interest, news organisations often do a monthly or yearly wrap. Information for these stories comes from MetService, the National Institute of Water and Atmospheric Research (NIWA), or from private forecasting companies like Blue Skies Weather, often triggered by a press release. Generally, recent weather details – temperatures, rainfalls, hours of sunshine and the like – can be gleaned from MetService; more detailed analysis and trends, including historical, can be elicited from NIWA (McFarling, 2006; Hicks & Campbell, 2012).

Personal drama is the most graphic way of showing how a disastrous event affects ordinary people. Be on the lookout for heroes.

Reporting disasters

Stories on any disaster event require a lot of hard work. You may have to cover things taking place over a large area, and to build up the story by contacting many sources. Note that weather in one area can have an effect in another: heavy rain falling in the hills can mean that rivers flood on the plains many kilometres away. A big event like a volcanic eruption may involve several reporters.

Think laterally about the effects conditions will have. Gather facts over a wide field – then select the most interesting and significant. Seek out the stories and facts that lend impact, drama, and/or suspense. Try hard for eyewitness accounts.

Areas to be particularly looked at are: effects on humans (death, injury); disruption to lives (evacuations, power cuts, effect on farmers, water problems, transport disruptions); property and economic damage (stock and crop losses, damage to bridges, roads, buildings); details of how much rain fell, how high the winds blew, how much snow fell, how high the rivers came up, etc.; and eyewitness accounts of narrow escapes and damage. For weather events, MetService should be able to talk about the path of storms and indicate the worst-hit areas. Research the vulnerable: hospitals, schools, highways, power stations, etc., are good starting points. Local knowledge is priceless: make it your business to know spots in your paper's or station's area that are prone to flooding, slips, etc.

Who you gonna call?

In covering science and environment, be guided by the fact that "news is news". Go to as many sources as necessary to fairly cover the story. The round is fortunate for having clear organisational experts to go to (see Further Reading). Reporters also have recourse to the Science Media Centre, which offers useful advice on good science reporting at: https://www.sciencemediacentre.co.nz/deskguide/.

As with all news, "fairness, accuracy and balance" should be the mantra.

Writing the story

There can be temptation to over-write. Don't. An active piece with short, punchy sentences conveys the necessary sense of drama much more effectively.

Whether writing for print, online or broadcast, the angle is often obvious: casualties sensibly come first, along with details of the dead and injured. The effect on humans is *always* important. Look out for evacuations of housing, or destruction of property. These will usually be the lead if there are no deaths or significant injuries. Civil Defence calling a state of emergency might also make a good intro.

What is it about the story that is having a significant effect on people? Roads and rail lines may have been cut, power lost, air flights cancelled, ferry sailings disrupted, etc. Focus on the most important:

> A Westport woman was killed when her car was swept off a bridge by a flash flood in the Buller River last night.

Use subsequent paragraphs to give all the details of the story not in the lead and then act as a transition to the other storm details. A print example might be:

> The dead woman was Mary Jayne Vaughan, 39, a teacher. She was driving her Fiat Uno over the Crags Head Bridge, 5km north of Westport when the flood struck at 11.09pm.
>
> The flash flood was the result of the heavy rain and strong winds that hit the South Island last night.

Think colour. Short sentences and active verbs add pace, urgency and drama:

> Winds of up to 160 kmh ripped trees out of the ground

is better than:

> Trees were blown over by the heavy winds, which reached speeds of up to 160 kmh.

Watch terminology. A wind is not a gale unless it is 34–40 knots (63–75 kmh). Note: "knots" are no longer style for most news media, so stick with "kmh". And don't write "gale-force winds", just "gales". Avoid overstating things by describing a run-of-the-mill flood as a "disaster".

Checklist

A checklist to be ticked off could be:

- Anyone killed or injured or in danger? Any heroes?
- Estimated death and injury toll?

- What were the causes of death/injury?
- Any eyewitness accounts?
- Are there any lingering dangers/problems?
- What relief operations are under way? Evacuations, unusual equipment used or remarkable rescue techniques, and how many rescuers have been deployed?
- What are the official warnings (ie, from the Ministry of Health, Civil Defence, police or utility companies)?
- Any looting? Any arrests? Any police investigations?
- What clean-up activities are under way?
- What's the property loss (ie, homes, land, utilities, long-term damage)?
- How many insurance claims, and their worth?
- Any long-term environmental effects?

Earthquakes

Between 10,000 to 15,000 quakes occur in New Zealand every year – although overwhelmingly they are too small to feel. Check the website of the Geological and Nuclear Sciences Crown Research Institute – www.gns.cri.nz (GNS Science, n.d.) – or the official hazard information site – www.geonet.org.nz (GeoNet, n.d.) – to get an up-to-date record. Everybody's aware of the big Christchurch and Kaikōura earthquakes, but note, too, that experts have for years predicted an imminent big one in Wellington, fears unassuaged by the 7.8 shake-up of 2016.

Twist and shake

What is *big* in respect of an earthquake? If a large quake happens in a populated area, the people there will know it, and that should be the first test of whether it's worth writing about. Were people affected in a way or to a degree that others will want to talk about it?

The complication in understanding quake size is that earthquakes are not measured on a linear scale, but a logarithmic one. For each number on a logarithmic scale, the amplitude goes up 10 times: a magnitude 5 results in 10 times the level of ground shaking as a magnitude 4, and 32 times as much energy is released; an 8.7 quake is 794 times bigger than a 5.8.

The logarithmic model has a period of rapid increase, followed by a period where the growth slows, but the growth continues to increase *without limit*. But all you need to concentrate on is the effect: in a measurement from 1 to 10, an earthquake of 3, 4 or even 5 is pretty small. Even the 5 may be of no great moment, although may shake things from shelves. Over 7, and the tremor is a huge one; 8, as has happened nearby before, could seriously damage much of Wellington. The equal-largest New Zealand earthquake to be *recorded* was the 1931, 7.8 Napier quake. Others have been as big, including Kaikōura in 2016, but none of these came near to matching Napier's 256 fatalities. Much larger tremors have occurred here before instrumentation. The impact of an earthquake will be affected by its depth and its proximity to a population centre.

In earlier days, the earthquake scale used was reported as the "Richter" scale, but

The Richter scale was devised by American seismologists Charles Richter and Beno Gutenberg, reportedly after the former grew weary of journalists repeatedly asking, "How big?"

If the quake is in a big city, you may get good descriptions by ringing offices in the top floors of bound-to-be-shaking tall buildings.

this term is no longer used here. Scientists just refer to "magnitude", recording the wave-form picked up on a seismogram, and the distance of the earthquake from the station that recorded its seismic trace (Ansell & Taber, 1996).

Earthquakes are created when two sides of a fault grind past each other. Wellington is known to sit above several such fault lines. Thankfully, most earthquakes are barely noticed; when one is felt, even if it rocks the newsroom, it may still be of little significance. Geological and Nuclear Sciences is pretty good at posting important details quickly. Unless you're an early-morning radio reporter, before calling, give GNS time to cope with the initial rush of work they face in the monitoring.

What you will initially need is:

In 1953, 151 train passengers died near Tangiwai when Ruapehu's crater lake collapsed, causing a mudslide (lahar). The lahar weakened a rail bridge, which caused the train to plunge into the river below.

- magnitude
- place (onshore or offshore)
- exact time
- depth (a shallow quake is felt much more severely)
- how far afield it was felt
- first reports of damage.

Early on, contact a workplace in the township closest to the epicentre. A trick is to go to the Yellow Pages to find a supermarket or liquor store where, even with a mid-range quake, foodstuffs and bottles are likely to dramatically crash from shelves. Or a pub: get the bartender to call out your question across the bar. Ring the police for more in-depth detail. Remember, they, too, may have personal stories to tell.

Once again, try hard for personal accounts: disruption to people's lives such as evacuations, power cuts, effects on farmers and city life, water problems, and transport difficulties; property and economic damage, such as to high-rises, bridges, roads, buildings; as well as eyewitness accounts, including of narrow escapes.

The personal drama is the most graphic way of showing how a disastrous event affects ordinary people. But think, too, of what the story will be when the drama has died down. Are there any long-term *effects* on the environment? Is there any *science* to be explained? Think follow-ups.

Under the volcano

The North Island has a number of active and potentially active volcanoes. Although the probability of an eruption affecting a large area of the island is relatively low in any one year, scientists agree the probability of an eruption occurring in the future is high.

Auckland sits on a series of volcanoes. But the active sites sensibly most watched are the ever-steaming White Island, off the North Island's east coast (pictured), Taranaki-Egmont, Ruapehu, and Ngauruhoe.

Use the GeoNet site – http://www.geonet.org.nz/ – (GeoNet, n.d.) to keep an eye on a volcano's "status". Volcanologists use a system of alert levels to define the current status of each volcano, ranging from 0 (minor background activity)

Photo: Stuff

to 5 (hazardous large volcanic eruption in progress). They run two tables, one for frequently active volcanoes like Ruapehu and White Island; another watching for signs of re-awakening of dormant volcanoes like Mayor Island, Tarawera or Taupō.

White Island is continually belching ash and smoke, its status frequently fluctuating. Ruapehu is also worth watching: it erupted severely in 1995 and 1996, scattering ash and volcanic rock – and acid rain – as far afield as Taupō. Check GeoNet on a quasi-regular basis.

The bigger picture

So are all the important environment and science stories being told, and told well? In a sense, big weather events and disasters are relatively easy fare, thanks to collegial support and reporting assistance, as well as the healthy dose of adrenalin that invariably kicks in. The blind spot for many reporters is the necessary persistence with longer-term issues. A valid criticism of many newsrooms is that too many environmental and science stories burn brightly, but vanish quickly. "Think follow-ups" could usefully be tattooed on every reporter's forehead.

Writing about the environment and science isn't always easy. Apart from the complexities of understanding detailed research variables and the dangers of oversimplification in the telling, there is also what could be described as a Mexican standoff between the scientists and the reporters – probabilities versus outcomes. There is also a strange disconnect where many reporters seem wary, if not nervous, about tackling science stories. Don't be! There is a wealth of good stories awaiting discovery.

Further reading

www.mbie.govt.nz, www.mfe.govt.nz, www.doc.govt.nz Websites for a range of useful government ministries and departments: the Ministry of Business, Innovation and Employment, Ministry for the Environment and Department of Conservation.

www.sciencemediacentre.co.nz Reporters should make use of the Science Media Centre, which provides research, science and technology information, useful direction to expert voices, and its *Desk guide for covering science*, a guide for journalists.

www.sciencenewzealand.org This is the website representing all the Crown Research Institutes. Individual CRI websites:

AgResearch: http://www.agresearch.co.nz

Callaghan Innovation: www.callaghaninnovation.govt.nz/ – an organisation dedicated to boosting national economic performance through science

ESR (Environmental Science Research): http://www.esr.cri.nz

Geological and Nuclear Science Institute: http://www.gns.cri.nz

Landcare: http://www.landcareresearch.co.nz

New Zealand Forest Research (trades as Scion): http://www.scionresearch.com

NIWA (National Institute of Water & Atmospheric Research): http://www.niwa.co.nz

Plant and Food Research: http://www.plantandfood.co.nz

References

Ansell, R., & Taber, J. (1996). *Caught in the crunch.* Auckland: HarperCollins.

Blum, D. (2006). Writing well about science. In D. Blum, M. Knudson & R. Marantz Henig (Eds.), *A field guide for science writers* (pp. 26–33). Oxford: Oxford University Press.

Frome, M. (1998). *Green ink.* Salt Lake City: University of Utah Press.

GNS Science. (n.d.). *Natural hazards.* Retrieved from www.gns.cri.nz/Home/Our-Science/Natural-Hazards

GeoNet. (n.d.). *Felt quakes.* Retrieved from http://www.geonet.org.nz/

Hall, S.S. (2006). Human cloning and stem cells. In D. Blum, M. Knudson & R. Marantz Henig (Eds.), *A field guide for science writers* (pp. 197–203). Oxford: Oxford University Press.

Hansford, D. (2016). *Protecting paradise.* Nelson: Potton & Burton.

Hicks, C., & Campbell, H. (2012). *Awesome forces.* Wellington: Te Papa Press.

Kunzig, R. (2006). Gee whiz science writing. In D. Blum, M. Knudson & R. Marantz Henig (Eds.), *A field guide for science writers* (pp. 126–131). Oxford: Oxford University Press.

Lyprinol firms admit guilt. (2000, September 22). *The New Zealand Herald,* p. 1.

McFarling, U.L. (2006). Climate. In D. Blum, M. Knudson & R. Marantz Henig (Eds.), *A field guide for science writers* (pp. 243–250). Oxford: Oxford University Press.

Meduna, V., & Priestley, R. (2008). *Atoms, dinosaurs & DNA.* Auckland: Random House.

Ministry of Health and TVNZ. (2000). Retrieved from http://bsa.govt.nz/decisions/4027

New Zealand Media Council. (2014). *NZ Media Council Statement of Principles.* Wellington: NZ Media Council.

Regalado, A. (2006). Investigative reporting. In D. Blum, M. Knudson & R. Marantz Henig (Eds.), *A field guide for science writers* (pp. 118–125). Oxford: Oxford University Press.

Samson, A.M. (2001a, January 31). Call for public to vote on modified food. *The Dominion,* p. 8.

Samson, A.M. (2001b, February 20). Key witness accused of misrepresentation. *The Dominion,* p. 2.

Samson, A.M. (2001c, February 8). Repeat my work, challenges scientist. *The Dominion,* p. 5.

Science Media Centre. (2008, September 19). *Genetic modification explained.* Retrieved from www.sciencemediacentre.co.nz/2008/09/19/genetic-modification-explained/

Science Media Centre. (2012, November 14). *Unravelling your genome.* Retrieved from www.sciencemediacentre.co.nz/2012/11/14/briefing-unravelling-your-genome/

Science Media Centre (UK). (n.d.). *Briefing notes on human stem cells.* Retrieved from www.sciencemediacentre.org/wp-content/uploads/2012/09/SMC-Briefing-Notes-Human-Stem-Cells.pdf

Science Media Centre (UK). (2009, November 4). *Nanoparticles in medicine.* Retrieved from www.sciencemediacentre.org/nanoparticles-in-medicine/

Science Media Centre (UK). (2012, May 31). *10 best practice guidelines for reporting science & health stories.* Retrieved from http://www.levesoninquiry.org.uk/wp-content/uploads/2012/07/Second-submission-to-Inquiry-from-Guidelines-for-science-and-health-reporting-31.05.12.pdf

Taylor, R., & Smith, I. (1997). *The state of New Zealand's environment.* Wellington: GP Publications.

Tully, J. (2008). Objectivity. In J. Tully (Ed.), *Intro: A beginner's guide to professional news journalism* (pp. 303–308). Wellington: New Zealand Journalists Training Organisation.

UN Sustainable Development. (1992). *Agenda 21: United Nations conference on environment & development.* Retrieved from http://sustainabledevelopment.un.org/content/documents/Agenda21.pdf

UN Framework Convention on Climate Change. (n.d.). *Kyoto Protocol.* Retrieved from http://unfccc.int/kyoto_protocol/items/2830.php.

UN Framework Convention on Climate Change. (n.d.) *The Paris Agreement.* Retrieved from http://unfccc.int/paris_agreement/items/9485.php

10

Reporting business and economics

Covering an important and widely read round

Allan Lee, AUT University

A *Dominion Post* front-page story in 2017 explained how recent natural disasters had disrupted the capital's businesses. Impacts included property and stock damage, building closures and demolitions, loss of sales and displaced staff. A Chamber of Commerce survey found only 34 per cent of businesses expected Wellington's economy to improve over the year, down from 62 per cent two months before ("Disasters hit city business confidence," 2017). The editor decided this business story rated ahead of everything else in the news that day.

Today, business stories regularly lead broadcast bulletins and grab front-page headlines. If it's not business fortunes, it will be interest rates, personal debt levels, the gyrations of the sharemarket or other investments. But there was a time when financial and economic news was mostly for men in suits – professionals working in commerce, industry and banking. For reporters it meant writing corporate news for a corporate audience, covering speeches by the president of Federated Farmers and boardroom changes at Westpac or Fletcher Building.

Times have changed, and today it seems everyone wants to know about power prices, family trusts, dairy exports, financial planning, share prices, the latest economic indicators affecting the dollar and the nation's spending and savings habits. Business journalism has broadened to include trends in retailing, people and opportunities in the wine and tourism industries, developments in technology and property, and new thinking in marketing and social media. The business desk also covers personal finance news and advice aimed at helping people manage their mortgages, loans, investments and retirement savings.

Knowing the basics

It seems that business touches just about every part of our lives.

All journalists need a basic grounding in reporting financial affairs, because regardless of whether they are covering health, education, science, environment or politics, sooner or later they will be writing stories about money. Much of the stream of news associated with the rebuild of Christchurch is centred on business issues like insurance, property development, capital funding, employment and the regeneration of local industries. Reporters working the health round need to understand and report their local district health board's annual reports, which include income statements and balance sheets.

Even journalists covering sport and the arts cannot escape the reach of business, as stories about sports franchises and arts organisations often focus on the money. One *Dominion Post* story on the Sports pages looked at whether a golf tournament should be rescheduled for summer in future to improve its business success. The most recent event had been hit by bad weather, which meant the tournament had to run an extra day and incur significant extra costs ("Open date change possibility," 2017). On stories like these business journalists may work alongside their non-business colleagues to pool their expertise.

Public and private sectors

Political journalists regularly write about financial management in the public sector.

Depending on their round, some reporters will deal mostly with agencies in the public sector – district health boards, schools, emergency services, social welfare, local councils, police and suchlike. The affairs of these agencies are clearly of public interest and consequently of interest to the media in its watchdog, fourth-estate role. When the media reports on the financial affairs of the Northland District Health Board, the Civil Aviation Authority, the Invercargill District Council, the Earthquake Commission, the New Zealand Tourism Board and Auckland Transport, there is an expectation of accountability and transparency to taxpayers and ratepayers.

Business journalists operate mostly within society's private sector and so are dealing with organisations that are not under the same moral or legal obligation to open themselves to public or media scrutiny. As long as companies are operating within the law, they are generally accountable only to their shareholders and, to a lesser extent, their employees. Business information, records and correspondence are not subject to official information laws. This presents a significant challenge for journalists: how do you get information from sources who are under no legal obligation to tell you anything? The answer is that business journalists have to win the trust and confidence of businesspeople if they are to get stories from them. Achieving that is in part about understanding the business world and having a reputation for reporting fairly and accurately.

Why the interest in business?

There are several reasons why audiences have become more interested in business-related news. One stems from the sharp rise in property values and rents, particularly in the main centres. Under financial pressure and keen to understand how best to manage their money, Kiwis turn to news sites and weekend business sections for news and columns about personal finance. There they find stories on which bank is offering the best mortgage deal or the cheapest credit cards. There are stories on what's happening in the financial markets and whether it's a good time to buy shares in the government's privatised power companies. There are columns by expert commentators advising readers on where to park their savings, how to finance a car purchase, how to minimise the tax they pay and how to get the best out of the KiwiSaver scheme, which now has more than 2.7 million members. As people's KiwiSaver balances grow, they want to know where their funds are invested and so get interested in how the sharemarkets are performing.

When there are shifts in interest rates, or the Kiwi dollar suddenly shoots upward, or there is a change to marginal tax rates, people are anxious to know how these changes will impact on jobs, housing affordability and food prices. They look to business reporters to explain these issues in ways they understand.

Audiences today are also interested in what is labelled "consumer news", which serves up advice on how to get the best deals on insurance, broadband services, household appliances and power prices. Journalists or invited experts test the latest tablets, smartphones or cloud computing services, and speculate on whether Apple or Google is at the leading edge of design. Consumer news can be cautionary, warning of problems with quality or poor practice by tradespeople. It can also be in-depth, for example taking on a property developer on behalf of apartment owners who have a building damaged by leaks resulting from a poor design and shoddy building work.

When media organisations cover financial issues where there is broad public interest – for example, the government's Budget announcement (see below) or the bailout of a large company – they will often split the reporting into two parts: a top-of-the-bulletin, simplified, plain-English version in which the emphasis is on explaining the significance of the issues; then in the business section, a more detailed look at all the financial angles in the story, written with a specialist audience in mind.

Different media outlets take different approaches to covering business news. TVNZ and Newshub cover business news on their morning news shows and summarise financial market news in their evening bulletins. RNZ runs several business slots throughout the day, while Newstalk ZB and Radio Live both run multiple business stories and market summaries daily, regarding business listeners as part of their target markets.

In print and online, the metropolitan dailies all run stand-alone business sections comparable with sport in their size and prominence, while the Sunday papers run

If a government agency or official fails to provide journalists with information, reporters can demand copies of a wide range of documents under the Official Information Act and the Local Government Official Information and Meetings Act. And if they are not satisfied with the response they can complain to the Ombudsman (see Chapter 12).

Consumer news can be found in the pages of the daily newspapers. There are also specialist outlets, such as *Consumer* magazine, which has print and online versions (www. consumer.org.nz), and popular TV programmes such as *Fair Go*.

combined business and personal finance sections. *National Business Review* is a specialised business weekly, in print and online. Online only are interest.co.nz and businessdesk.co.nz. The top international publications include *The Wall Street Journal*, the *Financial Times*, *Businessweek* and *The Economist*.

The business media also spans a wide range of trade, technical and professional magazines and websites, and in total it employs more journalists than any other round, including sport.

Business stories are everywhere

So what are business stories and where do you find them? Local media outlets report business stories every week: an Auckland Council agenda reveals a plan to build a Bunnings warehouse in a central-city suburb; a sign pinned to a door in Whangārei announces the closure of the last independent book store in town; a public notice details a planned new retail and office complex in central Dunedin. For national media, a lot of business news is "diary stories", like the scheduled annual profit announcement from AMI Insurance, or the release of the latest dairy price payout from Fonterra.

An angle for the AMI story could be: How does AMI's profit compare with other insurance companies, and does this year's profit top last year's performance? If the Fonterra payout is better than expected, what impact will this have on the rural economy and communities? Will it create jobs in the rural sector and related industries? Will it lead to more land going into dairy production? Other news might include an update on the free-trade deal with China, an upward spike in energy costs thanks to a threat to oil supplies from the Middle East, or the appointment of a new chief executive at Spark New Zealand.

Local and national media would be all over a strike by port workers in Tauranga, Wellington or Lyttelton. News stories coming out of a strike would include business angles: how it affects the supply chain for essential raw materials, and the impact on exporters with goods stranded on the wharves. When Mainzeal, a major New Zealand building company, collapsed in 2013, the media covered a range of angles, including the 500 jobs lost, the financial impact on hundreds of contractors, the effect on householders who had made leaky-building claims against the company, plus the impact on Auckland ratepayers when their council, in the words of its lawyer, became "the last man standing" to pay out on multi-million dollar claims ("Mainzeal failure," 2013, para. 3).

So finding business news sometimes comes down to identifying specific business angles within broader news stories. But things can work the other way too. Sometimes reporters turn what looks like a narrow piece of financial data into a broader story that impacts on the lives of ordinary people. One of the more obvious examples is when the Reserve Bank, a government agency, lifts interest rates. Who will be affected by this? When will the higher rates be passed on to mortgage holders? What will the extra weekly payment amount to for a typical household? Will higher interest rates push up the value of the dollar, as has happened in the past? And will a higher-valued dollar result in job losses in manufacturing and tourism?

Many stories will only interest the business section audience, such as commercial property stories, routine bond and share price movements, changes in taxation rules and personnel changes at leading companies.

Reporters have to be careful when writing stories about a single company. They can seem a bit PR-ish, especially where the story has a positive angle. The solution is usually to also quote another source – another company operating in the same sector, or a significant customer or supplier to the company.

Translating the jargon

One of the biggest challenges for business reporters is conveying in meaningful terms what is happening in the complex world of finance and business. Good business stories are not abstract or theoretical. Like any other journalism, business reporting needs human interest.

While on the surface business stories are about profits, infrastructure or the price of sheep meat, ultimately they need to say something about people. People's lives are being affected positively or negatively by shifts in economic fortune or financial trends, so people need to be at the heart of business stories. The very best business reporting is a blend of quantitative and qualitative material. Numbers are powerful, but when they are combined with their impact on people they take on a greater significance. If credit card debt levels have risen, the business reporter finds someone who is struggling to survive because they are weighted down by their credit card payments.

Bringing business news to a wide audience requires that reporters use vocabulary that people understand. It is easy for business journalists to assume too much knowledge of their audience and to slip into using the terminology of their industry contacts. Even when they are writing for a business audience, they need to avoid using overly technical terms and industry jargon. While some in the audience might know what is meant by "the money supply" or "the Trade-Weighted Index", many would not. And straight news reporting is sometimes not enough to tell a story. At times reporters in search of more latitude to explain or give context to a technical story will produce a background feature or interpretive article, or perhaps turn out a commentary piece to help convey what's going on.

Of course there are times when a business story is highly technical and difficult to simplify. If New Zealand share prices move sharply because of something a German banker said about the Greek economy, it may be difficult to join the dots for the casual reader who has not been following stories on New Zealand exports to Europe. But while simplifying financial matters can be tricky, it's no excuse for not trying. Often reporting in technical language is just lazy journalism. In the case of business magazines or financial news websites aimed at a business audience, reporters can assume a higher level of knowledge and avoid constant explanation. While all business stories need numbers, don't swamp them with too many detailed figures. If a lot of numbers are needed, tables and graphics are good options.

If they are to shine a light into the linguistic fog of business, reporters first have to fully understand the jargon themselves. That understanding comes with experience, but a starting point is reading everything you can find on the topics you are covering. It also starts with meeting and talking to lots of contacts in your first few months on the business desk. Business writers must be able to speak the technical language used by share traders, bankers and accountants without falling into the trap of writing overly technical stories. Without the necessary knowledge, reporters struggle to ask the right questions or recognise a newsworthy answer.

Names make news in business as they do in other rounds. Among the best-known business personalities would be Sir Richard Branson, the founder and chairman of the Virgin Group, and Elon Musk, founder of Tesla and SpaceX.

Locally, names in the headlines include transport industrialist and philanthropist

If you need some help with the jargon, check out the resources listed at the end of this chapter.

Sir Owen Glenn, commercial property owner and columnist Sir Robert Jones, Megaupload founder Kim Dotcom, former Air New Zealand chief executive Rob Fyfe, reality television producer Julie Christie, investment expert and frequent campaigner Gareth Morgan, and the wealthiest Kiwi, Graeme Hart. The annual publication of *National Business Review*'s Rich List (Figure 1) always creates a lot of public interest.

A lot of bread-and-butter news in the business world comes out of the corporate sector. There is the annual or six-monthly reporting of companies' results, the expansion and closure of factories, service centres and retail outlets, their environmental impact, mergers and acquisitions, breakthroughs in technology, plus the launch of new products and services. Whether it's expansion or closures, changes in companies' employment can make for big news.

Figure 1

Rich List — Wealth order 2017

1. Graeme Hart $7.5 billion
2. Peter Thiel $3.7 billion
3. Todd family $3.5 billion
4. Richard Chandler $2.0 billion
5. Erceg family $1.7 billion
6. Sir Michael Friedlander $1.6 billion
7. Goodman family $1.5 billion
8. Christopher Chandler $1.4 billion
9. Stephen Jennings $1.1 billion
10. Sir Michael Fay $920 million

Source: *National Business Review*

It's important to show the significance of business stories, answering the question "Who is affected by this event or development?" Explain why the news event matters to the company, or the industry, or the country, or the audience.

Dealing with sources and public relations

As with all journalism, the very best stories come from having good contacts, but building a range of well-placed contacts takes time. That's because there is a lot at stake for business contacts and understandably they will open up only with those they trust. Always keep the lines of communication open. Your business sources would prefer you keep going back to them to check your understanding rather than get something wrong.

It is not unknown for businesspeople to exaggerate about their business ventures or to rubbish their competitors. So it pays to be a little sceptical. Don't believe everything you're told and don't take material at face value. When reporters make factual errors they do huge damage to their personal reputations and the reputation of their news organisation, so it pays to check everything you can in the time available.

With business stories it can be hard to find sources who are not in some way compromised or conflicted. If you are writing a story about a trademark dispute between two companies, you have to seek comment from both parties. Beyond that, you will want sources who can clarify the complexities and put issues in a wider perspective. Academics are the traditional independent source here. Lawyers or business analysts at broking firms are potential sources for a trademarks story, but remember they could be conflicted by their current or potential business relationship with one of the parties.

Former employees can be a good source, as are competitors or suppliers, but they could all have their own agendas. Trade associations or chambers of commerce are potentially good sources for broader context, but they too can be compromised by their self-interest.

A novice business reporter calling a company for an interview can initially expect to be directed to a public relations officer. PR people can be helpful, and a good one will locate the best person to interview and negotiate on the reporter's behalf to make sure the interview is a success. Of course, they may be less cooperative if the story is likely to paint the company in a bad light.

Over time business reporters build relationships with company executives to the point where the contact will take calls and talk freely either on or off the record. The ideal relationship is one built on mutual understanding and respect – close but not so close that you cannot ask some hard questions.

Remember who is paying the PR person and that their job is to ensure that stories published are as favourable as possible to their employer or client.

The financial markets

Print and online media cover the markets in-depth, with daily reports on price movements on the stock exchanges in New Zealand (the NZX50 index), London (the FTSE 100 index), New York (Dow Jones Industrial Average) and Tokyo (Nikkei 225 index). While these sharemarket indices are well known, there are hundreds more financial markets trading small companies' shares, bonds, government debt and currencies, and commodity markets trading metals, rubber, paper, dairy products, wheat, sugar, coffee, corn and even pork bellies.

The financial markets are a restless, sometimes volatile force with a reputation for profoundly impacting on businesses, governments and ordinary citizens.

This was evident in the global financial crisis of 2008, considered by many economists to be the worst since the Great Depression ("Worst crisis since '30s," 2008). The crisis brought the collapse of financial institutions, major banks worldwide were rescued by their governments, housing markets collapsed, sharemarkets plummeted and unemployment queues lengthened around the globe. In New Zealand the impact was limited, but the government had to prop up the financial system by introducing bank guarantees and temporary wage subsidies for smaller business, as well as financing job-creating infrastructure projects (OECD, 2009). The country still experienced five consecutive quarters of negative economic growth (The Treasury, 2012).

These markets are central to the functioning of our economy, so it is hardly surprising there is public interest in their daily gyrations. Mainstream media coverage of the financial markets is regular, if not in-depth. Throughout the day radio and TV routinely update movements on the local sharemarket and bigger overseas markets, as well as shifts in the value of the dollar against our trading partners. They also report prices and movements in other commodities – the world gold price and the price for Brent crude oil, for example.

A \$5 rise in the Brent crude oil benchmark price on world markets soon translates into higher petrol prices over here. Similarly, a fall in dairy prices on the Global Dairy Trade auction (www.globaldairytrade.info) translates into a lower payout to farmers in the following season.

If you think the numbers don't add up, ask why. That's how Bethany McLean, for instance, was able to break the Enron story (see Chapter 12).

Understanding the sharemarket

Companies whose shares (also known as stocks or equities) are traded on the stock exchanges are called public or publicly listed companies. The New Zealand Stock Exchange goes by the brand name NZX.

Financial markets are where businesspeople buy and sell assets like shares, bonds and commodities (like oil or gold).

The overall value of a public company is known as its "market capitalisation", a figure arrived at by multiplying the current share price by the total number of shares on issue. The ownership mix of public companies is constantly changing as investors buy and sell shares every day on the sharemarket. But often companies have a handful of large investors, who are named in their annual report, including mutual funds, pension schemes, founding directors and other large companies. For example, the top six shareholders in The Warehouse Group are (The Warehouse Group, 2016):

Shareholder	Shares owned	% of total
Sir Stephen Tindall	93,687,096	27.01
The Tindall Foundation	73,920,496	21.31
James Pascoe Limited	57,030,600	16.44
Cash Wholesalers Limited	10,373,363	2.99
Foodstuffs Auckland Nominees Limited	10,373,363	2.99
Wardell Bros & Coy Limited	10,373,363	2.99

A share is a share in the ownership of a company. A shareholder can receive a share of any profit the company makes, known as a dividend.

In contrast, a private company is owned and controlled by a small group or family. Shares in a private company are not traded on an exchange, and the value of the company is set by its owners.

Information on private companies can be difficult to obtain. In the interests of transparency to their shareholders, public companies must publish an annual summary of their financial affairs and accounts in their annual report, but there is no such obligation on private companies. All companies – public and private – have to file information with the New Zealand Companies Office. Smaller enterprises only need to file information about their directors and directors' shareholdings and their addresses, while bigger companies (defined by the Financial Reporting Act 1993) also have to file their financial statements.

The media's daily coverage of the local sharemarket is based on data from the NZX exchange. The screenshot (Figure 2) from the NZX exchange (www.nzx.com) captures a day's trading in shares in Auckland International Airport (AIA):

- $7.035: the latest price on the shares, down 0.14% on the day
- Trades: the number (213) and value ($7,829,812.44) of share trades that day plus the current value of the business/capitalisation ($8,394,300,000)
- Performance: the opening price, the day's high and low prices, bids and offers
- Fundamental: P/E (29.090) is the share price divided by earnings per share; EPS ($0.242) is the earnings per share in the latest reporting period; NTA ($3.310) is the net tangible assets in the business (assets minus liabilities) per share; the gross dividend yield (3.746%) is the latest dividend divided by the share price; shares issued (1,193,219,685) is the total number of shares held by investors.

Figure 2

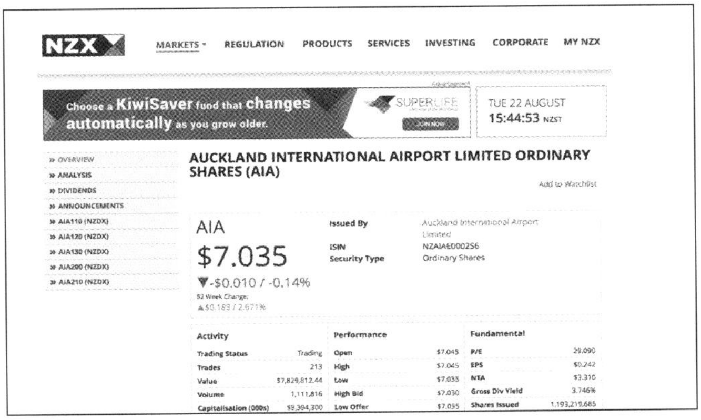

Source: www.nzx.com

Business journalists soon get to know that the news flow can have a big impact on share prices. Individual shares are sensitive to news, rumour and speculation about a company's business prospects or the prospects of its competitors. If a company has high levels of debt, the prospect of rising interest rates can drive its share price down. If the government proposes further investment in the broadband network, shares in Spark New Zealand are likely to move higher. The mere suggestion of a possible takeover can inject life into the target company's share price as investors see they might benefit from a bidding war. Many New Zealand companies are vulnerable to commodity price movements. Agricultural exporters are price takers, which means they cannot influence the price they receive for their products and just have to cope with price fluctuations beyond their control. If there is a drop in worldwide demand for logs, there could be a consequent drop in the Port of Tauranga share price, given the port's reliance on log exports.

The regulators of the financial markets and the broader business world are occasionally a source of some very big news stories. The NZX equity markets are overseen by the Financial Markets Authority (FMA), which monitors the functioning of the market, assesses risks to investors and the financial system, checks for money laundering, and reviews the financial reporting of companies listed on the markets. The FMA featured heavily in news stories on the collapse of multiple finance companies in New Zealand during the global financial crisis. The FMA receives in excess of 4000 complaints and inquiries a year. As finance companies collapsed, New Zealanders also got to know another financial regulator, the Serious Fraud Office (SFO), which laid charges against a number of failed companies. The SFO concentrates on the most complex cases where there are multiple victims (usually investors) and the sums involved exceed $2 million (see www.sfo.govt.nz).

GLAD SHE BECAME A BUSINESS REPORTER

Sophie Boot is a reporter for online business news organisation businessdesk.co.nz.

"When I became a business journalist, my experience was limited to what I'd picked up from headlines I'd skimmed over. I studied politics at university and the business journalism module on my postgrad journalism course. I was aware of the stock market, currency exchanges and big companies releasing their earnings, but that was about it! It was definitely a steep learning curve when I took the position as a business reporter, but I realised pretty quickly that the concepts are generally not all that complicated – it's learning the language that presents the biggest challenge.

"The part of my job that terrified me most when I started is also the part that has proven the most useful – our stock-market report. Every day at about 4pm I call a broker or a trader and talk about the day's news and price movements. At 5pm, the market closes, at 5:30pm the numbers are settled. My story is due at about 5:31pm!

"While initially nerve-wracking, it meant that from day one I was talking to experts with years of experience, improving my ability to build contact relationships and getting to understand what it all meant – I would frequently hang up and frantically Google a phrase somebody had used!

"Business journalism can have a stuffy reputation, but I have found no two days are the same. I cover commercial court cases, and being in Wellington is great as I get to go to the Court of Appeal and the Supreme Court. I also go to annual meetings, select committee meetings, and have the opportunity to write longer features. I've had the opportunity to travel to Shanghai for a six-week internship through the Asia New Zealand Foundation as a business journalist, which was great.

"I never thought I'd become a business journalist. At journalism school, we covered a variety of areas and, while I knew sports wasn't for me, I was open to anything. I was always interested in politics and took the business-reporting job as a chance to learn more about the way our society functions. I'm glad I did. It has given me a broader and deeper understanding of every story I read and every event I attend. And I no longer skip the business stories!"

Writing an analytical piece on the detail of a large corporate's financial performance would be left to business journalists with some years' experience.

Business-results stories

Even a fairly raw business journalist would be expected to write a news story on a public company's financial results. These results are supplied to markets soon after the company's financial year ends and are later included in its annual report. A reporter with just a basic understanding of the numbers in financial statements can reach some preliminary conclusions about the company's business operations, and these conclusions will help inform the questions put to company management and to experts such as brokers and industry sector analysts.

Prior to their release, financial statements are checked and verified by auditors, who follow financial reporting principles set out by the New Zealand Institute of Chartered Accountants. Auditors ensure the financial reports show a "true and fair view" of a company's financial position and performance. "The financial statements are the instrument panel of a business enterprise. They show the success or failure of the business and, like the plane's instruments, the financial statements flash warnings of impending problems" (Smart, Awan & Bourke, 2008, p. 200).

Annual reports can be a starting point for many stories, but keep in mind that while they include financial information that companies are legally required to publish, they are essentially marketing documents. They are basically trying to present the company in the best possible light, and that might mean masking or downplaying any bad news.

Annual reports put the best possible spin on the company's performance so need to be read with an open mind and a sceptical eye. Anything out of the ordinary might be in smaller type or located near the back of what can be a lengthy document – perhaps a comment in the auditor's report or somewhere in the footnotes.

The financial information in an annual report includes the income statement, which shows how much profit or loss the company has made from its operating activities in the past year; the cash flow statement, which tracks the cash movements into and out of the business; and the balance sheet, or statement of financial position, which is a snapshot of the company on the last day of the financial year, detailing all the assets the company owns and all the liabilities it faces.

Fixed assets represent the infrastructure of the business, like buildings, vehicles and equipment. They are held for a long period and are employed to generate revenue. Current assets are short-term, like stocks or cash. A long-term liability could be a 10-year bank loan, while a short-term liability might be rent that is due.

Accompanying the financial statements might be various performance ratios that provide insights into the health of the business – for instance, measuring profitability by geographic region, return on assets, return on equity, debt levels and the solvency of the company (assets vs liabilities). The annual report will also set out how the board of directors plans to distribute profits. How much will be reinvested in the company and how much will be returned to shareholders in a dividend payment?

Journalists working for specialist magazines and business news sites will delve deeper into the financial results, revealing how profit performance is trending across different divisions of the business, as well as commenting on changes to revenue, capital investment, cash holdings, debt levels and productivity.

News about the economy

A steady stream of data tracking the performance of the economy is published by Statistics New Zealand, a government department. Economic statistics underpin a lot of business news, but the challenge is always making such stories intelligible to the wider audience.

There is a wealth of information available about companies on the Companies Office website (www.business.govt.nz/companies) and on individuals' financial health (www.insolvency.govt.nz). You can set up a dashboard to monitor such information.

Many in your audience will be shareholders or would-be shareholders in the company, so focus on the company's financial performance, compare it with the previous year, and include expert commentary from business analysts.

A number of parties have a stake in a company's financial results – as well as management and employees, there is interest from investors, competitors, creditors and lenders, union officials, investment analysts, politicians and government agencies including Inland Revenue.

Headlines like "Productivity falls as wages rise" or "Balance of Payments deficit blow-out threat" sound scary, but it's up to the reporter to explain to ordinary people what these events mean, rather than resorting to the jargon used by economists. The starting point again is that the reporter needs to fully understand what the statistics are measuring and what they mean. Here are five important numbers that are routinely reported in our media.

Gross Domestic Product (GDP) measures the value of all final goods and services produced in the economy in a given period, either annually or quarterly. Statistics New Zealand bases its published measure of GDP activity on what is called the production-based series, which is calculated on estimates of the market value of all final goods and services produced within the economy. GDP is also based on constant prices, to get a measure of real changes in production without the influence of inflation. This is called Real GDP, and changes in Real GDP show if the economy is growing or shrinking (Figure 3).

Changes in the Consumers Price Index (CPI) is the official measure of inflation within the economy. Changes in the CPI (Figure 4) show changes in prices, based on a basket of goods and services that represent typical purchases made by households. There are about 700 goods and services in the basket, including food, clothing, health, transport and recreation. It is a weighted index so purchases representing a higher proportion of household spending are given a higher weighting. Because Kiwis spend more on petrol than on newspapers, a 2 per cent rise at the petrol pump would have a greater impact on the CPI than a similar price rise in newspapers. Food currently represents about 17 per cent of the index. Changes in the CPI tracks progress in the battle against inflation led by the Reserve Bank.

Balance of Payments (BoP) statistics measure New Zealand's financial dealings with the world. The BoP picture is sometimes confused with balance of trade data, which measures only the value of the country's exports and imports. "The BoP is an amalgam of the balances of merchandise trade (export/import figures), trade in services, international investment income, and so-called 'invisibles' payments, which include foreign debt and interest repayments, and insurance and freight charges" (Smellie, 1997). The figure in the BoP data given the most airplay is the current account deficit, which is reported as a percentage of GDP. This measures how much New Zealand is in debt to the rest of the world. In the 2016 calendar year, New Zealand's current account deficit was $7.1 billion, or about 2.7% of GDP (www.stats.govt.nz).

Unemployment data comes from the Household Labour Force Survey (HLFS), which is based on data from 16,000 homes around the country. The HLFS provides data on those who are employed, unemployed and those not in the labour force by age group, ethnic group and region. It shows those in full-time and part-time employment, those not in the workforce, the unemployed (those without a job but seeking one) and the total hours worked in the survey period.

The official HLFS unemployment rate (Figure 5) is one used for international comparisons. The figure for those on an unemployment benefit from Work and Income is not internationally comparable.

Figure 3

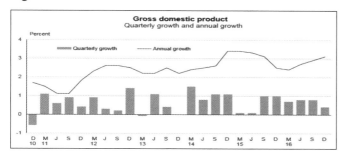

Figure 4

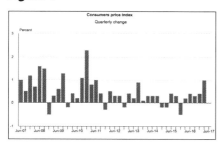

Figure 5

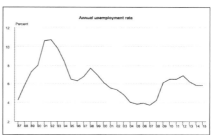

Source: Statistics New Zealand

Public, private and foreign debt are measured in various ways. There is public debt owed by government, and therefore by the taxpayer, which is revealed in the government's annual Budget. There is significant public interest in public debt. Private debt owed by companies is of less public interest unless the share or property market is in trouble. Public and private debt can be domestic or foreign, and are therefore held in both New Zealand dollars and foreign currencies. Of course, debt is only one side of the equation, as governments and companies also have assets to offset their debt. Statistics New Zealand publishes foreign debt figures covering public and private borrowers. The Reserve Bank publishes data on domestic private debt levels.

For more on statistics, see Chapter 13.

Monetary and fiscal policy

Beyond the statistics, economics news frequently makes it into the papers and on the television news. Two regular big stories centre on monetary and fiscal policy.

Monetary policy is the government's use of credit and interest rates to control inflation in New Zealand. The policy is undertaken by the Reserve Bank, an independent government agency charged with keeping inflation between 1 and 3 per cent per annum on average over the medium term. To do this, the Reserve Bank sets the official cash rate (OCR), an interest rate that influences other interest rates in the economy.

The Reserve Bank Governor issues quarterly monetary policy statements and the bank reviews the OCR eight times a year. These events are always reported, as interest rates and inflation affect virtually everyone. If interest rates change, news reports may explain the change in terms the ordinary person can better understand, such as how the change will affect repayments on a 20-year, $200,000 home loan. Indeed, reports on the housing market generally are also very popular.

Fiscal policy is the government's spending and revenue-raising activities. The government spends billions each year on such items as healthcare, welfare, education, defence, etc. To cover the cost, the government raises taxes, charges fees for its services and borrows. The government annual accounts are called the Budget, which are prepared by the Treasury, the government's chief economic adviser.

Again, these activities are widely reported as they impact on virtually everyone. As well as giving the big picture, including whether the Budget is in surplus or deficit, many reports look at how changes in the Budget will affect ordinary New Zealanders. As with so many business stories, reporting the Budget is a balancing act between providing solid technical information for the specialists and accessible material for the interested layperson.

Further reading

Black, J., Hashimzade, N., & Myles, G. (2017). *A dictionary of economics*. Oxford: Oxford University Press. An excellent guide to business and economics terms.

https://www.nzx.com The stock exchange website gives details on the market, plus tips on investing.

www.business.govt.nz/companies/app/ui/pages/home/dashboard An online system that allows you to manage your access to the Companies Office database, including setting up watches on companies.

www.consumer.org.nz The online version of *Consumer* magazine.

www.qv.co.nz Government agency Quotable Value generates many statistics on the housing market, including house prices and sales.

www.rbnz.govt.nz The Reserve Bank's website has lots of useful material on monetary policy and the banking sector.

www.sorted.org.nz The Commission for Financial Literacy and Retirement Income's guide to investing.

www.stats.govt.nz Government agency Statistics New Zealand publishes many of the country's main business and economics statistics.

www.treasury.govt.nz The Treasury's website includes all Budget material, plus analysis of the government sector and the economy generally.

References

Disasters hit city business confidence. (2017, January 16). *The Dominion Post*, p. A1.

Mainzeal failure lands ratepayers with millions more leaky homes debt. (2013, February 8). *The New Zealand Herald*. Retrieved from http://www.nzherald.co.nz

Open date change possibility. (2017, October 3). *The Dominion Post*. p. B5.

Organisation for Economic Co-operation and Development. (2009). *Policy brief: Economic survey of New Zealand 2009.* Retrieved from http://www.oecd.org

Smart, M. J., Awan, N., & Bourke, D. H. (2008). *Principles of accounting* (3rd ed.). Auckland: Pearson Education.

Smellie, P. (1997). Economic statistics. In A. Lee (Ed.), *Business reporting: A New Zealand guide to financial journalism* (pp. 36–45). Wellington: New Zealand Journalists Training Organisation.

The Treasury. (2012). *New Zealand economic and financial overview 2012.* Retrieved from http://www.treasury.govt.nz

The Warehouse Group. (2016). *The Warehouse Group annual report 2016.* Retrieved from http://thewarehouse.co.nz

Worst crisis since '30s, with no end yet in sight. (2008, September 18). *The Wall Street Journal.* Retrieved from http://www.wsj.com

11

Sports journalism

Not as glamorous as many imagine, but rewarding

Jim Kayes

"How was the game?"

It's a question I'm often asked, but for those asking there's always something they don't realise. For a sports journalist it's not "How was the game?" but "How was the game *to report on*?" It's the fan who gets to enjoy sport for just being sport. For the sports journalist there is the need for an angle, which usually means the need for a turning point in a game, or a decisive moment, injury or key mistake.

And there's an editor who wants your story filed quickly so it can go online and make the paper's first edition, thanks. So if you're a player and you're going to break a leg, please do so in the first half and get off the field quickly; there's nothing worse than a long injury delay when the printing presses will be running before the game finishes!

And, to both teams, save the thrills for the first 60 minutes, thanks. That way, I can get most of my article written before the final whistle. The curse of a sports journalist is the fan's delight – a game that goes down to the wire. Sport has no respect for the sports journalist's deadline.

Sorry, if you're a sports fan who wants to watch sport for the thrill of it and get up close to athletes for the buzz of it, then skip this chapter because sports reporting is

All Blacks first-five Andrew Mehrtens once recalled arriving at a test match and seeing some mates walking into the ground, laughing and relaxed. He envied their freedom to enjoy the moment. His joy had to be earned. It's the same for sports journalists.

not for you. A sports journalist isn't there to cheer and do the Mexican wave.

Sure, you have to enjoy sport but if you want to be a good sports reporter – and I mean one of the best – then you have to be a good reporter who just happens to cover sport. The best sports reporters could move to any round in the newsroom and succeed because they have a good grounding in news, so if you want to be a good sports reporter, don't make the sports editor's desk your first port of call, head instead to the chief reporter or editor.

I began my career as a news reporter, covering transport and the defence forces for the *Waikato Times*, then as the paper's police reporter – a position I continued with a shift to *The Evening Post* in Wellington. It's the same story with other sports reporters. *The New Zealand Herald*'s Wynne Gray was an excellent police reporter, as was Tony Smith from *The Press*, while *The Dominion Post*'s Toby Robson was a business reporter at *The Evening Post*.

And it swings both ways. Steve Deane has moved from the *Herald*'s sports desk to being a fine news reporter, while Mike McRoberts covered sport in radio and then for TVNZ before shifting to news and current affairs at TVNZ and TV3 (now Newshub). Those reporters based overseas for TVNZ and Newshub are expected to cover sport and news on a daily basis, and do both extremely well.

That's because reporting on sport is fundamentally no different to reporting any news. The basics are the same – who did it, why, when, where and by what means – though sports reporting offers more than that, much more. A decent sports reporter can cover anything that touches their round – whether it involves crime, finance, tragedy and triumph – because modern sports reporting is a lot more than just what happens between the white lines, on the track, in the pool or across the court. Pick a sport, any sport, and you'll find it requires a journalist who is multi-skilled, versatile and adaptable, with a keen sense of news and an ability to work to extremely tight deadlines and cover a wide range of topics.

Just look at the careers of Tiger Woods and Lance Armstrong, or do a quick internet search for New Zealanders Julian Savea, Jesse Ryder and Zac Guildford to get a glimpse of the range of stories that are there to be covered. A good sports journalist can write news, colour, profiles, features and opinion, and feels comfortable walking in many worlds – from a chief executive's office to the sideline chatting to the baggage handler.

If you think you've got what it takes, keep reading.

Sports reporters covering the 1972 Olympics in Munich suddenly had to report a terrorist attack on the Israeli team.

The different types of sports report

Previews

A preview is a story about an upcoming sports event. They are the bane of most sports reporters' lives. My preview for the 2003 Rugby World Cup semi-final against Australia ran through a fairly lengthy list of reasons why the All Blacks would win and skimmed over a couple of ideas as to why they might not. Australia won 22–10. Four years later in Cardiff I wrote about how the All Blacks had averaged 40 points in their last eight wins against France and that this quarter-final should be no different. The All Blacks lost 18–20.

But that didn't make either preview poor. It's just a reality that predicting what might happen in a sporting event is about as reliable as predicting the weather. A good preview has a strong angle, presents the facts and has an opinion. Delving back into history is fine, and statistics are okay, but steer clear of basing your preview around the weather or the pitch because it's lazy (there has to be a better angle than whether it will rain or the ball will seam). The best previews, just like the best match reports, have a strong human element in them. There's a person in the story. It might be a player on debut, in their 110th game, or coming back from a long injury layoff, pregnancy, a death in the family, or time away from the sport. Or it might be based on an old-timer who will talk to the team before the match and present the shirts, jerseys or bibs. Whoever it is, if there is a person in the preview, you're halfway there.

Sports reporters must write about the action as it is happening.

Reporting the game

Newspapers and online require match reports filed on full-time, so you will need to learn how to write about an event while it is happening. The simplest way is to provide a run of play for the first half that will anchor your story with the top of the piece covering what happens in the second half. When you have your head down writing, you need to still be aware of what is happening late in the match, so listen and the crowd will tell you when to look up. Keep a close eye on key action that might provide the hook into your story.

Keep things simple. On deadline is not the time to get clever. Be accurate with the score. Don't over-write, especially if filing for a newspaper, as all you're doing is handing a bigger job to a sub-editor who is also on deadline. Go into the match prepared – know your history, milestones, records, etc., so you can weave relevant facts into your copy.

The follow-up

Once the first edition or the online piece is written, you should have the chance to expand your piece with quotes and insight from the coaches and athletes. Look for a side-bar on a key player or moment. Move beyond the simple angle of what happened, to look at why, what the implications are, who stood out and what injuries will matter. Now is the time to take a bit more time and add some polish.

It's important to remember that you are there – the reader isn't – so take them into the arena. Paint a picture that's wider than just the game, race or event. Give them the history to what's happened, provide the context, add colour and emotion.

Sure, for your paper's first edition and website you might have to write that the Warriors broke an 11-game losing streak, but after that, find out why. Was there an inspirational speech before the game or a death in the family that inspired the players to lift their performance? Equally, what's behind a losing streak or a surprise defeat? Don't just settle for the superficial result.

In this age of internet, Twitter and texting, the result is quickly and widely known; to be a good sports reporter you have to take your reader, listener or viewer beyond that. Paint them a picture of what happened and explain why it happened. Give them more than what they can see on their television.

Features

Feature writing is an area where a sports journalist should have an advantage over their news-writing colleagues because it is a regular part of the sports brief, whether it is for newspapers or online. It is also one of the areas where sports journalists most frequently get it wrong, chewing up valuable space with overlong and directionless single-source interviews.

The scope for quality feature writing is vast. It could be a profile, an issue-driven series of features, a retrospective, deep analysis, or whimsy. What they all have in

A reporter has to be a problem-solver. When it comes to technology, if it works in the office it'll almost certainly fail in the field.

ADVICE ON WRITING SPORTS FEATURES

The New Zealand Herald's head of sport, Dylan Cleaver, says good features must be well-constructed.

"You can tell a well-written feature because it has a clear structure: a compelling hook, fresh information cleverly presented and an end that leaves the readers with few questions and a far better understanding of the subject. Ideally, you should have just as clear an idea of how you want to end the story as how you mean to start it.

"You can just as easily tell a poor feature because the chances are you'll give up long before the end. While there is more freedom to try different things because the 'rules' of shorter-form journalism do not apply, that freedom should not be abused with meaningless quotes and filler material."

Profiles are a staple of sports features. *Rugby World* editor Gregor Paul says to write a good profile you must have empathy with your subject.

"Emotion is the lifeblood of sporting theatre. A feature that can tell us how an athlete felt – throw light on their insecurities, doubts and triumphs, highlight their anxiety, tension and elation – is one that will capture an audience."

It's the same for television pieces, explains Mark Crysell of TVNZ.

"Stories have arcs, journeys; you weave people in and out, get to know their characters, signpost and build in reveals and surprises that give an audience something to discover and own.

"Write the way you speak and write to the pictures. Not always, but sometimes you'll need to tell people what they're seeing, but don't use too many words. Pictures always win, and once you've written the script, go through it again and lose more words. Your job as a reporter is to lead us through success and tragedy, rising and falling, sadness and laughter, conflict and resolution, and not get in the way. TV is a team game, talk to your editor, shooter, field producer or executive producer – without them you can very easily look like an idiot."

common, though, is the need for exceptional planning and gathering. Road-mapping features – the practice of setting out what you want to say, the points you need to cover off and the information you need to source – is a useful way of keeping on topic.

Readers need to connect with their subject, an often difficult link to make in the modern sporting context where the stars tend to be removed from humdrum normal life. Yet it's their fallibility, unseen ordinariness and universal pressures that draw us to them.

And as it's feature writing, be prepared to break every journalism rule in the book, as this excellent piece does: http://sportsillustrated.cnn.com/vault/article/magazine/MAG1015865/1/index.htm.

Opinion

Writing opinion pieces is what sets reporting on sport apart from almost every other round. When it's done well it is compelling, and in this age of saturation coverage of sports events, good opinion writing can provide a key point of difference for your newspaper or website. For me, the rules are simple. Never write anything you don't believe; never write something about a person you're not prepared to say to their face (this separates you from the nameless talkback or online responders); and base your opinion on facts.

Covering large international sports events can be less glitzy than you might imagine.

Covering major events

So you want to go to the Olympics, or maybe a Football World Cup? How about an All Blacks tour? Ah, the glitz and glamour. Flash hotels, fancy restaurants, shopping, travel.

Yeah, right. Covering an Olympics is two weeks of bedlam, in a time zone that often makes your deadline a nightmare and – if you work in television or radio – usually with no rights to be inside the ground or interview the athletes after the event. So get used to waiting outside stadiums or in hotel car parks. All Blacks tours can be a succession of hotel lobbies, airports and training fields, with lots of hanging around. Yet events and tours like these are what covering sport is all about.

It's the pinnacle, and when it's done properly it can set you apart from the pack.

The keys to covering major events are preparation, having great contacts within the team, patience, endurance and an eye for an angle.

Sometimes you need a bit of gumption too. At the final of the 2011 Rugby World Cup in Auckland, TV3 had broadcast rights to be sideline before the match, but not after it. We ignored that, storming the field to interview almost every player and getting vision that was different to what the host broadcaster was providing. We did this despite being asked four times to leave, and it worked. Our coverage was unique and so different from the sterile press conference reaction we'd relied on throughout the tournament.

WRITING A GREAT OPINION PIECE

One of New Zealand's best sports writers is freelancer **Richard Boock**. Here's his advice on writing opinion pieces.

"The best opinion writers are independent; independence is the mother of originality and creativity. Those who are truly independent will take greater ownership of an opinion, put more energy into representing it and will tend to express it in a more forceful and persuasive style. Not only that, over a period of time their work will reveal a consistency of judgement. This has a value.

"On the other hand, those who allow themselves to write opinion to suit, as an example, a boss's stance, or to promote an undisclosed agenda, leave themselves vulnerable. They generally won't feel as territorial about the subject-matter, they risk misunderstanding and misrepresenting it and – if writing opinion on a regular basis – can expose themselves to accusations of inconsistency, if not hypocrisy.

"News reporters are encouraged to be objective. Opinion writers need to be subjective. It's about one person's thoughts on an issue. It's not supposed to be a summary of public thinking.

"The best opinion pieces are always highly subjective, biased even, in that their authors are not denying taking sides. The quickest way to make an opinion piece boring is to try to be objective.

"Actually express an opinion. Explaining an issue and reporting the differing views surrounding it is not offering an opinion. It's offering a synopsis. There's no point in trying to write opinion and sitting on the fence. The whole point of opinion is personal judgement; call it bias if you want. Good opinion can even lack balance – it might take the shape of a rant. But the sub-text always needs to be asking readers, do you agree with this or not?

"The best opinion topics invariably involve sustainable arguments. Opinion pieces should never be able to be checkmated. They shouldn't be so much a matter of right or wrong as agree or disagree. Opinion is about explaining, defending or promoting a belief or judgement. Therefore, the subject-matter should be based on things less certain than absolutes.

"And have a thick skin. Opinion writers can never please everyone. There will be those who cheer and applaud them, and those who call for them to be horse-whipped through the town square."

A few tips

Don't be a cheerleader

You work for a news organisation, not a sports body. Report the sport – the good and the bad – accurately, and in the long run you'll be held in high regard. You're a journalist first, a fan second. You're working for your readers, not the sportspeople.

Learn to hang out

The best stories often come from mingling with those involved in sport. Talk to the baggage handler, the physio, the assistant coach, the injured players, and the bloke who fills the water bottles. It's amazing where stories come from, and in sport you will spend a huge amount of time watching training sessions, waiting for aeroplanes and being bored senseless at a hotel, so use that time to get to know those in and around the team, athlete or sport you are covering. You'll be amazed at what you learn.

Understand who you're dealing with

Sportspeople come in all shapes, sizes, hues, creeds and life stories. Getting to know them helps immeasurably in getting the best from them. I covered the Hurricanes rugby team from 1998 to 2008. Frank Oliver was their first coach. He was a big, tough guy, whose nickname in the All Blacks had been "Filth". I struggled for a long time to interview him adequately until Peter Lampp, from *The Manawatu Standard*, told me to swear at him. Peter then gave me a quick demo with questions laced with language that would've made a sailor wince. But I tried it, and when the swear words were deleted from Frank's replies, we were left with superb quotes that made a lot of sense. I can vividly remember watching Frank being interviewed by TV crews and he was stilted and hesitant – perhaps because he was losing track as he mentally deleted the swear words. I tried the same trick on his successor, Graham Mourie, and was promptly told that swearing demonstrated a lack of vocabulary! So know who you're dealing with.

Show empathy

Athletes don't try to make mistakes but, unlike other professions, their errors are magnified. So don't treat athletes who play badly as pariahs. Sport should be 90 per cent heroes, 10 per cent villains. We don't read sports pages for wall-to-wall doom and gloom (although, used sparingly, a doom-and-gloom story can enhance your pages or bulletin).

Be tenacious

It's as important in sports reporting as it is in any other round. If you break a story, stick with it, hammer the follows-ups hard – own the story. *The New Zealand Herald*'s Dana Johannsen did a superb job of this with her series on netball brutes. Read it here: www.nzherald.co.nz/sport/news/article.cfm?c_id=4&objectid=10876285.

Park the arrogance

Be brave, bold, prepared and ready to take a risk!

Sport is filled with people who know best. On the sports desk at *The Dominion Post* we had a motto: "No one has a mortgage on an idea." In other words, it wasn't important where a story came from, what mattered was that we ran it. So listen to other people's views. One of the great things about sport is the ability to debate it – don't be so arrogant as to presume that your view is the right one.

Be aware of current trends

Too many of our sports journalists cover sport the same way they did in the days

BE ORGANISED

When **Michelle Pickles** was a television sports reporter she loved the challenge of being a non-rights-holder broadcaster. Organisation was crucial.

"During the London Olympics we interviewed many of our medal winners live on *3News*. This didn't just happen because they won and we asked for them to agree to a live interview: nine months before the Games even started I had gone through every sport we were involved in, and highlighted who I thought might win a medal. I then put in a request with the New Zealand Olympic Committee for those athletes to do live interviews with us first, before our competition had access to them."

When Kiwi BMX rider Sarah Walker won silver at the Games, Michelle was watching it on a TV in a London bar.

"Six hours later, at around 8pm, I was with my cameraperson, hanging around outside a shopping centre that was close to Olympic Park and convenient for Sarah to get to. We got an interview and some shots of her wonderful medal around her neck.

"We finally got what we needed around 10 and headed back to the hotel. It took me two hours for what should have been a 30-minute trip. At midnight I started shot-listing what I had, I scripted my story, my editor cut it and I fell into bed at around 2.30am.

"At 4.30am I was up and getting ready to go live into *3News*."

Other times, everything can change. When Michelle went to San Francisco to cover the America's Cup in 2013, she suddenly found herself covering a plane crash at the city's airport.

before our major sports went professional (in the mid- to late 90s). At its worst, sports journalism can seem resentful of players who earn high salaries. Taken with a grain of salt, players' managers and agents are valuable sources. And take notice of what the crowds enjoy. Don't be afraid to pander to that.

Go easy on the jargon

It's important to know the difference between a birdie and a duck, but remember you're trying to attract a wide audience. Don't write in a way that leaves people feeling stupid. Of course, if you're writing for a specialist publication you can let more of the lingo stand as is.

Be a fast and accurate typist

A lot of sport is played in the evening and finishes bang on your deadline. The importance of being able to write while the game is being played and to file accurate copy to the length required can't be over-stated.

Avoid clichés

Athletes don't "step up" unless they have a ladder, and while it might be a "game of two halves", to say so is to open yourself up to ridicule. And there is never a "new record" set. If it's a record, by definition it's new.

Show the emotion

This is particularly true of television. This could be the sight of All Blacks lock Brad Thorn weeping as he talked about how it felt to have at last won the World Cup or Julian Savea breaking down as he admitted to assaulting his partner. It could be watching a runner collapse with the finish line in sight, high-speed crashes in car races, crunching tackles or terrific goals. Television portrays emotion better than any other media format can.

Let the moment tell the story. Over-writing is a sin in all television reporting but especially when it's a key moment. Use natural sound or the commentator's call to augment your story. Less is more when it comes to a voice-over in sport.

Sport is not war. Don't denigrate those who fight in wars by using the tired clichés of battles, fights and wars to describe sport. It's insulting and inaccurate.

The final whistle

The vote for who would host the 2011 Rugby World Cup was held by the International Rugby Board in a hotel in Dublin. Having spoken with several of the IRB's directors during the week, I'd written that if South Africa lost in the first ballot, New Zealand would beat the third contender, Japan, because South Africa's votes would head New Zealand's way. It wasn't a widely held view, especially in the English press, who were convinced Japan would win. I'm pleased to say my contacts were right.

When it was announced that New Zealand had won the rights to host their second

---

GETTING THE BIG STORIES

The organisers of major sports events only grant coverage rights to certain news organisations. The others have to use imagination and contacts to get their stories.

When Andrew Gourdie covered the 2010 Football World Cup in South Africa for TV3, the station didn't have broadcast rights, so Andrew couldn't have a camera at the matches. So he'd buy tickets to each game, watch it, then leave early to race the All Whites' bus back to their hotel to do interviews.

There was high drama following the match against Slovakia, when All Whites' defender Winston Reid equalised at the end of extra time. Andrew was already out of the ground, walking to his car. His sister told him about the goal in a text! After getting fan reaction, he and cameraman Billy Paine raced to the team's hotel to interview Reid at 8pm.

Andrew got the interview because he had earlier done an exclusive story on how the Denmark-based Reid was available for the All Whites (who hadn't realised he was). Thanks to that existing relationship, Andrew was able to do an exclusive follow-up story with Reid's mother the day after the match.

A WOMAN'S PERSPECTIVE

Too few women cover sports. One who does is *The New Zealand Herald*'s Dana Johannsen. Here are her thoughts on the industry.

"Despite the advances in gender equality in the media over the past 20 years, sports journalism remains dominated by men. Women who venture into sports journalism are considered an oddity in the newsroom. Even now I am asked by colleagues whether I chose to be a sports journalist, the implication being I was somehow forced into this unworthy job.

"It can be challenging working in a profession where you are the minority, though I am lucky to have been part of a supportive team over the past six years. The sports industry as a whole is a largely male domain and sexism is rife – whether it be the patronising attitudes of some coaches or administrators; readers who claim I should write about something I know, like shoes or hair straighteners; or someone assuming you are at a sports function as the partner of one of your colleagues. It can be frustrating that male sports journalists are automatically given a certain level of respect, while women must continuously prove themselves.

"There seems to be an unofficial quota system of one female per sports desk in New Zealand newsrooms. Often a female sports journalist has to resign or leave for there to be an opportunity for another woman.

"Sports editors are coming to realise having female reporters on staff is important for reasons that go beyond social responsibility. Market research has shown that women are increasingly becoming sports consumers and therefore publications and broadcasters risk alienating a large chunk of their potential audience by not including female voices.

"Women can offer a very different perspective to men. Due to basic traits acquired through gender, we generally have greater empathy and understanding."

Rugby World Cup, the second-best day of my journalistic career kicked off. In a flurry of fingers, I wrote a front-page lead, a page-three lead, the sports-page lead, and a 1000-word feature on Jock Hobbs, the New Zealand Rugby Union chairman, who'd missed captaining the All Blacks when they won the inaugural World Cup in 1987 because he'd been forced to retire from playing because of persistent concussions. It was an exhausting, exhilarating and intensely satisfying experience.

That Dublin day was topped when the All Blacks won the World Cup in 2011. I wrote two stories for TV3's news breaks and then another for the sports break. It was six minutes of television – a massive amount – that was a superb team effort, as all good television is.

They were such different days – winning a victory in the boardroom and winning another on the footy field, covering one for print and the other for television – but

Remember to have fun. Sport, after all, is about enjoyment.

they sum up the wide scope for stories in modern sports journalism.

I'm often asked if after all these years I still like my job. My response is always the same: "Yep, it sure beats working for a living."

I would like to thank all those who gave their time and advice in the writing of this chapter: Dylan Cleaver, Mark Crysell, Andrew Gourdie, Matt Hunt, Dana Johannsen, Gregor Paul, Michelle Pickles and Gregory Robertson. Any errors are mine.

Further reading

Agassi, A. (2009). *Open: An autobiography.* New York: Random House.
One of the great sports autobiographies from one of the great tennis players.

Coleman, N., & Hornby, N. (1996). *The Picador book of sports writing.* London: Macmillan.
Excellent anthology of international sports journalism.

Columbia Journalism Review. Available at www.cjr.org/. A leading US commentary on journalism, including sports journalism.

ESPN's Ombudsman column. Available at: http://espn.go.com/blog/ombudsman.
ESPN is a world leader in sports journalism and engages an ombudsman to critically assess the quality of its coverage.

Lewis, P., & McLean, J. (2010). *TP: The life and times of Sir Terry McLean.* Auckland: HarperCollins. A fascinating, warts-and-all biography of one of New Zealand's great old-school sports journalists.

Stout, G. (1991–). *The best American sports writing.* Boston: Mariner Books.
An annual anthology of US sports journalism.

Veysey, A. (1974). *Colin Meads, All Black.* Auckland: Collins. A classic New Zealand sports biography.

Plus any sports journalism written by Frank Deford and John Fernstein. In fact, every article and book on sport you can lay your hands on!

12

Investigative journalism
A six-step guide to journalistic investigations

James Hollings, Massey University

Investigative journalism is sometimes called the first draft of legislation (Burgh, 2000). That's because it often brings about change, usually through giving official bodies – such as the police, the courts or Parliament – the evidence they need to act. But that's usually after the investigative journalists' articles have first led to a public outcry for change.

The term "investigative journalism" became popular in the 1970s. It was used to describe a wave of hard-hitting, carefully researched journalism that seemed to shake the foundations of society. The most famous was a series of articles by *Washington Post* reporters Bob Woodward and Carl Bernstein on a secret slush fund used by US President Richard Nixon's administration to run a dirty tricks campaign against his rivals. The affair was called Watergate and led to Nixon's resignation. These "typewriter guerrillas" (Behrens, 1977), lionised in the film *All the President's Men,* became popular heroes for exposing wrongdoing.

Woodward and Bernstein didn't bring down Nixon on their own, but they brought to light information that other public institutions, such as the Senate, could then act on, and thus provided a check on the abuse of power.

Besides leading to Nixon's resignation, the scandal also sparked a host of laws designed to prevent similar abuses of power (Schudson, 2004). It was a classic example of the power of journalism to bring about change in society.

Woodward and Bernstein didn't invent investigative journalism. There was already a long tradition, in the United States and many other countries, of journalism that dug deeper, and tried to go beyond official denials to establish a truth. But they helped popularise and romanticise the term, and they demonstrated the crucial role of journalism in society as what some have called the "court of last resort" where other institutions fail.

Before them, and after them, journalists in many countries have lost their marriages, health, and even lives holding power to account. There are now institutions that fund and support investigative journalism, and a global network of investigative journalists helping each other. Among the many important issues they have brought to light are the use of torture by American forces in Iraq and the CIA's secret rendition campaign, the role of the French government in the bombing of the *Rainbow Warrior*, the torture and murder by Russian forces in Chechnya and by the apartheid government in South Africa, and thousands of stories exposing corruption, pollution, murder and other wrongdoing in many other countries.

In New Zealand, investigative journalists such as Pat Booth, Nicky Hager, Phil Kitchin and Donna Chisholm have helped free people wrongly imprisoned, exposed a secret spy network, and sent dozens of people – from ordinary citizens to MPs – to jail.

Many investigative journalists say there is nothing special about what they do. Carl Bernstein calls it simply "An attempt at attaining the best version of the truth" (Behrens, 1977, p. 29). New Zealand investigative journalist Pat Booth describes it as a Rolls-Royce form of ordinary journalism (Hollings, 2008). Experts differ as to whether it has to reveal secret information to count as investigative journalism, but most would probably agree with John Pilger's definition, that it "Not only keeps the record straight, but holds those in power to account"(Pilger, 2004, p. xiv).

There is no secret formula for investigative journalism. The many books on the topic all emphasise different approaches. Here is a six-step process that sums up the important steps, and helps budding investigative journalists get through a long, sometimes frustrating, but usually deeply satisfying process.

1. Find a topic

The first step is to find a topic you care about. In big news organisations, with a team of journalists, a topic may be assigned. Perhaps it is a big story of the day that the editors want more information on. There may be intriguing questions that suggest a lurking scandal. Watergate was an example of this; the newspaper's investigation was prompted by the arrest of six burglars who claimed in court that they were working for the CIA.

But many significant stories start out as small, almost inconsequential items that happen to catch a reporter's interest. Nicky Hager's exposé of former National Party leader Don Brash's links to a secret campaign by the Exclusive Brethren Church, in the run-up to the 2005 election, came after Hager became curious about a mysterious pamphlet that started appearing in letterboxes. A common factor, and one essential to any investigation, is that you must care. You can only keep going through months

What is investigative journalism? Investigation that "goes beyond allegation and denial to establish facts, which, if possible, decide the issue one way or the other", writes investigative journalist David Spark (Spark, 1999).

Another phrase that is often used by US teachers is "Start from the outside in". By this, they mean imagine the target of your investigation is the centre of a series of concentric circles. You start with the outermost circle, which may be documents, or books about the subject, and gradually work your way closer.

of work, and surmount obstacles, if you are genuinely interested in and care about the topic. Don't choose a topic because it is worthy, or someone tells you it is important. A good rule of thumb is that it is about something you have on your bedside table, ie something you enjoy reading about even when you are in bed.

Learn to listen to your inner voice. Often, if you find something odd, or curious, it may be a sign that it is worth pursuing. Some of the most interesting investigations have started not because a journalist thought there was something wrong, but simply because they were curious, and wanted to know more. US investigative reporter Bethany McLean had no intention of causing the bankruptcy of giant US energy trader Enron when she began her investigation into its balance sheet. She just couldn't understand its financial report. Only when she asked financial experts for help, and realised they were mystified too, did she start to suspect something was wrong. The result: a devastating report that caused the collapse of Enron, put several people in jail for fraud, and eventually brought down one of the world's biggest accountancy firms (McLean & Elkind, 2003).

You may be puzzled why the buses are always late in your suburb. Or why your local council doesn't recycle plastic waste.

The passionate belief that something is wrong, or an outrage, is also an inner voice worth listening to. That passion can help sustain you through a long and arduous inquiry. Wherever you find your inspiration, make sure it is something you believe in, and want to know more about.

2. Become an expert

This is a term used by investigative journalist Nicky Hager. It's a great description of a very important step in any investigation. You have to immerse yourself in your topic. You have to know as much or more than anyone about it. You need to become an expert.

Read everything you can about it. Look in your library for books. Google it. Start with general reading. Every time you read something, look at the references – where did they get their information from? Can you read that, too? Read any newspaper articles you can find. Make a list of all the experts quoted. Google them, and find out if they have written more, and if so, read it. Once you have done some general reading, start burrowing down into more specialist literature. Find out if there are documents available – perhaps a government report – and read them. Read any academic articles you can find. Again, make a note of the important points, and any unanswered questions, and especially of any names of experts you can contact later. Google Scholar (www.scholar.google.com) is a fantastic tool for finding academic articles. Search for articles and books on your topic, then see who has cited them. That way you can find the very latest writing on your topic. You may find that someone has already researched and answered the questions that inspired you. If so, great; move on to another topic. Or it may raise more questions. You may find that you spend several weeks or even months reading before you even think about going further.

A good question that I often ask my students to ask is "How is it done in Australia?" Of course, I don't necessarily literally mean that – what I mean is, find a country that has grappled with something like this before, and see what they do. This can often give you questions to ask, and clues to what things should be like. Then you can ask why it is not the same here. Often it also helps you to identify an overseas expert who can guide you with the right kinds of questions.

3. Find a sounding board

Look for overseas journalists who have done a story on the same topic. This will give you ideas about how to proceed. You could even contact them for advice.

It's very common, especially when you're in the early to middle stages of an inquiry, to become overwhelmed. You may think the story is far too big, or has so many angles you can't possibly research them all. Or someone may have tried to intimidate you, or put you off the story. If you're having these kinds of feelings, even if you are an experienced journalist, then having a mentor, or at least someone you can share your thoughts and feelings with, is essential. It might be your partner, a close relative or friend, or another journalist that you can really trust.

If you are new to investigations, you should find an experienced investigative journalist you can trust. They can help you on some of the technical details, like how to find people or documents, and what to do when you get stuck. More importantly, they remind you why you are doing this when many of the people you talk to are calling you a troublemaker or conspiracy theorist. They can also help you focus on what's important, and not get side-tracked by tangents. You would be surprised how many senior journalists are willing to give advice and encouragement. They've been there, and faced the same struggles. Obviously, you won't share the names of your sources, and you'll want to make sure they keep the fact that you are investigating something confidential.

4. Round up the witnesses

The New Zealand Centre for Investigative Journalism can provide advice or mentors for journalists – get in touch: http://cij.org.nz

Once you understand the background to a topic thoroughly, by reading everything you can find that has been written about it, start approaching people who may be able to help you. There are many kinds of people who may help. For example, many investigators talk about the value of "formers" – former employees, who have secrets but no longer obligations. Before you approach someone, however, a little bit of forethought is advisable. Are they likely to want to help you? Will they be afraid, or hostile? Generally it's best to leave until last anyone who may be embarrassed about what you think you might find, or to whom you may wish to pose some difficult questions. Many people you approach will be happy to talk. You will find the time you have spent learning about the topic makes them more likely to want to discuss it with you. But some will not. How do you approach them?

Famous US journalist Seymour Hersh was asked for his best tip. "Follow retirements," he said. People who have just left a job are often open to talking.

The art of getting people to talk to you is one of the most important skills any journalist can have. In my years as a journalist, I developed some very good contacts, and a couple of what might be called Deep Throats, who took considerable risks to give me highly sensitive information. Some years later, in talking to one of them, I realised I had little understanding of why they had helped me. This led to an investigation, of a different kind, for my research on why whistleblowers make the decision to speak out (Hollings, 2011).

Pat Booth's epic nine-year investigation into the murder conviction of Waikato

WHAT IT TAKES TO BE AN INVESTIGATIVE REPORTER

Phil Kitchin has won more awards for investigative journalism than any other New Zealand reporter, and sent several fraudsters to jail. He says investigative journalism is in the blood.

"I think you have to want to be one. There has to be a certain passion. You have to be patient, sometimes you have to take a knock, but then not give up. Patience is one thing, but taking a knock and continuing is another."

As for dealing with sources, he says, "You really have to know how to keep your mouth shut. And you have to be absolutely honest with your sources.

"Sometimes you have to be quite hard-arsed with the questioning. You have to be prepared to be calm, and you have to ask the hard questions. You have to be methodical in your record-keeping."

Louise Nicholas blew the whistle on a group of police officers who had sexually abused her. She says it took her a long time to trust Kitchin, who told her story. "He was just very honest, like he would ring me and he'd say 'Now Louise I've heard this, but I can't tell you where I've heard it from' ... He kept me informed all the time. Any lead, any break, any conversation, if he was able to tell me, he did. The more he delved, and the more he uncovered, I was able to open up a hell of a lot more because he just proved to me his honesty and integrity."

farmer Arthur Allan Thomas blew a series of holes in the police case (Booth, 1997). It led to a Royal Commission that concluded police had planted evidence. As a result, Thomas was pardoned.

Booth says investigative journalists need two main qualities. The first is persistence. "You've got to be prepared to work at it. I just had this compulsion." The second is scepticism. "There's also this necessity never to accept things at face value ... You've got to dig. I can say quite honestly that I just wanted to find out. You get a hunch, but hunches can be wrong ... Was there a document? I love to see pieces of paper. I always get a somewhat warmer feeling when I can actually see words or figures, and do the arithmetic myself."

Before you contact potential sources, think about their situation. How will they feel about an approach from a journalist? If they have had bad experiences already, they may instinctively distrust all journalists. Sometimes, in these cases, you are best to approach them through a friend who you know they trust. You can then explain what you are doing and why it is important to talk to the person, to someone less likely to have an overwhelmingly negative response.

In other cases, it is likely the person will never want their name revealed, and want no one to know they have talked to you. In these cases, you are best simply to approach them face-to-face, tell them what you are doing and why you would like

A whistleblower is someone who reveals secret information.

Deep Throat was the codename Woodward and Bernstein gave to their main secret source in the Watergate investigation.

to talk to them, and give them time to think about it. In his work dealing with spies, Nicky Hager would sometimes approach them on the street, perhaps on their way home from work, or at their homes. This way, there was no phone record that he had contacted them and no possibility of anyone listening in. He was amazed at how often they did want to talk, when approached carefully and treated with respect and care.

If you are able to get to talk to someone, there are important things to remember if you want them eventually to open up to you:

Be informed: People who hold sensitive information take it very seriously. To gain their trust, you need to demonstrate that you are serious too. Being an expert in their topic is important. By this, I don't mean that you tell them how much you know, but that you ask intelligent, informed questions. People like to discuss something important to them with someone else who is interested.

Be honest: Tell them what you are doing, or as much as you can. If you can't tell them some things without compromising your investigation, tell them that. Doing this helps you determine their motives. Usually, honest people don't expect you to tell them everything; they respect you for keeping some things confidential, because it shows you will value their own confidences. It also shows that you are independent, and it is very important that people realise you are going to make up your own mind.

Be scrupulous about promises: If you promise to keep their name secret, do so. Don't write it down. Don't tell anyone. If you promise to keep them informed about the progress of the investigation (as much as you can), then do so. Don't promise anything you can't deliver.

Be determined: It doesn't matter how nice you are, and how trustworthy, if you are too scared or lazy to pursue an issue you are not an investigative journalist. If someone is contemplating taking a considerable risk in trusting you with important information, which could well see their name made public (and despite your promises of confidentiality, most whistleblowers have in the back of their mind that this could still happen), they want to at least make sure something will come of it. A phrase I use that sums it up is: If they are going to stick their necks out to blow a whistle, they want it to be heard.

It is important to remember that when you ask someone to talk to you, you are beginning a relationship, and that requires communication and trust. You must communicate promptly, reliably and honestly. And like any relationship, it develops over time. Potential witnesses, or whistleblowers, often need time to think through the implications of what they are doing. Quite often, after they have had time to think, a kind of righteous anger will bubble up, and help them decide to speak out. It is important you give them time for this to occur naturally, if it is going to happen. You must be patient and, to a degree, allow them to set the pace. If you bully or harass people, they will turn off. On the other hand, you also have to keep in touch, to help answer questions they may have about your story or approach, and to remind them that you are still interested. If you are not persistent, they will think you are not serious. How do you know where to set the balance? By communicating with them; if you have deadlines, explain them, and ask for their opinion. Research shows that

> If you are approaching someone who may want to remain confidential, leave no digital tracks between you and them. Police can easily access your "metadata" – records of who you've texted, phoned or emailed, and when and where you did so.

witnesses use the course of the relationship to test whether a journalist is reliable (Hollings, 2011). They may reveal some small thing at first, and if the journalist shows over the course of several meetings and exchanges that they are reliable and trustworthy (ie, they keep every promise they make), the witness will feel safer about revealing deeper truths.

Tools for digging

It's a bit of a myth that investigative reporters have special gadgets that help them prise out hidden information. It's true that some do make use of computer search tools, and occasionally hidden microphones. But much investigative reporting is still done the old-fashioned way – going and talking to people, and reading through documents. As Carl Bernstein said about the Watergate investigation: "Woodward and I used the most basic, empirical techniques similar to those we first learned when we were very young ... What was really extraordinary about it ... was not the methodology but what was yielded by the methodology" (quoted in Behrens, 1977, p. 35).

However, while a telephone, car and notebook and a clear understanding of how to relate to people are still your most important tools, there are some techniques that can help you find documents and people relevant to your investigation.

Some investigative journalism textbooks try to list every source of documents for every kind of subject. There is not the space to do that here. Also, digital aids for investigative journalism are developing so quickly it is impossible to be an expert in all of them. You are much better off seeing yourself as a kind of coordinator, or team leader, seeking expert advice when you need it on the array of investigative tools out there. Nowadays, there are some fantastic websites and investigative journalism organisations that can help you. You can also contact an investigative reporter and ask for their help.

If a potential source is likely to be scared or reluctant to talk to you, consider approaching them through a friend of theirs, or a family member you know they trust. Be patient, honest and reliable. Communicate and negotiate.

Getting information from documents

Google is still a good tool. But learn how to narrow your search, by linking search words with +. For example, adding "New Zealand" will narrow the search to just pages relating to New Zealand.

Here are some useful websites for finding New Zealand documents:

The National Archives: This is a government website that has billions of papers and artefacts, all carefully organised. You can search it here: www.archway.archives. govt.nz/.

Companies Office: If your story involves business, you will want to search the Companies Office site. Any company must list its directors and shareholders, with their contact details. The site also lists anyone who has been banned from running a company: www.business.govt.nz/companies.

Official Information Act: Using this law, you can request any information held by most central and local government organisations or employees. They are required to give it to you within 20 working days or give you a specific reason why they won't. If they refuse, you can appeal to the Ombudsman. This can be a powerful tool for extracting official documents (and even information in officials' heads!), but does

A good place to start is the Global Investigative Journalism Network: http://gijn.org/

There are also many tools for searching documents and databases, and generating relevant data from them. This is "data journalism". For more on this, see Chapter 13 and http://gijn.org/

take time, and there are many exceptions. Some bodies, such as the courts, are not subject to it. If you want to access court records in New Zealand, you have to apply to the courts. Although the OIA doesn't apply to non-government organisations, private individuals or companies, you can still apply for any correspondence they may have had with government. Probably the most important point to remember when using the Act is to seek help from the Ombudsman's Office if you meet any obstacles. A quick phone call can often yield results. You can find more tips on how to use the Act and appeal process here: www.ombudsman.parliament.nz/.

Finding people

Investigative journalists have special tools for searching social media. Again, look at http://gijn.org/

A Google search is a good place to start. Also, the electoral roll records all registered voters in New Zealand. You can find these at your local library. There is also a list called a habitation index, which is an electoral roll in which the names of electors are shown under the numbers and addresses of the streets or localities in which they are currently registered. This tells you the name and number of electors currently registered in each dwelling. For privacy reasons, neither is available online, but you can ask a friendly reporter at a newspaper.

Facebook and other social networking sites are also very good. If your target's page is locked, check their friends. One of them may have a phone number that you can call and ask to be put in touch. Many journalists find Facebook incredibly useful. Many also use Twitter to tell people they are interested in a topic, and make initial contact with people in the area who are interested. They then follow them up by email. LinkedIn is a business directory that can provide a lot of information about people in business. It's like Facebook, but for professionals.

Another helpful tool, if you know their car, is motochek: www.nzta.govt.nz/motochek/. This will give you the name and address of the owner of any registered company motor vehicle in New Zealand. You can also find who owns a property, and how much they paid for it, here: www.linz.govt.nz/survey-titles.

Going undercover

Remember there are still some people who do not use computers. A web search will not find them. Sometimes the phone directory, electoral rolls, and simply calling all people of that name in the area can find them. Sometimes you can find relatives by tracking their family through a genealogy site.

For some stories, where you need evidence that something is happening but know that people are unlikely to tell you, you may need to go undercover. For example, you may be investigating someone offering an illegal service, like cage-fighting, or someone offering bribes to officials. Sometimes the only way to prove this is happening is to disguise your identity, and pose as a member of the public. This technique is widely used by British tabloids, with great success.

Going undercover requires strong nerves, and careful planning, to ensure your cover story is accurate and can't be challenged. There are a few important things to remember.

First, you must be satisfied that you cannot get the information you need in any other way. This is important, because if you are challenged in court for deception, you need to be able to show there was a good reason for it.

Second, you must also be satisfied that the information you need is not just *of* public interest, but *in* the public interest. Exposing the secret sex life of a politician may be titillating to some, but unless you can show that it is in the public interest – for example, that he lied about it – then you may be criticised for prurience or even sued for invasion of privacy.

Third, you must not break the law, for example, by forging documents. An undercover probe into unsafe food handling in the United States by the ABC went horribly wrong when the company successfully sued the ABC for fraud, because its reporters lied to get jobs at the food company.

Fourth, remember that if you wear a secret recording device, you are only legally allowed to record conversations you are a party to. In other words, the people you are recording must reasonably expect that you are listening (but they don't have to know you are recording it).

Fifth, keep good records. Write careful and detailed and legible notes afterwards of what you see and hear, including dates, times and places, and names, as soon as possible afterwards (eg, the same night). If it comes down to your word against theirs in court, your detailed notes could be vital.

Although the UK tabloids have been rightly pilloried for the phone-hacking scandal, over the years investigative journalists at the tabloids have also exposed major crimes, including by going undercover.

5. Concluding your investigation

Approaching the core figure

Often your investigation will be into a person or an organisation. You may have gathered a lot of information, and are confident that it raises some serious questions that need to be answered. You then have to decide whether you will approach the core figure, the main person your investigation is about, to get their side of the story.

Not all reporters do this. Nicky Hager often chooses not to seek a reply from people or organisations he has investigated. He feels that if he has enough information to prove his case, there is nothing to be gained from seeking a routine denial, and quite a bit to lose. For example, the core figure may take out an injunction preventing publication – providing they can persuade a court to grant one. Then all your hard work may be wasted while it drags through the courts.

British-based investigative legend John Pilger is another who believes that routine denials, when the case is overwhelming, only muddy the story, and give undue space to the corrupt or evil.

However, former *Dominion* editor Geoff Baylis gives the example of a probe into British Leyland boss Lord Ryder, who was alleged to be operating a slush fund to bribe officials. A newspaper obtained apparently incriminating letters, including some signed by Ryder. The paper had the letters checked by a handwriting expert, who confirmed it was Ryder's handwriting. The paper ran the story, only to find out that it was all a hoax by a former employee. If it had simply approached Ryder for comment, he could have saved them the trouble.

I also am firmly of the belief that you should approach the core figure of any investigation for their side, unless there are absolutely compelling reasons not to, such as your own safety. It is not uncommon for investigators, fed material by one side, to develop an emotional investment in one side of the story and generate an entire case against someone, only to find they are entirely wrong. Sometimes it is

If you go undercover, make sure your personal safety is paramount. Discuss your plans with experienced people first.

UK tabloid the News of the World thought it had a good story when it ran a sting showing World Formula One boss Max Mosley dressing up in Nazi uniforms for a bondage session with prostitutes. He sued them, not for defamation, but invasion of privacy, and won. The judge said there was no public interest in showing sex between consenting adults ("Max Mosley," 2011).

KEEPING SECRETS

Nicky Hager's exposure of the Echelon spy network between New Zealand, the United Kingdom, the United States, Canada and Australia was only possible because of his high-level sources (Hager, 1996). He also used a secret source to reveal close links between the National Party and blogger Cameron Slater (Hager, 2014). He's had to learn not to be too paranoid when protecting his sources' anonymity, but there are some things he is very careful about.

"I never talk about my sources. I don't write down the names of my sources ... their phone numbers and addresses. I don't have a telephone track between us because the main way that police follow up things is not by bugging phones, but just by going through the phone logs and seeing who rang who.

"So I'm very careful about not leaving tracks between us, and not leaving interview notes in the house. I have a highly encrypted hard drive so that I can assure someone that no one can walk into my house and blow their career for them. If there's something that's required to protect sources and protect the story, I will take maximum care, and everything else I just try to be relaxed about."

If you do decide not to seek comment from the target of your investigation due to the risk of an injunction, you should seek advice from an experienced editor or preferably a media lawyer before you publish.

much better to find this out sooner rather than later. If you approach the core figure and they are open and forthcoming, this does not always mean they are good liars. Sometimes they are simply wronged, or the victim of a whispering campaign. You can often gauge from their reaction – cagey or helpful – to determine whether they have something to hide.

If you decide to approach the core figure, plan your approach carefully. You may only get one chance to talk to them. If you have tried phone or email, and had no response (perhaps they are filtered by receptionists, or junk email filters), then a personal letter can be very effective. Almost everyone gets a personal letter. It gives them the opportunity to carefully think about you, rather than making a snap decision to ignore you. If you craft it carefully, a letter can be very persuasive, if only because they want to hear what you know. Set out a brief outline of what your story is about, and the reasons you want to talk to them (eg, to hear their side of the story). Be honest, and keep it brief. Keep in mind that they may well show it to other people you have approached, so don't say anything you wouldn't want made public.

If they agree to an interview, make sure you record it. You might start with some warm-up questions, but don't hedge your questions. Some investigators argue that there are no embarrassing questions, only embarrassing answers. In reality, however, the way you ask a question does matter. A simple phrase such as "I'm sorry to have to ask you this ..." or "This has been raised, so I want to give you the opportunity to respond" lets the interviewee know that you are not against them, and genuinely want to hear them. If they are still evasive, hostile or defensive, that may indicate they are hiding something. For more on these kinds of interviews, see *The investigative reporter's handbook* (Houston, Bruzzese & Weinberg, 2002).

Making sense of the story/finding an independent expert

So, you have become an expert, rounded up your witnesses and developed a line of questions based on solid evidence that goes beyond mere allegation and denial. You put your questions to the core figure, and they come back with plausible and convincing arguments that seem to blow your inquiry out of the water. What do you do? This is where seeking some kind of independent overview can be very useful. Try to find an expert in the topic, who is not involved in the investigation. It may be an academic, lawyer, medical professional, former police officer or journalist. You want someone with an independent, critical mind, who understands the technicalities of the subject. If it's about pollution, or medicine, you'll need a scientist, or a doctor. If it's about crime, you'll need a lawyer, or a police officer, or both. Often these people will help you see the subtle evasions in a response that you have missed. If they're prepared to go on the record with their assessment of the evidence, that can make your story much stronger.

6. Write the story

If you have been pursuing a story for months, chances are you'll have a mountain of notes, files, pictures and so on. How do you turn this into a crisp, hard-hitting 3000-word masterpiece that your readers can't tear themselves away from?

There's no one formula for writing a long feature, or long-form journalism, but there are a few tips that will help you.

Know your material thoroughly. Take some time to read through it all, and think about it. Don't feel you have to understand it all, but just let yourself soak in it.

If you haven't done this already, make sure your material is well-organised. Label your files and documents with the right date. Categorise and sort them by date and source.

Discuss the story with someone. Tell them in one sentence what you have found. This is particularly important if you feel the story is too big, or has many angles that you need to explore. Talking to someone can help you focus on what matters, and not get side-tracked by tangents.

Once you have a feel for what the story is, think about ways of telling it. You might want a hard-hitting newsy approach, or perhaps more of a human angle – following one person's story. An important point to bear in mind is why the reader should care about this story; what does it mean to them? Find some examples of features that seem to tell the story the way you like it and analyse them. Don't be afraid to copy their approach.

Sit down, turn off your email and phone, take a deep breath, and write the first draft from memory. Don't stop to rummage for a good quote you know is in your notes somewhere – it will just slow you down. Mark the place and keep writing.

Now go back and skim through your notes, and add in those juicy quotes and

YOUR FIRST INVESTIGATION

Young journalists Julia Hollingsworth, Amanda Fisher and Rory MacKinnon published major investigations while still at journalism school.

Julia investigated how the Privacy Act was contributing to suicides, by preventing families from finding out about how sick their family members were.

"It differed from my other work a lot – I was writing something that seemed useful and interesting ... I was surprised at how easy it was to get people to talk to me and how everyone I spoke to thought writing on this topic was really important.

"Most of all, I learnt a lot about people, how they're willing to talk even in dire situations, and how showing interest, compassion and a little of your own life helps people open up."

Amanda and Rory were part of a team of journalism students who exposed a toxic waste site being used for residential housing in Masterton. They had to deal with a lot of highly technical scientific reports, and what seemed like plausible answers from the local authorities as to why nothing had been done. But when they contacted independent scientific experts for their interpretations, the answers were clear: something *had* to be done.

"It's time-consuming and you have to be really persistent," Amanda says. "We kept motivating each other. That's the only reason it really came out."

Rory adds: "Collaboration is hugely helpful. It's so much easier to divide up the tasks. If you have got an issue that is quite broad, it's quite easy to get overwhelmed. If you are working by a committee, surprisingly it actually makes for a better story, and better collective knowledge of the issues."

You can read Julia's article by going to www.stuff.co.nz and searching for "Privacy versus patient health under spotlight".

You can read the Masterton investigation here: www.nzherald.co.nz/wairarapa-times-age/news/article.cfm?c_id=1503414&objectid=10988280.

Don't worry too much about legal issues while you are writing. The worst thing you can do is self-censor and kill the passion that drives your story. A good editor should be able to spot any legal problems. But make sure someone with a sound knowledge of media law reads your story before it's published!

telling details that popped into your head as you were writing, but which you couldn't quite remember.

Give your draft a brief edit, then give it to someone you trust to read. Do they understand it? Are there unanswered questions? Make any necessary changes, then repeat as necessary until you feel confident about sending it to an editor.

Think about running it as separate stories. Some papers like to keep back some of their most explosive material for day two or three. This keeps the story alive and makes it more likely to be picked up by other media, such as television. Wellington's *Dominion Post* newspaper often uses this approach.

After that, sit back and see what impact your story has.

Further reading

Booth, P. (1997). *Deadline: My story.* Auckland: Viking. The best book written by an investigative journalist in New Zealand. The accounts of the Thomas investigation are still hair-raising, 40 years later.

Cropp, A. (1997). *Digging deeper: A New Zealand guide to investigative reporting.* Wellington: New Zealand Journalists Training Organisation. This was the first-ever how-to guide to investigative journalism published in New Zealand. It came out before the internet era, but still has some useful practical information about New Zealand law, some interesting case histories, and a lot of sound advice.

Hollings, J. (Ed.). (2017). *A moral truth: 150 years of investigative journalism in New Zealand.* Auckland: Massey University Press. A great collection of the best of New Zealand's journalism. It includes introductions with comments from the journalists about how they did their stories.

Houston, B., Bruzzese, L., & Weinberg, S. (2002). *The investigative reporter's handbook: A guide to documents, databases and techniques* (4th ed.). Boston; New York: Bedford/St Martin's. This is the best textbook on the topic. Published by Investigative Reporters and Editors Inc, it includes a lot of detail about where to find information in the United States, but is also a well of distilled wisdom about approaching people, dealing with people, and getting people to talk and other general issues that an investigative reporter needs to know.

Northmore, D. (1996). *Lifting the lid: A guide to investigative research.* London: Cassell. This was one of the first textbooks on how to do investigative journalism. It still contains much useful information, but mainly for journalists working in Britain.

Pilger, J. (Ed.). (2004). *Tell me no lies: Investigative reporting and its triumphs.* London: Jonathan Cape. This should be on your bookshelf. It is full of astonishing, inspiring examples of investigative reporting from around the world.

Price, S. How to use the Official Information Act. *Media Law Journal.* Retrieved from www.medialawjournal.co.nz/?page_id=30

Shapiro, B. (Ed.). (2003). *Shaking the foundations: 200 years of investigative journalism in America.* New York: Thunder's Mouth. Some of the stories are riveting, and the introduction is a good overview of the development of investigative journalism in a country where it is practised assiduously.

Spark, D. (1999). *Investigative reporting: A study in technique.* Oxford: Focal Press. Mostly applies to Britain, but is simple, clear, and has much useful general advice.

Tanner, S., & Richardson, N. (Eds.). (2013). *Journalism research and investigation in a digital world.* Melbourne: Oxford University Press. This is the most recent Australian textbook. Includes a lot of political and historical context, but much useful material on how to do investigations, too.

www.linz.govt.nz/survey-titles A website you can use to find owners of land and buildings in New Zealand.

www.nzta.govt.nz/motochek A website you can use to find New Zealand car owners' names.

www.ombudsmen.parliament.nz A useful website on finding New Zealand government information.

www.tcij.org, https://www.revealnews.org/, http://gijn.org, http://helpmeinvestigate.com Useful websites on how to do investigative journalism.

References

Behrens, J.C. (1977). *The typewriter guerrillas: Closeups of twenty top investigative reporters.* Chicago: Nelson-Hall.

Booth, P. (1997). *Deadline: My story.* Auckland: Viking.

Burgh, D. (2000). *Investigative journalism: Context and practice.* London: Routledge.

Hager, N. (1996). *Secret power.* Nelson: Craig Potton.

Hager, N. (2014). *Dirty politics: How attack politics is poisoning New Zealand's political environment.* Nelson: Craig Potton.

Hollings, J. (2008). Interview with Pat Booth. Wellington: Massey University.

Hollings, J. (2011). *The courage to speak: How investigative journalists persuade reluctant whistleblowers to tell their stories.* (Unpublished doctoral dissertation). Massey University, Wellington, New Zealand.

Houston, B., Bruzzese, L., & Weinberg, S. (2002). *The investigative reporter's handbook: A guide to documents, databases and techniques* (4th ed.). Boston; New York: Bedford/St Martin's.

Max Mosley privacy ruling due in Strasbourg (2011, May 10), *The Guardian.* Retrieved from http://www.guardian.co.uk/media/2011/may/10/max-mosley-privacy-ruling-strasbourg

McLean, B., & Elkind, P. (2003). *The smartest guys in the room: The amazing rise and scandalous fall of Enron.* New York: Penguin.

Pilger, J. (2004). *Tell me no lies: Investigative journalism and its triumphs.* London: Jonathan Cape.

Schudson, M. (2004). Notes on scandal and the Watergate legacy. *American Behavioral Scientist, 47*(9), 1231–1238.

Spark, D. (1999). *Investigative reporting: A study in technique.* Oxford: Focal Press.

13

Statistics for journalists

What journalists need to know about numbers

Grant Hannis, Massey University

This chapter arms you with the tools you need to use and understand statistics in news stories. We'll be discussing rounding, percentages and percentage changes, averages, and understanding official statistics, graphs and surveys.

The only way to really understand maths is to do it. For this reason, this chapter contains lots of exercises. It is important that you work through the exercises, as this is the only way to really learn the material. All the answers are given in Appendix 2. Once you have worked through this chapter properly, you should feel confident you can handle the maths required of any good journalist.

Rounding

As a journalist, you'll often round figures in your stories to make the numbers simpler to understand and the story punchier. Unfortunately, journalists frequently do not understand how to round. They think rounding the number 77.963 would give us 77. That is incorrect. The rounded figure is 78, because 77.963 is much closer to 78 than to 77. Here's how to round correctly.

Every number is a string of digits moving from left to right. Each digit is said to have a "place" in the line. Take the number 89.73. It has two places before the decimal point (8 and then 9) and two places after the decimal point (7 and then 3).

Unless otherwise stated, all the data presented in this chapter is hypothetical. The sources of the real-world examples are given at the end of the chapter.

The term "decimal place" refers to numbers after the decimal point. We round to what is called the "significant digit", the number we decide to round to. The basic rule with rounding is to look at the number immediately to the right of the significant digit. If that number is 0, 1, 2, 3 or 4, we round down (in other words, the significant digit does not change). If it is 5, 6, 7, 8 or 9, we round up (we add one to the significant digit). Let's say we want to round to one decimal place (the significant digit). In the example here – 89.73 – that number is 7, so we must look at the number to the right of that number. This is 3, and so we round down to 7. So, 89.7 is the rounded number.

We can round to other significant digits. For example, the number 77.963 could be rounded to two decimal places, in which case it would be 77.96 or to zero decimal places, in which case it would be 78. You can also round numbers to the left of the decimal place.

Don't chain round. This is when you look at the numbers further to the right of the one you are using to round, and use those figures in your rounding calculation. For instance, consider the number 67.49. If we round this figure to zero decimal places, it is 67. That is because the number immediately to the right of the significant digit is 4. If we chain round, we decide that, as the number to the right of the 4 is a 9, then the 4 should be a 5 and therefore the rounded figure should be 68. That is incorrect. You must ignore any numbers to the right of the number you are using to round. After all, 67.49 is closer to 67 than to 68.

A good way to quote rounded numbers is to say "nearly", "just over" or "about", such as saying 77.963 is "nearly 78" or 65.3 is "just over 65".

Percentages and percentage changes

A percentage represents the relationship between two numbers, expressed as a proportion of 100. For example, "80 per cent of male students wear lace-up shoes" means that, irrespective of how many male students there are, for each 100 male students, 80 wear lace-up shoes. In news reports percentages are often used as a measure of change. For example, the statement "Exports have risen by 20 per cent in the past year" means that, irrespective of the actual number of exports, for each 100 units of exports last year, there are 120 this year.

The term "per cent" means "per centum", or "for each 100". Numbers are expressed as percentages because this gives us a common baseline to start from: 100, a nice easy-to-understand number.

Calculating one number as a percentage of another
To do this, divide the first number by the second number and multiply by 100. We can state this as a simple formula:

(Number to be expressed as a percentage ÷ Number to be expressed as a percentage of) x 100

For example, let us say we wish to express 8 as a percentage of 9. The calculation is:

(8 ÷ 9) x 100 = 89% (rounded to zero decimal places)

Calculating a figure, when we know what percentage it represents of a total
Here the formula is:

(Percentage ÷ 100) x total

Let us say we want to calculate 10 per cent of 75:

(10 ÷ 100) x 75 = 7.5

Exercise 1: *Round the following figures to zero decimal places.*

    1) 1.2

    2) 2.456

    3) 100.5

    4) $12.4m

    5) 23.4%

    6) 6.778

    7) 5.499999999

Exercise 2: *Round the following figures to the second digit.*
            Now repeat the exercise, rounding to the third digit.

    1) 344

    2) 23917

    3) 120

    4) 343.67

    5) 3400

Percentage changes

All percentage changes can easily be calculated using the formula:

    ((New figure – Initial figure) ÷ Initial figure) x 100

For instance, let's calculate the percentage rise from 3800 to 4000:

    ((4000 – 3800) ÷ 3800) x 100 = 5.3%

Similarly, to calculate the percentage fall from 4000 to 3800:

    ((3800 – 4000) ÷ 4000) x 100 = -5.0% (ie, a 5% fall)

It is very important to note that percentage falls are shown as negative numbers. The importance of this becomes clear in the next section.

Calculating the new figure, when we know the initial figure and the percentage change

To conduct such calculations, we use this formula:

    ((Percentage change ÷ 100) + 1) x Initial figure

With all these calculations, start with the figures in the innermost brackets first, and then work outwards.

The logic here is that we are calculating the percentage increase, and then adding the initial figure back in (that is why we add 1).

    So, if we know that a bus fare was $1.60 and has increased by 10 per cent, what is the new bus fare? Using the formula, we must:

    Divide the percentage change by 100

    Add 1

    Multiply this by the initial figure

PERCENTAGE POINTS AND BASIS POINTS

Sometimes we want to describe changes in percentage figures themselves, such as increases in the inflation rate or interest rates. To do this, we can quote **percentage points**. To calculate percentage points, we simply treat the percentages as if they were numbers without percentage signs after them. For instance, an increase in interest rates from 4 per cent per annum to 7 per cent per annum is:

- An increase of 3 percentage points: 7 – 4 = 3.
- A 75 per cent increase: ((7 – 4) ÷ 4) x 100 = 75%.

Financial journalists often measure changes in indexes using **basis points**. This is used when an index number has two digits after the decimal point. The digit immediately to the left of the decimal point and the two to the right are treated as a three-digit number.

Say the NZX50 rises from 1002.34 to 1003.50. This is an increase of 1003.50 – 1002.34 = 1.16, or 116 basis points. This is done simply because it is easier to say "116" than "1.16".

So, divide the percentage change by 100: 10 ÷ 100 = 0.1
Add this to 1 = 1.1
Multiply this by the number that is changing: 1.1 x $1.60 = $1.76

When quoting any changes in statistics make it clear the periods you are discussing. You cannot simply report that the number of international students has increased 10 per cent. Report all the relevant facts: "In the year to March, the number of international students increased 10 per cent."

If it is a percentage fall, don't forget to put the negative sign in front of the percentage change. So, to calculate the new figure after a 10 per cent decrease in the bus fare from $1.60:

Divide the percentage change by 100 (as it is a fall, we use a negative number): -10 ÷ 100 = -0.1
Add this to 1, giving: 0.9
Multiply this by the number that is changing: 0.9 x $1.60 = $1.44

Calculating the initial figure, when we know the new figure and the percentage change

Here, the formula is:

New figure ÷ ((Percentage change ÷ 100)+1)

So, let's say we want to know the initial figure, following a 15 per cent rise to 105:

Divide the percentage change by 100
Add 1
Divide the new figure by this

Divide the percentage change by 100: 15 ÷ 100 = 0.15
Add this to 1: 1.15
Divide 105 by this: 105 ÷ 1.15 = 91.30

To calculate the initial figure following a 15 per cent fall to 105:
Divide the percentage change by 100: -15 ÷ 100 = -0.15
Add this to 1: 0.85
Divide 105 by this: 123.53

Summarising data

When we are confronted with a large set of numbers, there are a number of statistics we can calculate to summarise the data. Knowing how to calculate these is very helpful when you want to summarise figures to make your article punchier and shorter. It's also important that you understand these different terms, as they often turn up in media releases and statistical reports.

The figure most often used is the mean (or average). It is easy to calculate. You add up a set of figures and divide by the number of figures in the set. Let us assume we have asked 10 students how much cash they have on them, coming up with the following figures: $0 $2 $3 $6 $9 $10 $15 $15 $15 $25

The mean of the above figures would be the sum total of the figures ($100) divided by the number of figures in the sequence (10). Using the mean, we can say the students had, on average, $10 cash each. That seems a fair summary of the data.

But let's assume that the 10th student had done something rare and skewed the data. Let's say she had $100 on her that day, because she is treating herself: she is off to buy a mobile phone. The mean amount the students have would therefore be $17.50 ($175 ÷ 10). That does not seem to be a fair reflection of the situation, as we know the event was rare. The $100 figure is called an "outlier", a figure whose value is much higher (or lower) than most of the rest of the set. The outlier has dragged the mean up, which may make the mean a misleading summary of the data because it represents a rare event.

It is possible to display lots of numbers in interesting ways online and even to make the material interactive. This is called "data journalism" and is an emerging field in journalism. The *Herald* has embraced the idea. For great examples and ideas, check out insights.nzherald.co.nz

THE NUMBERS BEHIND THE PERCENTAGES

Treat percentages with caution. Although percentages are a helpful way of showing the relationships between numbers, they can be misleading. Quoting percentage changes may not be appropriate when the actual numbers behind the figures are small.

In a front-page story, a local newspaper proclaimed unemployment in its area had increased 66 per cent ("Economic crunch," 2009). That sounds like a massive increase in the number of people out of work. However, the actual article said the number of unemployed in the area had increased from 41 a year ago to 68 now. That means the 66 per cent increase represented just 27 people!

Exercise 3: *Percentages*

1) What is 10 as a percentage of 20? What is 20 per cent of 80?

2) What is the percentage change if the number of violent offences rises from 50 to 70?

3) What is the percentage change if the number of violent offences decreases from 160 to 84?

4) The cost of a ticket to a rock concert has increased 20 per cent from $50. What is the new price of the ticket?

5) The price to ride on the local tourist cable car has dropped by 30 per cent from $2. What is the new price of a ticket?

6) The average number of apples in a box at the supermarket has risen 12 per cent to 110. What was the average number of apples in a box before the increase?

7) Two hundred students want to play soccer this year, 25 per cent fewer than last year. How many students wanted to play soccer last year?

8) Let's say you hear this on the TV news: "The inflation rate has increased 2 per cent over the past year, from 2 per cent per annum to 4 per cent per annum." Is this true?

Exercise 4: *GST*

GST is a tax levied on goods and service in New Zealand. It used to be 12.5 per cent, but increased to 15 per cent in 2010. At the time of the rise, both TVNZ and TV3 reported the increase. The reporters said, for instance, that:

> A $2000 item would now cost $2050
> A $40,000 item would cost $41,000
> A $1500 item would cost $1537.50
> (TVNZ, 2010; TV3, 2010).

How had the reporters calculated these figures? Are the figures correct?

Clearly, then, the mean can be a deceptive measure. When the data are skewed the mean can be high (or low) if there are a few very high (or low) outliers in the data. In cases like this the outlier(s) may be removed. Alternatively, other measures can be used. The first is the median, which is the middle figure in a sequence. We must first order the figures from lowest to highest and then find the figure in the middle. If there are 11 figures in the list, for instance, then the median is the sixth figure. When there is an even number of figures, choose the value halfway between the two middle figures (by summing them and dividing by 2). In the list of numbers above the numbers are already ordered lowest to highest. As there are 10 numbers in the list, we look at the fifth and sixth values, $9 and $10. The median will be the halfway point between these two numbers: (($9 + $10) ÷ 2) = $9.50. Here, the median is a much fairer measure of the typical value.

Another measure is the mode, which is the most common item in a group of values. In the above case, the mode is $15. That's because there are three $15s, so it is the most common figure. A group of values could have more than one mode. So, if the mean is affected by outliers, the median or the mode may be better measures.

An index number can be thought of as a special type of mean. For instance, the Consumers Price Index (discussed below) is a single number that summarises a range of prices. If the index goes up, prices generally have risen.

Understanding official statistics

The government and other agencies generate masses of statistics each year. Although many of these are only of interest to specialists, others have wide public interest and are reported in the daily news media. When you are covering a specific round, such as business or transport, it will be up to you to understand what the statistics mean and their significance. To get you started, here are brief explanations of some of the major statistics regularly produced in New Zealand:

Consumers Price Index (CPI): This is the index of the price of a basket of goods

---

Exercise 5: **Averages**

Assume you are covering a pay dispute at a local firm. Here is where the firm's annual payroll goes:

Staff member	$ salary
Chief executive	$450,000
General manager	$200,000
Advertising manager	$200,000
Production person	$60,000
Production person	$60,000
Production person	$60,000
Sales rep	$45,000
Sales rep	$45,000
Sales rep	$45,000
Sales rep	$36,000
Worker	$32,000
Worker	$32,000
Worker	$32,000
Receptionist	$32,000

1) What is the mean salary of the workforce?
2) What is the median salary of the workforce?
3) What is the mode of the salaries of the workforce?
4) The chief executive is negotiating with his workers' union over whether they should be paid more. The chief executive is arguing that pay increases are not needed because the mean salary at the business is very good. Is this argument a good one? Why? What figures would you put to him in your interview to challenge his position?

Exercise 6: *Expense accounts*

A Sunday newspaper ran an article on ministers' use of self-drive cars, the bills for which are picked up by the taxpayer. The biggest spender was Judith Collins, who spent $11,536 over a two-year period on petrol for her self-drive car. The next biggest spender was Tariana Turia, who spent $7216 over the same period. A spokesperson for Collins said her spending "was within the rules" ("Big petrol bills," 2011).

The newspaper ran an editorial on the matter. It said Collins' spending equated to "roughly $200 a week" on petrol, more than 100 kilometres a day. "What is going on?" the paper asked, adding that Collins spent five times more than any other minister. The paper labelled Collins the "Minister of entitlement" and said her spending was "nothing short of a disgrace, a shameful example of a minister out of touch with reality" ("Minister of entitlement," 2011).

Do you agree?

For more details on economic statistics, see Chapter 10. For explanations of the different measures of unemployment, see "A Guide to Unemployment Statistics", which is available on the Statistics New Zealand website, www.stats.govt.nz

and services consumed by households, from ice creams to cars. The most common measure of inflation in New Zealand (often known colloquially as the cost of living) is changes in the CPI, most often the percentage change per annum.

Unemployment rate: The most meaningful measure of unemployment in New Zealand is that obtained from the Household Labour Force Survey, published by government agency Statistics New Zealand. This survey measures the unemployment rate as the number of people without a paid job and looking for work, as a percentage of the labour force (those people of working age either employed or unemployed).

Gross Domestic Product (GDP): The total value of all the final goods and services produced in New Zealand. These are the goods and services purchased by consumers, so it excludes all the goods produced and consumed by firms in the production of final goods and services. Both dollar values and indexes of GDP are produced.

Balance of Payments: In simple terms, this measures the amount of money New Zealand receives from overseas less the amount we spend overseas. It is usually expressed as a percentage of the country's GDP.

Trade-Weighted Index (TWI): This is an index of the value of the New Zealand dollar against a basket of overseas currencies, weighted by the size of each country's economy and its share of trade with New Zealand.

NZX50: This index is produced by the NZX, the New Zealand Stock Exchange, and measures the value of the shares and dividends of the 50 largest companies on the exchange.

Crime rate: The most commonly quoted figure here is the number of recorded offences per 10,000 people in the population. This number is dependent on crimes being reported: if more people report crimes then the numbers go up, even if the actual number of crimes committed has not gone up.

Road toll: The number of deaths on the roads over a given time period. Usually,

---

Exercise 7: **Crime and drink**

1) A major national magazine ran a cover story on Asian crime in New Zealand (Asian Angst, 2006). The article spoke ominously of a "gathering crime tide" (p. 40) and "the Asian menace" (p. 41). The statistical evidence the article provided was that "from 1996 to 2005, total offences committed by Asiatics (not including Indians) aged 17 to 50 rose 53 per cent, from 1791 to 2751" (p. 44).

   What do you think of these figures? Do they prove the existence of a gathering Asian crime tide?

2) A major newspaper ran an article headlined "Men over 50 nation's biggest drinkers", going on to say men over 50 are "consuming more alcohol" ("Men over 50," 2012, p. 5).

   What do you think of these statements? What do they tell us about the drinking habits of older men?

---

a running total is collected as the year progresses. The figure for this year is then compared with the figure for the same time last year.

Net migration: This records the number of people who arrived in New Zealand to stay long-term or permanently minus the number of people who left New Zealand to live overseas long-term or permanently.

Adjusting the figures for seasonality and inflation

Two common adjustments are made to official statistics in order to make the results more meaningful.

The first is that figures may be "seasonally adjusted". Figures such as retail sales may be adjusted to take into account seasonal factors throughout the year that affect the figures. For instance, around Christmas retail sales spike as people buy masses of goods over the holiday period. It may appear that retail sales have suddenly risen, but, of course, in reality it's just a seasonal blip. Statisticians estimate the extent of this seasonal blip by averaging the figures over time, thereby smoothing out the seasonal peaks and troughs.

The other correction is to calculate "inflation adjusted" or "real" figures. For instance, let's say wages generally increased by 2 per cent in the economy over the year. The nominal (ie, not adjusted for inflation) wage index would therefore increase by 2 per cent. But let's say prices also increased by 2 per cent over the year. That means workers are no better off: they have more money to spend, sure, but that increase is exactly offset by rises in the prices of the products they buy. The workers' real (ie, inflation-adjusted) wages have remained the same.

Price indexes are used to create a whole range of real indexes, including an index of Real GDP.

Changes in Real GDP tell us whether an economy is growing or shrinking. As the effect of inflation has been removed, any increase in the Real GDP index means the economy is producing more goods and services.

> ### Exercise 8: *Inflation*
> Assume the Consumers Price Index in year one is 1000 and in year two is 1015.
>
> Assume the Real GDP index for the same period has gone from 1023 to 1010.
>
> 1) What is the inflation rate over the period?
>
> 2) Does this mean prices are generally rising?
>
> 3) What is the percentage change in Real GDP over the period?
>
> 4) What does that tell us about the economy?

Graphs

Statistical information is often represented in graphical form. A well-drawn graph can explain the key points of a story very quickly and strikingly. On the other hand, graphs can mislead your readers if they are not drawn carefully.

As a reporter, you are unlikely to be involved in actually drawing graphs for your stories, but you should take the opportunity to suggest how best to represent the data. You will want your articles to tell clear, accurate stories. Let's start with a few general points.

First, all graphs must be clear and simple. Don't cram too much information into one graph and don't clutter the graph with trite pictures and other gimmicks. Avoid 3-D effects, which can make charts difficult to read and even distort the figures (as I'll show in a minute).

A way to remember the y axis is the vertical line is that the letter "y" also has a vertical line in it.

Each graph should be self-explanatory – your readers should not have to read the accompanying story to get the point. Give each graph a main title stating what the graph is telling your reader (think of it as the graph's angle), a sub-title giving the technical details, and the source of the data. For instance, the main title of a graph on unemployment could read, "Unemployment rate drops to 20-year low", with the sub-head reading, "Number of unemployed as a percentage of the total labour force, 1999–2019" and the source, "Statistics New Zealand".

The vertical axis on a graph is called the y axis; the horizontal is the x axis.

Make sure the axes are both labelled (unless it is obvious what the label would be), and, usually, that the increments on the x and y axes are regular. The y axis should usually start at zero, as starting above zero can distort the results. If you do start above zero, you need to clearly state somewhere on the graph that you have done this.

This section looks at the main types of graphs, explaining what type of data they are best suited to present and the pitfalls to avoid.

Bar charts

A bar chart presents numerical data as a series of bars, either vertically or horizontally. Bar charts are easy to understand and are useful for comparing one category with the others, as the reader can compare the height of the bars. Often the data is ordered left to right from highest to lowest.

Figure 1 clearly shows the relative expense of the five banks' interest rates, including that Bank 1 is the most expensive and that Bank 5 is alone in offering the cheapest rate. Note that the x axis is not labelled, as it is obvious this axis would be labelled "Banks".

A special form of bar chart is called a histogram. This shows the frequency (or relative frequency) of each value. For instance, imagine you want to graph the percentage of people in each age band of a population. You could use a histogram to show this age distribution (Figure 2). Note that the mid-point of each age band is at the centre of each bar.

You can present multiple comparisons in a bar chart, as appropriate. For instance, Figure 3 is a histogram showing the percentage of the population by age and gender.

The legend (or key) tells the reader which bars represent males and which represent females.

Sometimes bar charts are presented in the form of pictographs. These graphs use pictures in place of the bars. Used with care, pictographs are fine, but they also present their own problems and pitfalls. See Exercise 9 for an example of the dangers.

Line charts

Line charts are a very good way of showing changes over time, including changes in several variables simultaneously. Figure 4 is a line chart showing numbers of native birds and feral cats in a native reserve over one year.

This graph makes a lot of complex data easily understandable. It clearly shows changes in two variables – the native bird population and the feral cat population – over time.

Note the two populations are of different orders of magnitude (the birds are measured in thousands and the feral cats in tens). If both sets of data were shown on the one y axis, the feral-cats line would be very close to zero and basically flat. So, to show both populations on the same graph we have two y axes, the left-hand one is for the birds, the right-hand one for the cats. The legend makes it clear which axis applies to which population.

Pie charts

These are useful when you want to show how much each piece of data contributes to the whole. The sum of the

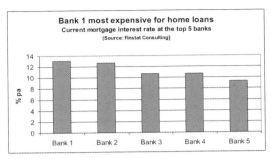

Figure 1

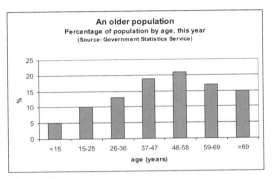

Figure 2

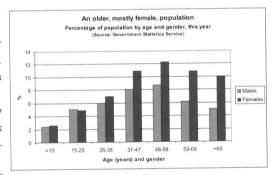

Figure 3

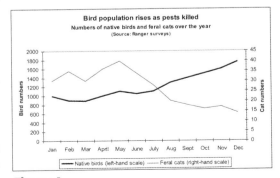

Figure 4

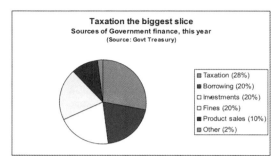

Figure 5

data must therefore be a meaningful concept. Pie charts usually present data in percentage form, meaning, of course, that the percentages must sum to 100. It is usually best to order each piece of the pie clockwise from largest to smallest, followed by "other" at the end – regardless of the size of this final category. For example – this pie chart (Figure 5) shows the various ways the government raises money.

Surveys

News organisations frequently commission surveys, especially opinion polls. These are an excellent way of generating hard news – finding out what the New Zealand public thinks about a particular hot issue or tracking support for political parties.

Most opinion polls involve the research company telephoning a random sample of people, say 1000, to measure the mood of the nation. Tomorrow's bulletins or newspapers will then lead with: "Support for the government has increased, according to a poll taken over the past week."

Polling or sampling involves taking a sample from the target population, such as all New Zealand voters, and drawing conclusions about the population as a whole based on the sample. The target population need not be the whole country – it could be voters in one electorate or one category of voter, such as women.

When designing a survey or reporting on one, there are two main issues you need to consider: First, has the sample been properly chosen and, second, what was the margin of error?

The sample

A common question people ask when they are considering commissioning a survey is: How large should the sample be? People expect that a sample should be a high percentage of the target population. But this isn't the case. Most political opinion polls, for instance, have a sample size of about 1000 – far less than the population of voters but still able to produce accurate results. What's far more important is that the sample is randomly selected from the population. That is, we want the sample to accurately reflect as much as possible the population it is drawn from, and not be biased in any way.

Surveys are a good form of publicity for a news organisation. Typically, a news organisation will commission a research company to conduct the poll and produce the results. The poll is then branded with the names of both the research company and the news organisation.

In "simple random sampling" every member of the target population has an equal chance of being included in the survey. This is the technique most often used in opinion polling, at least for sampling households. But just using the White Pages to find a random sample of telephone numbers to call won't generate a random sample of voters. For instance, it won't catch those in the home who don't answer the phone, those with unlisted numbers, or those who don't have a landline (such as those who rely on their mobiles). To help get around at least some of these problems, surveyors may use random telephone number generators to produce a list of numbers to call, including mobile phones.

Exercise 9: *Can you see any problems with this pictograph?*

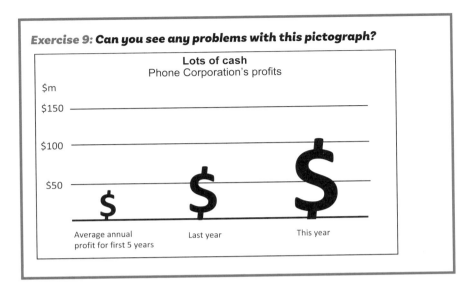

Likewise, surveyors may need to check that each potential member of a sample is indeed drawn from the target population. If you're conducting a political poll, there's no point including teenagers too young to vote.

A possible weakness of simple random sampling is that it is not possible to control sample sizes for all the sub-groups within it. "Stratified sampling" is one way of countering this shortcoming. It involves dividing the population into a number of groups (or strata), with members of the sample being randomly chosen from each stratum.

Make sure your report details the sample size. You owe it to your audience to tell them just how many people your report is based on. The bigger the sample size, the more confident your audience can be that the results are a good reflection of the population. Also tell your audience when and where the survey was conducted, and how the survey was conducted (telephone calling, face-to-face interviews, etc.). When you come to report the results, make sure you clearly tell your audience exactly what questions were asked. This all helps your audience judge for themselves how good the survey is and to understand the results.

Your report should also detail the response rate. This is the number of people who actually responded to the survey, as a percentage of the number of people asked

Exercise 10: Axes
The line chart (Figure 4) shows the bird and cat populations on two different y axes. Are there any ways the two populations could have been graphed using just one y axis? Which graph do you think better represents the situation?

to respond. For example, if you send survey forms to 700 companies and only 50 respond, this is a response rate of only 7 per cent. This could well affect the validity of your results. If the response rate is low, it is possible the results may be biased in some way. For example, the low response rate for the companies may be because you polled them over Christmas when most businesspeople were on holiday. It could be that your survey is really only reporting the views of retailers and others working over the holiday season.

The margin of error

The term "margin of error" is something of a misnomer, suggesting some sort of mistake. This is not the case. The margin of error simply reflects the fact that there is always a chance that a sample does not reflect the population from which it is drawn. This is not because of any kind of flaws in the sampling procedures; it is simply because the sample is not the population. We can never know for certain that the sample is an accurate representation of the population. There will always be sampling error – all we can do is minimise that error. Reporting the margin of error is very important, as it emphasises that sampling is inexact.

Be sceptical when reporting surveys conducted by other organisations. Are the organisations reputable? Does the survey detail all the important information – the questions asked, the sample size and sampling procedure, the response rate, the margin of error? Is this a proper, scientific survey or just a bit of advertising fluff dressed up as a survey?

Say we had many thousands of marbles of various colours randomly distributed throughout a vat. Fifty per cent of the marbles are yellow. We open the spout in the vat and pour out 2000 marbles into a large jar. We record the percentage of yellow marbles in the jar and then put all the marbles back into the vat. We mix the marbles up in the vat and then pour out another 2000 marbles. We do this over and over. After we've done this many times we look at what percentages of the marbles in each pour were yellow.

Not surprisingly, we'd find that in most cases the percentage of yellow marbles in each pour would be roughly 50 per cent – some pours had a slightly higher percentage, others a slightly lower one. In a few cases, however, the percentage of yellow marbles would be much greater or lower than 50 per cent.

In fact, you would find that, on average, in 95 per cent of cases the jar would have between 47.81 per cent and 52.19 per cent yellow marbles. Now, we know that the actual percentage of yellow marbles in the vat (the population) is 50 per cent, so the varying percentages we got in our jar (the samples) are solely due to the fact we were sampling. Another way to say this is that, on average, in 95 per cent of the pours the percentage of yellow marbles was 50 per cent ± (plus or minus) 2.19 per cent. This ± 2.19 per cent is the margin of error. Each sample proportion has a margin of error, to reflect the fact we cannot be certain that the sample proportion is the same as the population proportion.

So, just because one pour produced 49 per cent yellow marbles and another produced 48 per cent doesn't mean that the percentage of yellow marbles in the vat has changed. Yet many news reports claim this is exactly what has happened, when you hear comments like, "Support for the Yellow Party is down 1 per cent on two months ago", when the drop is within the margin of error. Of course, it makes better news to say that support for a party has dropped 1 per cent since the last poll, rather than say that it is very likely support is unchanged. But journalists owe

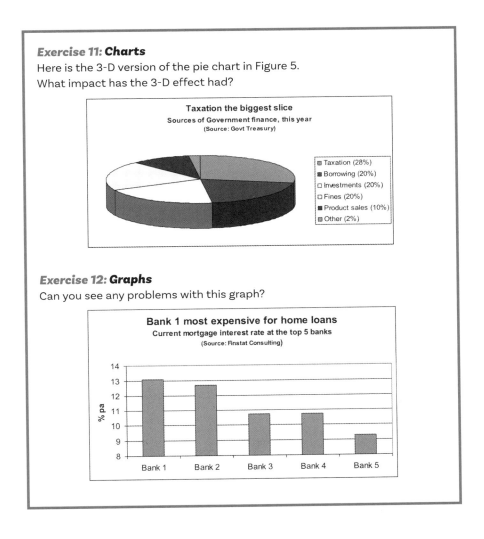

Exercise 11: **Charts**

Here is the 3-D version of the pie chart in Figure 5.
What impact has the 3-D effect had?

Taxation the biggest slice
Sources of Government finance, this year
(Source: Govt Treasury)

- Taxation (28%)
- Borrowing (20%)
- Investments (20%)
- Fines (20%)
- Product sales (10%)
- Other (2%)

Exercise 12: **Graphs**

Can you see any problems with this graph?

Bank 1 most expensive for home loans
Current mortgage interest rate at the top 5 banks
(Source: Finstat Consulting)

% pa

14
13
12
11
10
9
8

Bank 1   Bank 2   Bank 3   Bank 4   Bank 5

it to their audiences to produce accurate reports, not beat-ups.

Even if one poll finds a big change in support for a party – a change that is outside the margin of error – it may simply be that this survey is one of the 5 per cent that produces results that are way off. Most surveys calculate the margin of error at 95 per cent, as this is a reasonable trade-off between the cost of conducting surveys and the need for useable results. We could be 99 per cent certain that the percentage of yellow marbles in our samples includes the actual population percentage by increasing the margin of error to ± 2.87 per cent. But we can't eliminate the margin of error entirely because there will always be that chance, no matter how small, that the sample percentage is way off the actual percentage. The only way to be certain about the actual percentage of yellow marbles in the vat is to survey the population itself – count all the marbles in the vat to work out what percentage of them are yellow. That is a census and is usually far too expensive and time-consuming to be undertaken.

Strictly speaking, in this example the margin of error is 2.19 percentage points, but for some reason statisticians often don't use the term in this context.

Exercise 13: *Reporting research*

In 2016, a major New Zealand magazine published the results of research comparing births where a doctor led the process with births where a midwife led the process (including where a doctor took part in the delivery) ("Birth control," 2016). As midwives now play a greater role in births, a policy long advocated by feminists, the magazine's cover declared: "Where the revolution went wrong. The dangers of midwives in charge." The article reported the research on 244,047 births between 2008 and 2012, where 92 per cent of births were first registered with a midwife as lead maternity carer. The article said "babies delivered by midwives are at a higher risk of poorer outcomes than those delivered by doctors", that "babies delivered by midwives are 55% more likely to have oxygen deprivation ... a 39% higher chance of neonatal encephalopathy ... and have a 48% higher chance of a low Apgar score, which indicates a baby is unwell" (p. 18).

The article quoted one of the female researchers saying that, although the findings were alarming, adverse outcomes were rare and she, in fact, would use a midwife should she have another baby. The article also noted that the maternity system "isn't performing badly enough to suggest that the hard-fought battle of the feminist social movement to overturn doctor-led maternity care has been a costly and harmful failure" (p. 18).

What do you think about the article's use of statistics and its conclusions?

Exercise 14: *Surveys*

A leading newspaper ran an item based on a survey it conducted on its online news site ("Mother's Day," 2012). With Mother's Day approaching, the survey asked respondents whether they intended to give mum a card, a meal, breakfast in bed, or do nothing. The newspaper reported that 5000 people responded and the results showed "Almost half of New Zealanders won't be celebrating Mother's Day" (para. 1). The article's headline confidently declared, "Mother's Day off the cards for most: poll". Do you agree? Why?

Exercise 15: *Polls*

Imagine you work for a big metropolitan newspaper. The paper commissioned a poll last month that found 43 per cent of respondents supported the government. The margin of error was ± 3 per cent (at 95 per cent confidence).

The paper commissioned another survey this month, which found support for the government was 41 per cent, with the margin of error again ± 3 per cent.

"A-ha," your editor says. "Support for the government is slipping."

Is your editor right? Why?

What say the second poll found support for the government was at 35 per cent, with a margin of error of ± 3 per cent. Would your editor be right in this situation? Why?

Further, and this point is rarely made, when opinion polls are conducted there will be a different margin of error for each proportion within the sample (Labour support, National support, Greens support, etc.). When a margin of error is quoted in the media it is usually the one for a 50 per cent proportion. That is because this is the highest margin of error, and a good rule of thumb for proportions of between 30 per cent and 70 per cent. However, for proportions less than 30 per cent and greater than 70 per cent, the 50 per cent proportion overstates the margin of error.

For example, say there is only 1 per cent of purple marbles in our vat. The estimated proportion of purple marbles can't be 1 per cent ± 2.19 per cent, as we can't have a jar with -1.19 per cent purple marbles! In fact, the maths shows that at the 95 per cent confidence level the margin of error is 1 per cent ± 0.44 per cent.

My thanks to Professor Steve Haslett, Statistics New Zealand and the University of Auckland's Department of Statistics for their valuable comments on this chapter. Any errors or omissions are my responsibility.

When you hear a reporter saying a party is polling "within the margin of error", that is nonsense. Never say it!

Further reading

Rowntree, D. (1991). *Statistics without tears.* London: Penguin. Available as a free download here: http://archive.org/details/StatisticsWithoutTears. A very accessible guide to statistics for non-statisticians.

www.rbnz.govt.nz The Reserve Bank's website contains a wealth of statistical information, including a helpful inflation calculator.

www.stats.govt.nz This is Statistics New Zealand's website, which has myriad official statistics and guides.

www.statschat.org.nz A useful guide to the use and misuse of statistics in New Zealand, produced by the Department of Statistics at the University of Auckland.

References

Asian Angst. (2006, December). *North & South*, pp. 38–47.

Big petrol bills can be a sign of saving money. (2011, May 8). *Sunday Star-Times*, p. A2.

Birth control. (2016, October 8). *New Zealand Listener*, pp. 18–25.

Economic crunch hits home: Unemployment figures leap by 66%. (2009, May 12). *Ashburton Guardian*, p. 1.

Men over 50 nation's biggest drinkers. (2012, July 5). *The New Zealand Herald*, p. 5.

Minister of entitlement a disgrace. (2011, May 8). *Sunday Star-Times*, p. C6.

Mother's Day off the cards for most: poll. (2012, May 13). *The New Zealand Herald*. Retrieved from http://www.nzherald.co.nz/lifestyle/news/article.cfm?c_id=6&objectid=10805541#

TVNZ. (2010, February 9). *One news* [Television broadcast]. Auckland, New Zealand: TVNZ.

TV3. (2010, February 9). *3 News* [Television broadcast]. Auckland, New Zealand: TV3.

PART B

Telling the news

14

News writing

Mastering the essential journalistic writing skill

Grant Hannis, Massey University

News writing is a specialist form of writing, often written quickly. It is designed to be read by busy people, who'll only spare you a few moments of their time.

It is also the bedrock upon which so much other writing in journalism is based. Journalists who work in the glamorous worlds of, say, feature writing or broadcasting, often learnt their craft by first being newspaper news reporters.

A skilled news writer knows how to hook their reader into the story, how to write logically and concisely, how to use quotes and striking details, how to weave in background information, how to use correct grammar and punctuation, and much more.

And a great news writer can make any story interesting, from the fall of a president to a cat up a tree.

The inverted pyramid

Typically, news stories are written as an inverted pyramid (see Figure 1). That means the story starts with the most newsworthy information. As the story progresses, so the information becomes progressively less important. There are four parts to the story:

The headline: A very brief summary of the story, designed to catch the reader's

This chapter focuses on writing news for newspapers. Other chapters look at writing for other news media, like online and radio.

This chapter should be read in conjunction with Appendix 1, which looks at grammar, spelling and punctuation. Good writing and good grammar go hand in hand.

THE SLUG AND THE BYLINE

The first thing you'll write in any news story is usually the slug – that's the name you're going to call the story. Make sure the slug is unique, not generic. Don't name your article "council", as the chief reporter or news editor will handle many council stories. And don't use a slug that suggests you're biased, such as naming a court story "Guilty as sin", even as a joke. If your newspaper is sued for defamation, the plaintiff's lawyers could get their hands on the story and argue that your slug shows you acted with ill will.

The second thing you'll usually write is your byline. That is simply your name – the line that says who the article is by. Few journalists ever lose the thrill of seeing their byline in print!

There's another good reason to become skilled in news writing: most jobs in journalism, especially for new journalists, are as news reporters.

For more on writing headlines, especially for online, see Chapter 19.

attention. Headlines should be punchy and arresting ("Canterbury wins Ranfurly Shield", "PM to announce reshuffle"). Sometimes a very brief direct quote, repeated in the story, may be used ("Principal made 'rash' decision").

The intro: This is the key sentence and must grab the reader's attention. It also tells the whole story, focusing on the most newsworthy aspects of the who, what, when, where, why and how (the 5Ws and H). The intro states the story's angle and, thus, determines the rest of the story.

The bridge: The transition sentence, bridging the intro to the rest of the article. It answers any remaining 5Ws and H, gives proper attribution and identification, supplies any relevant background, and gives balance to controversial leads.

The body: This gives more information, quotes and details.

As developments occur in a breaking story, a reporter may update the intro of an existing online version of a story. Only later will the reporter post a complete, new updated story.

Think back to the last time you told a great piece of gossip to a friend. Most likely, you started off by saying, "You're not going to believe this." You then told them the juiciest bit of gossip. Astonished, your friend began asking you questions to get the whole story, and you obliged.

News journalism is glorified gossip – telling its audience what is going on. So, an inverted pyramid is written like a juicy bit of gossip. The "You're not going to believe this" bit is the headline. The juiciest bit of gossip is the intro. You then answer the questions in your audience's mind, fleshing out the whole story.

The abbreviation "par" stands for "paragraph".

Each par of the story is no more than one or two sentences long. You build your story sentence by sentence, with each flowing from the one that has gone before. Along with the inverted-pyramid story, the reporter may write a side-bar, which adds further background information, and a caption for an accompanying photo. We'll talk some more about those in a minute.

The inverted-pyramid structure means readers can quickly skim stories, taking in the most important information from the first few sentences. If they are particularly interested in a story, they can choose to read it to the end.

If you're not sure what information to place where in a news story, imagine you're telling it to a friend. What would you say first, second, third, and why?

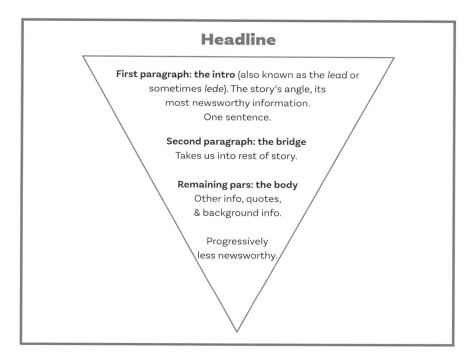

Figure 1. Structure of a typical inverted-pyramid story. Each paragraph is usually only one or two sentences long. A story may also have a side-bar and/or a photo caption.

Angles

The intro states the angle of the story. That is, the intro reports the most newsworthy aspect of the event you are covering.

Writing the intro of hard-news stories like plane crashes or stock-market crashes is easy:

> Twenty-two people died when an Air Kākāpō plane crashed while attempting to land in appalling weather at Stewart Island airport today.

That's because the angles in such stories are usually obvious. What's not so easy is finding the strongest intro when reporting the 23rd annual fair of the Sunnyglen Primary School. Perhaps it's the amount of money the fair has raised, the record turnout of people at the fair, the fact this is the last fair the long-serving retiring school principal will be at, that a popular singing star performed at the fair because her child attends the school, that one child at the fair said a quotable quote while having their face painted, etc. Finding the best intro here can involve thinking more creatively.

Once you've decided a story is newsworthy, you can then interrogate it using the 5Ws and H to decide what is most newsworthy of all in the event. This is what your intro should focus on. For instance:

Some stories are very small and so are written up simply as a brief – a couple of sentences, usually run down the side of the page.

Who?

If a prominent person is involved, the who may become the main aspect of the intro:

> Prime Minister Jane Bloggs has set up her own Facebook page.

Other ways of writing leads

Although the inverted pyramid is the most common structure for writing the news, it is not the only approach.

Another is the **partial quote**. An intro can be made more dramatic if you can lead with a strong partial quote from a newsmaker:

> The Prime Minister said yesterday he would rather "rot in hell" than continuing working with his deputy.

Here, the partial quote has been attributed (to the Prime Minister), but you don't always need to do that, just so long as you return to the quote, either as a direct quote or reported speech, later in the story and make it clear there who was speaking. Here is an example:

> In a move designed to "clean out the dead wood", the senior management team of Phoneco was fired yesterday. The chief executive, chief financial officer and three other top executives were all dismissed following the company's string of woeful financial results, which have seen its share price lose half its value over the past five months.
>
> The chair of Phoneco's board, Sir Loftus Ringworth, announced the dismissals at a hastily arranged media conference at the company's head office in Auckland.
>
> The firings were designed to remove the dead wood from the organisation, he said.

Partial-quote intros can be effective, but can become repetitive if used too much in an article. Also, of course, they only work if you have a strong partial quote to use. Another approach is called the **delayed intro**. Here, the first sentence refers to the news in an indirect way, designed to pique the reader's interest. A conventional intro usually then appears in the second sentence. Here's an example:

> Paula Lee may look like your average 13-year-old, but she is anything but. The Avondale teenager has more than a million friends on Facebook, all thanks to the videos she posts giving her quirky take on life.

Delayed intros tend to be used for profile stories or just for some variety in the news pages. They should be used sparingly, as readers will not bother to read many stories with obscure leads.

Another approach is called **foreshadowing**. This can be used in the rare cases where a news story is about two topics, rather than one. The intro leads into the first topic, but also foreshadows the second, which appears later in the story:

> Two armed robbers were caught by Wellington police yesterday, but robbers elsewhere in the country are still on the loose.

The story should then go on to report the Wellington incident fully, before moving on to the other robberies. But remember: this approach should be used sparingly. That's because, usually, a news report should only be about one topic.

Note that what the PM did – set up a Facebook page – is commonplace. Everyone does it. It is the fact that the PM did it that makes the story newsworthy.

What?

If a person is not well-known, it could be that what happened should be the intro's focus:

> A man knocked himself out when he ran into a power pole while trying to escape police yesterday.

Where?

It could be that the location of an event is the most newsworthy aspect. This intro would be of interest to Wellingtonians, but not Aucklanders:

> Wellington had its warmest February in a decade, MetService says.

When?

Many intros include some aspect of time, because timeliness is fundamental to news. The unconscious escapee mentioned above ran into that power pole *yesterday*. But sometimes the when is so important it starts the intro:

> Within minutes of the sharemarket opening this morning, the Phoneco share price fell 15 per cent as rumours continue to swirl about the corporation's precarious finances.

Why?

Sometimes it is why an event has happened that is the most newsworthy aspect:

> Following a spike in hospital admissions, parents are being advised to take their children to their doctor immediately if they show any signs of the deadly meningococcal disease.

How?

Other times, it is how an event has unfolded that makes it newsworthy:

> Arson has been blamed for a fire that destroyed the Greymouth Tennis Club's rooms last night.

Writing intros

The intro is the news angle written down, stating the news angle in a single sentence. In an inverted-pyramid story, the rest of the article simply serves to reinforce the intro. Indeed, before they sit down to write a news story, a news reporter often has the intro in their head, at least in draft form. Begin by writing your intro, at least in draft form, and then ensure the rest of the article serves that intro.

The intro should be a single sentence, no longer than about 25 words. It should express a single idea. If your intro is longer than this or includes more than one idea, edit it down.

The intro must immediately tell the reader what is happening:

> More than $5000 was raised at the Sunnyglen School fair on the weekend, to be used to help buy new computers.

Sometimes, there's a sixth W – "What's next?" This doesn't appear in the intro, but can appear in the body, reporting what's expected to happen next, such as: "The rescued boaties are likely to be back home tomorrow."

WATCH THE SIMPLE STUFF

Debbie Gregory is chief reporter at the *Gisborne Herald*. She began her career as a journalist in the 1980s. She says novice reporters struggle with intros, when what a good intro needs is "fewer words, more punch".

And new reporters often don't check the simple things. "Incorrect names of organisations, events, places, street names (that info is only one click away on Google). Names spelled incorrectly – this happens often and is a major golden rule: always ask the spelling of names."

And make sure you know your punctuation, she advises. Some of the problems she sees are "capitals in the wrong places; apostrophes in the wrong places".

But young journalists are still an asset to any newsroom, she adds. They "bring fresh new perspectives, positivity. And the good ones, who are hungry for a good story, are eager and keen. All good for a tired newsroom!"

Reporting local community news is great practice for writing strong news stories, because you often have to think harder about identifying and writing the strongest intros for your stories.

This is better than the following, where we are told the why before the what:

> Because of the need to buy new computers, Sunnyglen School has decided to put the more than $5000 raised at the school fair towards this.

Make the intro as detailed as possible:

> An Auckland man is lucky to be alive after he drove the wrong way along the northern motorway and slammed into an oncoming bus yesterday.

This is better than:

> A car collided with a vehicle on the motorway yesterday.

Look for the detail that makes this story different from stories about similar events. If the victims of a robbery tell you that the robbers were "gentlemen" because they spoke respectfully, that's unusual. Put it in your intro.

Attribution

Attribution (sourcing information and quotes) is very important. It gives your stories credibility and tells readers whose opinions are being quoted. Quotes allow the reader to "hear" the voices of the newsmakers.

If you don't attribute, you own the information. If you report that a new government policy is a bad idea, but don't make it clear it was the Leader of the Opposition who said that, then it's *you* saying the policy is a bad idea. Make sure any opinions expressed in your stories are attributed to those making them.

In an intro, attribution can go either at the beginning:

> Prime Minister Jane Bloggs today announced that France had ended nuclear testing in the Pacific.

Or the end:

> France has ended nuclear testing in the Pacific, Prime Minister Jane Bloggs said today.

Its placement depends on what is the most newsworthy part of the sentence, the statement or the person making it.

Sometimes attribution can clutter up an intro, in which case wherever possible it should be left until later in a story. One technique is to give a shortened form of attribution in the intro, with full attribution in the bridge. For instance:

> Christchurch ratepayers face an annual bill of $90 million to subsidise the city's buses, a new study says.
>
> The study was prepared by accounting firm PWC for the Christchurch City Council's transport sub-committee.

Generally, attribution used later in a story should be placed at the end of a sentence. That's because the statement is more important than who says it, and having a number of sentences beginning "He/she said" is repetitive.

Never put the attribution in the middle of a sentence:

> Electricity prices, she said, would continue to rise.

That's because it is not the news-writing style (you will see it in features, which are written in a more novelistic fashion).

Verbs of attribution

News stories generally attribute in the past tense. That means they use "said", not "says". It also means other verbs in the reportage are generally written in the past tense too:

> The dog was a cross-breed, she said.
>
> The decision would be made on Friday, he said.

> Don't include your opinions in your news stories. Just report the news. Let your editor give the newspaper's opinion in their editorial or, if appropriate, you can tweet your opinion online.

BURYING THE LEAD

Make sure you identify the best angle for your story and make that your intro. Let's say you've written a news story and submitted it to your chief reporter. She looks through the story and, in the seventh par, reads something far more newsworthy than what's in the intro. "You've buried the lead!" she exclaims. In other words, a far better intro (lead) than the one you chose is hiding in the story. You'll be asked to rewrite the piece with the new intro at the top, and the rest of the article rewritten to serve this new intro.

Not:

> The dog is a cross-breed, he said.
>
> The decision will be made on Friday, he said.

An exception is in intros, where news stories may attribute in the present tense, to convey immediacy:

> A decision on the new motorway must be made by the end of the week, the Transport Minister says.
>
> Speaking in Parliament yesterday, the minister said …

Never change the tense of verbs in direct quotes. In a news story, write:

> "The dog is a cross-breed," he said. (*This is what he actually said*.)

Not:

> "The dog was a cross-breed," he said.

The best verb to use for attribution is "said" because it is a neutral verb, it contains no implied judgement.

Verbs that carry implied judgements about the speaker's view – like "admitted", "asserted", "hinted", "demanded", "protested", "maintained" – should be avoided. That's because the speaker may say the words imply they felt one way when in fact they didn't. Avoid "according to" as well, as it sounds like the reporter doubts the speaker.

Over-attribution

Once you have identified a source in your story, do not overdo the attribution. It slows the story down:

> Foster said the budget would be approved at the next meeting.
>
> "I am sure special interest groups will be out in force. Council will have to weigh both sides carefully. (*No attribution needed.*)
>
> "After all, environmental policy was the most important issue to come before council this year." (*No attribution needed.*)

The attribution in the first par tells readers who the speaker is. We do not need to repeat that information.

DNA (designation name attribution)

When you introduce a source, state their job title (or role), name, and give the verb of attribution, in that order:

> Traffic engineer Steve Spence said Wellington City carpark fees would increase 50 per cent next month.

Most news outlets usually don't use honorifics (Mr, Ms, etc.). However, if yours does, then DNA still applies, with the honorific being the D: "Mr Smith said."

On subsequent mentions, state their surname, and give the verb of attribution, in that order:

> The increase was unavoidable, Spence said.

This is known as DNA:

- **Designation (job title/role):** Traffic engineer
- **Name:** Steve Spence, Spence
- **Verb of Attribution:** said

Note there are no commas between the DNA elements:

> Traffic engineer Steve Spence said

Not:

> Traffic engineer, Steve Spence said

You only use commas if the designation is a description of them, starting with "the", "a" or "an". In this case, commas go either side of the source's name:

> The traffic engineer, Steve Spence, said

Note the designation comes before the name:

> Protester John Smith said
> Mayor Jane Jones said

Not:

> John Smith, a protester, said
> Jane Jones, the Mayor, said

Quotes

Quotes are an important aspect of any news story. They are the lifeblood of stories, allowing the audience to hear directly what the newsmakers say. Reporters are always looking for strong quotes when interviewing.

There are three ways of reporting a quote:

1. Direct quote (using speech marks, also known as quotation marks or inverted commas):

> "Taxation cuts are likely to be introduced next year," the minister said.

2. Reported speech (also known as paraphrasing):

> Taxation cuts were likely next year, the minister said.

However, be careful that in reported speech you get the exact meaning of what the person is saying. Excessive paraphrasing can lead to errors of meaning.

Don't follow reported speech with a direct quote that simply says the same thing:

> The accident was horrific, Rousseau said.
> "It was really horrific," she said.

3. Partial quote (when only a word or a short phrase appears in speech marks):

> The minister said taxes would "almost certainly fall" during the next 12 months.

With children (typically taken to be those aged 16 years or younger), use their first name and surname on first mention and their first name only on subsequent mentions – for instance, "Gracie Smith, 6," and then "Gracie". It would look ridiculous to refer to her as "Smith".

As the example above shows, it's usual to give children's ages in stories. Don't do it for adults, unless it is relevant to the story.

If two or more people in a story have the same surname – two brothers, for instance – introduce the first person with first name and surname. Thereafter, refer to each of them using their first names only.

Partial quotes are useful for highlighting a few quotable words someone says in a sentence. They can work very well in intros:

> The Transport Minister says he is "staking his reputation" on the motorway proposal getting the green light.

Make sure the partial quotes are interesting, pithy expressions, not just dull words. Don't write:

> The chairman said he was "attending" the meeting tomorrow.

Changing direct quotes

Generally, a direct quote must depict exactly what the speaker said. However, there are three possible exceptions:

1. Correcting bad grammar (unless it is essential to the story). Spoken English is much less formal than written English. It's not usual practice to make people look ignorant by printing their mistakes.

2. Deleting voiced pauses ("Umm" or "Aah") and, depending on your publication's policy, obscene words.

3. Eliminating excessive wordiness. Unimportant meanderings can be edited, but make sure you do not change the essential meaning or structure. Any deletions should be marked by three dots (called ellipses), any text you add to clarify a quote should be in brackets:

> "[The National Party] will fight on ... we will fight to win," she said.

Descriptions of people can come after their name if the description is long: "John Smith, who wrote the initial letter of complaint to the council, said ..."

If you have to significantly change a quote to make it usable, rewrite it as reported speech. A combination of reported speech and direct quotation can be used to make sense of a rambling direct quote from the notes:

Original notes quoting Fred Smith: "Hang on, let me think, the train was coming from the south, out of Wellington and towards Johnsonville and, I think, although no, hang on again, it had gone past Crofton Downs, just past Crofton Downs and it was going really fast. Well, it seemed to me it was going really fast ... then it hit the bus and sliced through it like a tomato."

This can become:

> The train had just gone past Crofton Downs, heading for Johnsonville, Smith said. "It seemed to me it was going really fast ... it hit the bus and sliced through it like a tomato."

Punctuating direct quotes

Unless followed by attribution, the final sentence in a direct quote ends with a full stop and closed speech marks:

> "This is the end."

If the direct quote is followed by attribution, the final sentence ends with a comma, closed speech marks, and then attribution:

"This is the end," he said.

When you are running a long quote on from one par to another, do not close the speech marks at the end of the first par:

"The tax rate is too high for the lower paid worker," Finance Minister Ray Smith said.

"What we need are lower taxes for the poor and higher taxes for the rich. *(No speech marks.)*

"To this end, we will be bringing in a new tax regime in next year's budget. *(No speech marks.)*

"What is needed is the political courage to make these changes."

When doing this, the quotes must recount exactly what was said in the order it was said.

If attribution comes before the direct quote, you can use a comma or a colon to introduce the quote:

He said, "I know this is correct."

He said: "I know this is correct."

Punctuating reported speech

If a passage of reported speech is followed by attribution, it concludes with a comma:

This was the end, he said.

If attribution precedes the reported speech, no punctuation mark is required:

He said this was the end.

Punctuating partial quotes

With partial quotes, any final full stops, commas, etc., go outside the quote marks:

Gribb said the Kiwis should "go for gold".

The Kiwis should "go for gold", Gribb said.

Handling quotes

When you switch from one source to another in a story, you must introduce the new source with attribution then reported speech. Otherwise, the reader assumes the original speaker is still speaking. For example, write:

The closure of the shopping complex has hit the retailers hard.

"It's just terrible to see our life's work end," Flamingo cafe co-owner Jean Williams said.

But fellow co-owner Carol Jones saw a bright side to the closure. "At least I'll be able to spend more time with my children," she said.

Williams agreed. "Yes, I guess that's one bonus for those in our team with young families," she said.

WRITING COMMUNITY NEWS

Many new journalists will start their careers writing for community newspapers. Here's some advice from **Simon Edwards**, who edited community newspapers for 30 years.

"Community news can have a slightly different style and tempo to daily news reports," he says. "Writing for a distinct, and often smaller, community can open opportunities to write more informally – for example, reverting to first names after a first mention of a full name and using the colloquial names for locations."

But being accurate, fair and balanced is still vital. "It is no defence to say 'but we're just a little community newspaper'. If a journalist lets these standards slip they – and their publications – will earn the contempt of readers as untrustworthy, and perhaps end up in court trying to defend a defamation case."

Don't be afraid to go back to interviewees to check your facts. "If the journalist doesn't understand technical details given in an interview, he or she will not be able to write it up in a way the reader will understand. Go back to the interview subject for clarification. No one minds being called again if it means the story will be accurate and clearer."

And accuracy includes the little things. "Check the spelling of names, even when it seems obvious what it is (Smith, Smyth, Smythe). Get the name wrong, and the entire reading experience is soured for your subject and those who know him/her. They'll think, 'If the paper can't even get the name right, what else have they botched?'"

His final thoughts. "Readers might affectionately call your paper the local rag, but they'll do so with pride if you strive for excellence."

Not:

> The closure of the shopping complex has hit the retailers hard.
>
> "It's just terrible to see our life's work end," Flamingo cafe co-owner Jean Williams said.
>
> "At least I'll be able to spend more time with my children," fellow co-owner Carol Jones said. *(Until we get to the end of the sentence we assume this is Jean speaking.)*
>
> "Yes, I guess that's one bonus for those in our team with young families," Williams said. *(Until we get to the end we assume this is Carol speaking.)*

As much as possible, keep reportage (including reported speech) separate from direct quotes. Do not blend the two. Instead, have pars of reportage and pars of direct quotes. For instance, in a story about a visiting musician, Manola, write:

This was the first time Manola has toured New Zealand.

He was looking forward to getting some sightseeing in while he was here, he said.

"I've heard New Zealand is a beautiful country and I want to check out if that is true.

"I've seen all the *Lord of the Rings* movies, so I'm keen to see the locations where the films were shot."

Not:

This was the first time Manola has toured New Zealand.

He was looking forward to getting some sightseeing in while he was here.

He had "heard New Zealand is a beautiful country" and wanted to "check out if that is true", he said.

"I've seen all the *Lord of the Rings* movies, so" was keen to see the locations "where the films were shot", he said.

Re-read this section to make sure you understand it. Young journalists frequently pepper their stories with partial quotes. Break the habit!

By blending direct quotes with reportage, the above text simply does not read like news.

If you have multiple sources quoted in a story, avoid ping-ponging between sources. As much as possible, give all of the first source's quotes, then all the next source's quotes, and so on. For instance, that cafe story above would read like this:

The closure of the shopping complex has hit the retailers hard.

"It's just terrible to see our life's work end," Flamingo cafe co-owner Jean Williams said.

But there would be one bonus for those in her team with young families, she said.

One such person was fellow co-owner Carol Jones.

"At least I'll be able to spend more time with my children," Jones said.

Writing the news

A news reporter makes their stories easy to read by using short, simple sentences; active verbs; relevant facts and details; logical flow and concise writing.

Short, simple sentences

Keep your sentences short, with only one idea per sentence.

Generally, your sentences should average about 17 words. You'll need some variety, of course. If you write only very short sentences, your story will have a staccato, clipped feel. If you write only long sentences, your readers will get lost and bored.

Having some variety in sentence length will give your writing rhythm and balance. But even your longer sentences shouldn't exceed about 25 words. Use plenty of full stops!

Be organised when you write sentences. Keep all related information together:

Judge Roy Bean lectured the law students about drinking and driving in the District Court today.

Avoid excessive use of ellipses in quotes, as it makes the text look bitty. Recast the material as reported speech. Never start or end a quote with ellipses. Don't write: "... I was working," he said.

This sounds like the students were drinking and driving in court! The sentence would be much clearer like this:

> Judge Roy Bean gave the law students a lecture in the District Court today about drinking and driving.

If you use subordinate clauses, use no more than one in a sentence and make sure you mark them off with commas:

> The man, who police say should not be approached, was last seen heading towards Omaha beach.

Not:

> The man, who police say should not be approached *[missing comma]* was last seen heading towards Omaha beach, which is north of Auckland *[second subordinate clause].*

Active verbs

Verbs are the most important words in sentences. They give sentences energy and directness. Indeed, "verb" is Latin for "the word". Always favour verbs over nouns:

> The council is establishing *[verb]* a working party to investigate *[verb]* the matter.

Not:

> The council is undertaking the establishment *[noun]* of a working party for the investigation *[noun]* of the matter.

Because it uses verbs, the first sentence is punchier and shorter.

Verbs can be expressed in either the active or passive voice. To understand this, we need to identify two grammatical ideas:

The doer of the action. This is the person or thing undertaking the action (the verb).

The recipient of the action. This is the person or thing that receives the action.

In an active-voice construction, the doer comes before the verb and the recipient after it:

> I *(doer)* see *(verb)* the cat *(recipient).*

In a passive-voice construction, the order of the doer and recipient is reversed. The recipient comes before the verb and the doer after it:

> The cat *(recipient)* is seen *(verb)* by me *(doer).*

In the passive, the doer may disappear from the sentence altogether:

> The cat *(recipient)* is seen *(verb).*

Generally speaking, news writing uses the active voice. That's because the active voice is shorter and easier to understand. Write in the active voice.

> ## HOOKED
>
> When a reporter applies for a job at *The Dominion Post*, editor-in-chief Bernadette Courtney says she scrutinises the applicant's portfolio of published articles.
>
> "I look for strong intros, whose voices are heard in the stories – in other words, how much depth the stories have – and strong quotes. I want readers to be hooked in by the stories, so that they'll read to the end of each one."

However, the passive has its uses:

- To focus on the recipient if that has greater news value: Tokyo was rocked by an earthquake today.
- When you do not know or wish to say who the doer was: The Eastpac bank branch in St Heliers was burgled overnight.

As these two examples suggest, when the passive voice is used, it's usually in the intros of stories.

Relevant facts and details

A news story should be loaded with facts and details. These create images in the reader's mind, allowing them to visualise the news you are reporting.

Don't write:

> Strong gales caused major damage in Christchurch yesterday.

Write:

> Winds gusting at more than 160 kmh sent roofs flying and trees crashing in Christchurch yesterday.

Name names, give speeds, dates, times, costs, ages, dimensions, colours, etc.

Don't write:

> The huge, multi-million dollar mall sits in a sea of car parks.

Write:

> The $16.5 million mall covers three acres and has enough parking for 2300 cars.

In some cases, the statistics are so large as to be meaningless to the average reader. Recast them in terms they can grasp:

> The city's debt is $50 billion. That is $10,000 for every man, woman and child living in the city.

Avoid contractions (such as "can't" or "won't") in news writing, as they look too informal. You will only see them occasionally in the body of news articles. The most common times to use contractions are: (1) in an intro, to give it more energy, and (2) if the contraction is in a direct quote.

Write "about", not
"around": "There were
about 25 people at
the meeting."

Write "more than",
not "over": "There
were more than
25 people at the
meeting."

Write "past", not
"last": "For the
past two years
no possums have
been found in the
sanctuary."

Similarly, focus on people in stories, not abstract concepts. That's why every Budget day, the newspapers show how the government's economic announcements will affect ordinary New Zealanders.

Logical flow

Make sure your article proceeds in a logical fashion, so that the reader implicitly understands why each subsequent par is there. That is, make sure you set your reader up to expect something and then deliver on that expectation. Look at this extract from a report:

> Jones said he was unhappy with the police's handling of the situation.
> "I hope my son gets bail."

The first sentence sets up the expectation in the reader's mind that Jones will be quoted as saying something about his unhappiness. Instead, the quote is about something else. This lack of logical flow is known as a non sequitur.

Now, it could be there is a logical link between them – perhaps Jones feels the police have unfairly portrayed his son's actions and that is why he thinks the boy won't get bail. If so, that link needs to be made clear in the story:

> Jones said he was unhappy with the police's handling of the situation.
> Despite what the police were saying, his son was not violent and he hoped the judge would see this, he said.
> "I hope my son gets bail."

Concise writing

Edit your own work
ruthlessly. Prune it
back to the absolute
essentials. Begrudge
every word you have to
use. For a start, you can
usually delete the word
"that" from sentences.

Space is tight. Your readers' time is tight. That means you must report the news with as few words as possible.

Liberate your writing from waffle. Consider this sentence:

> Members of the public would be given the opportunity of examining the proposition more closely in order to get a better understanding of the complicated problems involved, she said.

It can be cut right back, making it far more likely to be read and understood:

> The public would have a chance to examine the proposal more closely, to understand the problems, she said.

Check every sentence you write for verbiage – that is, excess words. Look out for:

Tautology (also known as redundancy): This is using two words to say the same thing, like "true facts" or "5am in the morning".

The test here is: Does the opposite exist? Can you have untrue facts? Can it ever be 5am in the afternoon? If not, the original phrase is tautological.

Long phrases in place of short words: Don't write "adjacent to", use "near". Don't write "at the present time ", use "now". Don't write "not in favour of" use "opposes".

Drifting off topic: Once you've finished everything that serves your intro, stop.

REMAIN EVER DILIGENT

Jonathon Howe is Stuff's Manawatu regional editor. He says young journalists have a tendency to over-write, filling their articles with adjectives and overly punctuated sentences. "Sentences should be clear, concise and free of jargon and cliché … We should always remember that we are being paid to write for our audience, not to indulge our own passions."

It's important to personalise stories, he says. "One thing I've seen in novice reporters is a penchant for focusing on the issue rather than the people it affects. Often, personalising stories can be harder because you have to go the extra mile to find an affected person. But the internet and social media allow us more access to people's private lives than ever before, so there are plenty of tools to help us."

Novice news writers can have a "she'll be right" attitude, he says. "I've seen many instances where student reporters have brushed over details perceived as minor (names, places, titles). Often it's more of a case of that individual being eager to impress by banging out copy as quickly as possible. Writing at speed is a good skill to have but I think accuracy is a far greater asset. We all make mistakes, but nothing can be more personally and professionally embarrassing than getting something as simple as a name wrong.

"Mistakes I made as a junior still haunt me today, and I think the fear of making mistakes is crucial in ensuring you remain ever diligent with the facts."

Your article is complete. Don't allow your article to drift off onto a related topic. If you find there is a lot more you want to say, decide whether it's information that could go in a side-bar, a follow-up news story or a news feature.

Side-bars

Many news outlets like to have information compartmentalised: most of the information is in the text, but some is separated out into side-bars or boxes. Breaking up the text like this makes it easier to read and more attractive on the page. Material in a side-bar should be basically complete in itself. Do not repeat information in the main text.

Good information to put in side-bars can be case studies, a bullet-point list of the main facts, or background information (such as a timeline of events to date).

Captions

Increasingly, it is the reporter's job to obtain caption details for photos and to write the caption. Indeed, these days, reporters may be expected to double as photographers.

A photo can catch the reader's eye, so is a strong way to attract reader interest in your story. The reader will then want to know what is going on in the photo.

Avoid acronyms. Rather than write "WCC", write "Wellington City Council" and then "the council". Definitely do NOT create acronyms in your stories – "Wellington City Council (WCC)" – that you do not subsequently use!

The caption must stand alone. Describe what is happening in the photo without descending into irrelevancy. Write in the present tense.

There are three types of caption:

- **Label:** Usually this is simply the name of the person underneath a photo of their face.
- **Caption:** Usually this comprises one or two sentences and a photo credit (stating, in capital letters, who took the photo):

Molly Jones (left) and Ngaire Long, both 7, from Sunnyglen School hold jars of polluted water from the local stream, which runs alongside their school. PHOTO: JOHN SMITH

The caption must identify everyone in the photo (and ages for children), usually left to right. It's a good idea after taking the photo to ask everyone to stay in the same position as you get their names (and check spellings!).

It is important that a caption tells us something more about what's going on in a photo, not just telling us what we can see for ourselves.

- **Caption story** (also known as a fat cap): The story is effectively a long caption, accompanying a large, dramatic photo.

House style

It is up to you to learn your news organisation's house style and to comply with it.

Although good grammar will serve you in excellent stead when writing the news, there are many points on which the grammar books do not give a definitive answer. To cover these, each news outlet (or "house") has its own house style, a list of how it handles tricky points.

For instance, a publication's house style may make it clear that:

- If there is choice of spelling a word "-ise"/"-ize", use "-ise" ("criticise", not "criticize"); same with "-yse"/"-yze" ("analyse", not "analyze").
- On first mention the word "million" is spelt out, but on subsequent mentions it is shortened to "m". Same with billion, kilometres, etc.
- Dates are written as day, month, year.
- Abbreviations and honorifics do not take full stops (eg, "am" not "a.m.")
- Use "am" or "pm", never "o'clock", unless it is a direct quote.

Do not write "$50 dollars" – that reads "Fifty dollars dollars"!

Sometimes, the numbers one to nine are written as words, and 10 upwards as digits. There are some exceptions: any number that starts a sentence is written as a word, and dates and ages are often written as digits.

Many news organisations use news-writing software, which automatically applies at least some of the house-style requirements. Such software can also require writers, for instance, to confirm the spelling of names is correct.

While all this may seem technical and rather daunting, like most things it gets easier with practice. A good news writer is a valued member of any news team, as someone who can be relied on to produce clean copy under time pressure. And once you have sharp, accurate news-writing skills under your belt, you can adapt your technique to other writing challenges, like producing features.

Further reading

Greenbaum, S., Whitcut, J., & Quirk, R. (1996). *Longman guide to English usage.* Harlow: Longman. An excellent guide to writing clear, accurate English.

Any mainstream daily metropolitan print newspaper. You'll find plenty of inverted-pyramid stories, well-subbed (this last point, sadly, cannot always be said about the material that appears in online news). You should also have at least two good dictionaries. At least one should be an up-to-date edition of the *Oxford English Dictionary.*

www.dictionary.com This free online dictionary is helpful, but remember it has a US English focus.

www.maoridictionary.co.nz Increasingly, journalism organisations in New Zealand are spelling Māori words using macrons. These are the short lines above vowels to indicate a long vowel sound. You will need a Māori dictionary to make sure you spell Māori words correctly. This free online one is excellent.

15

Feature writing
Mastering the long form of written journalism

Charles Riddle and Richard Walker, Waikato Institute of Technology

---

This chapter should be read in conjunction with Appendix 1, which looks at grammar, spelling and punctuation. Good writing and good grammar go hand in hand.

If news writing is the bread and butter of the journalist's day, then feature writing surely is the feast. After the strictures of news writing, features offer an opportunity to have fun with language, to be creative in approach, to experiment and take risks as a writer, and to sink your teeth into a topic.

Features offer the journalist the opportunity to revel in ideas and face up to the challenge to see if, in a world of information bites and nanosecond attention spans, they can hook a reader, and reel them in.

Kinds of features

Features are usually longer-form stories published online, in magazines, and in special sections of newspapers. They can be divided into three main categories: news features, profiles and lifestyle features.

News features

These provide the chance to look behind the news. A news feature may take the form of a backgrounder, in which a reporter fills in detail left out of the breaking news. It may also involve developing a news story by talking in-depth to key players or those affected, providing context and answering questions such as, "Why is this

GREAT TRAVEL WRITING

Ex-newspaper editor Venetia Sherson is now an award-winning travel writer, and spends as much time as she can in southern Europe. For her, the secret is in the old adage: show, don't tell.

"To stand out from the mundane, you have to tell readers something they don't already know. That means eliminating every fact that is already known ('white sands', 'dense bush', 'vast plains', and 'hearty fare') and finding details that are quirky, colourful, dark or funny. Good travel writers convey a scene in words so readers feel they are present.

"In a story I wrote about mountain towns in Italy, I described the houses as 'leaning into each other like crooked teeth'; when I wrote about helping out at a farmers' market on a chilly morning, I eschewed the phrase 'wrapped up warmly' for 'appeared like Michelin woman'.

"Travel writing evokes an experience. It shows rather than tells. Readers want to feel as if they're eavesdropping on a conversation, or being shown something very different and special.

"A good travel story also needs a plot and characters. For me, travel is always about the people, so I like to draw detailed sketches of characters who encapsulate a place: an eccentric Englishwoman who restored an Italian castle by day and hosted cross-dressing parties at night; a woman who owned a B&B but couldn't cook; and even a dog that kept me awake at night, baying at Sicilian ghosts.

"Research is essential. Read before you go, during your travels and after you return home. When I met a Cuban woman on my travels, I downloaded Ben Corbett's *This is Cuba*, so I could ask intelligent questions. I rarely stay in hotels. I like to live as the locals live; eat where they eat, and ride the buses and trains.

"It also helps to have tension. I often start with an anecdote but don't reveal the ending until later. One travel feature began with me getting into what I believed was a taxi, alone, after dark in a city I had never visited. Bad move. But it produced a great story. The man (who was not a taxi driver) invited me back to his home to have dinner with his wife. It served as a backdrop for a story about the perils and pleasures of travelling alone."

happening?" and "What does this mean?" In both cases, the reader can expect to be better informed about a story they may already be aware of.

Profiles

As the word suggests, these focus on a single person. Sometimes they can be a type of news feature in which a newsmaker is profiled in some depth. These "newsmakers" can be just about anyone: celebrities, sportspeople, politicians, your neighbour, or a musician promoting a new album.

In all cases they should give the reader an insight into the profile subject – what counts is a sense of the person. They are not necessarily the definitive take on that individual – more often than not, they are a picture of how the writer found the individual at the time they interviewed them.

Lifestyle features

Trends, fads and events are all possible subjects of a lifestyle feature, which will be lighter in touch than most news features. Travel is a special category. These features typically appear in special pages or supplements of newspapers, on specialised websites, and in any number of magazines.

Starting out

Start by reading. Read novels, short stories, poems. Read features. Read whatever you enjoy. Think about how your favourite writers are putting the words on the page. Pick them apart, put them back together and imitate whatever you most like. Not word for word, but the attitude, or the short sentences, or the long sentences, or the humour, or the moment when they stop you short in your tracks. Keep doing that, and keep reading, and you'll develop your own way of doing it.

Feature-writing elements and structure

Feature writers have plenty of storytelling devices at their disposal. The inverted pyramid used for news is not one of them. A feature is a story, but it is not just a long news story. It is surprisingly common for journalists, sunk deeply in the trade of hard news to deadline, to struggle with the more expansive form of the feature.

Good writers beguile their readers through the feature as if they were reading a short story.

Facts accumulate along the way, and the reader should know more at the end than before they started, but they should not have had to work at it. The writer, on the other hand, must work hard. Indeed, those features that are the easiest, smoothest reads are often as not the ones writers sweated most blood over.

One idea

A feature needs a theme running through it. You should be able to write a sentence summarising your story idea (answering the question: What is this feature about?). That should give you the theme, and anything that doesn't contribute to it should be cut out.

That theme should be established early in the feature. Within the first five paragraphs your reader should have a clear sense of what the feature is about. Sometimes this can come in the form of a summarising paragraph (occasionally known as the "nut par") after the intro. Often it becomes apparent without that device.

The standfirst can help, but that doesn't give you licence to ramble for paragraph after paragraph with the reader unsure where you're headed. By the fifth or sixth par, they should know.

CAPTURE THE MOMENT

Freelance feature writer **Aimie Cronin** talks about stumbling across the right angle for a feature.

"'Day of Reckoning' was my first court feature. I arrived at the trial after being told it would go on for days, so I envisaged long periods spent observing the family, building a relationship with them slowly over time, getting to know the case intimately. I had a day to do this in the end.

"I approached the family with a thumping heart – there's a lot at stake when you're on a short deadline – and was lucky some of them agreed to talk. They really opened up.

"I decided while talking to Candi Hepi, that she would lead the story. You are always piecing things together as you go. And painting a picture. That doesn't mean you understand everything about them and their situation, but that you capture the day they were sitting on the steps outside the court, and you get little windows into their lives, at best.

"I always strive to capture the person in that moment as best I can. This means taking everything in. Every detail. I also want the reader to be able to hear the person speaking, as much as possible, when they read a quote. This means noticing the rhythm of their speech, any slang they use, any words they emphasise, and using it in the story. There is a fine line here. You never want to mock the person, or use quotes to show inadequacy – always be conscious of that.

"Remember your job is to be as nosey as you possibly can (respectfully). It's the perfect job for curious people.

"And work hard on learning the ropes, then develop your own voice.

"A good feature, I think, comes down to a strong idea, a stronger interview, and writing with heart."

You can read "Day of Reckoning" here: www.stuff.co.nz/waikato-times/news/8466344/Day-of-reckoning.

Standfirst

The standfirst, sometimes known as a precede or supra intro, is a sentence or two before the feature, invariably in a bigger font. It gives a sense of what the feature is about, an angle or hook for the reader, and the byline. Think of it as a window display enticing the reader in. For a freelancer, it doubles as a way of selling the feature to a prospective editor.

Keep your standfirsts short and sharp, and make sure you include your byline (that is, your name).

Here are a couple of examples (Stephenson, 2017, p. 66; Macdonald, 2017, p. C1):

> Sharon Stephenson joins a circle of compulsive over-spenders at a meeting of Debtors Anonymous.

> Is the short stay rental boom worsening the housing shortage? Nikki Macdonald reports.

In terms of structure, and put simply, a feature needs a beginning, middle, and an end.

The beginning

Get your reader hooked with the human story.

There are plenty of ways to start a feature. Beware the summarising intro, similar to a news intro and often favoured by beginners. Unless expertly handled, it risks being dull.

It's almost always more successful to start a feature with a simple, detailed account of someone doing something, as long as it is relevant to the story. That way you've got your "being there" detail right up front – the detail that makes the reader feel like they're there with someone. Your story is about a kayaker training for the Coast to Coast? Start with them out paddling on the harbour or wherever else they train.

Here's an example from the *Waikato Times* (Cooper, 2011, p. B7):

> Standing in muddy grass on the edge of a murky lake, wearing gumboots a couple of sizes too big and clutching a microphone in her right hand is not the kind of glamorous situation most television presenters find themselves in, but Amanda Harper is loving every minute of it.
>
> With the resounding boom of shotguns going off every time a duck dares to fly overhead, Harper and camera operator Manuela Kornell are recording an interview with two Conservation Department staff about the successful restoration of Lake Kaituna.

Colour is not about being flowery. It's about concrete detail or description that links to the story's theme.

Similar, but more difficult, is starting with a description of a scene or person. Be careful and stingy with your words when writing a colour intro of this type.

The fact someone is wearing a crisp white shirt might be useful if it turns out the last time they wore it, it was covered in blood. Then it provides a telling detail. Otherwise, it's probably superfluous and just getting in the way of a good story. Similarly, the fact someone has blue eyes is unlikely to be of value unless one of those eyes is false and the feature is about the intricate operation the person had to fit this ground-breaking piece of bionic technology. Otherwise, keep blue eyes out of it.

Some features are driven by analysis of a topic. But you can and should still have a person in them. For these features you might start with a person, preferably someone directly affected by the topic, rather than a "talking head" expert. That way, you get buy-in from the reader. If you're writing about breast cancer, who better to tell it than someone fighting the disease? You might start by describing the person or something they do, as long as your detail ties them directly into the theme of the feature.

Here's an example from the *Herald on Sunday* (Powley, 2013, paras. 1–3) in a feature about water charges:

> Despite one of the driest months in decades, the flowers and veges are thriving

on avid gardener Yvonne Dabb's 1230sqm property. Yvonne has a guilty conscience though. The 77-year-old grandmother, president of the Blockhouse Bay Garden Club, is fretting about the amount of water she has been pouring on to her climbing beans, shrubs, sunflowers and dahlias.

After 30 years in this house she has come to love its garden, but this summer the shine has worn off and she is even thinking of giving it up. That's because this summer, for the first time, the water bills arrive monthly – and when they do, Yvonne's guilt sets in.

Yvonne and Graeme Dabb's January bill from Watercare was a "horrifying" $126.83 compared with the usual $40 or so of recent months. Last January's invoice was $141.29, but that covered three months. That change to monthly billing helps disguise a big increase for many Aucklanders: council-owned Watercare has increased charges for drinking water and wastewater across most of the new SuperCity.

Imagine if the writer had started with the third paragraph. It's got plenty of information but is hardly likely to hook the reader.

The middle

Once you've got your reader hooked, you are free to start exploring the theme. Remember that everything you write should relate to that theme. Avoid side issues, however intriguing – you are not writing the final word here. In general, features require several voices. A rule of thumb is that you should have interviewed at least three people on top of your research. This should ensure you have a good grasp of the subject, and enough material to tell the readers something new.

Try to group content from a person you interviewed – if they had the best stuff to say about some aspect of the theme – in one section. It's much easier for your reader to keep track this way, and less distracting than having the same person pop up five or six times in different places in the same feature.

Let's take a hypothetical example. Say you're doing a follow-up feature on a spate of car accidents on a particular stretch of road. As a minimum, you have probably talked to someone from the Transport Agency, at least one person from emergency services, a victim or family of a victim, and people who live on the road. Give each of those people a section to themselves, or at least make them the dominant voice in a particular section. The Agency spokesperson might be talking about how the road ranks in terms of danger and whether they're planning to make changes. The cop or ambo driver will hopefully be giving you detail about having to deal with such accidents. That's two sections of your feature. Another section will be taken up with the victim's family talking about the accident and presumably saying something about the stretch of road. And people living on the road may have talked about the fact they've been warning about this for years.

Make each section lead naturally on to the next. Pay attention to how you transition between sections. In our example above, for instance, if you have someone complaining about the hazards on the stretch of road it will probably make sense to immediately follow that with comments from the Transport Agency about the hazards. Get each section to set up the next, and each following section referring back to its predecessor. It's surprising how often adding a simple linking phrase at the start of a section can achieve this (the likes of "in any case" in the next sentence). In any case, you're highly unlikely to lead with the Agency spokesperson before you report what the victim's family has to say.

The end

There are two very simple devices for ending a feature. Use them at will. One is to return to the beginning. In our road accidents example, you might return to someone from the family talking about the victim again, preferably in a way that develops something that was said earlier but without repeating it. The other device is a direct quote. Of course, both can be combined. Avoid the temptation to end with your own summary of the subject.

Sections

It's best when starting out as a writer to plan an outline of your feature before you begin writing: it will not only help you shape your feature but also organise your thoughts. You must group your material, which means your feature is likely to be organised in sections. As suggested above, sections can be based on different aspects of the feature's theme. They can also be based on the different people in the feature. Some people say the best way to organise your material is to find your strongest quotes, copy them out and work from there. Whatever approach you take, each section should follow naturally from the one before, just as sentences do.

Start writing

The best time to start writing your feature is immediately after the final interview. The key is to write while the interview is fresh in your mind. As you drive back to the office, think through what you've got. What was the most telling thing you were told – perhaps because it was funny, or unexpected or revealing? That might give you your intro. If you're lucky, by the time you get back to base you've mentally discarded a couple of possible intros and come up with a workable one – unless you're really lucky and your first intro is your best one. Write it up as soon as you get to a computer.

Once the intro's in place, other material tends to follow. Put your notes and your recording to one side. Skim your notes if you need to, but only to remind yourself of the key points. Don't listen to the recording. Write quickly at first and don't worry about getting names and other details right. You can go back and do that later. At that later stage, you can read properly through your notes or listen right through your recording for killer quotes or to remind yourself of anything you've missed first time round. You can also write yourself a story plan, making sure you have the key points in a sensible order, and reshape your story if you need to.

Narrative

This approach emphasises the short story possibilities of feature writing. Each section is likely to be treated as a chapter, with each chapter finishing with some sort of climax or cliffhanger. There is likely to be use of flashback and prefiguring. Dialogue is particularly valued. Be warned: the reporter needs to accumulate a great deal of detail to pull off this kind of writing.

Nikki Macdonald made good use of these techniques in a Canon Media Award-winning feature she wrote about two people who died in extreme conditions in the Tararua Range (Macdonald, 2010, paras. 10–22). It is written as a narrative, with "chapters" about the two central characters covered chronologically, intercut with chapters providing context, including elements of flashback and foreshadowing.

From that feature, here's an example of attention to detail:

> Back into the pack went a sleeping bag, cooking gear, 1997 Tararua Park map, warm clothes and waterproofs, chocolate afghans, four apples, half a pineapple, streaky bacon, four eggs coddled in newspaper, rice, the remains of that night's freshly baked bread and the new camping coffee plunger he was keen to try out. The tent stayed out.

But it's not detail for detail's sake. Macdonald immediately follows that paragraph with the point:

> It was the logical decision – why take four extra kilograms when you're heading to a hut in a range only 90 minutes' drive from central Wellington, where the highest peaks are a piffling 1500 metres?
>
> But it was a decision that might have cost two lives.

The key is to get as much detail as possible.

Narrative requires detail, and a great amount of reporting. But even if you can't write an entire feature as a narrative, you may still be able to have some narrative within it.

Development of character

The point of profiles and many features is to reveal something of the person you are writing about. This may be shown through the way they talk, the way they dress, the things they do. In Nikki Macdonald's tramping feature, mentioned above as an example of narrative, by the end the reader is left with a mystery that can't fully be resolved, but also a sense of what might have driven the two central people – their motivation.

You won't often have that amount of detail to work with, but you can still reveal things about the person. Remember that it's about "show, not tell". Don't just have your kayaker talking about how much she loves kayaking – show how much she loves it by describing her actually there on the water. Be observant. When you're with the person, you're looking above all for the telling detail, the more incongruous or unexpected the better.

Anecdote

Few human beings fail to respond to a story, and anecdote is at the heart of feature profile writing. A feature writer has the space to tell stories, not just deliver dry facts. Anecdotes could be in the form of stories told about the subject, or by the subject. So

MAINTAINING THE NARRATIVE

Editor-at-large at *North & South* and senior staff writer at *New Zealand Listener*, **Donna Chisholm** is an award-winning feature writer. For her, one of the biggest challenges in feature writing is maintaining a compelling narrative structure to carry the reader through the story.

"I think in long-form feature writing (magazine pieces of 3000–6000 words, say, as opposed to newspaper features of 2500 words or less), maintaining a narrative structure can be achieved in a number of ways.

"I make sure I vary the pace of the sentences – delivering the occasional short sharp shock to bring the reader back on board if the story is becoming too predictable

"Also, resist the temptation of long wadges of direct quotes in favour of distilling them right down and using only those that 'sing'.

"And understand your theme and stick to it. One of the biggest mistakes young feature writers make, in my opinion, is writing 'catch-all' type essays about a subject rather than understanding why the subject is relevant now and sticking to that.

"Of course, originality is the hardest part. The attraction of the cliché can be quite strong! Personally, I find observational/descriptive writing incredibly difficult so tend to avoid it. I think that's wise, because there is nothing worse than forcing it – so much bad writing is done in the name of 'colour'. Urgh.

"I prefer specific descriptions wherever possible in my writing. For example, instead of 'lunch', make it 'raspberry Mountain Dew and a cheese sandwich' – if, for example, that particular food tells you something about the people you're writing about. Mountain Dew and cheese sandwich tells me 'blue-collar lunchbox'. Butternut broccolini and a sauvignon blanc says Ponsonby Road. I remember being particularly pleased to see a forestry worker's witness report in a murder story I was doing call his torch not just a simple old torch but a '12v rechargeable Big John lantern'. Gold! In this way, you don't need adjectives to describe.

"It's easy to forget the value of the 'nut par'. The one or two sentences that tell the reader, fairly early in the story, what it's about and why it might matter to them. For example: 'This isn't simply a story about one woman's drug overdose. It's the story of a greedy pharmaceutical company and the compliant doctors who are putting thousands of us at risk'.

"And resist the urge to put too many voices into a story just because you've interviewed them at length. Sometimes you need to ditch people completely and that can make you weep for the lost time you spent on them.

"But the best feature writing is about the best stories, and the best stories usually involve the best ideas. One of the biggest failings of young feature writers I have seen is that they don't have any ideas. Seriously! They can write beautifully about all manner of things but they're usually stumped about first base – how do I actually get a story? That's why I think it's invaluable ▶

for would-be feature writers to get a solid grounding in news first. Obviously there are exceptions to this.

"But what a news background does provide is the skills to nurture contacts who can give you ideas/exclusives/access to people, improve the speed and sharpness of your writing, understand how features can spin off the back of news and, finally, become familiar with a subject or round and use this understanding to become something of an expert in an area – science, medicine and police come to mind."

the reporter should be looking for them. If you end up with two or three anecdotes for the feature, you're halfway there. This is a variation of "show, not tell".

Here's an example from feature writer Aimie Cronin (Cronin, 2013, paras. 10–22) in a profile she wrote of a long-serving traffic cop, Leo Tooman, who was retiring.

There have been countless bad nights, but the worst is indelibly lodged in his memory.

A call came through one night shift about a collision in Piarere by the Tauranga turn-off. Tooman was coming from Tirau and it was 2.15am. "I arrived to find I was the only person there in the middle of the night. We actually had seven people killed in that one.

"And, ah …"

He pauses.

"It was bloody lonely out there all on your own. Bloody lonely. There was bugger all I could do because most of them were dead."

He remembers the dead of the silence as he waited for colleagues to come and share the load of what he'd witnessed. Real, eerie silence. It took about 20 minutes till he heard them coming from Matamata and Cambridge. He remembers feeling *pretty hopeless, to tell you the truth*. Just the long wait for the sound of sirens. And then the *Thank God they're coming* sound when they finally appeared from empty highways.

He supposes he's so relieved because, well, at least he's got the company out there now for the long night ahead.

"We cleaned up. And it must have been about five in the morning or some time around then when one of the guys said, 'I can hear something'.

"I said, 'What can you hear?'

"We walked along the highway and found a little baby in the drain. So we raced it through to Waikato Hospital and the guy that was nursing the young one, he must have only been in the job a week, he got through the door and the baby passed away in his arms.

"He walked in that Monday morning and resigned. 'Can't pay me enough to do this job,' he says."

Tooman remembers. Takes a deep breath.

"It is a pretty lonely place when you're out there on your own."

Quotes and dialogue

Quotes add voice. Use them but watch out for overuse. Transcribing a recording of an interview can be a trap. Once you have laboriously transcribed, it is easy to copy and paste quotes – plus it may feel like it justifies all those wasted hours taken up by transcribing. The simple solution is not to transcribe, but use your recording to check facts and to find particularly good quotes. The quotes you use should convey something about the person, perhaps their humour, or their distinctive voice. But be careful about capturing every nuance of a quote, particularly colloquialisms. So what if they say "gotta"? Most people do, and you're not telling the reader much by writing it that way – but you are making them pause, however momentarily. Write "got to".

Beware a repetitive pattern in which every second or third par is a direct quote, usually expanding on or developing the preceding paragraph – this becomes tiresome for the reader. It's easy to avoid: go back, have a look, and if you find you've been doing it then paraphrase the quotes. Even worse is to say something and then say the same thing, in slightly different words, in a quote.

Dialogue is a special category and is treasure for the feature writer. This refers to those times when you record two people talking to each other – maybe if you're out in the field with a person and there's a co-worker there as well, or if you're out with someone who's door-knocking and they are chatting to a householder. If the conversation is even remotely interesting you should consider including it in the feature. It is a narrative device used, most obviously, by fiction writers. It puts your reader in the room with the person – or, in the following example from the *Waikato Times*, out in the field. Remember that intro earlier in the chapter about TV presenter Amanda Harper? Here's how the story continues (Cooper, 2011, p. B7):

> It's the first time in front of a camera for DOC staff Kathryn Duggan and Justin Wyatt and Harper spends several minutes encouraging them to speak naturally and to look at her, rather than the camera, during the interview.
>
> "Have you done this before?" she says. "Don't be nervous. It's easy, especially when this is something you are so passionate about."
>
> The interview then runs into its first unscheduled problem: the camera isn't working right.
>
> A couple of minutes later, Kornell has the problem sorted and the interview begins as she counts Harper in.
>
> "Five, four, three ..."
>
> "Tell me about the background of the wetlands here," Harper prompts.
>
> But just a couple of minutes into it, Kornell pipes up with an "oops, sorry" because the camera battery has gone flat. Wyatt takes the opportunity to ask if everything is going all right.
>
> "Yep, that sounded good," Harper says.
>
> Both Wyatt and Duggan say it's a nerve-wracking experience being interviewed on camera. Indeed, Wyatt fluffs his lines several times.
>
> "I just forgot what I was going to say. Sorry, this is really bad," he says, before being reassured about his performance.
>
> "You're doing really good," Harper insists as they get under way again.

If they've said something in a way that can't be bettered, by all means write it as a direct quote.

LOOK FOR THE TELLING MOMENT

Award-winning Stuff feature writer **Adam Dudding** reflects on the value of the anecdote.

"Stalin supposedly said the death of one person is a tragedy but the death of millions is just a statistic. Anecdotes reverse the order. When you read about a telling moment from someone's life, they are transformed back from statistic to tragedy, from banal generality to sharp reality.

"It's okay to include an anecdote simply because it's funny or heart-rending – it's your job to keep the reader entertained. But it's better still if the anecdote does something else at the same time: reveal character, demonstrate hypocrisy, perhaps echo a line from elsewhere in the article.

"I recently wrote a feature about a 13-year-old who shot his grandfather's partner dead. A friend of the victim told me how a few weeks before the murder she'd watched killer and victim chatting away, about some eels the boy had caught in a stream. In just a few sentences, the tale shed light on both the victim (maternal and kind) and the killer (seemingly compliant and an outdoors kind of kid), and restated the central mystery of the crime: that there didn't seem to be a motive.

"During an interview for an arts profile, the subject – an elderly poet – suddenly stopped and hauled me outside to show me a praying mantis on her back porch. It was a surprising, sweet moment which revealed her spark and inquisitive intelligence. It also linked nicely to the fact that her new collection had many poems about insects.

"And sometimes anecdotes, particularly ones involving dialogue, sum things up so you don't have to. After the funeral of Sir Paul Holmes I ended up next to Jonah Lomu at a pedestrian crossing and eavesdropped as he chatted to a woman. I quickly scribbled it down, and it became the closing line: 'It's an interesting day,' said Lomu. 'This is sad. And now I'm going to my son's birthday.'"

Profile writers sometimes use a variation of this, writing up part of their own conversation with the interview subject. This can work well as a way of varying what could otherwise become a very one-dimensional piece of writing. But use it judiciously. Remember that you are not the subject of the feature.

Multimedia

If you have the opportunity to work alongside a videographer, or if you are writing specifically for the web, you need to incorporate the advantages of these forms of presentation into your writing. Web-published features have the obvious advantage of hyperlinks to relevant material. And cooperation with a videographer can lead to

IT'S THE LITTLE THINGS

Author **Kingsley Field** was bureau chief for *The New Zealand Herald* before going freelance. A keen hunter and backwoodsman, he has learnt the importance of fine detail.

"Focusing on something small, something that may be a core part of the whole, and then letting the story build naturally around it – that's what I like to do when writing a feature. And doing that tends to make the whole business so much less complicated – starting off with one little observation about the weather, or the location, or an individual, or a sensation of taste or smell or sight or comfort or even uneasiness.

"All of these things are simple, easily described, are immediately identifiable by readers, and are something to which they can instantly relate. And I believe it is good to tell it like it is, not in complicated words and sentences, but just how it appears to be, whether what is being described is a person, a group, a location or an event.

"The English language is one of the most rich and diverse in the world, with a raft of descriptive words which provide exactly the right nuance. Being a good observer means often sitting quietly and just looking or listening or feeling – and then seeking those specific words to describe that right nuance for the reader.

"Never, ever be too self-important to use reference books on subjects you're not clear about: dictionaries, thesauruses, atlases, books on flowers, or birds or Greek mythology, or music or medicine or Māori language. It may take 20 minutes to find the right reference and/or the right word, but doing that sort of research and getting it right is, I believe, the art of good writing. Building a library of good reference works is fundamental to this sort of work.

"With proper research you're not selling readers short. You're providing them with accurate and reliable information, while at the same time producing material that is enjoyable and easy to understand.

"In the process you're building your own reputation as a writer of informative information that is always a pleasure to read."

some stunningly good overall effects, such as those from multi-Canon award winning videographer Mike Scott. In 2017, he and reporter Olivia Carville won for "Black Gold" (Carville & Scott, 2017).

Background planning the profile interview

Always get the available background on your subject before you interview them. A number of websites will help you dig up information about individuals.

It pays not to rely solely on the internet for your research – you may miss out on information that can still only be found in government departments and offline databases. And sometimes finding authoritative information online can be like searching for a needle in a haystack. But the internet is without question a great starting point. The much-maligned Wikipedia, for example, can give you some excellent leads to start your research. And try newztext as a search engine – it does a great job of searching through articles published in the New Zealand media.

There is no shortage of search engines we can use: Google, Yahoo, AltaVista, Bing (the search engine launched by Microsoft to challenge Google's supremacy) and Pipl. com, a search engine that specialises in searching for people.

All can be effective for researching a person, allowing you to track down documents, news stories, social media profiles, blog posts and comments, for example. Sometimes a Pipl.com search will turn up a person's username, which in turn will let you find them on Twitter, say, or Facebook, or the bookmarking site Delicious.com.

However, there are three golden rules for online research:

- **Check the source is authentic and authoritative:** Is the website credible, does it link to other authoritative websites, is the author credible, does the author have an axe to grind, did the author generate the information or have they copied it from somewhere else?
- **Check when information was last updated:** If it's old, find a newer source or check that it's still valid.
- **Verify the information:** Unless you get information direct from an official source, such as statistics from statistics.govt.nz, you should always corroborate your information by looking at one or two other sources.

Editing

Editing is a key part of writing. No matter how well you think the initial writing is going, it will need tightening. Here are some things to watch for during the editing process.

Clichés

Avoid them (like the plague). Go back through your feature after you've written it and take out all clichés – even some of those fine phrases that felt great when you first put them down. It's fine to write them in the first place – it's almost impossible to write without clichés at first draft. But a big part of writing is editing and, paradoxical though it may sound, that's where you can make your writing fresh.

Adverbs

Ditch them. Find the precise verb instead.

Adjectives

Keep them to a minimum. They clutter up the text.

START WITH YOUR HEADLINE

Staff reporter at *The New Zealand Herald* Steve Braunias has won numerous writing awards during his career, and suggests feature writers think about how the story will look on the page before they start writing.

"I always write the headline first, and then the standfirst. I want the blank page of the screen to resemble a piece of published writing as quickly as possible.

"Also, the headline and the standfirst can be really helpful in establishing the tone of the piece you're about to write. One-word headlines – so dominant, so confident – are good to look at when you're writing.

"I start a feature at the beginning and finish it at the end. I write each sentence at a time. And I only start when I've got all the information, and all the interviews. I never discuss the story with anyone. Their stupid ideas will only get in the way.

"I place a lot of importance in narrative and probably more importance in language. I'm always hoping that some good sentences will make themselves known to me.

"I often use long quotes – I love the sound of people's voices in print, the way they control the narrative for a while at least.

"I think a lot about how to proceed, what to leave out, when to quit showing the story and just tell it. Some of these things are simple decisions, like the issue of whether or not to include yourself in the story. Do it if you think your presence makes it a better story; don't if you think you're in the way.

"None of which is of any use if you don't have a good story. It's a game of two halves – get the get, and then get writing."

Context

Feature writing is a chance to stretch out and try things. If you enjoy it, your readers probably will too.

Have you given key context and ordered your story so your reader is never left wondering? Are there gaps? Remember that your reader doesn't know what you know. It's easy to absorb your subject so thoroughly that you forget to include basic facts.

Lengthy biographical detail is boring. Keep only that which is important for your story. You're not writing someone's CV. Add any such detail in the places it is important for your reader's understanding but preferably not too high up the story. If you find you are rehearsing someone's early life, ask yourself: Is this essential?

When you've finished

If you have time, it's a great idea to read what you've written out loud to yourself, preferably on your own in a quiet room. It's astonishing how often you hear a stumble that you hadn't seen.

If you get the chance, it's also good to put the feature aside for a while and read it fresh before handing it in. That requires some organisation, but having an hour with a feature the morning after writing it can help immensely with polishing.

Further reading

Cotton, B. (2012). *Feature writing: Notes, brief overview.* Retrieved from http://www. journalismtraining.co.nz/NZJTO/E-Learning/Feature-writing-notes-brief-overview

Cotton, B. (2012). *Feature writing: A full overview.* Retrieved from http://www. journalismtraining.co.nz/NZJTO/E-Learning/Feature-writing-full-overview

Pape, S., & Featherstone, S. (2006). *Feature writing – a practical introduction.* Los Angeles: Sage.

Spark, D., & Harris, G. (2011). *Practical newspaper reporting.* Los Angeles: Sage.

Sumner, D., & Miller, H. (2009). *Feature and magazine writing: Action, angle and anecdotes.* Hoboken: Wiley-Blackwell.

Tanner, S., Kasinger, M., & Richardson, N. (2012). *Feature writing: Telling the story.* South Melbourne: Oxford University Press.

References

Carville, O., & Scott, M. (2017). *Black gold.* Retrieved from www.nzherald.co.nz/indepth/national/black-gold/

Cooper, T. (2011, May 14). Broadcast news. *Waikato Times*, p. B7.

Cronin, A. (2013, April 5). *The lonely road travelled.* Retrieved from www.stuff.co.nz/waikato-times/life-style/8515084/The-lonely-road-travelled

Macdonald, N. (2010, October 23). *Lost: How tramp turned to tragedy.* Retrieved from www.stuff.co.nz/dominion-post/capital-life/features/4258473/Lost-how-tramp-turned-to-tragedy

Macdonald, N. (2017, October 14). Airbnb: Home-sharing or home-snaring? *The Dominion Post*, p. C1.

Powley, K. (2013, February 17). *The rising cost of our fresh water.* Retrieved from www.nzherald.co.nz/nz/news/article.cfm?c_id=1&objectid=10865847

Stephenson, S. (2017, October). Buy now: Pay for it later. *North & South*, pp. 66–70.

16

News photography
How to take great news photos

Greg Treadwell, AUT University

Many digital cameras can take video and still images. For guidance on video, see Chapter 18.

Photographs can linger in the minds of readers long after the words of a story have faded away. Often the real power of the story lies in its illustration, and famous images punctuate our histories and can be recalled by vast numbers of people in ways no written news story will ever be. Our collective memory is rich with pictures that have come to represent the pivotal moments and the great events of our time: moon landings, wars, natural wonders, natural disasters, political upheavals, the coronation of monarchs and the downfall of dictators.

In New Zealand we can think of classic news images, like the 1979 plane crash on Mt Erebus, the 1985 bombing of the *Rainbow Warrior* and Dame Whina Cooper leading the land march of 1975. And more recently, we've seen images of the Kaikōura earthquakes and the All Blacks' Rugby World Cup wins. News pictures still dominate the front page of every newspaper and most news websites. They're often the reader's first port of call in their journey through a story, which means pictures have to reveal their message quickly, and bring a compulsive response from the reader. One of their main purposes is to bring the reader's eye to the story, to hook them in. Pictures can draw focus with ease while nearby headlines struggle to stand out. They demand attention and can then take your breath away.

News photographers have not been immune to the effects of technological

Photos, like this one of the pitched battles fought in New Zealand streets during the 1981 Springbok rugby tour, record events in ways words cannot. Here, anti-tour protesters and rugby supporters clash on Sandringham Road outside Eden Park, Auckland.

Ref: EP/1981/3106/17a-F. Alexander Turnbull Library, Wellington, New Zealand

convergence and budget constraints being experienced by the news media (Ellis, 2010). The very nature of their job is changing. Video footage is now required for online news services, as well as still pictures, and so the need for videographers is increasing. If you can take both pictures and video, well that's all the better. Pictures are also now expected from a wider range of journalists, including reporters. So if you can write stories, shoot video and take pics, well, that's all the better too.

News photography is a highly skilled craft and anyone picking up a camera for the first time has much to learn. Their first task is to get to know the camera, probably starting at its manual. But because today almost everyone takes pictures and we live in an image-saturated world, many journalists start out with a strong understanding of visual media, and can quite readily take their photographs to the next level. We'll start off with the technical details and then look at the techniques for taking great news photographs.

Some news stories – called caption stories or fat caps – exist solely because they have a large, striking photo.

The equipment you should have

Fantastic pictures can be taken on almost any camera. Sometimes a point-and-shoot pocket camera, or even a mobile phone, will do the job. But if you are really interested in photography and the impact it can have, you will need gear that lets you work in the upper ranges of photographic decision-making and control.

There are dozens of suitable digital single-lens reflex (DSLR) cameras on the

Many New Zealanders will recognise this image of the *Rainbow Warrior*, sunk in Auckland harbour by French agents in 1985. A photographer, Fernando Pereira, died in the attack.

Greenpeace / John Miller
www.greenpeace.org.nz

market, either 35mm or the significantly more expensive medium-format, and there is no limit to what you can spend on the camera body, lenses, filters, tripods, lights, reflectors, bags, batteries and chargers. But if you do want to buy a basic kit for news and feature work, then you will need at least:

- a 35mm DSLR camera body, with built-in flash and shoulder strap
- two zoom lenses (one 18–55mm in focal length to capture wide-angled images and another 55–200mm or 80–400mm for pictures that magnify the subject)
- circular polarising filters for your lenses – these are used in bright-light outdoor settings, reducing glare and blown-out highlights, giving strong definition to clouds and eliminating reflections from surfaces like glass
- a tripod (handy for all sorts of long-exposure photos, but good photographers often improvise with a fence post or a pile of books)
- a camera bag, spare batteries and a charger, and memory cards.

Light

Flash, either direct or bounced off walls, can be used to fill out dark areas.

Without light, of course, there are no photos at all. Light falls in myriad circumstances: from the sun and stars, through clouds, through trees, off buildings, from neon signs or through an open window. It is both the ultimate material and enabler of all photography. When taking pictures, look for how the light is falling on the face of your subject. What happens if you move them to another room?

Watch how changing light changes your pictures. Work with highlights in the scene, things which the light is accentuating. Working with natural light produces the best pictures. Avoid using a flash if you can. If you have to, and have the gear capable of doing it, try softening your flash by bouncing it off a wall, ceiling or other reflector. Experiment with diffusing it through fabric. If you must use flash, make sure your subject is far enough away from the background to avoid harsh and ugly flash shadows.

Exposure

Once you understand that a picture is nothing without the light falling on its

GET YOURSELF A CAMERA AND USE IT

Qiane Matata-Sipu (Te Wai-o-Hua, Tainui, Te Arawa, Ngāpuhi, Cook Islands) is a freelance writer and photographer.

After she left journalism school for jobs at *Mana* magazine and then *Spasifik* magazine she found photography becoming an increasingly large part of her daily work.

"I hoped I would have some sort of pictorial element to my work because I loved photography. But I didn't expect it to have as much weight in my career as it has had. It just showed me you can't just be a reporter these days or you can't just be a photojournalist. You have to be more than one thing … otherwise you're just not as employable as you could be."

She taught herself basic camera skills, and with practice and determination became professional enough to conduct highly successful cover shoots. Among her best-known pictures are of Special Air Services hero Willie Apiata (Ngāpuhi) after he was awarded a Victoria Cross, and the Māori King, Te Arikinui Kiingi Tuheitia, taken as part of the first interview he gave after his coronation.

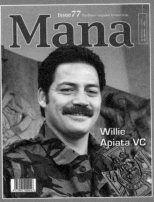

Not long out of journalism school, Qiane Matata-Sipu was taking cover shots like this one of Victoria Cross recipient Willie Apiata.

Photo: *Mana magazine*

Her advice to would-be photographers is to "learn how to use a camera and then use it – on anything and everything. Because the more practice you do, the better you get."

If you haven't studied photography, she suggests you attend a photography workshop. "Just to learn how to shoot in manual, because if you can't shoot in manual you aren't really going to be able to produce the best shots."

She revels in the world of photography. "You can capture an entire story in one image, and that image can say more than any of your work put down on a piece of paper. Because you can capture the emotion, the situation, the connection between people, you can capture all the unspoken things and the things you can't really explain in words. And that's the power of photography."

subject, you can begin to understand that letting the right amount of light into the camera is the secret behind a usable picture. Exposure refers to the quantity of light that enters the lens when the camera's shutter is activated. An overexposed image has had too much light brought to the image and has lost detail in the light parts of the picture, which are blown out. An underexposed image needed more light, and so is dark and has lost details in the shadowy parts of the picture.

There are three things that influence the final exposure – the shutter speed (how long light is let in for when the photo is taken), the F-stop aperture setting (how wide open the lens is when the shutter fires), and the ISO setting (how responsive the camera's light sensor is to light).

The best exposure for any picture is the result of all three settings working together to create a picture. All three need to be in balance – called the "exposure triangle" – and if one setting is changed, say the shutter speed shortened from 1/125th of a second to 1/500th of a second, one or both of the others will need to be adjusted as well to maintain an adequate exposure and make sure the picture comes out well.

The automatic settings on your camera will look after this for you, of course, and will almost always get you a serviceable picture. But you can have more control over your pictures if you work in manual or semi-manual settings, which allow you to prioritise the shutter in certain circumstances, the aperture in others, and in others still, the ISO setting.

Shutter speed priority

By turning your camera settings to shutter priority (the time value of the exposure) you can set the shutter speed at a certain speed to achieve some purpose (say, setting it at a fast 1/1000th of a second to freeze a fast-moving bird which would otherwise be blurry).

Aperture priority

Changing the aperture allows you to increase or decrease the depth of field, which is the area in the picture, from near to far away, that is in focus. Use a smaller aperture (counter-intuitively, that's the larger F-stop numbers on your lens or in your viewfinder, say F16 or F22) if you want things in both the foreground and the background sharp. Use a wider aperture (say, F2.8) to have your foreground and subject sharp and the background soft.

ISO priority

If you increase the ISO on your camera, it will be able to capture more in darker situations. But, also, the higher the number, the more grainy, or "noisy", the image will be. So in low-light situations, you might like to increase the ISO, which will let you shorten the shutter time and let you avoid camera-shake, but the price will be a grainier image. In well-lit situations, if you want very fine images, keep your ISO setting low, say 100.

Zoom lenses and focal lengths

Zoom refers to a lens's ability to move from one focal length to another, changing the visual approach to the subject from wide to narrow and back.

Wide-angled zoom lenses (generally from 16mm to 55mm in focal length) let the photographer get width and depth into an image and are best used when the wider, physical context of the subject-matter is important.

Here a wide-angle lens has allowed the photographer to also capture the diners in the background.

Here a telephoto lens has brought the distant peninsula apparently closer to the vineyard.

Long-focus lenses (often called telephoto, though for technical reasons not all are strictly telephoto) tend to have focal lengths from 70mm up to 400mm or above. They magnify the subject and make things behind it seem closer to it. They can turn a distant object into a fine photo.

The elements of a good news photo

Instead of recording a family holiday or proclaiming to be art, what news photos do is reveal events and issues in terms of news values – things such as entertainment, magnitude and relevance. Photos help promote the content of news and help us organise, interpret and understand the current affairs of the world.

For more on news values, see Chapter 2.

SPORTS PHOTOGRAPHY

Sports photographers favour very high-speed cameras and lenses with long focal lengths, for example 1000mm. This allows them to capture fast-moving people and objects in sharp focus and to fill the frame with images that are far away.

If you're covering a local game, don't take wide shots that feature lots of players on the field. These will look bland and lack a point of interest for the viewer. Concentrate on capturing a few players, one or two, locked in competition. Capture the determination on their faces, their concentration on the ball, the sweat on their faces.

You need to take many photos to ensure you capture all the crucial moments of the game: the match-winning goal, the defensive blunder, the delighted captain. It's usually a good idea to throw the backgrounds, especially of spectators, out of focus to concentrate on the foreground action. For inspiration, check out the sports pages of the main metropolitan dailies, which regularly feature great sports shots.

News organisations often ask the public for photos and video of big breaking stories, taken on mobile phones or other digital devices. For more on this, see Chapter 4.

Sometimes these news values may have little to do with the skills of the photographer. A very poor snapshot, taken with no thoughts of publication at the time, can become highly newsworthy if it is the only image available of an important event. But in general, newsrooms are after pictures that tell stories, are technically sound, have a clear centre of interest, have people in them, show emotion, have drama and in some way epitomise news.

Viewers tend to respond emotionally to pictures and may not be able to clearly articulate what makes them like the ones they do.

But there are plenty of hard-to-argue-with theories about what makes a great news picture. Here are some ideas that photographers seeking to improve their pictures can use.

Focus

A common mistake young reporters make is to submit out-of-focus photos to their editor. Never do it. Fuzzy photos of your subject will never be published. Submitting them wastes everybody's time.

With a DSLR camera you can choose to have the camera find its focus point itself or you can set the camera and lens to manual focus and use the focus ring on the lens. With automatic focus, the camera will find focus when you half-depress the shutter. Then press all the way to fire.

You can throw backgrounds out of focus to focus on a foreground subject. You can have part of a photo out of focus to suggest movement.

If you know something fast is going to happen in a particular place, pre-focus the camera and then capture the event as it happens.

Never, ever, submit a photo to your editor where the subject is out of focus. That is simply sloppy work.

Composition

Composing pictures, as opposed to just snapping them, is the first step towards effective photography. The rule for photographers and their compositions is: be bold.

Composition describes the jigsaw of things that make up your picture – that is, how its elements fit together and how the relationships between them create meaning. For example, one of the most common pictures in news is the environmental portrait, in which the photographer works to relate the human subject to the environment in which the picture is taken to reveal something of their life and character. It might be ex-servicemen at the RSA, a sex worker on a street corner or a chief executive in the boardroom, but what is common to all pictures is the articulated relationship between subject and background.

Landscape versus portrait

At each shoot, try experimenting with the basic format of your pictures. By turning the camera 90 degrees, you can try both a vertical frame (portrait) and a horizontal one (landscape) and consider their different virtues. In general terms, if you are photographing a quiet scene, the landscape format will enhance any sense of tranquillity, while the portrait format will enhance anything dramatic going on in your picture. But these are guidelines only, of course, because photography is experimental in nature and often great shots come from ignoring the rules. We'll talk more about portraits later.

A portrait of meningitis survivor and quadruple amputee Charlotte Cleverley-Bisman when she was less than two years old. Getting close and down low means Charlotte fills the frame and as a result the photo can honour her remarkable story.

Photo: *Gulf News*/Greg Treadwell

Fill the frame with your subject

Famous photographer Robert Capa once said, "If your photographs aren't good enough, you're not close enough" (Magnum Photos, 2017, para. 1). This is important advice. Tempting though it might be to try to capture an entire scene, most of the time it's better to get close, physically or with a telephoto lens, if necessary, and fill your viewfinder with the object of your attention.

Having too many competing elements in a picture is likely to weaken its impact. A news picture, which captures a moment in the story to help explain the whole story, needs a strong, clear centre of interest. Approach your composition boldly and affirmatively, and let your subject dominate the photograph.

But experiment with this rule too. Move the subject around inside your frame and take pictures as you do – try moving the subject towards the top of the frame to give more weight to the image's foreground. Then try to change the emphasis on the background, and shoot again. Another example: if you are photographing a moving subject, say a car or a sportsperson, then it's a good idea to leave some space in front of the subject in the picture so it doesn't seem about to hit the edge of the frame.

If you are attending a meeting, don't stand at the back and take photos of the backs of people's heads with some speakers way off in the distance. Get in close. Get dramatic shots of the speakers or of one or two members of the crowd.

Think carefully about the background

Novice news photographers are infamous for returning to the newsroom with a picture of someone with a power pole or something similar growing out of their head. At the time the photo is being taken it is easy not to spot the offending item in the viewfinder, as the photographer's attention is on the foreground, but it's impossible not to see it once the photo is captured and reviewed. It's an easy mistake to make, but it reduces the effectiveness of the picture considerably, often making it unpublishable.

So when framing your image, make sure you have considered its background. Is the subject you're photographing clear of such interfering detail? It's easy to move the subject, or indeed yourself, to solve any such issues. Often a plain background will enhance the definition of your subject, but sometimes a busy background might be just what you want – for example, when photographing a mechanic in his workshop it might be most effective to set him against a wall with dozens of hanging tools. Another effective technique is to throw the background slightly out of focus. This means the viewer concentrates on the image in the foreground, but can still recognise the background scene. Whatever your decision, don't leave the background to take care of itself.

Consider your angles

Always set your camera to the highest resolution, so the photo can be cropped and/or enlarged without loss of picture quality.

Photographers who take their pictures from a simple standing position too often produce dull pictures. Instead, make sure you regularly take pictures from below, looking up at your subjects (a low angle), and from above, looking down (a high angle), as well as moving your camera around them to good effect.

Low angles make subjects seem more powerful and give your pictures oomph, and high angles tend to imply less power. A politician celebrating an election win is best shot from below, arms in the air, while the loser contemplating what might have been could be taken from above. With children, get down to their level and frame the world as they see it. If you are at a retirement village, have a seat in the sunroom and try seeing things that way. Varying your angles emphasises the centre of interest in your picture – the thing at the heart of your pic – in different ways.

Experienced news photographers develop an instinct for their angles, and both think and feel their way through the taking of a photo. They respond to content, light, depth and detail all at once. Combine these variations with the different angles provided by lenses with different focal lengths and you will be able to inject energy into your pictures with success.

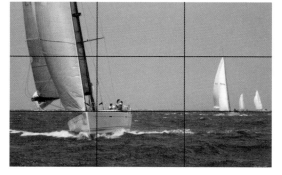

The rule of thirds helps organise a photograph's composition and creates a sense of interest that's pleasing to the eye.

The rule of thirds

An impulse to always centre the subject within the frame is also a common mistake. Of more interest to the eye are the lines that divide a picture into thirds, both horizontally and vertically. A picture has more energy when its points of interest lie on these imaginary lines and, even more so, at the places where these lines intersect. This is known as the rule of thirds. If the photographer hasn't quite placed something of interest – a pair of eyes, a face, a tree or a soldier at war – on these lines, this can still be achieved during the editing process with a calculated crop that will change the position of elements in relation to the frame.

Uncropped

Cropped

A judicious crop can shift elements in the image to better agree with the rule of thirds.

Photo: Björn Bechstein/Flickr

Photo: Dave Merrett/Flickr

Using leading lines and framing

If the scene you are photographing has natural lines – for example, the edge of a road, building or railway line – try using them to bring the viewer's eye to the centre of interest.

Framing the subject in a doorway, under an arch in a garden, through the branches of a tree or through a window frame are all handy ways of emboldening your subject.

The crop is the most significant alteration made to a photo once you have taken it. This is where you remove part of the photo to strengthen its composition.

Portraits

Portraits are some of the most common news images, despite the lack of action they might imply. It's a good genre to master – it involves skills required by all journalists: trust-building, honesty and empathy with your subject. Features and profiles on the famous, the infamous and the hitherto-unknown all require portraits so the reader can, to some extent, gauge the character of the subject for themselves. Of course, that judgement will likely be heavily influenced by the choices made by the photographer, who angles their photo much as a reporter angles their story.

The portrait photographer's job is to work the subject into a context that is more than the sum of its parts and helps tell their story. Good portraits reveal their subjects in subtle ways and have the viewer pause, look again and think. A master at this is New Zealand's Jane Ussher, whose work is acknowledged as among the finest.

Eye contact in a photo creates a connection with the viewer. It is like we are having a subliminal conversation with the subject. If there is no eye contact, we feel more like an observer on the subject. With portraits, it's often good to get both and decide later which works best.

Portraits should honour their subject, but don't have to always be serious. Here

Portraits do not have to be serious.

Photos: Greg Treadwell

Never take headshots against a window with strong light behind the subject. Their face will be hopelessly under-exposed.

Always check your photos before leaving the scene. Never leave a scene until you have good photos.

the late Malcolm Harrison, an extraordinary fabric artist whose work adorns Parliament Buildings in Wellington, lets us see his eccentric side as well as his serious side during a photo shoot. Notice too how the eye contact in the first two photos connects us to the subject, whereas the lack of eye contact in the third photo makes us observers.

Headshots

An important skill for any news photographer is to effectively and succinctly capture that most perfunctory of portraits, the headshot. It's often called a mugshot in the newsroom, but in fact anything akin to a square-on police identity photo will have the illustrations editor back at the office squirming.

Think about the light – do you want it coming from behind, in front or the side? Is it harsh, meaning the picture would benefit from a filter, say a gauze curtain? Is it too soft, and would it be better to move the subject outdoors? Ask your subject to turn their shoulders away from the camera and then their face back to the lens. That way you avoid the standard mugshot look.

Working with subjects

Sometimes the photographer is a passive observer, who tries to be as unobtrusive as possible, creating fly-on-the-wall photos documenting events. The idea is for the subjects to forget you are even there.

Other times, however, the photographer has to create a shot, a set-up, and must direct their subjects to achieve the desired end. Some subjects – like politicians and celebrities – are used to having their photos taken, but many others will not be. They will often be shy, awkward and keen for the whole experience to end quickly. It is up to you to take charge.

Make sure you interact with your subjects. Be open and friendly, address them by their names, tell them where you'd like them to stand. Think of some simple props they can use, or somewhere they can go, so that the photo reflects the accompanying story. Ask them for ideas. Smile.

Don't have too many set-ups. Decide on one or two and then take lots of photos of those. Have the camera set to take multiple shots, to ensure there are a few where the subjects are not blinking or looking odd.

When taking the photos, give your subjects encouragement. Say, "Yes, that's it, great. Lovely! Keep doing that."

If you're taking a photo of a group of people, ask them to stay in the same position afterwards so you can get all their names in the same order they appear in your photos. This will be needed for the caption.

Here the subject is lit from behind by sunlight. While the halo effect can work well, watch for glare and loss of detail in the face.

Here she is lit by direct sunlight – this approach tends to lack any subtlety and creates hard shadows.

Side lighting gives faces texture and character.

Soft, over-the-shoulders lighting creates a quieter, more moody portrait.

Make sure one of the first things you master is the headshot.

Don't be shy. If you're in a classroom taking photos of kids and you think you need to be higher up to get a better shot, get on a desk (ask permission first!). If you think the kids in the front row should sit down, ask them to do so. If the kids need to stand closer to each other, get them to do it.

For details on writing photo captions, see Chapter 14.

Be confident. If you're confident, your subjects will have confidence in you and will photograph better. Be enthusiastic and relaxed. Again, this will be communicated to your subjects and you'll get better images.

Editing

In general terms, less is much more when it comes to photo editing for news publications and websites. Software can be used to alter images to extraordinary degrees, to fraudulently present something as something else entirely if so desired, but the honesty required in all news means very little should be done to a news image in the post-production phase. Unless you are editing it overtly and signficantly for display purposes, say clear-cutting it (removing it from its background entirely) or adding text to it to form parts of a feature layout, then tweaking to optimise the image visually is all you should do. In editing software like Photoshop you can change the brightness, contrast and sharpness and make sure its colour mode is correct for the type of publishing (RGB for online, CMYK for print). You might also save it in an appropriate format (.jpg, .png, .tif, for example). You can also crop the photo and remove red-eye. But apart from these things, leave it alone.

TAKING COMMUNITY NEWS PHOTOS

Rhiannon McConnell often took the photos that accompanied her community news stories. Here's a behind-the-scenes look at some of her favourite shots (all photos courtesy *Wainuiomata News*).

"The most common thing I hear in my job is, 'Oh, I don't normally have my photo taken. I really don't like having my photo taken.' It's up to you to make your subjects feel comfortable, because it comes across in the lens if someone is feeling awkward.

"I will wait till the end of an interview to take a photo because by that time you've built up a little bit of trust and a relationship with your interviewee, so they've warmed up a lot. I'll then say, 'I'd like to take a quick photo.' I use words like 'quick' and 'small', so people realise it's not a big deal. I also tell them that a story is more likely to be read if it has a photo – many people understand that and so agree to being photographed.

"I will talk to them the whole time I'm taking the photo. If you stop talking and just take photos, they begin to be aware of the situation and start feeling awkward. I just make jokes, I talk about the interview, the weather, ask them what they're doing next – are they going to pick up the kids? It depends on the mood of the story. If it's a light story, where I want a smile or a laugh, I'll joke about a bit. If it's a serious story I'll talk more about the story and the issue, so the emotion will come across in their face."

River

"This story was about a man concerned about pollution in a river. I organised to meet him at the river. I talked through the issues with him and this photo was taken mid-point in the conversation. That's why he has a suitably serious look on his face.

"It is important to learn the rule of thirds and composition. In a lot of my photos I put the person slightly off to the side as that's a lot more eye-catching.

"I put him in the foreground with the river in the background. The human interest is the person in the photo; if they're too far back that gets lost. The composition would be wrong. The background needs to remain a background, but adding to the story. I asked him to crouch down. If he had been standing, again, it would have been bad composition. By crouching, I was able to get him, the river and the stones in."

▶

Chemist

"She was just standing up straight at first, so I told her to stand the way she is in the photo. The composition is better, as it creates a triangle. Your eyes go from the point at the top, her face, to the other two points, one under each arm.

"I often physically show my subjects what I want them to do, to crouch a certain way or lean a certain way."

Planting

"This was a spontaneous shot. I was out with a bunch of kids planting. I was walking around taking photos. I walked up to this little girl and said, 'Can I take your photo?' She looked at the camera, but carried on planting.

"I like eye contact because it engages the viewer. When you look at this photo you first look at her eyes, and you can see the emotion in her face and that she's really enjoying it."

Weet-Bix

"Props are really, really important. Often, I will have an idea in my head of what photo I want and then I can think about what props are needed.

"This story was about a school providing breakfasts for its pupils. The woman is a teacher at the school. I asked her to bring along some of the

boxes they had of the breakfasts. If it didn't have the Weet-Bix boxes in there, it would just be a woman in a classroom. But looking at the photo you can tell it's got something to do with breakfast and she's involved in it."

Cupboard

"I always try when I take photos to answer some of the questions created by the story. Part of this article was about a foodbank not having enough storage space for food. Readers would want to know how large the cupboard is – well, they can see."

▶

Road

"This one is an example of depth of field. First you see him, so you know he's involved in the story. Then your eyes follow the sign and see the road. The story was about how a subdivision was going to be built on the road."

Rugby

"This was a rugby story so I organised to meet him at the rugby club. I wanted to get the goal posts, the field and the club building in the background, and the ball. Without looking at the story or the headline, you know the story's about rugby."

Boxer

Always think about props you can use in photos (objects, animals, etc.). Have a look at Rhiannon's photos for inspiration on this.

"This is an example of side lighting and of me changing my plan halfway through a shoot. I first tried a few photos of her hitting a punch bag, but the background wasn't right and it was too dark. There were some guys sparring in the ring and the gym had strong fluorescent lighting. I put her next to one of the lights, with the ring in the background, and it turned out much better."

Apples

"I like the triangle composition. Also, a splash of bright colour – like red or blue – attracts the eye."

Rhiannon's final pieces of advice

"If, for some reason, we can't get a photo that adds to the story, I just take a headshot. For headshots, a good idea is to have plain, non-distracting backgrounds. I ask people to move around, so I get different lighting, then choose the best shot later."

Rhiannon uses a Canon 550D camera, but says any DSLR camera is fine. "It's how you use the camera and the lighting that matters. Some of my best photos have been iPhone photos. The iPhone has a rubbish flash, so it works best for outdoor photos or well-lit places." In fact, Rhiannon took the Weet-Bix photo on her iPhone.

The photo should back up and add to the story, she says. "The photo is what people will look at first. Then they will decide, even before reading the headline, whether to read the story. Look through newspapers and collect the photos that catch your eye. You'll soon see common themes. If they catch your eye, they'll probably catch other people's eyes too."

If you've attended an event and have a collection of great photos, you can also create a slideshow of your images. This can be loaded onto your news organisation's website.

The role of the news photographer

From the gruesome images of war to the awful behaviour of the paparazzi – the ethical issues in photography are never far away. As a US Supreme Court judge put it, ethics is knowing the difference between what you have a right to do and what is right to do. A photographer in a public place has strong, though by no means unlimited, rights to photograph what they see, even if what they see is on private property.

Check out the world's best photos in both single and multimedia presentations at worldpressphoto.org

They are working in the public interest. They are intent on making meaning with their photos to tell the stories that give rise to the public sphere. They are on the side of the repressed, in theory, and are a key part of the media's arsenal in speaking truth to power.

Photojournalists bear witness to our lives and urge us to engage with the realities they put before us. The subject might be children dancing in the streets or the impact of a nuclear disaster, but every news photo is in some way an argument about the nature of reality and the circumstances of the world. News pictures are not just a good way of making the website look pretty, accessorising the news, but are in their own right a powerful news platform.

The photographer's message is an important one, often intended to prick the conscience. They tells us not just about the scenes they are witnessing but about the people in them and how they cope in the world. Sometimes a picture is of a moment from the chaos of civil unrest and records the events for posterity. But on other occasions a photojournalist isolates subjects from the tapestry of everyday life in scenes that reveal meaning in the ordinary that we might have otherwise missed (Tom Ives' photo of Ecuadorian girls overleaf, for example).

Still images can truly embody the people side of news – they are rich in human interest, capturing both our triumphs and, perhaps more often than we would like, our pain and ability to endure suffering. Photojournalism is essentially a humanist endeavour and holds power to account by humanising the story. The best photojournalists work from a deep assumption of empathy with the people in their pictures and the people affected by the events they photograph. Though sometimes painful, their work is ultimately a powerful celebration of life and all sorts of people everywhere are the subject of their pictures. What's the most important thing? As the Māori proverb says, "He tangata, he tangata, he tangata" ("It is people, it is people, it is people").

For more on journalistic ethics, see Chapter 21.

For the final word, let's turn to Paul Martin Lester, whose book *Photojournalism: An ethical approach* is required reading for young photojournalists and camera-carrying reporters:

> A photojournalist is a mixture of a cool, detached professional and a sensitive, involved citizen … the technical aspects of the photographic process are not the primary concerns.

Photo: Tom Ives

GIRLS WITH CHICKENS

Not every great photo is of a major news event and not every meaningful picture is taken on a DSLR camera. This image, of young girls in Ecuador, was taken in 2013 by Tom Ives, known for more than 25 years of work specialising in human rights and social justice issues and shooting for news and feature magazines including *Time*, *National Geographic* and *Newsweek*.

But this picture was taken on a cellphone from across the street, and Ives says it is his favourite image from that year. In contrast to the dramatic work of his earlier years, during which he covered the homeless in the United States and the victims of nuclear devastation in Japan, this type of documentary journalism asks us more subtle questions about the lives of so-called everyday folk.

"These young girls are practising to be mothers," he explains. "They are holding chickens, the youngest with the slung-out hip of a mother carrying her offspring. The older sister is gazing lovingly at her baby brother in the stroller."

The image speaks of "the universal essence of why we are here – to have children, lots of them, so they will love us and nurture us with that love". It also speaks of the solace we can find in nature's rhythms if we raise our own chickens and don't forget where eggs come from, he says.

"This all came in a nanosecond of seeing them. Everybody looks at things, [but] seeing is intuitive, built on life experience: where you are, how it changes you, how it can change others through your personal vision ... There are just these three elements to all of this. If you don't have one of the three, look for other work."

A mother crying over the death of her daughter is not simply an image to be focused, a print to be made, and a picture to be published. The mother's grief is a lesson in humanity.

If the photojournalist produces a picture without a thought for her tragedy, the lesson is lost. But if the photographer cares for her loss, is made more humane, and causes the readers to share in her grief, photojournalism has reached its highest potential (Lester, 1999).

ADVICE FROM A PRO

New Zealand photojournalist Maggie Gould has captured images of people all over the world. Her famous portrait of Māori land-rights campaigner Dame Whina Cooper (right) is held at Te Papa. Gould's message to aspiring news photographers is to "love what you shoot".

Photo: Maggie Gould

"Have fun. Have interest in and patience with the subject. If you are bored, it will show in your images.

"Great distances are covered by sensible walking shoes.

"Taking photographs is a passion, not a career. Create your own assignments that are heartfelt – imagine your dream job and go and shoot it.

"Learn compositional tools from the work of master photographers and classical painters. Learn from the movies.

"Study and theory is useful, but you learn most by doing. Try not to look for pictures but keep yourself always open to really seeing."

Further reading and viewing

Lester, P. (1999). *Photojournalism: An ethical approach.* Available at http://commfaculty.
fullerton.edu/lester/writings/pjethics.html

Silver, S. (2010). *The bang bang club* [Motion picture]. Canada; South Africa: Adam
Friedlander. A drama about photographers in apartheid-era South Africa.

Ussher, J. (2004). *New Zealand Listener portraits.* Auckland: Random House.

www.voyagermediaawards.co.nz The Voyager (previously Canon) Media Awards are the
New Zealand journalism industry's awards for excellence. Every year, the award-winning
news photos are published online.

www.magnumphotos.com Magnum is a world-famous cooperative of photographers.

www.tepapa.govt.nz/WhatsOn/exhibitions/BrianBrake Brian Brake was a famous New
Zealand photojournalist.

www.worldpressphoto.org An international organisation dedicated to photojournalism.

References

Ellis, G. (2010, August). *Paying the piper.* Paper presented as part of the series "The end(s) of
journalism?" Seminar conducted at the University of Auckland, New Zealand.

Lester, P. (1999). *Photojournalism: An ethical approach.* Retrieved from http://commfaculty.
fullerton.edu/lester/writings/pjethics.html

Magnum Photos. (2017). *Robert Capa.* Retrieved from http://www.magnumphotos.com/C.
aspx?VP3=CMS3&VF=MAGO31_9_VForm&ERID=24KL535353

17

Radio journalism

Writing and presenting news in the fast-paced, ever-changing world of radio

Jo Scott

Radio is a rush. It is the fastest, most personal way to deliver news *en masse* and the industry is filled with passionate, dedicated professionals who relish the challenge of taking a complex issue and translating it to their audience within minutes.

Radio has immediacy, Lesley Deverall, editor at Newstalk ZB, says. "What's important one hour may pale into insignificance the next. It gives reporters huge scope to cover a variety of things, and I love the excitement of it, the pace and the adrenalin." The industry offers enormous scope to its reporters. The chance to cover breaking news instantaneously, the opportunity to front that coverage through live crosses and voice reports, as well as the creative licence to get into the field, record your own audio and craft longer pieces that really are theatre of the mind.

New Zealand has one of the highest numbers of radio stations per capita in the world, so there are plenty of job opportunities (Encyclopedia of the Nations, 2017). The main employers of radio journalists in New Zealand are the three major networks: the government-owned RNZ and commercial networks, Newstalk ZB (NZME) and Radio Live (MediaWorks).

Tight deadlines bring phenomenal pressure. What's more, the stories you produce have to be compelling – you will be competing for your audience's attention, so you have to cut to the heart of the issue, grab their ears and make them want to listen to more.

Radio is increasingly becoming multimedia. For instance, as well as its radio broadcasts and its website, RNZ these days broadcasts some of its shows with visuals on pay TV and social media.

What makes radio different?

Radio is the 24-hours-a-day medium that never sleeps. There is no lull between deadlines. If a major story breaks, it needs to be on-air as soon as its accuracy has been confirmed.

Often described as pressure cookers, radio newsrooms are places where words can be few, communication can be very direct and there's a quiet focus as stories are written and bulletins prepared.

The medium's portability is often touted as its biggest strength. Radio can be listened to everywhere – at home, at work, even while travelling. It is this portability that also poses radio's biggest challenge.

It is a personal medium – many listen to the radio while on their own, so those behind the microphone aim to speak directly to them. Radio is not oratory performance and it is not theatrical. It is simple, down-to-earth communication that informs and engages.

Radio journalism is not for the faint-hearted.

Covering a story on radio

Radio delivers news in a variety of ways – via bulletins, on-air interviews, live crosses and longer documentary-style packages.

Unlike a newspaper story, it won't have all of the aspects of a story in one report. Instead it will carry a story throughout the day, researching and developing new angles and covering off different elements over time.

"Radio is very powerful – it delivers a truckload of news in a very short space of time because you have to be so economical with words," says Tim Graham, a political reporter at RNZ.

Life in a radio newsroom starts early – about 4am. Breakfast time (6–9am) is the most listened-to time period for any radio station and a huge focus for newsrooms, with half-hourly bulletins and a dual focus on being across everything that has happened overnight and setting the news agenda for the day.

The activity level in a radio newsroom ebbs and flows throughout the day. After 9am there's a quiet hum before the next peak of activity around midday bulletins, the early afternoon is generally a quieter period before the hustle of "drive" (4–7pm). This delivers another peak in listeners as commuters drive home.

You can find yourself anywhere at any time – in the newsroom covering a story, out in the field on a breaking story, in court, at council meetings, wherever.

Radio reporters' focus is generally filing stories for the news bulletins, but you can also find yourself reporting live into the programme, filing content for your network's website or preparing longer packages.

Radio writing

Radio journalism is the art of writing something that will never be read by its audience, only heard. And it will be heard by people who are doing something else.

Radio news must be crisp, clear and immediately understandable.

New Zealand's three major radio news networks have clear policies governing their news – from the language that's acceptable to use, to the duration of each story and audio clip.

RNZ's style guide says its stories are simple but never simplistic. It uses the conventions of formal speech and demands each story be complete and remind

THE LIVE CROSS

A live cross is when a reporter at the scene of a news event reports on that event live. The reporter may speak directly to the audience or may be interviewed by the radio host or newsreader. Live crosses have two main uses: to take the listener to the scene of a breaking or major news story and to enable a reporter to succinctly summarise complex stories.

Reporting live is demanding – there are no second chances! Here is what **Tyler Adams**, a reporter at Newstalk ZB, advises.

"Start by understanding your issue. If you're at a protest, know what it's about. If you're at the scene of an emergency or breaking story, get your basic facts. If you're reporting on a day-long event (a court or Royal Commission hearing), identify the most pertinent points of evidence. If you're outlining a new report, understand its important points.

"Liaise with your programme producer. Do they want a lengthy live cross on-air with audio clips or just a quick update? Agree to a question line and clarify any aspects you need the host to stay away from.

"Gather the colour. You should take the listener to the heart of the story. Take some time to think about where you are so that you can paint that picture. Is it noisy? Quiet? Sombre? Vibrant? What can you see? Hear? Smell? Who's there with you? Who's not there that you might expect to be? Jot notes down so you can refer to them.

"Prep what you're going to say. Think about your structure – particularly your beginning and end. There must be a logical storytelling sequence. If you're using audio, identify your cuts and write or prep your cross around them. Some people warn not to script crosses but if that works for you, then do so ... but be careful that you don't sound as though you are reading. It's important to remember this is a *discussion* with the host, so if you script, be prepared to deviate. Bullet-pointing your main points is a better option.

"Relax. Take a moment to compose yourself.

"Be confident and own your information. You are the authority on this story. You must sound in control or you will lose credibility. If you're thrown a curve ball, divert it with 'I don't know that but what I can tell you is ...'

"Above all – have fun. Live crosses are one of the most exciting elements of radio!"

listeners of significant background. RNZ chief executive Paul Thompson says the network's brief is to be "a trusted and essential source of credible, high-quality news and current affairs and that relevant programming reflects and captures the diversity and dynamism of New Zealand".

Newstalk ZB describes its news as what listeners need to know, packaged with what they want to know. "We use idiomatic English – a conversational style with modern language. We credit our listeners with having some knowledge already, so we don't need to be pedantic all the time," Lesley Deverall, editor at Newstalk ZB, says.

Radio Live's news style is also conversational. "We want to grab the listeners by the ears and let them know we have something that's relevant to them. We inform them without talking down to or at them. We have a conversational style but if the story deserves gravitas, then that should be used," Melanie Jones, head of news and sport at the station, says.

There are marked differences in style between the three networks. This section will give you a good grounding in the general rules.

Three types of report

There are three main types of radio news stories:
- the written (or writ)
- the audio story
- the voice report (or voicer).

The length of each is measured in time, not word count. The rule is three words per second.

The written (or writ)

This is the most basic of all radio stories. It is written by a reporter and presented by the newsreader. A written on RNZ can be up to 50 seconds long; on commercial radio they are shorter. They must contain all the basic facts of the story – who, what, when, where, why and how. Here's an example:

> Rescuers are combing through rubble trying to find survivors in Christchurch. The city was hit by a magnitude 6.3 earthquake at 12:51 this afternoon.
>
> Mayor Bob Parker says the city has suffered major damage, buildings have collapsed, the spire has fallen off the Cathedral and buses have been crushed by rubble in the central city.
>
> He says a number of bodies have already been found but there's no official death toll yet.
>
> Civil Defence officials from Wellington are on their way to Christchurch to co-ordinate the emergency response.

The structure of a written story can be very formulaic:
- The intro must be as tight and hard as possible.
- The second par is often referred to as the context paragraph as it contains the background necessary for listeners to understand the story.
- The third par expands on your intro and often introduces your interviewee.
- The fourth par usually also quotes that person and adds further information with a final par rounding up the story and often pointing to where it will go next.

The audio story

Audio stories include a slice/clip/cut of audio from an interviewee. A reporter will generally record the audio, edit the clip and write the story. The duration of those clips differs between networks, with RNZ more open to running longer clips (more than 15 seconds). Here's an example (with explanations of the jargon given in square brackets):

Bloggs leaves – audio [This is the slug.]

One of New Zealand's biggest stars is leaving the All Blacks.

Fred Bloggs has just signed a contract with French club Toulon.

Bloggs says it was a hard decision to make.

[Now we have the audio clip. "CART" is the name the audio file has been saved as in the audio editor, "IN" are the first words of the clip, "OUT" are the final words and "DUR" is the duration of the clip.]

CART: Leaves

IN: I haven't slept in weeks

OUT: Now or never

DUR: 12 secs

Bloggs says leaving New Zealand will be one of the hardest things he has ever done. [This is the back announce, which finishes the report.]

When you come to write your story, identify the person in the clip in the sentence before it and ensure that sentence flows into the clip without repeating the information in it. If you are having trouble, listen back to your raw audio. Often the words your interviewee said leading up to the clip can be used to write into it.

Not every radio news network uses back announces. The rationale for them is that a compelling piece of audio can attract attention, so it makes sense to say who was speaking in the clip once it is finished.

Choose the most compelling piece of audio. More tips are in "The art of audio" section of this chapter.

> Muffled speech, strong accents and noisy backgrounds can make audio unusable. If you're not sure if a clip can be understood, play it to someone else once. If they don't understand it, your audience won't either.

The voice report (or voicer)

Voice reports enable journalists themselves to report the story. The two parts to a voice report are the "intro" or "head" (read by the newsreader) and the "voice report" or "voicer" (pre-recorded and read by the journalist). Here is an example (with jargon explained in square brackets):

Police voicer [This is the slug.]

The standoff between police and an armed man in Napier has just ended. [Intro]

The Armed Offenders Squad has confirmed the gunman, 51-year-old Jan (yarn) [Correct pronunciation of the man's first name] Miller is dead after a 51-hour siege.

Jack Brown reports.

> A "wrap" is a voicer that includes interview audio.

CART: Armed over
IN: Police went
OUT: For Basement Radio, Jack Brown
DUR: 27 secs

Voice reports are often used when a reporter is out of the newsroom covering a story. Here the journalist should endeavour to paint a picture. Explain what you can see, smell and hear. Voice reports are also a useful way to present complicated stories, for example, a report that has numerous findings and recommendations.

How long a voice report will be depends on the network it is being written for, although they hover around 30 seconds. Each has a standard sign-off, for example, *Jo Bloggs, Christchurch, Newstalk ZB*.

Rules for writing good radio

Keep it simple. Your listener only has one chance to hear your story. Use short sentences. Parenthetical phrases have no place in radio. Avoid jargon and complex language and remember you are *writing for the ear* so write the way you speak.

> **Bad:**
>
> The EcoClimate report, which is prepared by NIWA, reveals rainfall will be so low in Canterbury that, in a decade, the province will not be able to grow crops or raise livestock.
>
> **Good:**
>
> A new report is predicting no crops or livestock will be able to be grown in Canterbury within ten years.
>
> NIWA's EcoClimate report says rainfall will be so low in the region …

Get to the point quickly. The crux of the story must be clear in your intro. It must be hard and contain the very latest development or the most gripping piece of information you are reporting. It must also grab your listeners' attention. Make it punchy and leave out names that aren't immediately recognisable.

> **Bad:**
>
> Brad Johnson's family is laying a complaint with the Independent Police Conduct Authority.
>
> **Good:**
>
> The family of a Hamilton man shot dead by police wants an investigation into the tragedy.

Make it current. Radio is about what's happening *now*. Use the present tense wherever possible and the active as opposed to the passive voice.

> **Bad:**
>
> The Christchurch City Council should sell its assets to pay for the rebuild, said John Smith, Prime Minister.
>
> **Good:**
>
> The Prime Minister says the Christchurch City Council should sell its assets to pay for the rebuild.

Radio generally uses *says* instead of *said* and we pronounce it *sez*.

Keep your copy short, sharp and tight. You have limited time to tell the story, so don't waste a second of it. Go through your copy and remove any redundant words.

Avoid tautology – that is two words that mean the same thing. For example, *major disaster* (a disaster *is* major). Remove repetition – it sounds sloppy and wastes time.

Ask yourself whether the information is relevant to the angle of the story. You will cover stories where every facet seems interesting – managing to edit is the art of radio.

Make sure your copy makes instant sense. Include necessary context information. Don't assume your listener knows the background to the story. Be careful of ambiguity, particularly when using *he* and *she* (for instance is it clear who *she* refers to?). Interpret time and date references for your listener. So instead of writing *he will appear in court on June 16* write *next week*.

Be careful with statistics or figures – limit their use and keep them simple. *The report shows 53.7 per cent of the population is homeless* is better written *the report shows more than half of the population is homeless*.

Think of your newsreader. Your story *must* be easy for them to read aloud. Make sure there is a place for your reader to stop and breathe in long sentences.

Write out guides for any tricky names or words so their pronunciation is explicitly clear. For example: *Rambuccari [ram-book-a-rye]*.

Read every story to yourself, aloud, when you finish it. Make sure every sentence is grammatically perfect, clear and flows.

MAKING IT IN RADIO

New Zealand's vibrant radio industry is always looking for talented new reporters. So what are radio heads looking for in young reporters?

Paul Thompson, RNZ's chief executive, says you must "have fire in your belly about telling stories. You've got to have an interest in world affairs, national affairs and local affairs. If you're not curious about the world, always wanting to ask, 'Why is that like that? What does that mean?', it's going to be a pretty tough road being in a newsroom. You've got to be driven and want to be the best."

Lesley Deverall, editor, Newstalk ZB, says, "I want new reporters who can write clear and concise English. Who can spell and get it grammatically correct. I want them to have that gut instinct for what is news."

Belinda McCammon, chief reporter at RNZ, says learn from others. "Listen to other journalists' packages, from hard news to light colour pieces. You'll learn from them all."

Radio packages

A package is best described as a short radio documentary. Its intro is read out by programme presenters with the package scripted, voiced and edited by the reporter. Packages can be up to four minutes.

A radio package is a real luxury for any journalist, as it allows extra time to develop a story and also provides opportunity for creativity. So says Philippa Tolley, executive producer of *Insight*, RNZ's weekly current affairs documentary.

The reporter needs to add real value to this news form, rather than just using the package to round off the issue. Unlike voice reports or wraps, packages do not have to follow events in a linear way. The reporter can use interviewees, sound and writing to tell the story.

Introductions

A package's introduction should be short and straightforward. The first line is the most dramatic and newsworthy angle of your story. The entire intro should provide brief context and make your audience want to listen.

Be careful of repetition; do not make the classic mistake of repeating the last line of the introduction as the first line of the package.

Think carefully. How will the intro lead into the package? If the last line of your intro is *[name] reports*, the listener will expect to hear that voice. If the package is to start with audio, help the listener know what is coming next. For example, if the package starts with a clip of an interviewee, make the last line of your intro *[REPORTER'S NAME] has been speaking to [INTERVIEWEE'S NAME]*, or if it starts with sound, use *[REPORTER'S NAME] has been at [NAME THE PLACE HERE]*.

Package body

Think of the body of a package as a diamond. The top is the start of the package and needs to include the most newsworthy angle, the most evocative clip or piece of actuality to draw the listener in. If you don't start with sound, you need to script into it in about 20 seconds. A long and complex voice-over at the top will take the listener's finger to the off switch.

The middle of the diamond will contain a lot of information, but short links and tight clips (10–20 seconds) will keep up the pace of the package. Your package will need background information, but the proper place for this is when you've got them interested, not at the start.

Packages should have at least three voices in them and you should think about how to use sound, interviews and actuality creatively. Listen to other packages to get ideas. Above all, think about balance – all issues and events have more than one side.

Finally, the bottom of the diamond is sharp and pointy. It's time to bring the package to a strong end. One classic approach is to include a throw to what happens next.

Sound

All packages sound better with actuality. Take care to record your sound properly, getting clear interviews. Face-to-face is always preferable. When out in the field, record 40–60 seconds of natural sound or a buzz track. Sound isn't confined to something happening (a siren, babies crying, etc.), it is everyday life.

Such recordings shouldn't be used in chunks – they should flow in and out of your package. Tie the sound to your script subtly. Not an obvious *That's the sound of children in their classroom*. But *The students start each school day with maths*. Lead your listener to understand what they are hearing and the sound will help build a picture in their mind.

The art of audio

A variety of sound is crucial to any radio broadcast, from news bulletins to packages. Monotony does not make compelling listening. "I want audio gold," Lesley Deverall, editor at Newstalk ZB, says. "Ordinary people telling their story in their own words, so it's vibrant and exciting."

New Zealand's radio reporters record not only *people talking* but also *sound* to give life to their pieces – be it the thudding of machinery, the chants of marching protesters or the quiet sounds of native bush-life.

Slices of interviews enable listeners to hear directly from those involved in a story. Sound recorded in the field is used in voice reports and packages and in the documentaries that RNZ specialises in.

This section gives some overarching advice on how to record and edit good-quality audio – skills any budding radio journalist must have.

Recording in the field

Most New Zealand media use digital recorders and professional microphones to collect audio in the field. Increasingly, reporters use smartphones to collect audio. While such recordings are often of broadcast quality and can be emailed to the newsroom for cutting easily, a microphone and recorder will get clearer results.

Don't let anyone grab the microphone when you are interviewing them. Keep control of it.

Each network's equipment differs and you won't be expected to be an expert on day one. This section contains general rules that apply to recording audio – regardless of what gear you are using.

Check your gear: Ensuring your field recording will be a success starts before you leave the newsroom. Make sure you have everything you need, that it is all working and that you have spare batteries.

Get your recording levels correct: Each time you record, you will be in a different sound environment, so you need to check that your audio will be usable. Recording at the correct level is vital. If your levels are too low, the audio will require boosting, which may render it unusable. Levels that are too high result in distorted audio. Start by getting your interviewee to say their name and title into your microphone so you can check your levels. This will also mean you have a record of how the interviewee pronounces their name. Keep your eye on your levels throughout your recording, as they can change and you may need to adjust them.

You will record in infinite situations: sitting close to someone as you interview them, in a scrum of reporters jostling to record the same person, over the phone, in noisy sports stadia and parades, or in the soundproofed quiet of a radio studio.

Use your microphone correctly: Hold your microphone firmly and be warned – each time you move the hand holding it or knock its cord, you will get noise on your recording. Holding the cord will prevent this. Make sure your mic is the right distance

Mike Hosking
fronts the
*Mike Hosking
Breakfast* show
on Newstalk ZB.

VOICE WORK

Radio presenters have no easy task. They are alone, in a soundproofed studio with several computer screens, a complicated studio desk and a microphone.

On top of that, whether you're reading the news, interviewing the Prime Minister or a crying mother, the clock is ticking and you have to finish on time so the programme can move to the next element.

You need to be focused on what you are saying, listening intently, watching the time and thinking about what button you need to push next. It is multi-tasking on a very public stage.

You may be under pressure in an unnatural environment with an inanimate object in front of you, but when that microphone is turned on, you must remember you are talking to people. And you must engage them if you are to succeed.

Your arm is likely to get tired, so pause the interview while you change hands.

from the sound you are recording. Aim to have it around 20cm from an interviewee's mouth. Your mic will not distinguish, as the human brain does, between background noise and the sound you want to listen to. It will record it all and the background noise will be more obvious on tape than it was to you when you recorded it.

Background noise: "Intrusive background noise is obviously a problem, but good background sound can help transport the listener to the location of the interview or voice report and clearly underline that it is from the field," says Simon Dickinson, news technical and training manager, RNZ. Wearing headphones as you record can help you assess whether the background sound adds to the story or is rendering the audio unusable.

Do not be afraid to ask your interviewee to repeat themselves if something unexpected – a dog barking or a loud truck passing – interrupts the recording.

Always record a piece of natural sound – often called a buzz or wild track – that

INTERVIEWS

Dig deep for your interviews. That's what award-winning radio journalist **Amanda Snow** says.

"With the race to be first, it's easy to chase the usual suspects for a quick audio grab for the next bulletin. Politicians, police, and experts are among your instant hits. Some are even media-trained to speak in sound bites to make your life a dream.

"But though perfectly polished, if overused the formula can be predictable and dull. Radio bulletins are more compelling when they better reflect the human, diverse fabric of life.

"When covering a story, any story, ask yourself: Who is really affected? Who on the frontline will suffer the consequences of decisions made at the top? How will it affect their families or communities? What are the real implications? What are the costs and who is really paying?

"As a journalist, you have a duty to serve all citizens – here's where you need to hone your people skills. Here's where you go out of your way to give a voice to the voiceless.

"Naturally, victims of violence, sexual assault, financial crime, job cuts, funding shortages or whatever the situation are often the hardest to reach – let alone convince to talk on tape. But give it a shot. Play the long game. You are human, show empathy, be patient, be kind, be fair – and when the interview's over, stick to your word.

"Don't become the radio journalist who sees just another fatal, missing person, or brutal assault. People's lives are impacted, sometimes destroyed by these events – so stay human.

"Real people are left to pick up the pieces long after the media's left the scene. Do them justice."

you can use under your piece. While commercial radio tends to use these under voice reports or wraps only, RNZ uses them frequently in longer packages and documentaries. You can listen to many at www.radionz.co.nz

Be aware of your own noise: Don't "Hmm" and "Ahh" through your interview – communicate non-verbally with your interviewee by using eye contact, nodding your head or smiling. And remember, jangly jewellery is noisy, so don't wear it.

Think about small noises that may be affecting your audio – ask people nicely to stop clicking that pen, rapping their fingers on the table, etc.

Take charge: Don't be afraid to take control of the environment to record an interview that is clear of unwanted background noise. You may need to rearrange furniture to move chairs closer or ask them to turn off radios, fan heaters or noisy computers. You may even want to pull them out of a noisy room to a quieter space for the interview – just as a photographer would ask someone to move to a better light.

A BEGINNER'S GUIDE TO BEING ON-AIR

This advice is from Barry Holland, a voice consultant with more than 40 years' experience in New Zealand radio.

"Be comfortable in your own skin. Relax. Your job is to simply tell people what's going on. Don't put on a radio voice. If you start worrying about how you sound, you will sound unnatural and revert to awful patterned speech.

"Imagine who you're talking to. Tell yourself, you're not performing to thousands of people – you are simply talking to one person who's listening to the radio. If you can picture that person, you're more likely to sound natural.

"Be in command of what you're saying. You are your listeners' authority. You must sound confident to have credibility. That comes by understanding what you're reporting.

"Prepare. If you're reading the news, pre-read the bulletin and focus on difficult names, ensure you have any pronunciation guides needed. When you're new to the industry practise at every opportunity you can ... have scripts at home so you can rehearse.

"Breathe. Make sure it is from the diaphragm, not the chest, to ensure you have enough air to slow down or vary your pace. Breathing will also help you relax and ensure you're not constricting your mouth or throat.

"Find your best vocal pitch. Everybody has a vocal range and there's little you can do to change it. But you can alter your pitch. Your best pitch is probably in the middle of your vocal range. That means you are not throwing your voice up high or down low. Speak in that pitch. Young people have a tendency to start a sentence by pitching high and then dropping down. Start and finish in the medium range of your pitch.

"Warm up. Prepare both mouth and vocal cords by warming up. Go through the vowel sounds, 'ah, eh, eee, or, ooo', aloud and stretch your mouth by making the 'ooo' and 'eee' sounds.

"Use your voice to bring out your points. The point of each sentence will not be one word, it will be several. So use your voice to hit that *phrase*. Every sentence you read will be different, so it should be presented differently – don't deliver every story with the same melodic tone.

"Don't rush your story – that will lead to stumbling. Simply speak at a comfortable pace but vary it to make your points.

"Vary your tone. If you smile while you're reading, the audience will hear warmth in your voice. Be careful, though – warmth is hardly appropriate in sombre news stories. Don't be afraid to communicate urgency if you're reporting from the field in either a voice report or a live cross ... that will help paint the picture for your listeners. If you muck up, do not dwell on it. You'll digress and trip over something else and then you'll tie yourself in knots. Correct yourself quickly and move on."

Niva Retimanu, award-winning newsreader with The Radio Network, adds, "Never think you're reading to thousands – visualise just one. Make yourself comfortable. If you want to stand, stand. If you want to, use your hands to help emphasise key points. No one will see you."

Phone interviews

Many radio interviews are done over the phone, although field recording is of higher quality. Many of the rules outlined above also apply to recording over the phone. Start by doing a level check, and watch your levels during the interview. Background noise can cause as much difficulty in phone interviews as in interviews done face-to-face. The easiest way to avoid it is to get your interview subject to shush the noise or go to a quieter room. Always prefer landlines to mobile phones. If your interviewee is on a mobile phone, ensure there is good reception. Sometimes there are problems with the phone lines themselves. It is always worth calling back if you suspect there is a line fault.

Melanie Jones, head of news and sport at Radio Live, says, "Phone audio is not always great. But I think the audience, as a whole, is becoming more accepting and if we're taking them to the heart of the action they will forgive lesser-quality audio."

Never interview your subject on a speakerphone or hands-free kit – the quality will not be good enough. Ask them to use the handset.

Editing audio

All audio editing involves selecting "cuts" or "grabs" from a piece of audio. Sometimes these stand alone and sometimes they are joined to other cuts to make a longer piece.

Start by listening back and identifying the most outstanding cuts, the bits that leap out at you – they may even evoke an emotional reaction. Think carefully about your cut's start and finish – it must sound like a complete statement, not as though you have cut half a sentence out of someone's speech. Be careful to avoid clips that end on upward inflections – they're distracting and sound like errors on-air.

Sometimes, people speak in circumlocution. They start making a point but veer off on a tangent before coming back to their original point. You can edit out the middle of such statements to bring the point together.

Take into account the rhythm of natural speech. Edit out "Ums" and "Ahhs" or repetition, but ensure that the edited statement sounds like natural speech, not jumping unnaturally from one word to the next.

"There are times when gaps are more eloquent than words, and it's important that they're left in. Let the grabs breathe," says Melanie Jones.

Editing clips of audio together takes practice but the general rules include ensuring your clips are all of similar sound levels, and that each edit is clean and sounds natural. Sound or music is best faded in or out, under a voice, using multi-track functions.

Remember: good journalistic ethical principles apply to audio editing. You cannot take someone out of context and you must not change the meaning of what they're saying.

Radio in the online era

The internet is changing the way radio reporters go about their business. Each of the major radio news networks now has its own website: www.radionz.co.nz, www.newstalkzb.co.nz, www.radiolive.co.nz

And each of the networks requires its journalists to service the website, as well as its on-air product. Photos, audio and video can all be provided by reporters covering

Podcasts are a valuable tool anyone can use to broadcast their own radio pieces and create a portfolio to help get into the industry. For more on podcasting, check out Further Reading.

PODCASTING

Podcasting is an easy way for anyone to "broadcast" their own content via the internet, says experienced online editor **Edward Swift**.

"A podcast in its original definition is audio content delivered to the user via an RSS. However, the term now covers audio on-demand and can be any recording whatsoever – from an hour-long pre-recorded speech to short vox pops or a beautifully scripted and polished package.

"Collecting audio for podcast is the same as collecting it for broadcast – you want good-quality, clear audio that is well-edited and scripted so that it flows and tells a story. If it's not, people won't listen. Podcasts enable New Zealand's radio stations to provide extra news content. There is a demand for longer content, particularly when it comes to major news stories.

"The brilliant thing about podcasting is it's something that almost anyone can do. In days past, to create good 'radio' you required expensive recording equipment and editing gear, as well as a platform to broadcast from. Nowadays, a lot of the tools you need are free and easy to obtain.

"Most smartphones can record audio that is of broadcast standard. As well as recorders already built into the phone's operating system, apps like iRig make it very easy to record interviews, edit them on the go and email them to your computer.

"Most recorders and apps will give you the option to save the file as an MP3, which is the best format to use. MP3s are highly accessible and a compressed format that's easy to download. There's nothing worse than trying to download a 100MB podcast only to find out it's actually 30 seconds long, especially when you're using mobile data which can be expensive.

"If your device won't let you save audio as MP3, you can download an audio converter that will convert it for you. There are a number of other formats you can use, such as OGG (an open-source alternative) or even Windows Media Audio, but with the range of devices and applications, MP3 is universally recognised.

"There are a number of free audio editing applications available too. Audacity is one of them and is relatively easy to use. That can be downloaded from http://audacity.sourceforge.net.

"The final step in the process is uploading your audio to the internet. Again, there are a number of platforms. You can use an audio hosting service like SoundCloud or upload it to a blogging site like WordPress. Each is a free service that will store your audio and enable others to access it. From there, you can send people the links to audio, or get the RSS feed and submit it to iTunes' podcast directory for the whole world to find.

"Podcasting gives you an easy way to launch your radio career and build a portfolio well before your first job in the industry."

particular stories for online use, so multimedia skills are an asset.

The internet enables radio stations to reach a worldwide audience. Each network offers the opportunity for users to listen to their station via their website – and thousands do. A lot of effort also goes into packaging key features so they can be accessed on-demand. The internet has also enabled print and television media to challenge radio's position as always first with the news, which has meant radio reporters have had to lift their game.

Radio newsrooms monitor the web to ensure they have the latest news, with close eyes kept not only on news websites but also social media, including tweets. But enormous care is taken to ensure that speed never trumps accuracy.

"The internet, social media and citizen journalism have no doubt increased the pace of radio. But it's made us even more aware of accuracy. You have to check everything before you report it. You can't just repeat, retweet or share a Facebook status unless you've checked it out," says Lesley Deverall, editor, Newstalk ZB.

My thanks to Philippa Tolley, who contributed the section on radio packages.

Further reading

Ahern, S. (2000). *Making radio: A practical guide to working in radio.* Sydney: Allen & Unwin.

Cohler, D. (1994). *Broadcast journalism: A guide for the presentation of radio and television news.* New Jersey: Prentice-Hall.

www.newscript.com

www.newstalkzb.co.nz

www.radiolive.co.nz

www.radionz.co.nz

www.soundportraits.org/education/

www.thisamericanlife.org/about/make-radio This site contains excellent resources for podcasting.

References

Encyclopedia of the Nations. (2017). *Radio broadcast stations.* Retrieved from www.nationsencyclopedia.com/WorldStats/CIA-Radio-brodcast-stations.html

18

Television journalism

Reporting for the visual world of TV

Jo Malcolm, University of Canterbury; Vicki Wilkinson-Baker, New Zealand Broadcasting School

When news breaks in New Zealand or around the world, people expect to *see* it. Whether it be on a TV set or a mobile device, they want to watch events unfold.

Pictures are powerful. Who can forget the moment the All Blacks won the Rugby World Cup in 2015 or the champagne celebrations after Peter Burling and his team took out the America's Cup in 2017? What about pictures of the Christchurch, Wellington and Kaikōura earthquakes, or the carnage created by terrorist attacks around the world? How about Winston Peters' announcement in 2017 that he would form a government with Labour?

The image of a grieving mother carrying her dead child in the midst of a war zone needs no explaining.

But a good television story also needs words to give those pictures context. The images showing the panic and grief following the 2015 terror attacks in Paris were graphic, but viewers also needed to know when and where the attacks occurred, how many were killed, who was responsible. These are the facts a television reporter weaves into their story – the who, what, when, where, why and how.

A cameraperson or video journalist will film the best pictures they can. It's then up to the reporter to take those images and write a story around them. And that requires skill. The aim is not to tell viewers what they can already see, but to give them extra information that's relevant to what they're watching.

WHAT MAKES A GOOD TV REPORTER?

Here's what the country's top two TV news heads think.

Richard Sutherland, head of broadcast news at Newshub, says a good TV reporter never forgets they are visual storytellers. "No matter how important the story, without strong visuals, you are unlikely to hold your audience – and if you're not holding your audience, everything else is a waste of time. Sometimes the pictures are so compelling the story tells itself. Most of the time, though, they won't, and a large part of your day will be spent finding pictures and graphics that allow you to get the facts through to the viewer in a clear and informative way."

"Aside from the visuals, the basic rules of journalism apply – hard work, persistence, contact-building and being proactive are the key attributes. Don't expect the next Roastbusters or Watergate to fall into your lap. You won't find a story by sitting at your desk."

John Gillespie, head of news and current affairs at TVNZ, says: "Be curious and dig hard. Be prepared to dig up information others won't get, or that some don't want you to get. You will need to dig with alacrity.

"And while you want to be first, you want to be right, always. A good maxim, to quote American broadcaster and tutor Al Tompkins, is to 'Write for the ear, shoot for the eye, and aim for the heart.'

"You want to produce a story that stands out visually and is well told with strong voices. A story that's memorable and makes people care."

Television journalism is a craft and a very creative one. But it's also stressful because of the deadlines. The television news reporter has to pull many different elements together and do it quickly. It requires planning, communication and teamwork. The reporter also needs to be multi-skilled. Increasingly, they're filming and editing their own stories. There are big adrenalin highs when jobs go well. The feeling of getting pictures (or a story) out via a satellite feed or the new smaller LiveU units from some remote location back to your newsroom with seconds to spare is incredible.

As an eyewitness to events both here and around the world, the television reporter has to interpret what's going on for viewers at home. It takes hard work and practice to succeed but the rewards make it worthwhile. This chapter will focus on creating a standard TV news story, handling spot news and doing a live cross.

The average TV news story is just 90 seconds long, but it can take all day to establish the facts, get the right pictures and interviews, and put it all together.

Thinking pictures

Great pictures with plenty of action and noise usually make the best television. So, wherever possible, start with your best pictures and sound fx (effects) to grab the viewer's attention. Imagine you are assigned a story about a drought in Canterbury. Your first job is to verify the facts. You would ring Federated Farmers, some individual farmers and the MetService. You need to establish how bad the drought is, check all relevant facts and figures and find out their views. You discover the drought is the worst in 30 years – that sounds like a great angle.

The drought is widespread throughout Canterbury and farmers need urgent assistance from government. The Federated Farmers spokesperson puts you in touch with a local farmer, who says he is running out of hay and is about to send another load of sheep to the sale yards. This is perfect because it personalises your story. You know the farmer is articulate because you have spoken to him and his situation is typical of what other farmers are going through. You check he is happy to be interviewed on-camera, and because you need pictures to tell the story, you ask to film him feeding out, rounding up the sheep and loading the truck. You explain it could take a couple of hours.

You need to interview the Federated Farmers man, which means visiting another farm and organising some briefs shots of him working. You also want an interview with the Minister of Agriculture in Wellington to find out what the government is doing. You would phone the minister's press secretary to discuss the situation and then organise for one of the Parliamentary reporters working for your news organisation to do an on-camera interview. You'll now a have a broad idea of your angle, and the pictures and interviews you need to obtain (Figure 1).

Figure 1: *Initial plans for the story*

Angle	Pictures you need	Interviews
Canterbury has been hit by the worst drought in 30 years. Many farmers are running out of feed and are being forced to sell their stock.	• Farmer feeding out last of hay • Cracked and bare ground • Empty watering hole • Sheep being rounded up • Sheep in the yards • Sheep being loaded onto truck • Truck leaving the farm • Brief shots of Federated Farmers man working on his farm	• Farmer • Federated Farmers • Minister of Agriculture

---

Rough script or storyboard

Before leaving the newsroom it's useful to do a rough script or storyboard (Figure 2). This helps identify the angle and the key pictures required to tell the story. Having spoken to Federated Farmers and the individual farmer on the phone, you know what they're likely to say and you know what you're going to film. You can show this in your script as IV (interview).

Figure 2: *Rough script*

Pictures	Sound VO and IVs
	INTRO: (newsreader) CANTERBURY FARMERS ARE BEING FORCED TO SELL STOCK AS THE WORST DROUGHT IN 30 YEARS HITS THE REGION. FEDERATED FARMERS IS APPEALING FOR GOVERNMENT ASSISTANCE AND SAYS WITHOUT IT, MANY FARMERS WILL GO UNDER. JOHN SMITH REPORTS:
Farmer feeding out last bales of hay Wide shot	Sound fx of sheep baaing for couple of seconds **VO:** THESE ARE THE LAST BALES OF WINTER FEED. SHEEP STARVING.
Interview with farmer Ted Brown	**IV:** Upset about situation. This is really bad.
Set-up shots of Fed Farmers man on his farm	**VO:** FEDERATED FARMERS SAYS WIDESPREAD PROBLEM AND THEY NEED GOVERNMENT HELP.
Interview Fed Farmers	**IV:** Lot of others in the same situation.
PTC standing in field, talking about government	**PTC:** Talking about government assistance and what's going to be done.
Dry paddocks // empty sheep troughs	**VO:** LINE HERE LEADING INTO GRAB FROM THE MINISTER.
IV Minister of Agriculture	**IV:** With minister in Wellington
Loading sheep onto truck	More sound fx. Dogs barking at sheep **VO:** FARMER IS HAVING TO SELL STOCK, HOW MANY. MAYBE EVEN SELL FARM.
Interview Ted Brown	**IV:** This is a desperate situation. Would be awful if we had to sell up and go.
Truck driving off down the driveway	Sound fx. Truck driving off. **VO:** FINAL LINE ABOUT WHAT'S GOING TO HAPPEN NEXT. SIGN OFF.

GLOSSARY OF CAMERA SHOTS

CU (close-up): The close-up concentrates solely on the main subject, whether it's a person, an animal or an object.

Moving shot: Usually the camera stays still and follows the action.

MS (medium- or mid-shot): A relatively close shot that focuses more on the main subject.

Pan: The camera is stationary but moves horizontally on the tripod from one side of a scene to another.

POV (point-of-view): The camera shows what a person or animal is seeing. Often the camera is hand-held or it can be attached to a helmet.

Tilt: The camera is stationary but tilts up and down on the tripod.

Tracking shot: The camera is usually hand-held and the cameraperson walks along behind a person or an animal.

WS (wide shot): A view of the whole scene, including the main subject.

Zoom: The camera zooms in from a wide shot into a mid-shot or close-up. Alternatively, the shot is reversed and zooms out to a wide.

It's worth thinking about your opening and closing shots, any sound fx that could enhance your story and whether you want to do a piece-to-camera (PTC) or stand-up. We talk more about PTCs later. Also, think about what you want to say in your voice-over (VO). The voice-over is usually written in the present tense and is the part the reporter says. A rough script or storyboard can be done by hand in your notebook. It's often easier to divide the page in two. Write what you are going to say in capital letters and the interview grabs (extracts) in lower case. You will finish with a sign-off (which is where you state your name).

Now you've got a plan, do it

On the way to the location you need to explain the story to the cameraperson. Communication and teamwork are vital. The cameraperson needs to know the angle, the pictures required, the number of interviews, whether you are doing a PTC and whether there are any particular sound fx needed. The cameraperson also needs to know how long you have to film the story. When you get there, it's important to keep your eyes and ears open in case something unexpected happens which makes your story stronger. In this scenario, the farmer could be too embarrassed to say some stock have already died, but looking around you might see a couple of dead animals lying in another paddock.

For our drought story, the cameraperson would probably start filming the farmer feeding out from a distance. They would get a wide shot showing the sheep, the farmer and the brown paddock all in one picture. This would be followed by a pan, a shot starting with the farmer which then moves along the line of sheep. After that, some closer individual shots of the farmer working and the sheep. From there the camera operator would probably jump on the back of the truck and get much closer shots of the farmer picking up bales of hay, cutting the strings and throwing the hay over the back. You would also want a variety of shots of the sheep eating and maybe CUs of the wheels as the truck goes by.

Your cameraperson will know the basic shots needed for a news story, but it's important you are watching and checking that specific shots you want have been filmed (see our glossary of camera shots).

How to do an interview

We have already explained the importance of talking to the key people on the phone first to establish what they've got to say. You should take notes and use this information for scripting and working out your questions. In most television stories it's easier for the reporter to summarise facts and figures in the voice-over and leave the talent (the interviewees) to give their reactions to what is going on.

For more details on interviewing, see Chapter 3.

Basic camera angles for an interview

Establishing two-shot

Walking two-shot

Close-up of person being interviewed

Close-up of reporter or "noddy"

Most interviews are filmed as a CU, but several other shots are helpful for editing. First, there is a two-shot (2S), which shows the talent and the reporter together. This can be the establishing 2S, which often introduces the interview, and the walking 2S, used to add variety to the report. Second, there is the CU of the reporter. This is called a "noddy" and is used to cover the join if you edit two bits of interview together.

In the drought story we already know what the main people are likely to say. The farmer is struggling because he is running out of hay and his sheep are starving. He's upset about selling his stock and maybe selling his farm. Asking open questions will encourage him to describe what is happening and say how he feels about it.

Although there are instances where you want politicians or community leaders to answer "yes" or "no" to a specific question, it's not what you want in most television stories. If you ask the farmer if this is the worst drought for 30 years and he says "yes", it's not an answer you can use in your story. Instead you ask him how bad the drought is, what's it like when there isn't enough hay to feed his sheep, how difficult is it having to sell his sheep, and how upsetting would it be to sell the farm?

For a story like this, interviews should last three or four minutes. You don't want long, complicated answers, so if that's what you get, rephrase the question and ask it again or get the person to summarise their thoughts.

Doing a piece-to-camera (also called a stand-up)

A PTC is usually about 15 seconds long and shows that a reporter has actually been to the location. The best PTCs are those where you explain or show viewers something. For example, the reporter could be standing in a dry paddock talking about the drought or flicking through a pile of documents while explaining what is in them.

It's a good idea to write a PTC when you do a rough script. It can always be changed out in the field if you think of something better. Like all writing for television, the PTC needs to be conversational, clear and concise. Make sure it's easy to say out loud, and identify the key words that need emphasising. The next step is to work out with the cameraperson where it should be filmed. If the PTC is about farmers running out of hay, an empty hayshed would be appropriate. If the PTC is about budget cuts in hospitals, then outside a hospital would be suitable.

Going out on any job, reporters need to be tidy and appropriately dressed. In most cases this means a jacket for women with trousers or a skirt. A suit and tie is usually best for men. More casual clothing is acceptable when covering events like floods, fires or a drought story. In our example, an open-neck shirt and tidy trousers would

Reporters should avoid jewellery, such as big dangly earrings, as they distract viewers. On a windy day, long hair needs to be tied or clipped back so it doesn't blow in the reporter's face.

Piece-to-camera

Mid-shot

Slightly wider shot

be fine. Classic-looking clothes with simple lines work better on screen.

All reporters (male and female) should carry a basic foundation and some translucent powder. The foundation hides any blemishes and a light dusting of powder will stop a reporter's face from looking shiny. For women, using eye make-up and lipstick, and looking "natural", comes across best. It's important to try to relax when you're filming your PTC. Take some deep breaths and lighten the expression on

---

*Figure 3: **Shotlist***

Numbers represent the timecode in minutes and seconds of the raw footage.

0.00–0.55" WS truck in paddock / pan from truck to sheep
1.15" Ted Brown lifting bales of hay / CU cutting string
1.32" CU farmer's face
1.55" Various shots of truck
2.30" Sheep following truck (good sound fx – baaing)
3.10" Dry empty paddocks / empty watering hole
3.35" Ted rounding up sheep
3.50" CU dog barking (good sound fx)
4.12" Sheep into yards (various shots)
5.45" Sheep loaded onto truck
6.08" Ted watching sheep being loaded.
6.34" Truck driver getting into truck
6.52" Truck driving away (good sound fx)
IV Ted Brown
7.21" "It breaks my heart doing this, but I don't have any option. I just can't feed my own stock."
7.54" "I wish the government would step in and help. We are in a desperate situation here."
8.13" "There are times when I don't think I can carry on. This was my great-grandfather's farm and I'm worried I might have to sell the whole thing."
9.05" PTC (Best take) "With the MetService warning the drought's set to continue for weeks, maybe months, the government's looking at several options to help farmers, including sending feed down from the North Island."
IV Brian Black, Fed Farmers
10.17" "These farmers are in a desperate situation and they need help now."
10.46" "We are not just talking about one farmer here. There are hundreds in this region who are in a crisis."
11.16" Brian Black walking through gate, CU latch (sound fx)
11.35" CU Brian
11.55" 2S reporter + Brian
IV Minister of Agriculture (ex Wgtn)
3.17" "We haven't made a decision yet on assistance. Cabinet will be reviewing it next week."
4.05" Shots of the minister sitting at his desk looking at a weather map.

your face so you're not frowning. Have a couple of practice runs and then record two or three versions so you have choice when it comes to editing.

The shotlist

TV news writing is concise and conversational, like radio. And like radio packages, the story needs to flow from one grab to the next.

When you get back to the newsroom, you need to shotlist your material (Figure 3). This means looking through the pictures and interviews and writing down the relevant time codes. You need to identify the key shots needed to tell your story, especially your opening and closing shots. It's a good idea to highlight them, along with the best bits of the interview and any good sound fx. Interview grabs must be transcribed in full into your script. If there is time, it's useful to transcribe the entire interview.

A detailed shotlist means you can help the editor find pictures quickly. It's also easier if you need to find an alternative grab. The information contained in other answers is also useful when scripting. Shotlisting takes a while, so you have to make a judgement call on whether there's time to do it thoroughly or quickly jot down the main things you need.

Scripting

The generic template for a news story (Figure 4) shows just how brief the different components need to be to fit into one and a half minutes. The first thing you write is a two-paragraph introduction, which the newsreader will read. This summarises your story and clearly defines your angle. You then write your script.

Figure 4: *Generic script template*

Intro: This is about two sentences long, duration is about 15 seconds.

Sound fx if possible	
VO SCRIPT + PICTURES	10"
IV first interview grab	05"
VO SCRIPT + PICTURES	05"
IV second interview grab	05"
PTC WITH REPORTER AT SCENE	15"
VO SCRIPT + PICTURES	15"
IV third interview grab	10"
VO SCRIPT + PICTURES	05"
IV fourth interview grab	10"
WRAP-UP VO AND SIGN OFF	10"
TOTAL STORY DURATION:	1.30"

In this example the reporter talks in VO for 45 seconds (just 135 words). The entire script (including grabs and PTC) is 90 seconds (270 words).

Bad and good scripting

The biggest mistakes television reporters make are describing what viewers can see for themselves and repeating the words used in an interview grab.

BAD:

Sound fx as farmer feeds out hay to sheep

VO: TED BROWN FEEDING OUT HAY TO HIS SHEEP THIS MORNING NEAR DARFIELD. THE PADDOCKS ARE DRY AND BROWN.

CU sheep baaing

VO: HE SAYS HAVING TO SELL HIS STOCK WILL BREAK HIS HEART.

IV Ted Brown: "It breaks my heart doing this, but I don't have any option. I just can't feed my own stock."

Viewers can see he is feeding out and they can see the paddocks are dry and brown. Tell them information they don't know, information that complements the pictures. Below, we have also changed the lead into the grab, so the same words aren't repeated.

GOOD:

Sound fx as farmer feeding out hay to sheep

VO: THESE ARE TED BROWN'S LAST BALES OF WINTER FEED FOR HIS STARVING SHEEP.

IT'S BEEN WEEKS SINCE ANY RAIN HAS FALLEN AROUND DARFIELD. THE DRIEST SUMMER HE CAN REMEMBER.

CU sheep baaing

VO: LATER TODAY THESE EWES WILL BE OFF TO THE SALE YARDS.

IV Ted Brown: "It breaks my heart doing this, but I don't have any option. I just can't feed my own stock."

The order and duration will change for every story. Try to spread the grabs out through the story and instead of having long paragraphs of voice-over, talk for just one or two sentences at a time. If the PTC and interview grabs are longer, then the voice-over needs to be shorter. If there is no PTC, there's more time to play with. Before you start writing, think about your opening pictures. Television stories work best when pictures dictate the shape of the story. The skill is getting your script to relate to those pictures and telling viewers what they need to know. A good guide is to show viewers the problem at the start, then give them background and general information, and end on the future and possible solutions.

Including sound fx will bring your story to life, making the viewer feel like they have been to the location. Sometimes just a few seconds of natural sound is enough. But in a protest story, you might start and end with five or 10 seconds of chanting. If you are covering a singing contest, the viewers need to hear the songs.

The challenge with television news stories is fitting everything in. The pictures and words need to work together, plus you need to include the relevant facts. Most

Figure 5: *Drought script*

INTRO: CANTERBURY FARMERS ARE BEING FORCED TO SELL STOCK AS THE WORST DROUGHT IN 30 YEARS HITS THE REGION. FEDERATED FARMERS IS APPEALING FOR GOVERNMENT ASSISTANCE AND SAYS WITHOUT IT MANY WILL GO UNDER. JOHN SMITH REPORTS:

1.15" Farmer feeding out

VO: THESE ARE TED BROWN'S LAST BALES OF WINTER FEED FOR HIS STARVING SHEEP.

IT'S BEEN WEEKS SINCE ANY RAIN HAS FALLEN AROUND DARFIELD. THE DRIEST SUMMER HE CAN REMEMBER.

2.30" Sheep following truck (good sound fx)

LATER TODAY THESE EWES WILL BE OFF TO THE SALE YARDS.

1.15" Cutting string on bale of hay

7.21" IV Ted Brown, farmer: "It breaks my heart doing this, but I don't have any option. I just can't feed my own stock."

11.16" Fed Farmers man opening gate (good sound fx)

VO: FEDERATED FARMERS WARNS MANY OTHERS ARE IN THE SAME PREDICAMENT AND GOVERNMENT ASSISTANCE IS URGENTLY REQUIRED.

10.46" IV Brian Black, Federated Farmers: "We are not just talking about one farmer here. There are hundreds in this region who are in crisis."

9.05" PTC: WITH THE METSERVICE WARNING THE DROUGHT'S SET TO CONTINUE FOR WEEKS, MAYBE MONTHS, THE GOVERNMENT'S LOOKING AT SEVERAL OPTIONS TO HELP FARMERS, INCLUDING SENDING FEED DOWN FROM THE NORTH ISLAND.

3.10" Dry paddocks / empty watering hole

VO: FEDERATED FARMERS SAYS THEY NEED MORE THAN THAT, AND THEY NEED IT NOW.

Ex Wgtn 3.17" IV Doug Green, Agriculture Minister: "We haven't made a decision yet on assistance. Cabinet will be reviewing it next week."

3.35" Farmer rounding sheep (dog barking 3.50")

VO: THAT MIGHT BE TOO LATE FOR TED BROWN.

HE'S ALREADY SOLD HALF HIS EWES AND ANOTHER 250 ARE GOING TODAY. HE WAS FORCED TO SELL HIS LAMBS SEVERAL WEEKS AGO.

AFTER SPENDING HIS WHOLE LIFE ON "MALVERN DOWNS" HE SAYS THE FUTURE IS LOOKING BLEAK.

8.13" Ted Brown: "There are times when I don't think I can carry on. This was my great-grandfather's farm."

6.34" Driver into truck / 6.52" truck leaving (end shot)

VO: TODAY HE'S SELLING SHEEP. HE'S WORRIED NEXT WEEK IT'LL BE THE WHOLE FARM. JOHN SMITH, CHANNEL 4 NEWS.

The times in Figure 5 are not the elapsed time of the report as it progresses; they are where the grabs can be found in the original footage.

importantly, read each line out loud as you write it. If it doesn't sound right or it's hard to say, change it.

Opposite is the script for our drought story (Figure 5). Notice how the timecodes from the shotlist are included in the script so both the reporter and editor can find the relevant interviews, pictures and sound fx. Layouts for scripts vary in each newsroom. In some cases you can divide the page in two as you did earlier for your storyboard, but in many newsrooms journalists simply write it out on one page as it is on the preceding page.

Once the script is finished a senior producer will sub it. He or she will double-check the key facts to ensure nothing important has been left out. It's useful to have your research notes and shotlist handy in case the producer wants to make changes or include another grab.

Putting it together

Once your script has been approved, the next stage is to record a voice-over and put the story together. While some TV newsrooms are still using editors, increasingly reporters are required to edit, or partially edit, their own stories. If you're working with an editor, it's a team effort involving communication. If you are partially editing your own story, an editor will usually check the audio and polish the item before its broadcast.

In some newsrooms, reporters are increasingly being asked to partially edit their stories, with an editor checking everything has been done correctly and finalising the sound mix.

The fastest way to edit a story is to put the voice-over and grabs down in the correct order. This is basically the same as putting together a radio package. Any music or sound fx will also be included. This gives you a rough idea of the duration. If the story needs to be shortened, it's easier to talk to the producer and make the cuts at this stage. Using your script as a guide, the editor then puts in the pictures. Most reporters have a general idea of what shots go where, but it's up to the editor to put them in the correct order and ensure they are cut together properly.

When the story is completed, it's checked by the producer before going to air.

Spot news

Spot news is covering events as they are happening. It is really all about the cameraperson. It's their job to get pictures of the event, whether it's a fire, a natural disaster, a police emergency or a protest which has turned into a full-scale riot. It's your job as the journalist to put the event into context by getting the facts. That means who, what, when, where, why and how?

So, while your camera operator is filming, you will be busy finding people to interview. You need to find eyewitnesses who can describe what they saw and how they felt. For example, how big the fire was or how terrifying the noise was. You will also need to interview those in charge, like the police or the fire commander.

You won't have time to do a rough script because it's all happening too fast. But when you're at the scene it's helpful to make notes of good pictures to start and end your story with, and you may want to point out things to the cameraperson. For example,

THE LIVE CROSS

Live crosses are a staple of television reporting. But live links still generate fear and anxiety in many reporters, terrified of becoming a YouTube hit or the laughing stock of a national audience. Here's what **Jack Tame**, co-host of TVNZ's *Breakfast* show and former US correspondent for *One News*, advises.

DO:

- Communicate your plans clearly with studio staff and your camera crew.
- Feel free to use props or graphics, where appropriate.
- At the start of your live cross, justify it by explaining where you are and why you're there.
- Feel free to move and have the cameraperson shoot "off the shoulder" (that means taking the camera off the tripod and putting it on their shoulder to get a better variety of shots).
- Openly refer to notes if it makes you more comfortable. Checking a notepad can add immediacy and credibility to a cross.

DON'T:

- Memorise your words. By repeating a few sentences over and over and over before going to air, reporters set themselves up for disaster. If your brain is relying solely on memory rather than simply making a point, it's far more likely to go blank in the heat of the moment.
- Overthink. A live cross is never much more than a simple story delivered down the barrel of a camera. A story. A few sentences. That's all it ever is. Anyone can tell a story!
- Beat yourself up. One day you'll stuff up, everyone does. Just laugh it off, share the YouTube link with your mates and get back on the horse.

Don't make silly faces or hand signals, and don't swear. These can all end up going to air.

a teddy bear lying on the ground or people huddling together to comfort each other.

The PTC is also an important element of the spot-news story. This shows you were there witnessing the event. Make sure your PTC is relevant and tells viewers some new piece of information rather than just describing the pictures they will see in your story.

Let's go live!

When there's breaking news or a major story, reporters are often required to go live from the scene. You need to quickly confirm the facts and work out the key points you want to impart. Where possible, avoid technical terms or words likely to trip you up. Write the main facts neatly on a notepad as bullet points. This means if you forget what you're saying, it's easy to glance down and quickly find the information you need. If you write everything out in full, it's too difficult to find your place.

Once you know what you are saying, you need to practise how you are going to say it. Your delivery should be conversational, with just the key words emphasised. Don't speak too quickly or too loudly. Doing a live cross is similar to having a conversation with your neighbour over the back fence.

Just like doing a PTC, it's important that you are neatly dressed and your hair and make-up are sorted out early. If you are working with a cameraperson or live operator, they will usually try and set up about half an hour before going to air so they can do their technical checks. If possible, you should arrive then as well. This leaves plenty of time to make sure everything is working, including your earpiece (so you can hear the newsreader and director talking to you from the studio). If you are working as a video journalist and setting up your own live cross, it's advisable to get to the location as early as possible because you will have to set up and do the technical checks yourself.

With any non-visual story, make sure you do a PTC.

Just before going live, take some deep breaths, relax and lighten the expression on your face. You need to be looking at the camera when the newsreader starts introducing your story in case they cut to you early. And after you have finished talking, continue looking at the camera until the director gives you the all-clear.

Non-visual stories

Although television is a visual medium, sometimes TV reporters have to do important stories which don't have good pictures. For example, stories about interest rates, unemployment figures or an inquiry into a rest home where the home has refused you permission to film inside.

But all is not lost. You could, for instance, personalise the story by finding someone who is affected and use them as an example. Film that person at work or at home with their family. If you're talking about unemployment or obesity statistics, you could film people anonymously walking down the street – filming them from behind, or just their feet. You can use re-enactments. You can do vox pops, which is a series of very quick interviews with members of the public. You can film buildings and signs. To make the story as visually interesting as possible, get the cameraperson to film a variety of moving shots.

Another idea would be to find relevant library pictures or old black-and-white footage, newspaper headlines, photos or books. You could check YouTube for any suitable videos, or use graphics to show facts and figures.

If your story is about a report, show the title and relevant sections of the document, or someone flicking through its pages.

Further reading

Hudson, G., & Rowlands, S. (2012). *The broadcast journalism handbook* (2nd ed.). London: Routledge.

Kobre, K. (2012). *Videojournalism*. Available as an online resource by Googling the author and book's names.

Papper, R. (2013). *Broadcast news and writing stylebook* (5th ed.). London: Pearson.

Shook, F., Larson, J., & DeTarsio, J. (2009). *Television field production and reporting* (5th ed.). Boston: Allyn & Bacon.

Tuggle, C., Carr, F., & Huffman, S. (2011). *Broadcast news handbook: Writing, reporting and producing in a converging media world* (4th ed.). New York: McGraw-Hill.

19

Writing for news websites
The continuous-deadline world of online news

Helen Sissons, AUT University; Danielle Mulrennan, AUT University

Converged journalism is also called "backpack" journalism – journalists carry the new technology in their backpacks; "mobile" journalism ("mojo" for short) – reporters use mobile phones and various tablet devices to gather and publish news online; or simply "multimedia", "digital" or "online" journalism.

The once separate news media technologies of the newspaper (the written word and photographs), radio (audio) and television (audio with video) have converged on the internet. This means a newspaper's website looks much like that for a radio or TV news station.

This new "converged journalism" continues to evolve, requiring news writers and producers to adapt to the new digital technologies.

The reporter's job is to convert raw information into a journalistic narrative that brings real knowledge. A good reporter shouldn't be contributing to the online noise, but should step back and try to make sense of it. They should supply news that users can engage with and that sustains their interest, perhaps because of its interactive graphics, video, audio or photo galleries. In addition, it needs to be shareable information. Users want to show their social networks that they are connected to news events; they want news they can use.

In this chapter, we look at how you can write news for websites. The framework we'll use is the Associated Press's 1-2-3 filing system, in which variations of the same story are filed in three stages. But first let's look at the changes in the way the public now consumes the news.

Big changes

The evolution of anytime, anywhere news on web-enabled devices has caused media corporations to rethink how they distribute or "share" news. Newspapers increasingly use their websites for breaking news, and feature video and audio to enhance news stories. Television news organisations, like TVNZ, Newshub and Prime TV, no longer restrict their news menu to scheduled bulletins or "by appointment" viewing. Instead, they also provide online news "on demand".

This means more journalists will be creating news for online and mobile platforms in future. Convergence has altered consumer behaviour, with a majority of young adults now getting their news online (Pew Research Center, 2011) and a third accessing news on at least two devices (Newman & Levy, 2013). New Zealand research shows more than a third of journalists say their roles are now "digital first", where they're expected to break news online as it happens instead of holding it for the print edition. In addition, nearly a third say they develop multiple versions of the same story to utilise tools available online that aren't available in print, such as video and interactive elements (Ahmed, 2013).

Coverage of a story can be collaborative, where your content is combined with the published content of others – known as curation – into a multi-platform news story, containing written text with embedded video (such as from YouTube), images (Picasaweb, Instagram) and user-generated comments (tweets, Facebook). Increasingly, social media video applications are featuring in collaborations of this kind. One is Vine,

On-demand is a technology that allows users to access news material of their choice as and when they want it.

For details on social media sites, see Chapter 4.

CONTINUOUS DEADLINES

Old media, like newspapers or TV, have specific deadlines. The newspaper articles must be ready to go to the printing press by 2am, the TV reports must be ready to air at 6pm. Online news has no such deadlines, the news can be posted anytime. It also means the news can be reorganised anytime, as online editors monitor which stories are generating the most hits.

Let's listen in on the instructions from the news editor to an online editor at Stuff's Auckland Now online newsroom (www.aucklandnow.co.nz) as the site is constantly being kept fresh:

"I think we might flip around some stuff on the home page.

"The local news lead, let's bring that up into number five and put the piece about the skeleton found in Mt Wellington down as the lead item on local news.

"That's not really rating on two. Let's flick that around.

"And also in the local news about the woman's death, we just remove the 'Today' so that that doesn't date it.

"Are you cool to update the baby story?

"Actually, I've got something else that I'll get you to make a priority, just because it's a fresh story."

which allows you to create six-second video clips and post them in a way similar to tweeting a short message via Twitter. Another video tool is Vyclone, which uses GPS to link the footage recorded by a number of users for multi-angle coverage of an event without the need for post-production. For more on Vyclone, see http://bit.ly/1czIXKC.

1-2-3 filing

Much has changed about the way news is presented, and much has stayed the same. Newsrooms still emphasise the taken-for-granted characteristic of news: that it is new and that what is presented to the audience has the strongest angle and the most up-to-date facts. Online, we still put the new and most important information at the top of the story, and at the top of the news website. But with websites there are continuous deadlines. Stories are posted as soon as possible. Often the websites tell us when the stories were posted (5 mins ago, 2 hours ago), to emphasise this timeliness.

However, it is not only breaking news that wins an audience. The Associated Press in the United States carried out research that followed how a group of young people consumed news (Associated Press, 2008). Chief among its findings was that although the young people constantly checked for news, they were often dissatisfied. The users wanted more than just short updates, they wanted understanding and in-depth information on important events. This hungering for fresh, well-told and deeply researched stories is good news for journalists. It supports the argument that the real task for the digital mobile journalist is not simply to provide more updated information, but also to help people understand and make sense of events: to filter, process and arrange raw information into attractive, readable, understandable narratives.

One way to keep up with the demand for speed and accuracy, while still aiding understanding, is to publish stories incrementally (iteratively). That is, the journalist keeps adding to the story as they discover more, and allows the audience to add its voice. In this way the journalism is a process, rather than just an end-product. But if the journalist is not careful, this way of working can lead to a lot of repetition in news material, with a procession of long articles saying much the same thing with little new added.

To overcome this problem, the Associated Press came up with a third way. It changed how it presented its news in a manner that follows some of the ideas of "iterative", unpackaged, real-time journalism, but reduces repetition. It instituted a procedure called 1-2-3 filing, where reporters produce news content in three parts, which they file separately: a very short news report (called a websnap, often in the form of a tweet), a short present-tense story, and, when appropriate, a longer backgrounder or in-depth account.

The approach removes the duplication caused by filing a full-length article for every new story development. In 1-2-3 filing, each new element filed replaces the previous item: the short report is replaced by the present-tense story, which is then replaced by the in-depth account. It also institutes a way of tagging material that allows the related elements of a story to be electronically linked, enabling the reader to see all the threads and therefore the bigger picture.

In this next section, we are going to address the three ways of reporting highlighted in the Associated Press's 1-2-3 system of filing: The short report, which is best as a tweet, the short story, and the longer, more explanatory piece.

Step 1: The websnap/tweet

The first task is to join Twitter. When you sign up to Twitter, write a bio and attach a photo, remembering you are trying to attract followers. Someone will glance momentarily at your description and decide whether to follow you. Therefore, your bio should clearly and succinctly state who you are and what your purpose is. Your photo should show your face, probably smiling, as first impressions matter and many people are hesitant to follow those with impersonal icons or images as their avatar.

An avatar is the small picture on your Twitter profile.

You should view Twitter as a tool for showcasing your material. Your tweet's short burst of words should be as carefully crafted as if it were going to be read by your favourite writer. News must be timely and tweets make this explicit. Each tweet carries the time of the action in elapsed time, such as 5s (5 seconds ago), 5m (5 minutes ago), 5h (5 hours ago) or 5d (5 days ago).

It is important to use an appropriate tone in your tweets. If you adopt a light-hearted tone normally, change the tone if the event is serious or tragic. Do not use text shorthand or slang. This may work when you are talking with a friend, but on Twitter you are in a public arena and your language should be understandable to everyone.

These tweeting guidelines are adapted from Chilcote (2013) and Stahl (2013).

Always proof-read your tweets before you send them. Better still, read them aloud. If what you have written is hard to read, then it will be hard to understand and will need rewriting. Watch out for the most popular errors such as spelling mistakes and malapropisms. Not only do mistakes make you look uneducated, they ruin your credibility and people will go elsewhere. So, if you want to keep your followers, good grammar and a clear style are essential.

Research any hashtags you are going to attach to a tweet. For example, do a search using the hashtags to ensure they're not being used, if you want to start a new thread, or that they are, if you are joining a conversation. Don't overdo their use, and use them in-text when possible to keep the flow of the tweet, such as in the tweet below.

The immediacy of online news means poorly subbed work is often published. That is a bad look. See Appendix 1 for guidance on grammar and spelling.

Always try to be interesting in tweets and, if possible, original. If every one of your tweets is impersonal, and all you ever share are links, retweets or quotes from famous dead people, you will soon lose followers. And, if you can, leave space in your tweet for your followers. Although the character limit on Twitter is 280, it's worth leaving space for "RT @YourName:" so followers can retweet you and/or attach a comment. The more engagement you get, the better. One way to save space is to shorten any links you include. Sometimes these links use too many characters. You can shorten them with services such as Bitly, TinyURL or Google Url Shortener. These applications reduce the link to fewer characters to make it easier to share, tweet or email. For more, see http://goo.gl/. Below are examples of how Twitter can be used to its best advantage. The first example uses alliteration along with a skilful summary of the facts to attract the reader to a smuggling story.

This next tweet engages readers' emotions, helping to promote a news story and including a strong quote and a photo. Notice these two tweets use URL shortening devices.

Short version of the story

Once you have tweeted or posted a very short summary of the story, you are likely to be expected to produce a four- to six-paragraph version quickly. Often this is within five to 10 minutes. On the web, space may be unlimited, but the 250–350-word inverted-pyramid story is still king. This is because tight writing and an organisational structure that puts the most important information at the start of the story works very well online.

Headlines

Many online journalists have to write their own headlines. If this is the case with you, it's the first thing you should tackle after the tweet. This is the one chance to grab the attention of the user. If the headline is not good enough, is too vague or just clumsy, they won't bother to click onto it and read more.

An online story can have two headlines. The first is called the main headline. It appears at the top of the actual story and can be fairly long (up to 120 characters). It spells out the story explicitly. That's because this headline is designed for search engine optimisation (SEO). This means the headline must include the keywords somebody searching for the story is likely to use. These potential readers are making a Google (or similar) search for information they are interested in. To ensure your story appears at the top of their list of hits (in other words, to ensure SEO), your headline must include the words they would likely enter into the search engine. That is why the headline to the article on page 300 mentions "Hawke's Bay Hospital", "norovirus" and "confirmed". These are the sorts of words those seeking out the article are likely to enter into their search engine.

The second headline is called the index headline. It appears on the news website's homepage, if the story is featured there. This headline uses fewer characters (up to about 60) and can be a little mysterious and intriguing. It is designed to pique the interest of those already on the website idly looking for stories to read. Hopefully these people will then click through to the story. The index headline for the norovirus story was "Norovirus confirmed in hospital". By removing the reference to Hawke's Bay, the story is generalised. Hopefully, general readers will then be attracted to the story and click through to it out of curiosity.

When updating a story, a web journalist will refresh the top of a story to show the latest developments. The journalist will update the headline and the first few pars. The details lower down are likely to remain unchanged from older versions of the story. This technique enables updates to be rolled out more quickly than if publication were delayed until all the story is updated.

Body of the story

Once users have clicked into the story, research tells us that the majority get no further than the first four paragraphs or, if they do, they are not reading in detail (Weber, n.d.; Nielsen, 2008). Therefore, you have those four paragraphs to explain the most important elements of your story. You need to try to answer the news questions – who, what, when, where, why and how, and what next – so that if the user stops

Your aim is to make your prose attractive enough to persuade your audience to read on, turning a browser into an engaged reader.

reading after the fourth paragraph, they have enough information to understand the basics of the article.

To succeed, you will have to keep your language simple and punchy. Below is a good example from the stuff.co.nz site on a norovirus outbreak in Hawke's Bay (Chumko, 2017). The headline is straightforward and explanatory. The intro tells us the virus has been identified (the what), which people it has affected (the who), and that this has happened at Hawke's Bay Hospital (the where) this week (the when). The bridge gives us details on the ongoing restrictions (the what next), and the next sentence explains that norovirus is extremely contagious (the why/how). There are direct quotes from an expert and background about the outbreak. The reader can get all they need from these short, clearly written paragraphs. And if the reader is interested in learning more, they can click on the links to read related articles. They can also easily share it on Twitter, Facebook, etc., using the buttons at the top right.

Restrictions remain at Hawke's Bay Hospital after norovirus outbreak confirmed

ANDRE CHUMKO
Last updated 11:22, October 19 2017

A bad strain of norovirus has hit Hawke's Bay Hospital.

Norovirus has been confirmed as the illness which has affected more than 30 patients and staff members at Hawke's Bay Hospital this week.

Chief Medical and Dental Officer John Gommans said the outbreak appeared to be under control, however one ward continued to have restricted visiting, which would remain in place throughout Labour weekend.

Gommans said norovirus was extremely contagious and very difficult to contain, so hospital staff would have to remain vigilant with strict hygiene measures being put into place throughout the facility.

"We know norovirus is circulating out in the community, so again we remind people about the importance of hand-washing and not to visit friends or family in hospital if you have had a tummy bug for 48 hours after symptoms have disappeared.

READ MORE:
* Virus closes hospital wards and leads to warning ahead of annual show weekend
* Norovirus suspected in retirement village lockdown
* Norovirus outbreak in Nelson Lakes National Park contained DOC says

"Staff at the hospital had worked extremely hard to contain the outbreak, and we are now confident we are now over the worst," he said.

On Monday, norovirus was suspected to have led to the closure of some hospital wards and prompted Hawke's Bay medical staff to warn people attending the Hawke's Bay A&P Show this weekend to be vigilant about washing their hands.

Seven patients have suspected norovirus and about 30 hospital staff also had symptoms.

Source: Stuff

Longer version of the story

Once your short story is published (hopefully within 10 minutes), you can, if the story warrants it, go back and look for more details and context to add to the user's understanding. At the very least, you can provide links to background information

KEY FACTS

Republic of the Fiji Islands
Capital: Suva

Population 900,000

Area 18,376 sq km (7,095 sq miles)

Major languages English, Fijian, Hindi

Major religions Christianity, Hinduism, Islam

Life expectancy 67 years (men), 73 years (women)

Currency Fijian dollar

UN, World Bank

Source: BBC website

and earlier stories on the same topic. But many stories afford the opportunity to add other multimedia features.

Multimedia elements are increasingly important as users look for more in online stories than the text. The options include photographic slideshows (also called albums), graphics (for example, maps and diagrams), audio and video. The video could have been created by the news reporter, be a feed from a news agency (such as Reuters), be an embedded YouTube clip, etc. All these elements intensify the engagement of the reader, and can aid understanding. They also help to break up the text, as big blocks of writing are hard to read on a screen. Graphics can be especially useful to provide interest and context. For example, maps can show users the area or region affected by an event. You could even provide a bullet-pointed profile of a country if something has happened abroad. See the profile above of Fiji from the BBC's website: www.bbc.co.uk news/world-asia-pacific-14919066.

For details on writing news, taking news photographs, preparing news audio and news video, see Chapters 14, 16, 17 and 18.

Interactive maps can go a step further, showing change over time or allowing for comparisons, such as a map that displays annual crime statistics when you click on a region. A reporter may need help to produce such maps (see Further Reading for an easy-to-follow video on how to do it). Despite the technical challenge, it is important you come up with ideas like this, and then it is up to an editor to decide whether it should be produced. But what you can do is take your own photos, and perhaps record video and audio from an event you attend. Also, remember the part user-generated content can play (see below).

A good example of what can be done with some investment in time is a piece by Charles Anderson for the Stuff website. "Lost in the long white cloud" tells the story of the doomed trans-Tasman flight of pioneering aviators George Hood and John Moncrieff in 1928, and the search for their lost plane. It combines more than 7500 words, broken up into chapters, with photos, video and an animated graphic of the planned flight path. See www.lostplane.co.nz/main.html to read the full piece. Another excellent example of multimedia storytelling is from *The Guardian* about the

MULTIMEDIA COMPONENTS OF A STORY

A web editor in Stuff's aucklandnow.co.nz newsroom discusses the kind of multimedia material she uses on a story.

"My job is to upload a story, make sure it fits into the story format properly, and write the headlines. I sub and attach all the multimedia aspects.

"For this story, we've got a video that one of our videographers went out and filmed. He's just uploaded it to the system so you can attach that and it'll go across the top. There could be photos. If we have an album stream we can embed that into the story.

"So we are definitely making it quite visual, more than just a reading experience. You can have audio at the side sometimes and embed YouTube videos. All that sort of stuff, which is quite cool."

Holmes family's narrow escape from bushfires in Tasmania. The photographs of them hiding at the end of a wooden jetty were seen around the world. Again, the report combines several different forms of media: photographs, audio, video, interactive maps and background information about bushfires and the landscape of Tasmania (see http://bit.ly/1371QSa).

These are both lengthy pieces of journalism, but not all articles containing background and multimedia have to be this long. An article by the Associated Press published on stuff.co.nz about the birth of a baby boy to Prince William and the Duchess of Cambridge is just over 1000 words. It contains four videos and a photo gallery along with links to related stories. See the story at http://bit.ly/19dzVAY.

For more on using statistics in journalism, see Chapter 13.

Another approach that is becoming increasingly popular is called data journalism. This is where journalists undertake major statistical research projects, with associated news stories being published from them.

Go to www.insights.nzherald.co.nz to see plenty of good examples of data journalism.

Ongoing updates

There is a constant need to update online stories. This can be done in many ways, including through tweets, email or text alerts, and a news ticker (where big stories scroll across the page, as on the BBC's website www.bbc.co.uk). With an ongoing story you can use live-blogging. This involves posting stories, audio and images of an event on social media sites in short entries. After the Wellington earthquake in July 2013, *The New Zealand Herald*'s website team used ScribbleLive to deliver rolling live updates. They included information from scientists, transport authorities, the city council, and short reports and photos from *Herald* reporters and users. The updates also incorporated pictures and reports from Twitter. As after the Christchurch earthquake, Twitter users employed the hashtag #eqnz.

User-generated content

User-generated content is where users publish their own content online and thereby become active participants in the process of news. One of the first examples of this was when members of the public started generating content during the bombings in the London underground railway system in 2005 (Douglas, 2006). On the day of the bombings, the BBC received 22,000 emails and text messages, 300 photos and several videos from users who experienced the tragedy. As the events had happened in large part underground, the images from users' phone cameras were the only illustrations the BBC had of the day's horrific events. On-air, the dramatic images led the BBC's 6pm news bulletin.

The BBC had lengthy debates on how best to use user-generated content, following criticism that encouraging users to submit photos of potential tragedy was almost voyeuristic. There was also concern that users could put themselves at personal risk to get better pictures, so the BBC published a warning on its website to discourage this.

BLOGGING

A blog (short for web-log) is an online diary of commentary and personal accounts. Many journalists are required to blog on news and other topics that feed into the news agenda.

Blogging raises the profile of both the journalist and their work. It allows you to go behind the scenes of stories, profile people who may not get into the mainstream and highlight research not significant enough for the main news pages. It also allows you to connect with your audience on a new level.

Blogging is now accepted as part of the mainstream media; the number of reporters who blog is likely to grow. It's particularly useful for journalists wishing to promote their work beyond their media outlet.

This is crucial for freelancers, who need to keep a high profile to remind commissioning editors that they are there, but can also be helpful for specialists and those journalists who wish to show their expertise at a deeper level.

Greer Berry worked as a blogger for seven years.

"Blogging accidentally became important to me. I certainly never trained or had any ambition to become a blogger," she says. She enjoyed being able to write in a less structured way and how blogging created a strong bond between her and her readers. But on the downside, trolls (online bullies) criticised her work and she felt a lack of respect from some colleagues, particularly older journalists, who saw blogging as inferior to column writing.

For more on live-blogging, see Chapter 4.

Overall, though, she enjoyed blogging, saying it "provided me with a really unique bond with my readers".

To see examples of Greer's blogs, go to stuff.co.nz and search for "cold coffee".

Further reading

http://bit.ly/1dJTaYG A thought-provoking discussion about writing headlines for the web.

http://bit.ly/14mo6VC, http://nyr.kr/1e9h5OW and **http://slate.me/1afqjdl** Excellent articles on tweeting.

http://bit.ly/15zBq8o A thoughtful piece on journalism's role in the age of information overload.

http://bit.ly/17Ha1lt A very good video on journalists' use of Twitter.

http://bit.ly/19dVilB A step-by-step guide to making an interactive map.

http://nbcnews.to/1dJSrGY A must-read before dabbling in hashtags.

www.codecademy.com If you wish to learn how to design and build your own webpages from scratch, a useful skill for the modern multimedia journalist, you can teach yourself for free on this site.

www.visualisingdata.com/index.php/resources/ More information on data visualisation tools.

References

Ahmed, S. (2013, July 10). *Journalists say online doesn't make dollars or sense. Idealog.* Retrieved from http://www.idealog.co.nz/news/2013/07/journalists-say-online-doesnt-make-dollars-or-sense

Associated Press. (2008). *A new model for news: Studying the deep structure for young-adult news consumption.* New York: Associated Press & Context-Based Research Group.

Chumko, A. (2017, October 19). *Restrictions remain at Hawke's Bay Hospital after norovirus outbreak confirmed.* Retrieved from www.stuff.co.nz/national/health/98034316/restrictions-remain-at-hawkes-bay-hospital-after-norovirus-outbreak-confirmed

Chilcote, T. (2013, May 2). *13 style and grammar tips for Twitter success.* [Weblog message]. Retrieved from http://www.ignitesocialmedia.com/twitter-marketing/style-grammar-tips-tricks-best-practices-twitter/

Douglas, T. (2006, July 4). *How 7/7 "democratised" the media. BBC News.* Retrieved from http://news.bbc.co.uk/2/hi/uk_news/5142702.stm

Newman, N., & Levy, A. (2013). *Reuters Institute Digital News Report 2013: Tracking the future of news. Reuters Institute for the Study of Journalism.* Retrieved from https://reutersinstitute.politics.ox.ac.uk/fileadmin/documents/Publications/Working_Papers/Digital_News_Report_2013.pdf

Nielsen, J. (2008, May 6). *How little do users read?* [Weblog message]. Retrieved from http://www.nngroup.com/articles/how-little-do-users-read/

Pew Research Center for the People and the Press. (2011, January 4). *Internet gains on television as public's main news source: More young people cite internet than TV.* Retrieved from http://pewresearch.org/pubs/1844/poll--main--source--national--international--news--internet--television--newspapers

Stahl, J. (2013, April 15). *Thou shalt not stoop to political point-scoring. Slate.* Retrieved from http://www.slate.com/articles/technology/technology/2013/04/boston_marathon_bombing_all_the_mistakes_journalists_make_during_a_crisis.html

Weber, T. (n.d.). *Online journalism. BBC College of Journalism.* Retrieved from http://bbcjournalism.oup.com

PART C

Media law and ethics

20

Media law

Defamation, privacy, copyright and other aspects of the law journalists need to know

Ursula Cheer, University of Canterbury

This chapter is about the laws that govern the media and journalists. Journalism is a worthy and important profession that genuinely serves the greater public interest by seeking out and publishing news and current affairs stories the public needs to know about. This means that as much freedom of expression as possible should be granted to journalists. That freedom is accordingly recognised in section 14 of the New Zealand Bill of Rights Act 1990. However, it is important to remember that this right comes with a responsibility not to cause unlawful harm when publishing information. Our laws recognise that sometimes publishing can do great harm.

This chapter outlines the laws you need to bear in mind while collecting and publishing stories, whether for online, print or broadcast media. It will summarise the risks involved, give you real examples encountered by journalists, and discuss defences and strategies for avoiding risk. Generally, media laws should not stop you writing stories if you are aware of them and know how to manage risk and when to seek legal advice.

The laws discussed in this chapter are those relating to defamation, privacy, copyright and other civil liability, breach of confidence, and laws affecting investigation and interview methods. The chapter does not discuss other important laws, such as those covering what you can report in court, official information, and the ethical complaints codes and processes that also affect what you can do and publish. Those are discussed in Chapters 8, 12 and 21.

It is vital that you are familiar with both the laws and the ethical codes that are relevant to media. This is because observing the standards of ethical journalism, such as accuracy, balance and fairness, not only makes you a better and more trustworthy journalist, it also, in many cases, helps you avoid legal traps as well.

Difference between criminal and civil cases

It is important to understand the difference between criminal and civil court cases. Criminal proceedings brought against individuals (or corporate bodies like companies) by the state on behalf of its citizens are heard in court, and can result in state-imposed penalties, such as fines, or more significantly, imprisonment.

Civil proceedings are private claims made by individual citizens (including companies) against other citizens, using the state-provided court system. Such proceedings can result in private remedies, such as awards of damages, or orders affecting behaviour, but do not, as a rule, involve imprisonment. Criminal proceedings are prosecuted after an individual (or corporate body) is charged with an offence. In contrast, civil claims are filed, and in such claims a plaintiff sues a defendant.

Criminal and civil proceedings are quite different. However, sometimes the same conduct may make media liable to both types of proceedings. For example, secretly recording someone can be a criminal offence as well as a breach of privacy, which is a civil matter. This means even if the police decide not to prosecute, a civil claim may still be brought by the person who has been harmed.

Statute and common law

There is also a useful distinction to be made between statute and common law. A statute is an Act of Parliament that may cover all or part of an area of the law. The Crimes Act 1961 is an example of a statute that contains the main criminal offences in New Zealand. In contrast, the common law comprises decisions made by judges in the cases before them. Some areas of law are completely judge-made in this way, breach of confidence being one. Both statute and judge-made law are binding. Many areas of the civil law are covered by both statute and common law, such as defamation.

Penalties that affect media

Criminal

Sometimes media can be guilty of a criminal offence, for which penalties, such as a fine or even imprisonment, may be imposed. An example is failing to obey a court order suppressing an accused's name, as discussed in Chapter 8. Normally, the media company is found guilty, but individuals – such as the reporter and, in particular, the editor – may be personally penalised as well.

Civil

Civil claims, like defamation, invasion of privacy, breach of copyright, and breach of confidence, may result in civil remedies, including damages, injunctions, and other financial remedies.

Damages is an award of a sum of money to compensate an aggrieved person for the injury caused to him or her by the publication or other actions of the media.

Injunctions are orders made by a court directing that media which have been sued not do certain things (like publish an article) or do something (like destroy the remaining copies of a book or publish a correction). Media who do not obey risk criminal penalties.

An injunction can be permanent (it remains in force unless later lifted) or interim (temporary). Most applications against the media are for temporary orders. Interim injunctions are "holding measures", usually granted under some urgency to stop something being published until the issue is dealt with at a full hearing later on. They are quite hard to get.

Sometimes other monetary remedies are available. In copyright, breach of confidence, and breach of contract, for example, an order can be made to hand over the ill-gotten profits made as a result of the breach.

Regulation outside the court system

Some media laws are enforced by bodies other than the courts. For example, harming human rights or privacy can prompt complaints to the Human Rights Commission or the Privacy Commissioner, and possibly the Human Rights Review Tribunal.

Likewise, the Broadcasting Act 1989 lays down standards for broadcasting and sets up a Broadcasting Standards Authority (BSA) to enforce these. The Media Council, a voluntary body covering print and online media, hears complaints about breaches of ethical standards. The BSA and Media Council are discussed in Chapter 21.

With these introductory matters out of the way, we can now turn to the main laws which impact on the media.

Defamation

Defamation protects a person's reputation against unjustifiable attack. It is a civil action and the injured party can claim substantial damages. The law is technical and complex in places, and therefore impossible to deal with in a text of this kind in any detail. What this section sets out to do, therefore, is to alert you to the important features of the law, to allow you to make judgements in your work about when to publish material, and when to seek legal advice first.

Definition

A defamatory statement is one which is untrue and tends to lower a person in the estimation of ordinary members of society generally. The statement must also identify that person in some way. This need not be by name, but can be implied or obvious from the statement so that those who know the person would think it was him or her. The statement must also be published, although this needs only be to one other person who is not the plaintiff.

A company or other corporation can sue for defamation, but it must show additionally that it has suffered financial loss or is likely to. It is not defamatory to make disparaging statements about a dead person, but, remember, if the statement reflects on members of the family who are still alive, they might bring their own action.

Intention not necessary

It makes no difference whether you intend to defame or have simply made a mistake. Defamation can arise in either case. This means great care is required in preparing and publishing stories that might damage someone's reputation. You need to be sure the text and any implications that might arise are correct. Similarly, the placement and accuracy of images should be checked.

Disclaimers

It is possible that a carefully worded disclaimer could remove an inference that could otherwise be drawn from the words complained of. But disclaimers will not always remove risk. A common disclaimer is: "All characters in this book are fictitious, and any resemblance to any real person, living or dead, is purely coincidental." If the disclaimer is untrue and the resemblance to a living person is not coincidental, the disclaimer can be of no effect at all. But even if the disclaimer is genuine, it might not be effective if the character in the book bears many close resemblances to a real person, for readers will inevitably make the connection and the disclaimer will be useless.

The meaning of statements

You need to check that the words you want to use mean what you think they do. Although all the facts expressly presented in a programme or article in print or online media might be true, they could lead the audience to an inference or conclusion that is not.

Denials: Inferences can also arise from publications that grammatically state the opposite. This means a denial that facts exist might lead an ordinarily alert reader to suspect that they do. One example is an article in a women's magazine that took the form of an interview, containing photographs and a heading (the names have been removed from the quotes): "Tell me it isn't true, M". The article's opening paragraph began: "It's time to set the record straight and shut up the gossips – M is not having an affair with H!" The interview that followed contained several denials by M of the rumours. H successfully sued. It was held that in reading the article a notional, reasonable reader could feel there was no smoke without fire (*New Zealand Magazines v H*, 2005).

Bane and antidote: Everything depends on the overall impression created by the publication, and it may be that a denial could counter allegations completely. This is called the "bane and antidote doctrine" by which the *bane*, or negative part of an article, must be taken together with later words – an *antidote* – which puts things right. An example is an English case where the article complained of was made up of a large headline, two photographs, a smaller headline, photo captions, and the smaller

Before a court can say whether words are defamatory, it must decide what the words mean. What matters is the meaning that the ordinary reasonable person would as a matter of impression carry away in his or her head after reading, listening to or seeing the publication.

Real examples of false statements by media which were defamatory

Suggesting a government Treasurer was "for sale" (that is, corrupt); claiming a celebrity was a bad parent; tweeting that a top sportsman had fixed matches; publishing allegations by a third party that a company paid a substantial sum of money to an MP and another in order to protect the company's interests during a select committee inquiry; suggesting certain men were involved in a notorious abduction of a child; broadcasting a statement that a man was a convicted murderer when he had been pardoned; suggesting a person was suspected of an offence when there was no evidence to support it; wrongly attributing nude photos to an MP; accusing a mayor of being corrupt; suggesting an iconic company's products caused ill health; publishing a photograph of a woman and mistakenly describing her as wanted in connection with the presentation of a stolen cheque; publishing the wrong photograph of a person described as a gang member; and wrongly stating a company was in financial difficulties.

text of the article. The photographs and the main headline suggested that two well-known Australian actors were involved in the production of a pornographic computer game. The photo caption and the article itself made it clear that the actors' heads had been superimposed on the bodies of porn models and they had not consented to the use of their images. It was held that the article carried the antidote for the bane of the headline and photographs, and the ordinary, reasonable, fair-minded reader would have read the caption and article and seen at once that the defamatory material should not be taken at face value (*Charleston v News Group Newspapers*, 1995).

Innuendo: Sometimes the words may bear a further meaning (an innuendo), which would be appreciated only by a limited number of people who have special knowledge. Here the words used appear perfectly innocent to the ordinary reader. However, to certain readers who have what might be colloquially called inside information – knowledge of certain facts that do not appear in the passage concerned – these words take on a colour that is damaging. For example, a photo caption describing a man as being at the races with his wife, when he is actually there with his mistress, may be damaging to the man's real wife because those who know the wife will question her married status on seeing the photo.

Context: The meanings of words can be coloured by their surroundings, so they may be defamatory or not according to the context in which they appear. That is why in the example about the two Australian actors and the pornographic computer game discussed above it was held that a prominent headline, or a headline plus photographs, could not be looked at in isolation from related text even though some readers read only headlines.

Liability for publication on the internet

The issue of republication and the possibility of defamation on the internet is challenging. Worldwide communication by computer, in particular via email, allows the passing of messages between individuals without any other human intervention, and the use of blogs and social networking websites, such as Facebook and Twitter, which allow effortless multiple publication to large groups of people at the touch of a button, have exponentially increased the possibility of defamation occurring both intentionally and unintentionally. Most newspapers now publish internet editions, while broadcasters maintain websites too, and some media are purely online. Defamation can arise on media websites, but also in any comments solicited on such sites. Furthermore, although the law is not settled yet, even if you do not publish defamatory statements you know to be on other websites, it is risky to include in your article hyperlinks to those sites, as this may be seen as a form of publication in itself.

Similarly, breakouts, the journalistic practice of prominently isolating an extract from the body of an article, should not be read on their own. Here broadcasting is no different from print or online. For example, a hoax telephone call made by a radio station which coincidentally defamed a third party was held not to be defamatory because the station made it clear before and after the call that it was a hoax. The call was not looked at in isolation (*Thode v Coastline FM*, 1997).

This can mean extra care is needed though. Sometimes an article that seems inoffensive by itself assumes a defamatory meaning when read in conjunction with other articles or news items, whether in the same newspaper or in earlier or even (possibly) later issues of the newspaper, and whether in hard copy or online. In one case, a man alleged he was defamed by published reports branding him a fraudster. The court assessed all the publications, and in particular treated two broadcasts by TVNZ as parts of a story emerging over a two-day period. It considered the stories in print and in television broadcast as a coherent whole in looking at meanings (*McGee v Independent Newspapers*, 2006).

Repeating what others have said

It is not a defence to say: "But I heard it from her."

Even if all you do is to repeat words that someone else has spoken or written, you can still be liable if those words are defamatory. So, as a general rule, if media report defamatory words used by someone in an interview or in a speech or at a meeting, they are open to a defamation action. This means reports of rumours may land you in trouble. "It is rumoured in the capital that ..." or "usually reliable sources say that ..." may result in action against you if those rumours are false and are defamatory of some person.

It is not enough for you to prove that there were in fact such rumours; you can only escape by proving that the rumours were true. Furthermore, just as you can be liable for repeating the words of speakers, so you can be liable for repeating defamatory words that other newspapers, broadcasters or online media have used.

Links in a chain of publication

When a defamatory statement is published, all those concerned with the publication are liable – for a newspaper, for example, this includes the newspaper company, the editor, the reporter, and even the sub-editors. In practice, usually only the company is sued because the others are not worth pursuing. But media will be liable even if the writer of the offensive material was not a member of the media at all – for example, the writer of a letter to the editor, or someone commenting on an online story. Media are publishers of the statements too.

There are difficulties for broadcast media, where outside contributors often go to air live. On live interviews and talkback shows there is always the risk that the interviewee, without any involvement of the broadcaster, may make a defamatory off-the-cuff remark. Even here the broadcaster will normally be held liable, for it has assisted in publishing the remark – that is, in disseminating it nationwide. Use of a short delay button, whereby broadcast is delayed long enough to prevent publication of risky material, is highly recommended for such interviews.

In some situations, a talkshow host or interviewer might also be personally liable, although this would be so only if that person had made comments personally, or could be said to have been in some way responsible for the statements made by the interviewee.

Remedies for defamation

A number of remedies are available. The most common remedies are damages and apologies. Orders (injunctions) to prevent publication can be granted too, but these are rare (*TV3 Network Services v Fahey*, 1999).

Damages are money to compensate the person for the damage done to their reputation. Awards can range from $5000 to $50,000 where ordinary people are defamed. Where celebrities or public figures are involved, awards range from $50,000 to $500,000, though more commonly are at the lower end of the scale. Where a company has been defamed and its business damaged, awards can be very high, even in the millions. If the defamation has been deliberate and malicious, an additional award can be made to punish the publisher.

In a New Zealand case involving a newspaper deliberately defaming Ray Columbus, an ex-pop singer who latterly ran a business providing pre-rugby match entertainment, the award was $675,000 (*Columbus v Independent News Auckland*, 2000). The courts calculate the figures by taking into account such factors as how important the person is and whether they already have some kind of bad reputation.

Other remedies which are unique to defamation are also available. These are declarations, corrections, retractions or rights of reply. These orders are not claimed very often.

APOLOGIES

Apologies are a very good idea when you have definitely got the story wrong. They can stop a person from suing you or your media employer. But they require care. The following extract from a real apology (names changed) contained a serious typo that defamed the person complaining all over again. The word "his" should have been "this". The mistake was corrected the following week in a further apology.

"That story stated, wrongly, that Mr X had a personal interest in the ... Trust, which owned land close to [a certain property]. The article reported further allegations against Mr X based on **his** untrue statement. [The publication] accepts that Mr X held no personal or beneficial interest in the ... Trust. His involvement with the trust was as a professional trustee and as its solicitor ... unreservedly withdraw these statements. An apology is given to Mr X for their publication" (*National Business Review*, July 19, 2002, emphasis added).

Defences to defamation

Even though a person can prove that an untrue statement has been made by media that has affected his or her reputation, they will not succeed in a defamation action if media can present a recognised defence. The most important defences for media follow.

Truth: The media must show that the words were true or not materially different from the truth. This means minor inaccuracies will not destroy the defence. But it might be harder than you think to prove truth. It is safer not to make sweeping statements.

The standard of proof required is truth on a balance of probabilities, which is not as high as the criminal standard of beyond reasonable doubt. But the defence is useless if you cannot get your evidence before a court. If you are relying on witnesses, you need to know whether they are reliable in this respect.

Defence against attack: This form of privilege protects you if you have been defamed in a publication and wish to justify yourself to those who heard or saw the original statement. The defence can protect you if your justification contains defamatory material. You can be robust in your reply, but you must not go too far. If you go beyond what is necessary for defence you may exceed the privilege. Therefore, you should not make fresh or irrelevant accusations in your response (*Alexander v Clegg*, 2004).

Constitutional qualified privilege: Statements (true or otherwise) made about the actions and qualities of Members of Parliament past, present or future, are protected. Those actions and qualities must be relevant to their capacity to meet their public responsibilities. However, the story must not be motivated by ill will, nor must the opportunity to publish be misused – in other words, there must not be an ulterior motive (*Lange v Atkinson*, 1998).

Statutory qualified privilege: The Defamation Act 1992 contains far-reaching statutory privileges. A stronger kind of this privilege covers mainly Parliamentary

> What is ill will or misusing the opportunity to publish? Undue sensationalism in a report and headlines; inclusion of comment or irrelevant matter; disproportionate prominence to the report itself or aspects of it; publication at a seemingly irrelevant time (eg, some time after the event); repetition of publication or unnecessarily wide publication; recklessness or indifference to the truth.

and court reporting, for example, delayed broadcast, by any broadcaster, of proceedings in Parliament, a fair and accurate report of proceedings of the House of Representatives or of any of its committees, or a fair and accurate report of the pleadings of the parties in any court proceedings.

A weaker kind of qualified privilege protects reports of the proceedings of a large number of meetings and bodies, as well as certain publications that are statements supplied by someone in authority for the benefit of the public. An example of the latter would be a report based on a statement released by the police. In general, this defence only applies to reports that are fair and accurate, and it may be lost if publication is motivated by ill will of some kind. Journalists rely on the defence every day without necessarily being aware of it.

Honest opinion: One of the most important defences covers media opinion, such as the work of political columnists, and restaurant, book and film reviewers. This defence requires that the statements used must be opinion and not fact, they must be based on facts that are true, and must also be genuine opinions (again, ill will may destroy this defence). The more direct and bald a statement is, the more likely it will be seen as a statement of fact and not opinion. If it is a statement of fact, then it must be proved true and honest opinion cannot be used.

Consent: If a person has consented to the publication of a statement, he or she cannot sue. However, media will have to prove not just that the person suing consented (which may itself be difficult if the consent was given orally), but also that he or she consented specifically to the story as published.

Settlement

Many defamation suits are settled out of court. This means that the person suing, in return for the performance of some act on the part of the media, such as publication of an apology or payment of a sum of money, undertakes not to pursue his or her claim in court.

Public-interest stories

The constitutional qualified privilege defence described above may be developing into a general public-interest defence. There are cases supporting this in New Zealand

PUBLIC-INTEREST STORIES

Public-interest stories are about these sorts of issues: politicians in their public role, the spending of public money, the democratic process, public health and safety, crime, national security, the public behaviour of public figures, the operation of the economy, the management of public or monopoly businesses, the functioning of government departments and officials, electoral and other constitutional processes, exposing misleading claims made by individuals or organisations, and exposing seriously anti-social and harmful conduct.

Taking a photograph of a person in a public place without their consent does not normally invade privacy, unless they are very vulnerable in some way. Care is required when publishing, as shown by this picture from an article in *The Press* newspaper, June 3, 2013, about drinking in Christchurch.

and overseas. This sort of defence would apply to responsible communications about matters of public interest. Being responsible means you should not be reckless or carelessly indifferent to the accuracy of your story. If this defence becomes fully recognised, it will be very valuable to media wanting to publish general public-interest stories. Such stories attract good protection under the law. They should not be censored in a way that is unjustified in a free and democratic society.

Privacy

Privacy laws are increasingly significant because they restrict the methods by which a journalist may obtain and disseminate information and the content of that information. The media cannot afford to ignore privacy. This section will describe a civil action called a tort, privacy principles developed by the BSA, legislative requirements for collection, storage and use of personal information in the Privacy Act 1993, the requirements of the Harassment Act 1997, and a number of miscellaneous legal requirements.

A civil action in privacy

The existence of a civil claim for invasion of privacy was confirmed by the Court of Appeal in *Hosking v Runting* in 2005. This case was an attempt to prevent publication of photos of celebrity broadcaster Mike Hosking's twin daughters. The images were taken by a freelance photographer while the children were being pushed in a pram by their mother on a Christmas shopping trip on a public footpath, in a busy shopping mall.

Taking a photograph of a person in a public place without their consent does not normally invade privacy. This is because if you are in public, anyone can see you, and a photograph of you only replicates what the public could see. In the end, that is why the court rejected the Hoskings' claim. However, the court did say that in exceptional cases, such as where a person is particularly vulnerable, a privacy claim based on activities in public might succeed.

Although the Hoskings' claim was not successful, the case confirmed that a right to sue to protect privacy does exist in New Zealand. The action has these parts:

Private or public? Private matters are things like domestic behaviour, particularly if sexual or intimate, or personal or family circumstances, such as medical or financial records. Public matters are those such as criminal convictions, ownership of land, and marriage or divorce. However, criminal convictions can become private over time, depending on how serious the offence is and how much time has passed.

Privacy (Andrews v TVNZ, 2009)

This unsuccessful privacy claim involved a married couple who were filmed by a production company for a series commissioned by TVNZ while being rescued by firefighters following an accident in their vehicle. The accident occurred when the plaintiffs were returning from a party at which they had both been drinking.

The couple were trapped and had to be removed using the "jaws of life". They were unaware they were being filmed and were also unaware edited footage of the incident would be used about a year later in the TVNZ series *Fire Fighter*. The programme focused on the activities of the fire fighters, but also showed the couple interacting with their rescuers. Some pixilation was used but parts of their faces were shown, and statements of endearment made by the wife to her husband were broadcast.

Although the event took place in public, the court found footage of intimate and personal conversations did give rise to a reasonable expectation of privacy because the couple were vulnerable, the footage went beyond mere observation of the scene, and its extent was prolonged.

However, the claim ultimately failed because a reasonable person in the same position would not consider publication of the statements to be highly offensive. The couple were not able to show they were humiliated or embarrassed by the broadcast because it treated them sympathetically and did not disclose the drunk driving they had been involved in. The court also thought there was public interest in a programme about the lives of fire fighters even though the programme had entertainment value too.

- the existence of facts of which there is a reasonable expectation of privacy
- publicity given to those private facts would be considered highly offensive to an objective reasonable person
- the harm protected against is humiliation and distress
- there is a public-interest defence, described as a legitimate public concern in the information
- the primary remedy is damages, but injunctive orders are possible.

There have been successful privacy claims, however. New Zealand examples include an injunction granted to prevent a newspaper publishing the fact that a prominent person had been treated in a psychiatric hospital (*P v D*, 2000) and another made to stop a newspaper from disclosing the location of a policeman who had killed a young man during an incident and had been cleared of any wrongdoing (*Abbot v The Press*, 2002).

A convicted paedophile whose post-prison release location had been disclosed by police in a flyer, resulting in vigilante attacks and harassment, was awarded $25,000 for breaches of privacy and confidence (*Brown v AG*, 2006). And an order was made preventing the disclosure of the identity of a young man who had made a complaint

In privacy, the defence of public interest is very valuable to the media. Therefore, stories which deal with matters described here may well breach privacy but be excused because they are of legitimate public concern.

about a sexual offence against a Member of Parliament where no charges were laid (*A v Fairfax New Zealand*, 2011).

A civil action for breach of seclusion

The tort of invasion of privacy described above does not apply to intrusive behaviour. But in 2012, in a case called *C v Holland*, a young woman sued the male flatmate of her boyfriend who had secretly filmed her in the bathroom of the flat. As a result, New Zealand now has a claim called intrusion upon seclusion. To sue, a person has to show the act was:

- an intentional and unauthorised intrusion
- into an area of seclusion (namely intimate personal activity, space or affairs)
- an infringement of a reasonable expectation of privacy
- one that is highly offensive to a reasonable person.

The action does not cover unwitting or simply careless intrusion, nor consensual and/or lawfully authorised intrusions. Also, only intrusion into intimate personal activity, space or affairs is covered. This new action has the capacity to impact on media methods for collecting news and current affairs. It could apply, for example, to cases like taking photographs with a telephoto lens of the Duchess of Cambridge sunbathing topless on private property. A defence of public interest would likely be unsuccessful in such a case.

Broadcasting Standards Authority

Under the Broadcasting Act 1989, the BSA has jurisdiction to deal with complaints that a broadcaster has breached some aspect of privacy of the individual. Privacy complaints can be made by anybody, not just by those affected, and they go directly to the BSA. The BSA, which is discussed in detail in Chapter 21, can award compensation up to $5000 on upholding a privacy complaint.

The BSA has developed considerable expertise in dealing with privacy complaints and uses eight privacy principles for guidance (see http://bsa.govt.nz/standards/privacy). These cover much the same ground as the two privacy actions described above, but also allow complaints about broadcasts that encourage harassment. The person whose privacy is breached has to be identified or identifiable. There are defences of public interest and informed consent.

Under the BSA codes, children under 16 cannot give consent to the broadcast of private information about them. Additionally, even where consent has been given by parents or guardians on behalf of children, broadcasters still have to consider whether the broadcast is in the best interests of the child. To do this, broadcasters should address the nature and context of the information to be broadcast, the age and maturity of the child, and the potential effects of broadcast on the well-being of the child.

If disclosure of information will significantly expose or embarrass an individual in some way, it is likely that something about the information is inherently private, or has the characteristics of privacy. Privacy is usually breached where filming is surreptitious, for example, where the complainant has no knowledge of the existence

> ## Interests of children *(NS and Sky Network Television, 2015)*
>
> The BSA upheld a complaint based on its privacy standards which require broadcasters to consider the interests of the child before broadcast, even if one or both parents' consent has been obtained for the child to be filmed.
>
> In this case, a *60 Minutes* programme about a mother who had lost a child due to a driveway accident also identified and broadcast footage of the child's sibling. The item also included information detailing the descent of the mother into prostitution and drug addiction.
>
> Although the mother had consented, the father's complaint was upheld due to the need to take account of the interests of the surviving child. The point was that the child was a nine-year-old schoolboy, who would be subject to peer pressure as a result of the content of the programme.
>
> The disclosure of the information was undesirable and in breach of Standard 3 of the Television Code, in which privacy is intended to protect dignity, choice, mental well-being and reputation, and children's ability to develop relationships and opinions away from the glare of publicity.
>
> The broadcast also did not need to identify the child to tell the story.

of cameras, or the camera is hidden. BSA decisions tend to be very much based on the facts in the complaint.

New Zealand Media Council

The New Zealand Media Council, discussed in Chapter 21, also has a principle dealing with privacy (see www.mediacouncil.org.nz/principles, at 2).

This covers similar ground to the actions discussed above, but also requires care and discretion before identifying relatives of persons convicted or accused of crime where the reference to them is not directly relevant to the matter reported.

Also, these principles suggest that careful attention is to be given to those suffering from trauma or grief.

The Privacy Act 1993

New Zealand has comprehensive privacy legislation. The Privacy Act sets out 12 Information Privacy Principles as guidelines for agencies that collect, store, and use personal information about identifiable individuals.

The principles are drafted in general language, with a number of exceptions provided for (see http://privacy.org.nz/the-privacy-act-and-codes/privacy-act-and-codes-introduction/).

The Act also provides for the appointment of the Privacy Commissioner to whom complaints are made. But there must be some actual, significant effect on a complainant before a complaint will be entertained. Mere annoyance is insufficient to support a complaint.

WHEN IS THE PRIVACY ACT RELEVANT?

As a journalist, you are most likely to come in contact with the Privacy Act when seeking information for a story which is not released to you because "the Privacy Act applies". It will be useful for you to familiarise yourself with the main grounds for disclosing information under the Act so that you are able to judge whether withholding information is justified. The grounds are contained in Principle 11 of the Act and can be found at: http://privacy.org.nz/the-privacy-act-and-codes/privacy-principles/limits-on-disclosure-of-personal-information-principle-eleven/.

The media are often required to report about the status of accident victims. A special code made under the Privacy Act, the Health Information Privacy Code, allows hospitals to release certain information about accident victims: http://www.privacy.org.nz/the-privacy-act-and-codes/codes-of-practice/health-information-privacy-code/.

The Act applies to personal information. This is information about any live person who can be identified. The legislation covers both public and private bodies ("agencies"). Therefore, government departments and bodies such as banks or other businesses are all subject to the Act. Even individuals are covered. However, the Act does not apply to the media in general in relation to gathering, preparing and broadcasting or publishing news for public broadcast.

Harassment

It is normally not a legal wrong to badger or question a person persistently with a view to extracting information from them – provided, of course, you do not actually go to the extremes of assaulting or threatening them, or bailing them up and preventing them from going on their way.

It is an offence under section 21 of the Summary Offences Act 1981 to follow a person or watch or loiter near a person's house or place of business, but only if this is done with intent to frighten or intimidate.

The Harassment Act 1997 includes an offence of criminal harassment, and provides for the making of civil restraining orders where harassment is at a lower level. While it is clear that acts of members of the media may well fall within the definition of harassment, it is highly unlikely that the criminal offence would be applicable because of the requirement that there be a mental intent to cause fear in the victim or recklessness as to that result. Journalists who harass should not be journalists and are breaching ethical codes, if not the law.

Interception devices

Under sections 216A–C of the Crimes Act 1961, it is an offence punishable by

> ## The Teapot Tapes affair (*Ambrose v AG, 2012*)
>
> There are no reported cases of the interception offences applying to the New Zealand media. But the potential exists. Prior to the November 2012 election, then Prime Minister John Key referred an audio recording he said was illegally obtained to the police. Mr Key and a political ally, John Banks, had held a meeting to which media were invited in the week running up to election day. The two men enjoyed a cup of tea in a cafe, but prior to having discussions, media were asked to remove themselves to a position outside where they could film but not record the conversation.
>
> After the meeting, Mr Key discovered a recording device had been left on the table. A cameraman, Bradley Ambrose, who owned the device, obtained a recording remotely from it, which he later released to a newspaper when Mr Key accused him of deliberately recording the conversation. The question was whether Mr Bradley had intentionally intercepted a private communication between Mr Key and Mr Banks using an interception device.
>
> The police eventually announced they would not prosecute Mr Ambrose who had written a letter of regret, but delivered a warning to him and to media that his actions were probably illegal and any publication of the tape would be also. However, the tape had been leaked long since by prominent media law bloggers linking to it. There was a good argument that the meeting could never have been private, and that would mean any media publishing the tape would not be in breach of the criminal law either.

imprisonment for up to two years to intentionally intercept any private communication using an interception device. An interception device is any electronic, mechanical, electromagnetic, optical or electro-optical instrument, apparatus, equipment or other device that is used or is capable of being used to intercept a private communication.

Bugging devices, tape recorders and telephone taps are included, as well as hidden cameras and internet spyware. A private communication means a communication (whether oral or written) in circumstances that may reasonably indicate someone doing the communicating desires it to be between the parties only, but does not include circumstances where anyone would reasonably expect the communication could be intercepted by someone else. It is an offence to also disclose private communications that have been unlawfully intercepted in this way.

There is no law preventing participant recording (*R v A*, 1994). Therefore, the media can secretly record or film a person if the journalist (or someone acting on their behalf) is a party to the communication, bearing in mind the other privacy law risks outlined above.

Breach of confidence

The general principle of this area of the common (judge-made) law is that no one should be allowed to publish information which he or she has received in confidence. Not only the original confidant but also the media to whom he or she disclosed the

> ## Public-interest defence for breach of confidence (*New Zealand Post v Prebble, 2001*)
>
> In cases of breach of confidence the primary defence is public interest. This means when the public interest in disclosing the information outweighs the interest of the plaintiff in keeping it confidential, the defendant – including the media – will be permitted to publish it. Once again, because public interest is the most significant and useful defence, it is important for you to have a good idea of what makes a public-interest story. The defence applies only to matters that it is in the public interest to publish, which is not the same as matters which the public may find interesting. The same matters relevant to public interest for defamation and privacy are relevant here.
>
> In one case, New Zealand Post, a state-owned enterprise, tried to stop a Member of Parliament from disclosing the business case report in relation to the setting up of Kiwibank. This failed because its shares were held by the government on behalf of the public, and its expenditure of funds on a matter unrelated to postal services deserved public debate.

information may be prevented by a court order from publishing.

To be confidential, information must be inaccessible to the public, although it may be known to more than one person. It must also not be trivial or nonsense. The great majority of confidence cases involve a relationship between two parties where one entrusts the other with information on the understanding that it will go no further. These include professional relationships like banker–customer and doctor–patient, domestic relationships like marriage or close friendships, employer–employee relationships, business relationships, and dealings with police. Government secrets are also confidential, as is the relationship between journalists and their sources. So any information disclosed by either party in these confidential relationships to parties outside is likely to be wrongfully disclosed.

Because journalists rarely disclose their sources, it is unlikely that you will be sued for breaching the journalist–source relationship. The situation you do need to worry about, though, is where you have received confidential information and are wondering if it can be published. A number of situations can apply.

If a news organisation has used disreputable means to get the information from the confidence-breaker, all remedies will be available against it. An example would be where a journalist induced a person to reveal information in breach of his or her contract of employment, or paid the person for the information.

Where the media receive information *knowing* it to have been revealed in breach of confidence, even though the information is provided to them without any inducement, they are bound by the confidence and can be sued. In the *Argyll* case, the Duke of Argyll, on learning that his estranged wife was about to publish matrimonial confidences, successfully obtained an injunction against her and the newspaper involved. The content of the material was such that its confidential nature was obvious (*Argyll v Argyll,* 1967).

Media may even be liable if a journalist suspects, but does not know for certain, that the information is from a confidential source. This means you cannot deliberately close your eyes to the obvious.

If you have received the information innocently but learn of its confidential nature before publication, you may breach confidence by publishing once you have that knowledge. This is because it is wrong to decide to publish when you know.

Defences

There are two main defences that allow you to publish even if the information has come to you in breach of confidence. The first applies if the information is in fact circulating publicly already. If the allegedly confidential information is or has become public knowledge, the obligation to respect the confidence disappears. The second is public interest; see the box opposite.

Copyright

The Copyright Act 1994 provides that the owner of copyright in a work has the exclusive right to use and control use of the work. No one else may copy from it, or publish it, or otherwise use it, without the copyright owner's consent. In general, in New Zealand, copyright expires at the end of the period of 50 years from the end of the calendar year in which the author dies.

The author of a work is entitled to copyright. But if you produce work in the course of your employment, the employer owns the copyright.

Copyright exists not only in written work but also in works of art, including photographs and drawings, musical compositions, recordings, films, and now in a technology-neutral concept called "communication works" (which replaces previous references to broadcasting or cable programme services).

There is no copyright in news generally, but a newspaper that published an article verbatim which it had lifted from another publication or a website without permission would breach copyright.

It is a breach of copyright to lift parts of another person's work and incorporate them into your own. Although the part taken must be "substantial", this does not just mean quantity but also quality. The fundamental question is whether the essence of the copyright work has been taken. So the copying of a quantitatively small part of someone else's work *can* be a breach of copyright.

Just because something is publicly available on a social media site does not mean it is not subject to copyright. Lifting and using someone's photograph or substantial parts of other material from Facebook without permission or a defence could be a breach of the law. In all cases, you need to investigate the site's terms and conditions and any copyright policy to see what might be possible. For example, some videos loaded onto YouTube are available under a Creative Commons licence and will be labelled as such (see www.youtube.com/yt/copyright/creative-commons.html), but, otherwise, you cannot assume those loading the video onto the site had the right to do so.

Because Twitter (twitter.com) is a site which is based on sharing and retweeting of the material loaded on it, its terms and conditions require users to give Twitter the right to make users' tweets available to the rest of the world and to let others do the same. While this appears to allow copying within the Twitter context, this does not

> ## Fair dealing (MediaWorks v Sky Television, 2007)
>
> The court found in favour of MediaWorks and TV3, in a claim against Sky Television for using exclusive footage of Rugby World Cup matches to which TV3 had rights. Sky had used TV3's footage intensively in a number of different programme formats including news, current events and sports, and magazine-style programmes, and across a number of its channels. Fair dealing is a question of impression and degree. Length of the excerpts used may be relevant, but repetition of the footage and the nature of the programmes involved are also relevant. Here the excerpts used were short, but Sky's use was intensive – at times, viewers were able to access TV3 footage on Sky in excess of 48 times a day. Timing of the footage also coincided with intensity of viewer interest and was not limited to one channel as with TV3. The rate of repetition alone was excessive, the use in entertainment magazine-style programmes was unfair, and it was not reporting current events.
>
> In contrast, in *Sky v Fairfax NZ Ltd,* 2016, the High Court suggested use by the Stuff website of an automatic loading function that allowed its readers to see continuous clips from exclusive Sky coverage of the Olympics would probably not be fair dealing. However, after Fairfax disabled this function on the website, the court would not injunct its continued use of one-off clips of Sky coverage, even though that use went somewhat beyond what Sky had allowed other media to use.

mean anyone else can use the material for other purposes. Photographs in particular may remain the subject of copyright. These issues have not been tested in a court of law and so uncertainty remains. If you are in any doubt at all, you should seek legal advice. Freelance authors own their copyright and may decide whether or not they wish to give up the rights to their work when the story is sold. However, you may have little choice in the matter if the publication insists on taking the copyright as a condition of buying the story.

Defences to breach of copyright

Two fair dealing defences are useful for media. The first is fair dealing for the purposes of criticism or review that is accompanied by a sufficient acknowledgement. This exception extends well beyond literary criticism. For example, it would cover an online newspaper that publishes an article critical of the practices of an organisation and uses the organisation's own publications to prove this. In one case, the defence covered use of 13 photographs in a television programme which contained frequent shots of newspapers, their mastheads and stories, and pictures, as well as various film clips, showing the public presentation or public appearances of David Beckham and his wife, Victoria. The photos were used to demonstrate the coverage of celebrity, and to comment on that style in tabloid newspapers and magazines. It made no difference that the programme had entertainment value. The programme was not trivia dressed up as criticism or review, but genuine criticism (*Fraser-Woodward v BBC*, 2005).

The second defence is fair dealing with a copyright work for the purpose of reporting current events. However, in relation to newspapers, there are two very important conditions: the piece must be accompanied by a sufficient acknowledgement; and the defence does not apply to photographs.

Sufficient acknowledgement means an acknowledgement of the work by its title or other description, and a reference to the author if his or her name is known.

There is no recognised public-interest defence to justify copying a copyrighted work, although some courts have hinted at the possibility. It seems unlikely that a story which did not deal with a matter fairly would be in the public interest.

Other possible civil claims

Related risks to consider in publishing include:

False attribution: You should not write a piece and publish it under the name of a well-known or other author, or attribute words to someone that were not said.

Hoaxes: Publishing or broadcasting untrue statements with the intention of frightening a person can result in legal liability if the person suffers nervous shock, illness or bodily harm.

Negligent misstatement: Making a careless or negligent statement which causes financial loss can be unlawful.

False and misleading statements: Use of subterfuge or misleading statements by the media when *gathering* information could fall under the strict liability provisions of the Fair Trading Act 1986 if you are behaving so unethically as to not be seen as gathering news.

Passing off: Adopting a title that is confusingly similar to that of a rival publication, publishing a column pretending it is written by someone well-known who is not involved at all, or using a character created by someone else may be a form of passing off if the public are misled.

Plagiarising someone else's work, fabricating stories and interviews, and careless work may all give rise to legal liabilities as set out above. However, even if lawful, this behaviour would clearly be a serious breach of any employment contract and would justify dismissal, thus putting an end to any career in journalism.

Laws that impact on investigation and interview

A collection of laws restrict the methods journalists use to acquire and keep information. A brief discussion of these follows.

Observation and photography

Generally, there is no law against looking at, or taking photographs of, a property from any place outside it, for example, from an upstairs window next door, through a fence, from a plane, or from the footpath (*Bernstein v Skyviews*, 1978). However, if you interfere with the occupier's enjoyment of their land, it could be that the common law wrong of nuisance is committed. Also, photographing or filming coupled with other

Journalists trespassing

In one Australian case (*Rinsale v Australian Broadcasting Corporation*, 1993), it was held to be a trespass when journalists, having been refused an interview, entered premises with cameras rolling and then a room where the plaintiff's director was questioned by the reporter. Because an interview had been refused, it was held that there was a trespass from the moment of entry; there could be no suggestion that an implied licence existed.

It is also a trespass if reporters enter by trickery, eg, by misrepresenting their intentions or identity. In another Australian case (*TCN Channel Nine v Ilvariy*, 2008), Channel Nine broadcast a segment on its television programme *A Current Affair* intended to expose the allegedly incompetent building practices of a company. Employees of the programme pretending to be interested in building a home entered the business premises with cameras and confronted a managing director and franchisee of the company. The footage was broadcast together with the testimony of dissatisfied customers. Although a claim in defamation failed because the media were able to rely on truth, claims by the company for trespass were successful.

factors may be a breach of an individual's privacy and result in a suit or a complaint to the BSA or the Media Council (for example, secretly filming a person at the door of her house using a hidden camera, see Privacy, above).

Trespass

Unauthorised entry on to someone else's land is a trespass and is wrongful. However, you are not trespassing if you have express or implied permission to be there. So long as there is no sign forbidding it, we all have a right to go on to a property and knock on the door to talk to the occupiers. This means journalists do not trespass by going to a house and knocking on the door, or to the reception of business premises, intending to ask the occupier questions. If told to leave, you must do so, but you must be given reasonable time to do this.

It is different, however, if you initially entered the property not intending to

Disclosing sources (*Police v Campbell, 2009*)

This case arose from an interview with an alleged medal thief by broadcaster John Campbell on *Campbell Live* in February 2009. The interview had actually taken place earlier in the day in a hotel, where the alleged thief had been recorded on audio only, and an actor had been used to broadcast the interview that evening, using a transcript of the real interview.

The police, seeking the thief, applied for an order under section 68 of the Evidence Act 2006, compelling John Campbell and his production team to produce relevant information. The judge was inclined to make an order for disclosure. However, he asked counsel to consider the matter further and return to him with further submissions. About three weeks later, Mr Campbell produced a "will say" statement with some information in it that did not disclose his source. This meant that a disclosure order was no longer necessary.

communicate with the occupier but simply to "snoop" – then you would be trespassers from the moment of entry. This means door-stepping and secret filming are risky. Trespass can be a criminal offence, as well as a civil claim. It is also possible that you might be injuncted to stop publication of information obtained by using trespass.

Journalists and disclosing information

Generally, no one has to answer questions put to them by the police, unless you are in lawful custody under a charge, in which case you must supply identifying details. Journalists are no different from ordinary citizens in this regard.

In contrast to this, as a rule, a person must answer all questions put to him or her if giving evidence in a court of law. Failure to do so is contempt of court and can result in a penalty such as a fine, and even possible imprisonment.

There is a strong ethical principle that journalists do not disclose the identities of their sources. There is no special privilege in the law protecting this. However, judges try very hard not to compel such disclosure. Also, the Evidence Act 2006 contains a presumption that journalists will not be compelled to do so where they have given an undertaking to their source. Despite the presumption, journalists do remain ultimately compellable where a judge finds there is greater public interest in disclosure. That would likely be when the police need the information as evidence in a case and cannot get it any other way.

Obstructing the police

It is important to do your best not to get in the way of emergency teams at the scene of a crime or accident, or natural disaster. In such circumstances, the police can issue

---

Obstructing the police (*Mackley v Police, 1994*)

A television camera operator was taking pictures at the scene of a fatal accident in Christchurch when he was directed by a police officer to move further away. He refused for two reasons. First, he believed from experience that the officer who directed him was motivated by animosity against him because it seemed the police had unreasonably restricted his access to emergency scenes previously. Second, he said he had an arrangement with the ambulance service whereby he made film available to them for training purposes. He asked the police officer to speak to an ambulance officer who was present to confirm this, but the police officer refused.

The camera operator was arrested for obstructing the police and was convicted. His appeal to the High Court succeeded. The court found a person is only guilty of obstruction if that person *knows* the officer is acting in the execution of his or her duty and *intends* to obstruct the officer in the execution of that duty. If a person honestly believes that the officer is not acting in the execution of his or her duty, there can be no charge of obstruction.

The camera operator was found not guilty because he believed that the police officer had no right to move him, for the two reasons described.

Guidelines for police searching media offices

The High Court has laid down guiding principles for the grant and execution of warrants for the search of media premises (*Television New Zealand v Attorney-General*, 1995). These include:

- A search warrant should not be used against the media in trivial cases.
- As far as possible a warrant should not be granted or executed so as to impair the public dissemination of news.
- Only in exceptional circumstances where it is truly essential should a warrant be granted or executed if there is a substantial risk that it will cause the drying up of confidential sources for the media.
- A warrant should be executed considerately so as to cause the least practicable disruption to the business of the media organisation.
- The tapes or other material being looked for should be important for the progress of the prosecution. It must be likely that they will have a direct and important place in the court case.

instructions to the public to move away if they reasonably believe that is necessary to enable emergency services to function better. An unreasonable refusal to comply could be obstructing the police.

Searches of newsrooms

Certain statutes allow the police to search premises for certain things (in particular, firearms, drugs, and items used for espionage) without first obtaining a warrant. But, generally, before the police can search premises they require a warrant under the Search and Surveillance Act 2012. Police may also use production and examination orders, which put onus on media to make information available.

Warrants may be issued for the search of newsrooms, to look in particular for film or photographs of such events as riots or disturbances at protest marches. For example, in 1995, police obtained a search warrant to take from TVNZ offices all tapes filmed by TVNZ at Waitangi Day protests. And in 2008 police executed a search warrant of the headquarters of TV3 in Auckland, seeking information relating to an interview carried out by broadcaster John Campbell with an alleged medal thief. Nothing was found.

If you are subject to a search, you are entitled to check the warrant or order to ensure the police have the required authority. Police should also follow the guidelines set out in the box above. When applying for search warrants against media, police must disclose that they intend to search the premises of a journalist, and should advise the journalist of their right to protect their sources before the search is carried out. If the journalist exercises that right, all the materials seized by police must be packaged up and delivered to the court, to be held until a decision is made about the source-protection issue (*Hager v Attorney-General*, 2015).

Further reading

Cheer, U. (2015). *Burrows and Cheer: Media law in New Zealand* (7th ed.). Wellington: LexisNexis.

http://bsa.govt.nz Website of the Broadcasting Standards Authority.

http://inforrm.wordpress.com The International Forum for Responsible Media blog.

http://privacy.org.nz Website of the Privacy Commissioner.

Penk, S., & Tobin, R. (Eds.). (2010). *Privacy law in New Zealand.* Wellington: Brookers.

Price, S. (2007). *Media minefield: A journalists' guide to media regulation in New Zealand.* Wellington: New Zealand Journalists Training Organisation.

www.medialawjournal.co.nz Lawyer Steven Price blogs about media law and ethics.

www.mediacouncil.org.nz Website of the New Zealand Media Council.

Cases cited

A v Fairfax New Zealand. (2011). High Court Wellington, CIV-2011-485-569, March 28 and 29, 2011.

Abbot v The Press. (2002). High Court Christchurch, T9-02, December 13, 2002.

Alexander v Clegg. (2004). *New Zealand Law Reports,* Vol. 3, p. 586.

Ambrose v AG. (2012). *New Zealand Administrative Reports,* p. 23.

Andrews v TVNZ. (2009). *New Zealand Law Reports,* p. 220.

Argyll v Argyll. (1967). *Chancery Reports,* p. 302.

Bernstein v Skyviews. (1978). *Queen's Bench Reports,* p. 479.

Brown v AG. (2006). *District Court Reports,* p. 630.

C v Holland. (2012). *New Zealand Law Reports,* Vol. 3, p. 672.

Charleston v News Group Newspapers. (1995). *Appeal Cases,* Vol. 2, p. 65.

Columbus v Independent News Auckland. (2000). High Court Auckland, CP600/98, April 7, 2000.

Fraser-Woodward v BBC. (2005). *Entertainment and Media Law Reports,* p. 487.

Hager v Attorney-General. (2015). NZHC, p. 3268.

Hosking v Runting. (2005). *New Zealand Law Reports,* Vol. 1, p. 1.

Lange v Atkinson. (1998). *New Zealand Law Reports,* Vol. 3, p. 424.

Mackley v Police. (1994). *Criminal Reports of New Zealand,* Vol. 11, p. 497.

McGee v Independent Newspapers. (2006). *New Zealand Administrative Reports,* p. 24.

MediaWorks NZ v Sky Television Network. (2007). *Intellectual Property Reports,* Vol. 74, p. 205.

New Zealand Magazines v Hadlee. (2005). *New Zealand Administrative Reports,* p. 621.

New Zealand Post v Prebble. (2001). *New Zealand Administrative Reports,* p. 360.

P v D. (2000). *New Zealand Law Reports,* Vol. 2, p. 591.

Police v Campbell. (2009). Unreported, High Court Wanganui, CIV 2009-483-000127, August 7, 2009 and August 31, 2009.

R vs A. (1994). *New Zealand Law Reports,* Vol. 1, p. 429.

Rinsale Pty v Australian Broadcasting Corporation. (1993). *Australian Torts Reports,* p. 62377.

Sky v Fairfax New Zealand Ltd. (2016). NZHC, p. 1883.

TCN Channel Nine v Ilvariy. (2008). *New South Wales Court of Appeal,* p. 9.

Thode v Coastline FM. (1997). High Court Tauranga, CP31/95, October 1, 1997.

Television New Zealand v Attorney-General. (1995). *New Zealand Law Reports,* Vol. 2, p. 641.

TV3 Network Services v Fahey. (1999). *New Zealand Law Reports,* Vol. 2, p. 129.

21

Journalism ethics

A guide to help you decide how to behave as a journalist

Jim Tully, University of Canterbury and Massey University

New Zealand journalists do not practise their profession with unfettered freedom. They work within legal and ethical constraints. The law determines what is legal and illegal; ethics determines what is right and wrong.

The two are not always compatible. Behaviour that is legal may be considered unethical in certain circumstances. For example, it is legal to photograph a burial from a public place, but what is published may be considered an unacceptable intrusion into grief.

Codes of ethics are normally an expression of a profession's commitment to maintaining high standards and being accountable to the public. Think of it as an implicit bargain between the news media and society: in return for a high degree of freedom of expression, journalists in a liberal democracy are expected to behave responsibly.

This chapter discusses what we mean by ethics, looks at the main ethical watchdogs, and considers some of the major ethical dilemmas journalists face. It is non-prescriptive, recognising the many grey areas that exist in news media practice.

Making ethical decisions

The term "ethics" generally refers to the study of ethical theories that address what is good, both for an individual and for society. When we talk of media ethics we normally mean the codes and principles that guide the practice of responsible journalism.

It is important to acknowledge theories that have shaped our understanding of ethics over the centuries. They inform our moral reasoning and provide guidelines for making ethical choices. The writings of Aristotle, Immanuel Kant, John Stuart Mill, and John Rawls, for example, have been particularly influential, as has the Judeo-Christian tradition. Journalists should also draw upon and apply other ethical commentary, reflecting their own cultural traditions.

Making ethical choices can be daunting, but you need not take up the challenge alone. Journalists can enhance their understanding of ethics and ethical decision-making with the help of guidelines developed specifically for them and by discussing ethical issues with colleagues as they arise in the workplace.

Such guidelines are important because the nature of news, in particular, with its emphasis on immediacy and fast decisions, is not conducive to the reflection, discernment and discussion so often required when making hard ethical choices.

Journalists should be able to explain their ethical decisions. A journalist will want to be true to their own ethical values, but obligations to their news organisation, professional colleagues, their audience and society at large must also be considered.

Most discussion centres on written codes, but it is important to recognise the power of unwritten codes – conventions of practice absorbed through training and experience in the workplace. In newsrooms, ethical decisions made under the pressure of deadlines are likely to be intuitive, drawing on the team's collective experience.

A simple approach to making ethical decisions is to pose questions. In their excellent guide to media ethics, Black, Steele and Barney (1999) suggest the following questions in the context of three guiding principles, to seek truth and report it as fully as possible, to act independently and to minimise harm:

- What do I know? What do I need to know?
- What is my journalistic purpose?
- What are my ethical concerns?
- What organisational policies and professional guidelines should I consider?
- How can I include other people, with different perspectives and diverse ideas, in the decision-making process?
- Who are the stakeholders – those affected by my decision? What are their motivations? Which are legitimate?
- What if the roles were reversed? How would I feel if I were in the shoes of one of the stakeholders?
- What are the possible consequences on my actions both short- and long-term?
- What are my alternatives to maximise my truth-telling responsibility and minimise harm?
- Can I clearly and fully justify my thinking and my decision to my colleagues, stakeholders and the public?

The questions are leading you to consider ethical issues in a structured manner that identifies the facts, ethical principles, values, relevant stakeholders and editorial context.

A professional approach to ethical issues demands far more than a gut reaction or a "What can I get away with?" approach.

Other media ethicists, such as Lambeth (1992) and Patterson and Wilkins (1994), offer their own guidelines, but whatever framework you adopt, it is important to consider ethical choices in a reasoned, discerning manner.

Codes of ethics

It is easy to compose a list of expectations the public could reasonably have of responsible news media: accuracy, fairness, honesty, impartiality, independence, diversity, cultural sensitivity, compassion, and so on.

Professional codes are an attempt to standardise the ethical principles governing practice, and are integral to claims of autonomy and self-regulation.

The responsible journalist is a thinking journalist. What responsibilities do you accept as guiding principles for your journalism practice?

Since the 1970s, statements of standards have become a fact of life in New Zealand journalism. If anything, the pressure for written codes has grown as a result of changing journalistic practice in a more competitive news environment and technological innovations that raise new ethical dilemmas.

Several journalistic organisations – such as Stuff and the union of journalists, E tū – have their own codes of practice. For instance, E tū's code covers such topics as honesty, respecting individuals' grief, accuracy, etc. One part of the code states that E tū members will "use fair and honest means to obtain news, pictures, films, tapes and documents" (E tū, 2017, para. 8). Such codes may be enforceable directly through office supervision or disciplinary procedures.

The watchdog role of the news media is essential for a participant democratic society. If there is to be informed debate on public issues and policies, people must know what is going on. The performance of those who exercise power must be scrutinised. But who guards the watchdog? One answer is standards bodies, which have drawn up their own codes of journalistic ethics against which to hear complaints about journalists.

The watchdogs

Self-regulation means the industry has established its own complaints body. Statutory regulation means the complaints body was created by an Act of Parliament.

Newspaper and magazine publishers have been able to self-regulate through an industry-created standards body, the New Zealand Media Council (NZMC). This covers the print media's hard-copy publications and online news sites. The NZMC also covers broadcasters' news websites, as well as various bloggers.

Radio and television broadcasters, by contrast, are subject to statutory regulation via the Broadcasting Standards Authority (BSA). This solely covers the broadcasters' broadcast programmes. The reason the BSA does not cover the broadcasters' websites is that the law that established the BSA has not been amended to allow this.

New Zealand Media Council

The NZMC was established in 1972 as a response to the perceived threat of legislation to regulate the newspaper industry. The model used was the British Press Council, modified to New Zealand needs and conditions.

The flexibility of the NZMC meant it was easily able in 2017 to extend its jurisdiction to cover broadcasters' online news and current affairs outlets.

The NZMC has a statement of principles to which newspapers and magazines must adhere (NZMC, 2017). The statement covers such topics as fairness, accuracy, use of photographs, etc. For instance, it states that members should make a clear distinction between fact and comment in their publications: "An article that is essentially comment or opinion should be clearly presented as such" (NZMC, 2017, para. 4).

The NZMC comprises an independent chair (a retired High Court judge), plus representatives of both the industry and the general public. The industry representatives are in the minority. The NZMC is funded by its members from the press media industry. Those who have a complaint about the press media must first take their complaint to the news organisation concerned. If they are dissatisfied with the outcome, they can complain to the NZMC.

The complaints procedure is straightforward and at no cost to the complainant. For the complaint to proceed, the complainant must agree not to take or continue legal action against the newspaper/magazine. If the NZMC upholds a complaint, it can require an offending news organisation to prominently publish the decision.

Broadcasting Standards Authority

New Zealand broadcasters have never experienced the degree of self-regulation experienced by newspaper and magazine publishers. They have long known statutory accountability.

The Broadcasting Act 1989 established a formal complaints procedure with a statutory watchdog, the Broadcasting Standards Authority (BSA). As with the NZMC, the BSA has established a series of ethical codes to which broadcasters must adhere. There are numerous codes covering a wide variety of topics. The free-to-air broadcasting code, for instance, covers good taste and decency, law and order, privacy, violence, etc. One aspect of the law-and-order code states that "Programmes should not actively promote serious antisocial or illegal behaviour" (BSA, 2017, para. 2).

The BSA comprises four members appointed by the government. Members are appointed for three years on the basis of their legal experience, a background in media or community involvement. The chairperson must be a barrister or solicitor with not less than seven years' experience in the High Court. One is appointed after consultation with broadcasters and another after consultation with public-interest groups. The BSA is funded by the government and a levy on broadcasters.

Those who have a complaint about the broadcast media must first take their complaint to the broadcaster, unless it involves privacy alone or election programmes. If they are dissatisfied with the outcome they can complain to the BSA. The complaints procedure is straightforward and at no cost to the complainant. Complainants do not have to waive other legal options and the BSA's decisions can be appealed to the High Court.

The BSA can impose significant penalties when complaints are upheld. These include requiring broadcasters to run apologies on-air and, in some cases, imposing fines or even taking broadcasters off-air (see box below).

The BSA has sought to better inform its decision-making by exercising its statutory responsibility to conduct research about broadcasting standards matters.

If you compare the decisions of the two watchdogs you will notice the BSA's are legalistic in tone and format, and those of the NZMC are more informal. This reflects the fact the BSA is a statutory body with a more legalistic approach.

TAKEN OFF AIR

The BSA has only once been so appalled by a broadcaster's ethical lapses that it has ordered the broadcaster off-air (*Barnes and Alt TV*, 2007).

Small independent TV station Alt TV broadcast free-to-air in Auckland and nationally via Sky. On the afternoon of Waitangi Day, 2007, Alt TV broadcast live an Auckland concert. The programme was rated G.

During the programme, viewers were able to text messages to the station, which it broadcast along the bottom of the screen. Alt TV hired a person to moderate these messages before they were broadcast, but this person became drunk and did not perform their job. As a result, viewers began sending texts full of extreme expletives and racist hate language, which the station broadcast.

The BSA found that Alt TV breached a range of free-to-air TV standards, including good taste and decency, racial denigration and children's interests. Alt TV was fined $5000 and required to go off-air for an afternoon, instead running a silent message outlining the BSA's decision and apologising for its actions. Alt TV closed in 2009.

It has commissioned research, prepared discussion papers and/or held seminars on a variety of topics, including television violence, children's programming, taste and decency, and accuracy, fairness and balance.

Ethics in the workplace

Ethical issues, big and small, arise every day in the editorial departments of all news media. This section looks at some of the most common.

Accuracy, fairness and balance

Codes of ethics often insist that reports should be accurate, fair and balanced – see, for instance, the NZMC's Principle 1 (NZMC, 2017).

Accuracy is absolutely essential to credible journalism. Inaccuracies undermine any story and the credibility both of the journalist and their publisher/broadcaster. But accuracy, within the wider frame of truth-telling, means more than just ensuring facts are correct and correcting errors. It means reporting the under-reported, uncovering concealed facts, providing context and presenting the big picture. The NZMC upheld complaints about a column in the *Weekend Herald* that attacked all Māori as failing to educate their children and for bashing their babies. The NZMC said commentators were entitled to hold strong opinions but the information published must be accurate. The NZMC found that in this case, "the allegations against Māori as a race are inaccurate, and the opinions are extreme to the extent of being a gratuitous offence to Māori" (*Georgia Harrison against the Weekend Herald*, 2012).

Fairness means a lot of things. It means treating others how you would wish to be treated in their situation. It also means avoiding labels and stereotypes, and being inclusive of diversity and minority groups. No story is fair if it omits facts of major importance or significance, so fairness is also completeness. No story is fair if it consciously or unconsciously misleads or deceives the reader, so fairness includes honesty – levelling with the reader. No story is fair if reporters hide their biases or emotions behind such subtly pejorative words as "refused" or "admitted".

Balance means giving all sides in a debate or story the opportunity to be heard. There is more than one side to a story. If an opposition politician accuses a government minister of corruption, the reporter must put the accusations to the minister and report both in their story. Of course, judging how much space or time to give can be difficult. In an article on climate change, should climate-change deniers be given as much space as scientists, when the overwhelming consensus among scientists is that climate change is happening? Balance should reflect the relative strength of each side's arguments; it doesn't mean giving equal space and time. Indeed, in its free-to-air TV code, the BSA says "No set formula can be advanced for the allocation of time to interested parties on controversial issues of public importance" (BSA, 2017, para. 3).

In 2017, the *Northern Advocate* newspaper published what was purported to be reconstructions of skulls of non-Māori who had come to New Zealand long before the Māori. The story included no credible evidence or experts. In upholding a complaint about the story, the NZMC found the article touched on sensitive historical and cultural matters and "breached basic journalistic principles of accuracy, fairness and balance" (*Ewan Morris against Northern Advocate*, 2017, para. 12).

Deception

Much ethical discussion focuses on what is published or broadcast, but sometimes the way in which that information was gathered is the significant issue. When journalists gather information using dubious methods they can seriously undermine their credibility. When can journalists justify methods that involve some measure of dishonesty?

Journalists have practised deception in many forms over the years, including not identifying themselves as journalists, lying, impersonating others, using hidden cameras, eavesdropping, plagiarising and fabricating stories.

When can deception be justified? There's no easy answer, and each case has to be considered on its merits. Going undercover, a form of deception mostly used by investigative reporters, is usually justified as necessary to report a story in the public interest.

Fabrication is impossible to justify. A *Herald on Sunday* reporter was dismissed for fabricating a story about a South Auckland police officer. Likewise, plagiarism is never

Ethical journalism is also good journalism. News website Stuff was hoaxed in 2013 when it ran a report saying an oil company was donating a polar bear to Auckland Zoo. The information came from a fake media release. Nobody at Stuff thought it necessary to check with the zoo or the oil company before running the story (Scanlon, 2013).

OBJECTIVITY

Journalists are often attacked for not being objective in their coverage. But is this a realistic expectation? Is it possible? Should journalists even worry about being objective?

The concept of objectivity in journalism gathered force from the 1920s and has shaped its practice ever since. We have become used to an avowed separation of fact and opinion, the use of an apparently neutral voice in news writing, with an emphasis on independent verification and an expectation of fairness and balance. Even the use of shorthand for note-taking can be seen as a device to demonstrate a commitment to accuracy.

The claim to objectivity was integral to moves to enhance the standing of journalism. The public was encouraged to trust journalists who were independent, separated facts from opinion and imposed professional standards. An appearance of neutrality was desirable when publishers sought to appeal to mass audiences to attract advertisers and become more profitable.

Technology has also played a part. The introduction of the telegraph, which saw the rise of news agencies, put an emphasis on concise, accurate stories that could be published in non-partisan newspapers anywhere. Later, television, with its visual images, was seen to present an authentic eyewitness account of an event.

However, reporting will always be influenced by the values of journalists, who construct a reality shaped by linguistic, ideological, cultural, social, professional and organisational contexts. Journalists are not robots devoid of emotions, values and opinions, even if they do adopt the air of a detached bystander neutrally observing and reporting the world about them.

The notion of the detached bystander also fails to recognise that journalists should be actively involved in their community and attuned to the interests, aspirations and concerns of its people in all their diversity.

Further, people pay journalists for their judgement about the relative importance of things. In this information-rich age there is a growing public appetite for analysis by knowledgeable journalists who explain, interpret, even advocate from a point of view – which is inevitably subjective. When Newshub political editor Patrick Gower, for example, is reporting from Parliament he is expected to give his analysis of an unfolding political event or issue. When political journalists write blogs they express their analysis without the traditional constraints of reporting.

Given that absolute objectivity is impossible, a much more realistic goal is gathering accurate, independently verified facts, providing fairness and balance, and honestly acknowledging and addressing biases and prejudices.

A story which is accurate, fair and balanced is also compatible with advocacy journalism, which is where journalists are arguing a case or running a campaign. The information must be accurate, and the positions of all relevant parties must be sought and fairly presented. Any conclusions will be based on strong evidence gathered with an open mind, not to support a preconceived thesis.

acceptable, as a columnist at *The Press* discovered. He was forced to apologise when it was discovered his columns bore striking resemblances to columns written by others overseas. The same tough lesson was learned by a young reporter at *The New Zealand Herald* who lifted material from a website for a profile on a former rugby league star. The original source was an article in the *Waikato Times*. The *Herald* apologised and ran a prominent article reviewing the incident (Gleeson & Tully, 2004). For more on these examples and others, see Samson (2009).

Ambush interviews

There are times when journalists surprise a source who has been evading them, a technique known as "ambush" interviews or "door-stepping".

The practice does not sit well with the notion of fairness, but news organisations justify it in certain circumstances. Generally, door-stepping is seen as a last resort and the questions to be asked must have a serious purpose and be in the public interest.

The BSA's approach was set out in a 1994 decision when a person who managed an organisation under investigation complained he was approached by a TV reporter and crew on his driveway (*Smedley and TVNZ*, 1994).

The BSA did not uphold the complaint. But it did say people with little experience in, and no training for, appearing on television could be at a distinct disadvantage when appearing on television even with prior knowledge and consent. And that's to say nothing of opening a door to be confronted by a camera and reporter in what is usually an adversarial situation.

The BSA was also concerned that a broadcaster might decide to use door-stepping for the expected visual impact of the confrontation that was likely to ensue, rather than as a source of considered information and constructive comment. The BSA emphasised that it was a method which should not normally be used unless every alternative legitimate way either to obtain the information sought or to ensure that a person being investigated was given the opportunity to respond had been exhausted.

This can even apply when interviewing someone as media-savvy as the Prime Minister. The BSA found John Campbell unfairly ambushed then Prime Minister Helen Clark in an interview on genetic modification (*Prime Minister (Rt Hon Helen Clark) and 6 others and TV3 Network Services,* 2003).

Altering quotes

In some newsrooms people argue that it is simply a reality that reporters must sometimes alter direct quotes, at the very least to eliminate grammatical errors. However, other journalists would insist that direct quotes are sacrosanct and anything inside quotation marks should not be altered. If the statement is confusing, paraphrase it and remove the confusion.

Privacy

Each of us wishes to keep private certain things about ourselves. Our reasons for wanting to protect or disclose information will vary according to the nature of the information, the circumstances in which it is revealed, and our individual privacy threshold.

The news media at times have a legitimate interest in intruding upon that privacy because of who we are, what we have done or what has happened to us. The ethical dilemma for journalists is weighing their obligation to reporting and the public's right to know against their obligation to treat sources fairly and an individual's right of privacy.

Privacy is best addressed by distinguishing between public figures and ordinary people who may be cast, albeit briefly, into the media spotlight.

Interviews can backfire. In 1985, journalist Rod Vaughan helicoptered unannounced in to interview then politician Bob Jones, fishing in a river. Enraged at the intrusion, Jones physically attacked Vaughan and his cameraman. Vaughan was left bleeding profusely with his nose broken. Jones was later fined (NZ On Screen, 2017).

Always be careful when paraphrasing someone's comments. Do not change their meaning and include any qualifying comments they made.

Going undercover

A TV news story on the standard of care in rest homes in New Zealand saw the producer go under-cover as a caregiver for five days in a rest home on Auckland's North Shore. The rest home subsequently complained to the BSA about the deception.

The BSA said there was no doubt the broadcaster used deception to gain entry into the rest home. The producer lied to the rest home's management about why she was there and who she was.

But the BSA did not uphold the complaint. Instead, it said: "the Authority accepts that the broadcaster could not obtain this information by any other means. Further, it considers that, due to the rest home's history, the broadcaster had a justifiable basis for going into the home and that the use of deception on this occasion was in the public interest as a means to secure an unlaundered view of how well the home was operating" (*Turley and Television New Zealand*, 2009).

Public figures

People in public life must accept a higher level of media scrutiny and intrusion because of the power, influence, privilege and financial rewards they seek, exercise and enjoy. Even then, there are limits.

The test is whether the information is relevant to the performance of public duties or public confidence in the individual or the office itself. The Cabinet minister who is seen to be frequently drunk can expect scrutiny regarding their fitness to hold high office. The issue is competence. The politician who calls for a return to traditional family values can expect to have an extramarital relationship revealed. The issue is hypocrisy.

In 2013, outspoken blogger Cameron Slater revealed on his site Whale Oil that then Auckland mayor Len Brown had conducted a two-year extramarital affair. Brown's political career collapsed. Controversially, in 2014, Slater won the inaugural Canon Media Award for best blog for breaking the story (Hannis, 2016).

In our modern media age there is an even greater premium on reporting the lives and loves of prominent people from the worlds of entertainment, sport and royalty. This is no longer the exclusive world of the paparazzi – photographers who relentlessly pursue celebrities. Anyone with a mobile phone can photograph or film public figures and celebrities in embarrassing or compromising positions and place it on the internet or sell it to a media organisation.

The concept of the "limited-purpose public figure" provides a useful guide here. Individuals lose their right to privacy only in areas relating to their fame. This offers a measure of protection to both the individual and their families.

Ordinary people

What of people who get thrust into the media spotlight, albeit fleetingly and often without warning? Their inexperience in dealing with journalists and/or the circumstances which have made them newsworthy may leave them extremely vulnerable as victims or perhaps by virtue of their age (young or old) or disability. Beyond that, it may be that a person is simply embarrassed by what is published or broadcast.

The principle of fairness requires journalists to display integrity, sensitivity and compassion, while legitimately seeking information the public needs to know.

Victims of crime, disaster or other traumatic experiences, and people in grief, should be treated with particular care for such reasons as re-victimisation arising from inaccurate, intrusive or unfair coverage, the revisiting of past events, and the vulnerability of victims to say and do things they may later regret and find embarrassing.

Journalists can advance good reasons for interviewing survivors – for example, the high level of public interest. The same applies to the much-maligned "death knock" where journalists interview a bereaved family or friends. Some people are very keen to talk, some may even expect to be interviewed, but for others media intrusion can be extremely distressing and unwelcome.

Intrusion becomes particularly challenging when it involves images of dead or badly injured people. The experience of many news editors is the closer the connection to home, the greater the potential to offend. For instance, in many emergency situations TV camerapeople are close enough to film graphic images of people who are dead, badly injured or grieving after someone has died. It's normal for a cameraperson to film what they can at the scene without getting in the way or causing further distress.

When they return to the newsroom a senior producer must then decide what will be broadcast. Although people from other countries are often shown dead or injured, the New Zealand media don't usually show graphic pictures of local murders or disasters. This is out of respect to the families of those who have died.

Bodies are only shown once they are covered. If a person has been badly injured, an editor has to weigh up how upsetting it would be for the family to see those pictures broadcast or in the newspaper.

Hidden cameras

Imagine you are a journalist thinking of using hidden cameras and microphones for a story. It is important to discuss your story and what you propose to do with a senior producer or news executive. If you record someone secretly, you need to be able to show it's in the public interest and that you have been fair and balanced in your approach.

Say you're doing a story about a businessman who's allegedly ripping off customers. He needs to know the allegations and have a reasonable amount of time to respond to them. If he ignores your phone calls and emails then you might decide to film him, record his voice secretly or turn up at his office with the camera rolling. But if he lays a formal complaint, you have to be able to justify your actions.

The most famous case involved TV3 secretly filming a doctor, Morgan Fahey, accused of sexually abusing patients. TV3 hid a camera on a patient, who then met with the doctor and accused him of abusing her. TV3 broadcast the footage. The BSA did not uphold complaints about TV3's actions, holding that although Fahey's privacy had been breached, the story had a strong public-interest element (*de Hart, Cameron and Cotter and TV3*, 2000). Fahey pleaded guilty to rape charges and was imprisoned.

Children

Children are not competent to give informed consent for intrusions into their privacy, yet they frequently feature in the news stories that include revelations of a personal nature. For example, the *Sunday News* newspaper ran a story about a Family Court case, involving a female child. The child's mother complained to the NZMC that the article infringed her daughter's privacy (*Complaint against Sunday News*, 2010).

The *Sunday News* had not named the people involved in the case, but the NZMC determined that the paper had published other details that did effectively identify the child. The NZMC found the newspaper had not done enough to protect the child's privacy and upheld the complaint.

Who represents the child's interests in such cases? Can parents waive their child's right of privacy? If not, then who decides? There are no easy answers. Journalists should always consider what is in the best interests of the child.

Conflicts of interest

Independence is central to journalism. So when the independence of journalists or their news organisations is compromised, their credibility or believability is undermined, sometimes irrevocably. Hence journalists and news organisations should avoid conflicts of interest – situations that compromise or appear to compromise their independence.

The commercial activities and policies of media owners have created conflicts of interest that often impact on their journalists. Journalists may have to report on other interests and activities of the media corporation they work for.

For the working journalist, conflicts of interest generally arise from their affiliations or personal interests and financial inducements.

Affiliations

A long-held view in newsrooms was that journalists with known affiliations or allegiances could be accused of bias, making it difficult, if not impossible, to assign them to certain stories. It was better to avoid any real or perceived conflicts in interests by not joining groups or causes.

Would you trust the independence of a political reporter who is a member of a political party? What about one who simply votes? Does that mean the reporter is biased or just that the reporter is interested in politics?

But why should a journalist not be able to participate actively in community affairs and have the same freedom to express views as other citizens? Arguably, it is more honest for the journalist to openly state their position rather than pretend they were neutral. Besides, a professional journalist, trained to keep their personal values and prejudices out of a story as much as possible, could file a fair and accurate report. The problem is that the *perception* of a conflict of interest is as important as the reality.

On a personal level, friendships have the potential to create conflicts of interest, especially when friends are sources or are in the news. Journalists in small towns where the range of community, sporting and cultural groups is small are easily drawn into close-knit networks that can make it difficult to avoid conflict between personal and professional duties. Journalists on niche publications and broadcasting outlets serving a relatively small audience and narrow range of advertisers face similar complications.

A journalist has the right to participate in and contribute to the life of their community. The issue is where do you draw the line? Should a journalist serve on a school board of trustees, the local council, belong to a political party, an environmental group? Codes generally call on journalists to avoid affiliations or involvements in areas about which they could be reporting or exercising editorial judgements.

For instance, the Fairfax-owned *Sunday Star-Times* ran articles about a business retreat in Fiji, which attendees paid to attend. The articles, which painted a highly favourable picture of the retreat, were written by a long-time columnist at the newspaper. What the newspaper failed to adequately disclose was that the columnist was in fact the person organising the retreat. Following a complaint, the NZMC investigated. It concluded a conflict of interest existed because the author "has written the articles predominantly to promote a commercial event from which he will profit ... It seems incredible to the Council that the *Star-Times* would argue these articles stand alone on their news merit ... the articles should be clearly displayed as advertising, advertorial or sponsored content, so that readers can judge for themselves their rigour and exactitude. Anything less comprises Fairfax's independence" (*Tom Frewen against Sunday Star-Times*, 2017, paras. 27, 28, 30).

> If you come across a great story in a situation where you have a conflict of interest, give it to another, independent, journalist to cover.

Gifts

The independence of journalists and their news organisations is also compromised when they receive something of value from people wanting to influence the information subsequently published. Conflicts of interest would clearly arise if a journalist entered into a business relationship with a news source.

News organisations commonly accept free tickets to cover or review cultural and sporting events and receive books for review purposes. Sponsorship to cover the cost of reporting events such as the Olympics and America's Cup is increasingly common, normally with the proviso that editorial independence is preserved.

Journalists often accept free trips and accommodation – junkets – on the basis that they are offered to the news organisation rather than to an individual and that there is no promise to publish or broadcast anything. However, those who have enjoyed travel junkets know how hard it can be not to write anything. And when they do hit the keyboard the itinerary was such that they can only think of positive experiences to recount.

The Washington Post newspaper takes no free gifts and no free travel, declaring, "We pay our own way" (*The Washington Post*, 2017, para. 2). This might be the ideal way to preserve editorial independence, but for most New Zealand media editorial independence is inextricably linked with financial strength. They just can't *afford* to always pay their own way.

So if conflicts of interest are unavoidable, how best to deal with them? If responsible journalism means a commitment to honesty, a policy of disclosure seems appropriate. In resolving this ethical dilemma, journalists could usefully begin with the question, "Why should we not disclose this conflict of interest?"

Once the free travel is disclosed, it is then over to the reader to decide what value they place on the journalist's story.

Investments, including shares, can also pose problems, particularly for financial journalists. A journalist who owns shares in a particular company and then advises others to buy those shares, would benefit from any consequent rise in the share's price. At the very least, journalists must disclose such financial interests. The journalist may also use a blind trust – an organisation that invests on their behalf but does not tell the journalist what shares they have invested in.

Interviews

People selling their stories may be tempted to exaggerate, embellish, or even fabricate information, on the basis that the better the story the bigger the payment.

Paying for stories is almost inevitable in a fiercely competitive market. Chequebook journalism, where media pay for interviews for stories, is typically the province of the tabloid newspapers and gossip magazines. Most mainstream media refuse to pay for stories.

Usually, in exchange for paying for an interview, the media organisation involved has exclusive right to the story (that is, the interviewee cannot also take their story elsewhere). This premium on the scoop or exclusive is understandable, both in terms of the market and professional satisfaction. However, exclusive deals deny some people access to information in which they have a legitimate interest and about which they rightly feel entitled to be informed.

Sometimes, interviewees with big stories have considerable power to impose conditions on journalists, such as limiting the topics to be covered, declaring some issues off-limits, vetting the story and photographs before publication, or ensuring publication or broadcast coincides with the launch of the interviewee's new television programme/book/film/etc.

Such arrangements potentially damage the credibility of journalists, as journalists should be committed to independence in their information gathering. If the audience is left disappointed because the interview did not address or answer relevant issues, the journalist has done them a disservice.

Outside employment

Working journalists may freelance or write for other media outlets, or engage in other non-journalistic employment or contract work. This situation is both an employment and ethical issue. Codes generally offer these guidelines:

- Has the journalist's employer given them permission to do this?
- Does the outside work create, or appear to create, a conflict of interest?
- Does the work impinge on the journalist's duties?
- Does it benefit a competitor?

Matters of taste

In 1956, All Black Peter Jones caused a buzz when, straight after a test match against the Springboks, he declared during a live radio broadcast in front of fans that he was "absolutely buggered". The crowd roared with laughter, but the startled radio journalist said "we'll ignore that" and added Jones was "rough, but he's tough" (Te Ara, 2017).

Today, expletives are more acceptable in a variety of mass media. So what guidelines

Reporting on suicide

Reporting on self-inflicted deaths in New Zealand is a blend of legal requirements and guidelines voluntarily adopted by the news media. Although general discussions about suicides in New Zealand can be published, specific information cannot. These controls are designed to protect vulnerable people, such as those at risk of committing suicide.

Unlike comparable jurisdictions overseas, New Zealand has legislative controls on how suicides in New Zealand can be reported. Under the Coroners Act (as amended in 2016), the news media can report that a death in New Zealand is a *suspected* suicide, but cannot say it *is* a suicide until the Coroner issues his/her findings and states the death was a suicide. The media cannot report the method (or suspected) method of death or other details that may suggest the method of death (such as where the death took place). These controls apply beyond the news media – for instance, they include Facebook posts. People may apply to the Chief Coroner for an exemption to these restrictions on a case-by-case basis.

Beyond the legislation, the New Zealand news media, like media in comparable countries, also work to a series of guidelines they have voluntarily agreed to abide by. These include publishing helplines, avoiding language that sensationalises or trivialises suicide, and avoiding simplistic explanations as to why a person has committed suicide.

These controls have limitations. Self-inflicted deaths that have occurred overseas are not covered by the Coroners Act, and compliance with the voluntary codes can be fitful. Indeed, reports of self-inflicted overseas deaths can be graphic, especially in overseas media easily accessible online.

For more details, visit www.health.govt.nz/publication/reporting-suicide-resource-media.

can the journalist adopt? The gratuitous use of what is generally considered offensive language would find little favour in mainstream media. However, some four-letter words may be acceptable in court reports, when uttered by a prominent public figure, or when integral to an essential quote and where the meaning would be lost without them. Sometimes, the words are censored by the use of lines or asterisks.

Context and relevance are the two tests most likely to be applied in determining matters of taste. In terms of context, it makes a big difference if the material is broadcast on, say, a student radio station or RNZ. An item on late-night television news may not be suitable at 6pm when many young people are watching.

In terms of relevance, is the potentially offensive material essential to the story and, if so, how is the material used? For instance, a 6pm *3 News* report on a terrorist attack at a Tunisian beach resort included amateur footage of people shouting and running around in terror and confusion, gunshots and bomb blasts, the panicked breathing of the cameraperson, comments that there were "bodies everywhere" and the corpse of the gunman lying in the street. Prior to the item starting, *3 News* gave no warning to viewers that the item was going to include such graphic material. The BSA recognised the high public interest in the story and that the footage was important in showing the violence that, sadly, takes place in the world. However, the BSA noted that its standards require that in such circumstances viewers must be warned of the nature of the material beforehand. The BSA ruled that the item breached its standards on good taste and decency, and violence (*Cochran and MediaWorks,* 2015).

The BSA considers context and relevance within the wider frame of currently accepted norms. That, of course, is not an objective yardstick, and the BSA has commissioned research and surveys to identify prevailing public attitudes regarding language, sexual content and violence. Good ethical standards can be difficult to define and can change over time!

Further reading

Black, J., Steele B., & Barney R. (1999). *Doing ethics in journalism: A handbook with case studies* (3rd ed.). Boston: Allyn & Bacon.

Lambeth, E. (1992). *Committed journalism: An ethic for the profession.* Bloomington: Indiana University Press.

Patterson, P., & Wilkins, L. (1994). *Media ethics: Issues and cases* (2nd ed.). Madison: Brown and Benchmark.

Tanner, S., Phillips, G., Smyth, C., & Tapsall, S. (2005). *Journalism ethics at work.* Frenchs Forest: Pearson Longman.

www.bsa.govt.nz The BSA's website outlines its functions and complaints process, and provides a searchable archive of decisions.

www.mediacouncil.org.nz The NZMC's website outlines its operations and provides a searchable archive of decisions.

References

Barnes and Alt TV. (2007). Retrieved from http://bsa.govt.nz/decisions/2056-barnes-and-alt-tv-ltd-2007-029

Black, J., Steele B., & Barney R. (1999). *Doing ethics in journalism: A handbook with case studies.* Boston: Allyn and Bacon.

Broadcasting Standards Authority. (2017). *Free-to-air television code of broadcasting practice.* Retrieved from http://bsa.govt.nz/standards/free-to-air-code

Cochran and MediaWorks. (2015). Retrieved from http://bsa.govt.nz/decisions/7837-cochran-and-mediaworks-tv-ltd-2015-054

Complaint against Sunday News. (2010). Retrieved from http://www.mediacouncil.org.nz/display_ruling.php?case_number=2113

de Hart, Cameron and Cotter and TV3. (2000). Retrieved from http://bsa.govt.nz/decisions/1139-de-hart-cameron-and-cotter-and-tv3-network-services-ltd-2000-108a-113

E tū. (2017). *Journalist code of ethics.* Retrieved from http://www.epmu.org.nz/journalist-code-of-ethics/

Ewan Morris against Northern Advocate. (2017). Retrieved from http://www.mediacouncil.org.nz/rulings/ewan-morris-against-northern-advocate

Georgia Harrison against the Weekend Herald. (2012). Retrieved from http://www.mediacouncil.org.nz/display_ruling.php?case_number=2258

Gleeson, S., & Tully, J. (2004, July 30). Finding the right words; journalist's pillars – truth and trust. *The New Zealand Herald,* p. A18.

Hannis, G. (2016). The Len Brown Affair: The roles of new and old media in a New Zealand political sex scandal. *Pacific Journalism Review,* 22(2), 160–171.

Lambeth, E. (1992). *Committed journalism: An ethic for the profession.* Bloomington: Indiana University Press.

New Zealand Media Council. (2017). *Statement of principles.* Retrieved from http://www.mediacouncil.org.nz/principles

NZ On Screen. (2017). *Eyewitness news – Bob Jones punches reporter Rod Vaughan.* Retrieved from www.nzonscreen.com/title/eyewitness-news-bob-jones-punches-reporter-rod-vaughan-1985

Patterson, P., & Wilkins, L. (1994). *Media ethics: Issues and cases* (2nd ed.). Madison: Brown and Benchmark.

Prime Minister (Rt Hon Helen Clark) and 6 others and TV3 Network Services. (2003). Retrieved from https://bsa.govt.nz/decisions/3548-the-prime-minister-rt-hon-helen-clark-and-others-and-tv3-network-services-ltd-2003-055a-2003-061

Samson, A. (2009). *Plagiarism and fabrication: Dishonesty in the newsroom.* (Master's thesis, Massey University, Palmerston North). Retrieved from http://www.massey.ac.nz/massey/fms/Colleges/College%20of%20Business/Communication%20and%20Journalism/Staff/Staff%20research%20files/ASamson/Plagiarism%20thesis.pdf

Scanlon, G. (2013). W*hen Stuff hit an iceberg.* Retrieved from http://www.stuff.co.nz/national/blogs/from-the-newsroom/9080132/When-Stuff-hit-an-iceberg

Smedley and TVNZ. (1994). Retrieved from http://bsa.govt.nz/decisions/29-decision-number-1994-029

Te Ara. (2017). *English language in New Zealand.* Retrieved from www.teara.govt.nz/en/speech/40316/im-absolutely-buggered

Tom Frewen against Sunday Star-Times. (2017). Retrieved from http://www.mediacouncil.org.nz/rulings/tom-frewen-against-sunday-star-times

The Washington Post. (2017). *Conflict of interest.* Retrieved from http://www.washingtonpost.com/wp-srv/opinions/documents/conflict_of_interest.html

Turley and Television New Zealand. (2009). Retrieved from http://bsa.govt.nz/decisions/2601-turley-and-television-new-zealand-ltd-2009-037

APPENDIX 1:

Grammar for journalists

The main points of grammar all journalists should know

Grant Hannis, Massey University

Grammar is the study and rules of how a language operates. As professional writers, journalists needs to understand grammar, the tools of their trade.

In this appendix we consider:

- the sentence
- parts of speech
- spelling
- punctuation.

The sentence

A **phrase** is a group of words that has some sense but cannot stand alone. Some examples: "to the zoo", "above the TV", "can apply", "will be going soon", "the man", "the shabby house".

A **clause** is a group of words that have a subject and a predicate. The subject is what the clause is about and the predicate is what is said about the subject.

Although there can be one- and two-word sentences ("Damn!" "But no."), these are used sparingly and often reflect colloquial speech. Generally, a sentence is a group of words that is a complete thought on its own. Its meaning is complete and nothing needs to be added to it to make it seem right.

As with a clause, every sentence must have a subject and a predicate. The subject is basically the primary noun in the sentence and the predicate is built around the primary verb in the sentence. We talk more about nouns and verbs below.

Consider the following group of words:

"went to the movies"

This group of words, or phrase, feels incomplete. That's because it is a predicate with no subject. Now consider the following group of words:

"I went to the movies."

Why does this feel right? It is because the group of words now has a subject ("I") as well as a predicate ("went to the movies"). It is a clause. As the example above shows, a clause can be a simple sentence. But we can join main clauses (clauses that could stand alone as sentences) together to create compound sentences:

Main clause 1   **Main clause 2**

"Steve is going to the movies and John will join him later."

A subordinate clause has a subject and a predicate but cannot stand on its own. A complex sentence is one in which one or more subordinate clauses are added to at least one main clause:

Subordinate clause   **Main clause**

As it was such a lovely day, we went to the beach.

Parts of speech

Words are classified by their function in sentences. These word classes are called parts of speech. In English, there are eight parts of speech: noun, adjective, pronoun, verb, adverb, preposition, conjunction and interjection.

Sometimes a part of speech is made up of just one word, but it can also be made up of several words (a phrase).

Nouns

Nouns name things, such as people, organisations or qualities. There are four types of noun:

Common nouns name everyday, tangible things, such as "chair" or "child".

Proper nouns are given names, such as "John" or "Mt Victoria". Proper nouns always begin with a capital letter.

Collective nouns name groups of things, such as "team" or "jury". A collective noun may be singular or plural depending on whether it is regarded as a group acting as one or as individuals operating separately: "The jury reached *its* verdict." "The jury dispersed to *their* respective homes after the trial finished." Words like "council" and "school" are usually regarded as singular.

Abstract nouns name things we cannot touch, such as "joy" or "laughter".

Nouns can alter to reflect number, gender and case.

Number: This indicates whether there is one or more of the thing named: "one dog", "two dogs". Plurals are usually formed by adding an "s", but there are many exceptions. For instance, nouns ending in "s", "sh", "ch", "x" or "z" take "es" ("Jones" becomes "Joneses"). With the exception of proper nouns, nouns ending in "y" take "ies" ("pony" becomes "ponies", but "Mary" becomes "Marys"). Some change letters: "louse", "lice"; "mouse", "mice" for the animal, but often "mouses" for the computer hardware. Some plurals take "x", some take "a" and some take "n" or a version thereof: ("bureaux", "phenomena", "children", "oxen"). Some nouns do not differentiate between the singular and the plural: "series", "sheep".

Plurals of compound words (words made up of other words, often joined together by hyphens) can be confusing. Generally, the primary word takes the plural. "Governor-General" becomes "Governors-General", "court martial" becomes "courts martial", but "forget-me-not" becomes "forget-me-nots".

Nouns are often preceded by "a", "an" or "the". These words are called **articles**, and are often categorised as being adjectives (see below). The first two are indefinite articles – that is, they do not point out a specific article. The word "a" comes before a noun that begins with a consonant ("a horse"). The word "an" comes before a noun that begins with a vowel or vowel sound ("an echo", "an honour"). The definite article, "the", is used to point out a specific noun.

Adjectives

Adjectives tell us more (that is to say, they modify) a noun. They usually appear immediately before the noun but can appear elsewhere.

"This is a *beautiful* sunset."
"This sunset is *beautiful*."

Adjectives have three degrees: **Positive** (where nothing is being compared), **comparative** (comparing two things) and **superlative** (when three or more things are being compared). The usual ending for comparatives are "-er" and for superlatives "-est", but some adjectives take "more" and "most" respectively.

"That dog has a dark coat." (positive)
"That dog has a darker coat than the other dog." (comparative)
"That dog has the darkest coat of all." (superlative)
"That was a beautiful sunset." (positive)
"That was a more beautiful sunset than last night." (comparative)
"That was the most beautiful sunset I have ever seen." (superlative)

Some adjectives have no comparative or superlative, such as "unique" or "empty". You cannot say: "This was one of the most unique occasions I have ever attended." The occasion was either unique or it wasn't.

You can use nouns and verb participles (see below) as adjectives, and you can create compound words as adjectives by using hyphens: "*cattle* truck", "*working* holiday", "*10-year-old* girl". These forms do not have comparative forms.

Note that if we write "A 10-year-old girl" or "The girl was a 10-year-old", we use hyphens. In the first instance, that's because we have a compound adjective and in the second a compound noun. But if we write "The girl was 10 years old" we don't.

Pronouns

Pronouns stand in for nouns. If we did not have pronouns, we would have sentences such as:

> "When John went to John's study, John switched on John's light and began reading the report John's boss had given John."

We can substitute pronouns for the repeated noun in that sentence:

> "When John went to his study, he switched on his light and began reading the report his boss had given him."

There are several types of pronoun:

Personal (I, you, we, they, him, them, his, my, our, yours, etc.)
There are three persons with personal pronouns: first, second and third.

Singular
I (first person, referring to me)
You (second person, I am/we are talking to you)
He, She, It (third person, I am/we are talking to you about him, her or it)

Plural
We (first person, referring to us)
You (second person, I am/we are, we are talking to you)
They (third person, I am/we are talking to you about them)
Words like "one" and "a person" and "people" are all third person.

Reflexive (always end in "self" or "selves"). These are only used when the subject acts upon itself ("He kicked himself.") or to emphasise that the subject acted alone ("John did it himself.").

Relative ("who", "whom", "whose", "which", "that", "what"). These join a clause to information earlier in the sentence.

Interrogative ("who", "whom", "whose", "which", "what"). These ask a question.

Demonstrative ("this", "that", "these", "those"). These point out a specific noun.

Indefinite ("any", "each", "several", "some", etc.). These refer to nouns in general.

Increasingly, a plural pronoun is used to avoid sexist language and cumbersome language: "Somebody has left their book behind", rather than "Somebody has left his book behind" or "Somebody has left his or her book behind."

Use of "which" for non-restrictive and restrictive clauses

The word "which" is used to introduce a non-restrictive clause, and is marked off with commas:

> "I climbed the tree, which was an evergreen, last week."
> "We went to the market, which is open every weekend."

The subordinate clauses here ("which was an evergreen" and "which is open every weekend") are parenthetical. They add information, but they do not define. That is to say, they are non-restrictive. They can be removed from the sentence and the sentence would still have meaning. A non-restrictive clause must be introduced with "which" and be marked off with commas.

A restrictive clause does not have commas. It can be introduced with "which", "that", or neither:

> "I saw the car which the police were chasing."
> "I saw the car that the police were chasing."
> "I saw the car the police were chasing."

The clause "the police were chasing" is restrictive. It is not additional, non-parenthetical information. Instead, the information is vital to the sentence. It defines the car – there were many cars on the road, but I saw the specific car the police were chasing. The information cannot be removed from the sentence and the sentence still make sense.

Compare these two sentences:

> "The council owns 5000 houses, which remain unoccupied for at least part of each year."
> "The council owns 5000 houses which remain unoccupied for at least part of each year."

In the first, the clause "which remain unoccupied for at least part of each year" is non-restrictive. The council owns 5000 houses and, incidentally, they remain unoccupied for at least some of the year. The clause is thus marked off with a comma. In the second sentence the clause "which remain unoccupied for at least part of each year" is restrictive. The council owns more than 5000 houses, but only 5000 remain unoccupied for at least some of the year. The clause is thus not marked off with a comma.

Verbs

The verb is the most important word in a sentence. Verbs can be either action (doing) words or linking words:

> "The dog *chased* the cat."
> "The dog *is* brown."

Verbs are either in the active or passive voice. **Active** means the doer (also known as the agent or principal) is in the subject position of the sentence and comes before the verb, and the recipient is in the object position. **Passive** means the recipient is in the subject position and comes before the verb, the doer (if any) is in the object position:

"The council arranged a meeting to discuss the issue." (active)

"A meeting was arranged to discuss the issue." (passive, no agent)

Verbs have **tense** – that is, they express time. The simple tenses are past, present and future. However, by using additional words, we can create more complex tenses.

Present: "I see the car."

Present continuous: "I am seeing the car."

Present perfect (the "near past"): "I have seen the car."

Past: "I saw the car."

Past perfect: "I had seen the car."

Past continuous: "I was seeing the car."

Future: "I will see the car."

Future perfect: "I will have seen the car."

Future continuous: "I will be seeing the car."

The way a verb changes depending on person is known as how the verb is **conjugated**. Usually in English, the same form of the verb is used for all persons, except third person singular, which takes an "s" in the present tense:

Singular

I	talk
You	talk
He/she/it	talks

Plural

We	talk
You	talk
They	talk

An exception is "to be", which is conjugated:

Singular

I	am
You	are
He/she/it	is

Plural

We	are
You	are
They	are

Verbs must agree in person and number:

"A box of books *was* delivered today." (third person, singular)

"Bacon and eggs *is* my favourite breakfast. I love it." (third person, singular)

We can also turn verbs into nouns, such as "flying" and "dancing". These noun-verbs, which take the form of the present participle, are called **gerunds**.

Note that voice has nothing to do with tense. Active and passive voice can exist in the past, present or future tense:

Active
I saw the cat. (past)

I see the cat. (present)

I will see the cat. (future)

Passive
The cat was seen by me. (past)

The cat is seen by me. (present)

The cat will be seen by me. (future)

Adverbs

Adverbs modify a verb, an adjective or another adverb:

"The horse was galloping *fast*."

"The sky is *distinctly* blue."

"The horse was galloping *very* fast."

As with adjectives, adverbs can have **positives**, **comparatives** and **superlatives**, and these are usually created by adding "more" and "most":

"The girl was speaking beautifully." (positive)

"He is speaking more beautifully than she did." (comparative)

"She spoke the most beautifully." (superlative)

Some adverbs do not follow this pattern, such as "well" (positive), "better" (comparative), "best" (superlative) and "badly" (positive), "worse" (comparative), "worst" (superlative).

Prepositions

A preposition shows the relationship between two things. A preposition is always followed by a noun or pronoun.

"The child had to stay *in* the classroom to do detention." ("in" is a preposition showing the relationship between the child and the classroom; "in the classroom" is a **prepositional phrase**.)

"Jan is coming *with* David and me." ("with" is a preposition, and "me" is a pronoun. If you are unsure whether to use "me" or "I", take "David" out and see which word makes sense.)

Some words are always followed by a specific preposition. Here are some examples, but use your dictionary to avoid errors with others:

"adjacent to"   "different from"   "independent of"   "substitute for"

Conjunctions

These join words, phrases and clauses to show either similarity or contrast between them, or to create a sequence. Here are some examples:
"John *and* Steve played golf *or* tennis every weekend."
"John plays golf, *but* Steve plays tennis."

Coordinating conjunctions join clauses of equal importance, such as in the examples above. **Subordinating conjunctions** join a subordinate clause to a main clause:

Main clause	**Subordinate clause**
"I shall be at the station	*when* you arrive."

Conjunctions can also include transition words (sometimes called **adverbials**) that lead from one idea to another, such as "however", "nevertheless" and "moreover". These are marked off with commas:
"I like to play the piano. However, I only sing in the shower."

Interjections

These are words uttered in surprise, shock, joy, etc. They are marked off with commas, an exclamation point or a question mark:
"Oh! What a marvellous surprise."
"Really? I didn't know that."

One New Zealand interjection is frequently misspelled:
"That was a good win, eh?" (Not "aye" or "ay".)

More on parts of speech

The same word can be a different part of speech depending on how it is used. For instance, consider the word *fast*:
"Before the operation I went on a fast." (noun)
"Before the operation I need to fast." (verb)
"This is a fast boat." (adjective)
"The boat was stuck fast." (adverb)

Pronunciation of a word can change depending on whether it is a noun or verb. Notice the different pronunciations of "present" in this sentence:
"I will present *(verb)* her with a present *(noun)*."

Here are some other examples: "convict", "attribute", "contest", "convert", "graduate", "project", "subject", "reject", "content", "desert", "envelope".

Pronunciation can also change depending on whether a word is an adjective or a verb: "dogged", "learned", "aged", "moderate", "blessed".

Spelling

You may believe that spelling is not important – the computer will correct your errors. But that is not the case. For one thing, not all your writing will be on computers – you don't want to give your chief reporter or editor a handwritten note full of spelling mistakes! Also, computers won't protect you against malapropisms and homophones.

Malapropisms

A malapropism is a wrong word used for a similar-sounding word. The malapropism is spelt correctly, so the computer software won't say it's wrong, but it is the wrong word. For instance, if you write "He excepted the prize on behalf of his partner", you have used a malapropism ("excepted", when it should be "accepted"). Here are some other examples:

adverse/averse
advice/advise
affect/effect
begging the question/raising the question
bisect/dissect
brought/bought
cachet/cache/cash
definitely/defiantly
hone/home
internment/interment
imply/infer
incredulous/incredible
fortuitous/fortunate
fulsome/abundant
historic/historical
lose/loose
parameter/perimeter
sewage/sewerage
watershed/Watergate

If you don't know which word to use, look it up in a dictionary.

Homophones

Some words that sound the same (homophones) can have different spellings to denote their different meanings. Again, the computer won't catch this, so be aware of the different spellings and meanings. For instance, if you write "The North and South Islands are separated by Cook Straight" you have written a homophone ("Straight", when it should be "Strait"). Here are some more examples:

anyway/any way
awhile/a while
baited/bated
compliment/complement
currant/current
dependant/dependent
(A mnemonic with this one: "ant" is a noun, so "dependant" is too.)
everyday/every day
flu/flue
incite/insight
its/it's ("it's" is only ever a contraction of "it is" or "it has")
licence/license
(A mnemonic with this one: the noun is the one you can "c". It's the same with advice/advise and practice/practise. Note that "defense" is only ever a US spelling.)
may be/maybe
meter/metre
mussel/muscle
palate/palette
practice/practise
premier/premiere
principle/principal
programme/program
queue/cue
reigns/reins/rains
site/cite/sight
their/they're/there
tyre/tire
who's/whose
stationary/stationery

The following words are often misspelled. Make sure you use these correct spellings:

accommodate, acknowledge, allege, all right, altogether, anomaly, argument, calendar, cemetery, centre, colonel, committee, concede, conscience, disastrous, dyeing, embarrass, enrol, exceed, existence, February, foreign, forty, fulfil, government, graffiti, grammar, harass, inoculate, idiosyncrasy, irreducible, just deserts, library, manoeuvre, millennium, necessary, neighbour, occasion, occurrence, opportunity, parallel, permissible, persuade, picnicking, pneumatic, poplar tree, precede, privilege, proceed, pursue, recede, recommend, reconnoitre, resistible, rhyme, rhythm, secede, separate, sergeant, singeing, skilful, succeed, supersede, theatre, tomorrow, victuals, weird, woollen.

More advice on spelling

- Read. Standard books and texts have been professionally sub-edited. Observe the spellings of words as you read. By a process of osmosis, you will improve your spelling. Visualise the spellings of words you are unsure about. That way, if you misspell it, the word will look odd to you.

- Do spelling tests. Crosswords and other vocabulary-building exercises introduce you to words whose spellings may be unfamiliar. There are plenty on the internet and in newspapers.

- Make sure your computer's auto-correct dictionary language is set on English (New Zealand). For instance, this should prevent US "-ize" endings creeping in, when the preferred New Zealand spelling is "-ise": specialise, recognise, industrialise.

- Use a dictionary and other guides. If you are in any doubt, never assume a spelling is correct. Consult two dictionaries if need be. *Oxford* and *Collins* are standard texts. The free online dictionary www.dictionary.com is also helpful, but remember it has a US English focus.

- English usually dispenses with accents as a punctuation mark. You don't need to spell "cafe" with an accent on the "e".

- Increasingly, journalism organisations in New Zealand are spelling Māori words using macrons. You will need a Māori dictionary to make sure you get this right (www.maoridictionary.co.nz is excellent).

- Finally, remember a good speller has the following characteristics:
  – they know how to spell commonly misspelt words
  – they readily look up unfamiliar or unusual words
  – they are not fooled by malapropisms or homophones.

Punctuation

Good punctuation makes a story easier to read, so it is important to know how to use the main punctuation marks. We will consider the comma, apostrophe, hyphen, colon and semicolon, dash and brackets, question mark and exclamation mark.

Comma (,)

Journalists frequently use commas in their stories. Here are the main times you need to use them.

Quotes

If a direct quote is followed by attribution, the final sentence ends with a comma, closed speech marks, attribution:

"This is the end," he said.

If attribution comes before the direct quote, you can use a comma or a colon to introduce the quote:

He said, "I know this is correct."
He said: "I know this is correct."

If a passage of reported speech is followed by attribution, the reported speech concludes with a comma:

This was the end, he said.

For more on punctuating quotes, see Chapter 14.

Lists

Commas separate items in a list:

The boys ran, jumped, leaped about and generally enjoyed themselves.

Don't put a comma before the word "and" unless it is needed to make sense of the sentence, for instance:

They laughed, swam and played for hours.
The bands at the concert were Midnight Oil, Hunters and Collectors, and The Mutton Birds.

Without the final comma in the second sentence the reader could be confused by the bands' names.

Contrast

Use commas to separate subordinate clauses indicating some form of contrast:

New books were put on the shelves, but no one read them.

Parenthetical information

Commas mark off a noun or phrase from the rest of the sentence, putting it in parenthesis (additional information not essential to understanding the sentence). If you remove the section in parenthesis the sentence will still make sense:

Jane Smith, the new mayor of Wellington, began work today.
Ross Wilson, representing the unions, said …

Similarly, commas identify a relative clause that describes, but does not define. For instance:

His brother, who was in New York, was coming home at Christmas.

The commas make it clear that the man has only one brother and he is in New York. If the commas are removed, the meaning of the sentence changes:

His brother who was in New York was coming home for Christmas.

This sentence says the man has more than one brother. One of them is in New York and will be coming home at Christmas.

Addressing someone or something
Commas mark off any name used to address someone or something:
> Where are you going now, Roger?
> Behave, chair!

Clarification
Sometimes commas help to ensure a sentence is immediately understandable:
> He found a notebook and a pen, and set off for the media conference.

Numbers
Use a comma for numbers of five-digit orders of magnitude:
> $50,000

And for hundreds of thousands, millions and billions:
> 100,000
> 1,000,000
> 1,000,000,000

Apostrophe (')
Apostrophes have two main functions:
- to indicate contractions, that is, that words or numbers have been left out
- to indicate the possessive, that is, that something owns something else.

Before we look at that, note that the apostrophe never denotes the plural. The plural of dog is dogs, not dog's. The plural of tomato is tomatoes, not tomato's. The plural of MP is MPs, not MP's. The plural of 1970 is 1970s, not 1970's. The plural of journo is journos, not journo's.

Contractions
The apostrophe shows us that a letter or letters (or numbers) have been left out:
> isn't, can't, I'll, '72, a ne'er do well

Possessive
Apostrophes show that nouns possess something:
> He grabbed the dog's collar.
> She was alarmed at the government's policy.
> The women's group met at 8pm.

When forming the plural possessive, first create the plural form of the noun, then indicate the possessive:

> The children's books were on their shelves.
>
> He let go of the dogs' collars.

In modern journalistic use, all proper nouns that end in "s" take an apostrophe after the "s", for example:

> She did not like Keats' poem.

Possessive pronouns do not take an apostrophe, for example:

> They knew the money was not theirs, but they took it anyway.
>
> The tiger growled when the keeper grabbed its tail.

This means that "it's" is solely a contraction of "it is" or "it has". In all other cases, there is no apostrophe:

> It's a wise dog that knows its master.

The second "its" in the above sentence does not need an apostrophe as it is already showing the possessive, just as his, hers, yours and theirs also don't need apostrophes.

Periods of time

Words referring to a period of time take an apostrophe when used in the possessive sense, for example:

> They will go overseas in a week's time.
>
> He had to undertake eight years' study before he could call himself a specialist.

Hyphen (-)
Compound words

Hyphens are used to join two or more words to produce a compound word:

> The new legislation was ill-considered.
>
> The middle-aged woman sat in the park eating her lunch.

However, you do not need to use a hyphen when linking an adverb ending in "-ly" with an adjective:

> The argument was closely reasoned.

That's because the -ly ending is already indicating it is an adverb modifying the following adjective.

> Note that the meaning of a phrase can change if you use a hyphen, for example:
>
> A red-winged insect.

is not the same as:

> A red winged insect.

Prefixes
A hyphen joins a prefix to a word:
> The salesman described the car as "pre-loved", rather than second-hand.
> re-enter   re-read   pre-empt

In this regard, hyphens help distinguish between pairs of words that might otherwise be confused:
> Having reached the end of his employment contract, the man resigned.
> Having reached the end of his employment contract, the man re-signed.

Fractions, numbers and compass points
Use a hyphen when writing a fraction, two-word numbers as words, or mentioning secondary compass points. For example:
> She climbed three-quarters of the way up the mountain.
> Twenty-seven people took part in the search.
> The trampers headed south-west towards the hut.

Colon (:) and semicolon (;)
A colon can be used to introduce a list:
> In my desk I have three books: a dictionary, a textbook and an exercise book.

It can also introduce a direct quote:
> The Prime Minister said: "It is vital that we ..."

It can also introduce examples (as immediately above) and explanations:
> There was only one reason for this: revenge.

The semicolon is rarely used in journalistic writing. It separates clauses that are grammatically independent, but are closely connected in terms of subject-matter:
> In the old days people were very much tied to their own village; they often lived, worked, and died in the same place.

It is more common in such cases to use dashes or full stops.

Dash (–) and brackets
Dashes can be used to mark off a major interruption in a sentence. They suggest the interruption is more pronounced than a pair of commas would indicate:
> James Smythe – you remember him, surely – was born in this town.
> The children in the class – 15 boys and 10 girls – went to the museum.

A dash can also be used to add a thought to the end of a sentence:
> It was indeed a tragedy – a tragedy that could have been avoided.
> She has a special quality about her – enthusiasm.

Note that these dashes have spaces on either side of them. Hyphens do not.

Square (or sometimes round) brackets are used to insert explanatory information into a direct quote. Sometimes the original information is deleted in favour of the explanatory information, but strictly speaking it should be included:

"[Her father] is the greatest!" she said. (This is okay.)

"He [her father] is the greatest!" she said. (This is better.)

Exclamation mark (!) and question mark (?)

Exclamation marks indicate jokes, light-heartedness or interjections:

"You must be kidding!"

"Ow! That must have hurt."

Question marks indicate questions: "What is your name?" The question mark is not needed to indicate requests phrased as questions: "Would you please sit here."

APPENDIX 2:

Statistics answers

The answers to the exercises in Chapter 13

Grant Hannis, Massey University

Exercise 1
1) 1
2) 2
3) 101
4) $12m (make sure you retain the same units in your calculations: here it's millions of dollars)
5) 23%
6) 7
7) 5

Exercise 2
Second digit:
1) 340
2) 24000
3) 120
4) 340
5) 3400

Third digit:
1) 344
2) 23900
3) 120
4) 344
5) 3400

Exercise 3

1) 10 ÷ 20 x 100 = 50%   20 ÷ 100 x 80 = 16
2) (70 – 50) ÷ 50 x 100 = 40%
3) (84 – 160) ÷ 160 x 100 = -47.5% (Don't forget the negative sign!)
4) 1.2 x $50 = $60
5) 0.7 x $2 = $1.40
6) 110 ÷ 1.12 = 98.2
7) 200 ÷ 0.75 = 267
8) No, it isn't. An increase from 2 to 4 is a 100 per cent increase. What the reporter meant to say was that the inflation rate has increased by 2 percentage points.

Exercise 4

As GST had increased 2.5 percentage points, the reporters simply added 2.5 per cent to the cost of the items.

But, that's 2.5 per cent on the price of a product that already includes GST! The reporters needed to first calculate the GST-exclusive price (at 12.5 per cent) and then add 15 per cent.

In the first example, that would be:

GST-exclusive price
$2000 ÷ 1.125 = $1777.78

New GST-inclusive price
$1777.78 x 1.15 = $2044 (not $2050)

In each case, then, the reporters over-stated the effect of increasing GST. The TV stations later issued corrections.

Exercise 5

1) The mean salary is $94,929 ($1,329,000 ÷ 14)
2) The median salary is $45,000
3) The mode is $32,000
4) By quoting the mean salary, the chief executive is suggesting people working for the company are getting a good deal. However, nearly all the staff are earning considerably less than that. The wages paid to the three senior managers push up the mean salary dramatically. You could quote median and mode figures, which give a much fairer representation of the actual position, and ask the chief executive for a response.

Exercise 6

The newspaper seems to have calculated Collins' average weekly spend as being over one year: $11,536/52 = $222. But, as the article made clear, Collins' spending was over *two* years, making the weekly average $11,536 ÷ 104 = $111.

Even then, at $11,536, Collins' spend was not five times Turia's $7216. In fact, it wasn't even double Turia's spending.

The following week the paper published an apology.

Exercise 7

1) Well, for a start the increase was 54 per cent – the journalist did not round the figure correctly. Also, checking the source data reveals that the 2005 apprehension figure was actually 2752.

Far more importantly, the data on Asian crime ignores the fact that the number of Asians in New Zealand increased dramatically over the same period. It's hardly surprising the number of crimes committed by Asians increased – the number of Asians in New Zealand increased! Crime figures are routinely quoted as a crime rate precisely because we need to take changes in population into account. To calculate the crime rate we simply divide the number of offences by the population and multiply by, say, 10,000 to show the number of crimes for each 10,000 members of the population.

According to census data, the number of Asians (excluding Indians) aged 17 to 50 in 1996 was 78,513. Using 2001 and 2006 census data, we can estimate that the same population in 2005 was 142,527. This means the crime rates were:

> 1996: 1791 ÷ 78,513 x 10,000
> = 228.1 crimes per 10,000 Asians

> 2005: 2752 ÷ 142,527 x 10,000
> = 193.1 crimes per 10,000 Asians

So the crime rate among Asians went *down* by 15 per cent over the period (put another way, whereas the number of Asian crimes rose 54 per cent, the Asian population rose by more, 82 per cent). So Asians were less likely to commit crime in 2005 than they were in 1996. This is exactly the opposite from what the article claimed. Further, the crime rates for the whole New Zealand population aged 17 to 50 were:

> 1996: 801.9 crimes per 10,000 New Zealanders

> 2005: 772.4 crimes per 10,000 New Zealanders

In other words, in 2005 the crime rate for all New Zealanders was four times that for Asians. Asians are far more law-abiding than is the general population.

The article's inadequacies caused an uproar, but the magazine refused to back down. Complaints were eventually taken to the Media Council, which ruled the article was inaccurate and discriminatory. The magazine was obliged to publish the council's decision in its July 2007 issue.

2) We're not told how many in the population are men over 50. As the article itself went on to point out, men over 50 comprise a large proportion of the population so, of course, they consume a relatively large amount of alcohol.

The statements tell us virtually nothing about the drinking habits of older men. Just as "Asian Angst" needed to consider crime rates, so this article needed to consider alcohol-consumption rates.

Exercise 8

1) The inflation rate over the period is:

(1015 – 1000) ÷ 1000 x 100 = 1.5 per cent per annum.

2) Yes.

3) The change in Real GDP for the period is:

(1010 – 1023) ÷ 1023 x 100 = -1.3 per cent per annum.

Real GDP has fallen by 1.3 per cent over the period.

4) The economy has shrunk. That is, fewer final goods and services were produced in year two, compared to year one.

Exercise 9

There are many problems with this pictograph and the data presented on it. The use of dollar signs is ill-advised. It is unclear where on the dollar sign we read off the totals: is it the top of the S or the top of the line running through the S? Let's assume it is the top of the line. This means that the first dollar sign represents about $45m and the third dollar sign represents about $115m. That's an increase of 156 per cent. But the third dollar sign has grown in width as well as height. It is in fact 586 per cent larger than the first dollar sign, giving a hugely distorted impression of the size of the increase. If we must use dollar signs in this graph it would be better to use the same-sized dollar sign in each case (the tops of some of the dollar signs are cut off to accurately show the values they represent):

But the problems don't end there. The graph is unsourced – we have no way of knowing where the figures come from. Also, the dates on the x axis are irregular. The

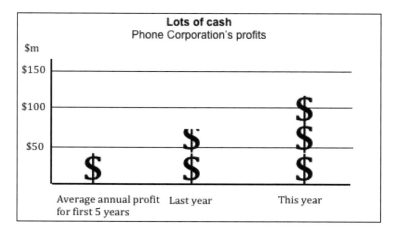

graph makes it look like profits have increased steadily over three years, but the first figure actually covers five years – we have no way of knowing what profits were like in each of those five years.

The data is also poor. Profit figures on their own tell us very little: we need to know the rate of profit: say, Phone Corporation's profit as a percentage of its total assets. If simple dollar figures are to be used, they should have been adjusted for inflation: one dollar today is not worth the same as one dollar several years ago.

Exercise 10

By dividing the bird population figures through by 100 you would quote the bird numbers in the same order of magnitude as the cats. You could then put them on the same axis (note that the correction is stated in the legend at the bottom of the chart).

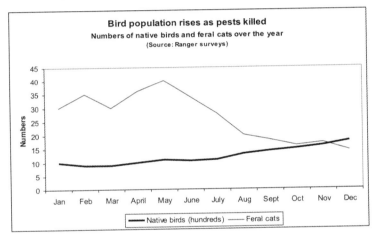

Notice how each graph shows a different picture, even though the underlying data is the same. You need to make a judgement as to which graph most fairly represents the situation. The graph in the textbook is probably better, as it shows the data in its original form, making it more intuitively obvious to the reader.

Exercise 11

The 3-D effect has distorted the segments. In particular, notice how the "Borrowing" segment looks bigger than the "Fines" segment, even though they both represent 20 per cent of the total, and the "Other" category looks disproportionately large.

Exercise 12

The data in this graph is exactly the same as the banks' graph in the text, except here the x axis cuts the y axis at 8, not at 0. This exaggerates the differences between the banks' interest rates – particularly the difference between Banks 1 and 5. It looks like Bank 1's rate is nearly 300 per cent higher than Bank 5's, when in fact it is only about 40 per cent higher. At the very least the graph should make it clear that the y axis does not go to 0.

Exercise 13

The article was confusing. The cover said the revolution went wrong, but the article said there was no evidence the revolution was a failure. Indeed, one of the researchers said she would still use a midwife.

The article talked about midwives delivering babies when it was meant to be referring to births where midwives were the lead maternity carer (known as the LMC). When the baby was actually being born, it could be it was another person, such as a doctor, who delivered the baby. The *Listener* published a correction on this point in its November 19, 2016, issue.

Although the article quoted greater risks of being born with the abnormalities mentioned, it did not say how many children *in absolute numbers* were born with the abnormalities. Indeed, the researcher said adverse outcomes were rare.

The College of Midwives complained to the Media Council about the article (*NZ College of Midwives against New Zealand Listener,* 2017). The council ruled the headlines on the magazine's cover were inaccurate and unfair, in that the headlines gave a much more negative view of midwives than that presented in the article.

Exercise 14

The paper had no solid evidence most New Zealanders would be doing nothing for Mother's Day. Although the number who responded to the poll was apparently high, 5000, it only comprised those who visited the website and chose to take part. This was hardly a random sample of all New Zealanders. We don't even know if these respondents had living mothers!

Also, the questions were poorly designed. Only those who planned to celebrate Mother's Day with a card or a meal or breakfast in bed could answer yes. Any other options – such as giving her flowers, visiting her or giving her a phone call – were excluded.

Finally, although the headline claimed "most" respondents wouldn't be celebrating Mother's Day, in the survey less than half said that (44 per cent, in fact). In other words, most respondents *would* be celebrating Mother's Day.

Exercise 15

The editor is wrong in the first example. Support for the government in the first survey is somewhere between 40 per cent and 46 per cent (43 per cent ± 3 per cent). Support for the government in the second survey is between 38 per cent and 44 per cent. It is entirely possible, for instance, that support for the government has remained the same in the overlap between the two surveys at 40, 41, 42, 43 or 44 per cent. It is even possible that support for the government has risen: from, say, 41 per cent in the first survey to 44 per cent in the second. We cannot say with any confidence that support for the government has decreased between the two surveys.

The editor is probably correct in the second example. In the first survey support for the government is somewhere between 40 per cent and 46 per cent, and in the second survey is somewhere between 32 per cent and 38 per cent. There is no overlap between these two ranges: the lowest possible support in the first survey is

40 per cent; the highest possible support in the second survey is 38 per cent. It's very likely support for the government has dropped. But this is at the 95 per cent confidence level. It is just possible this result is an aberration – the 5 per cent of off-the-wall samples. We would be more certain that support for the government has really dropped if other surveys produce similar results.

APPENDIX 3:
Additional science resources

Supplemental information for Chapter 9

Alan Samson, Massey University

Glossary of weather terms

Anticyclone (or high): An area of high air pressure, with winds blowing counter-clockwise around the centre. Usually means fine weather with light winds.

Cyclone: A rotating system of winds about a centre of low atmospheric pressure, often bringing heavy rain. Term should be used only where a cyclone is at least of moderate intensity, such as for tropical cyclones.

Depression (low or cyclone): An area of low pressure, with winds moving clockwise around the centre. In our latitudes, depressions may be 1500 kilometres across, with winds reaching gale force or stronger and with rain usually widespread.

El Niño: A four- to 12-yearly warming of the ocean surface off the western coast of South America linked to a large-scale shift of atmospheric pressure. It brings to New Zealand colder, stronger and more frequent winds from the west in summer (bringing drought in east coast areas and more rain in the west) and more frequent winds from the south in winter (bringing colder conditions to both the land and the surrounding ocean).

Fronts: Many depressions have two distinct masses of air – one warm, the other cold. The boundary between the two is called a "front". A warm front is one in which warm air is moving to displace cold air. A cold front is the reverse. Much of the rain and cloud in a depression is concentrated at the "front". The weather often clears after a front passes.

Hurricane (or tropical cyclone): Winds of force 12 (where mean speeds exceed 64 knots or 117 kmh) bringing heavy rain, and winds and rough seas. May form north of New Zealand between November and April and move south, but usually loses intensity before reaching us.

La Niña: Weather conditions characterised by a cold patch of sea surface temperatures in the central and eastern equatorial Pacific, but warmer around New Zealand. Air temperatures rise here, with anticyclones more frequent in the south-east, and north-easterly airflows becoming more frequent over the North Island and easterlies over the South Island. A pattern of greater monsoonal activity over Indonesia and northern Australia, sometimes bringing severe storms to New Zealand.

Lightning: An electrical current in the air. Sheet lightning is a current between clouds; fork lightning, a current from cloud to earth. Western areas (Taranaki, Westland, Northland) have 15–20 thunderstorms a year.

Pressure: The weight of air pressing down on the Earth. Measured by a barometer and expressed in millibars (mb), formerly inches.

Relative humidity: Amount of water vapour in a given volume of air (affected by temperature of air – warm air can absorb more water vapour than cold). Expressed as a percentage. Average relative humidity in New Zealand: 70–80 per cent coastal, 60–70 per cent inland. Uncomfortable humidity is 90 per cent plus.

Ridge of high pressure: Formed between two depressions, rather narrow and elongated. Generally means fine weather (similar to small anticyclone).

Tornadoes: Violent spinning air bred from thunderstorms. Wind speeds can reach 170–260 knots or 320–480 kmh. A funnel cloud descends, reaching towards the ground like a trunk and filled with dirt and debris where it touches the ground. Advances at speed of thunderstorm. Few last longer than half an hour. About 20–25 tornadoes occur each year in New Zealand, mainly in the west (Taranaki, Westland, Waikato).

Trough of low pressure: An area of low pressure in the shape of a trough, usually between two anticyclones. Moves from south-west to north-east. A cold front is often in a trough, preceded by a belt of north-west winds, rain, and cloud. South-west winds follow, with showers and lower temperatures.

Units of measurement

Weather
Rain: Measured in millimetres (25 mm = 1 inch). Know the average annual rainfall for your district – or at least how to get the information in a hurry.

Sunshine: Measured in hours (about 4380 hours' potential sunshine in a year).

Temperature: Measured in degrees Celsius.

Wind: Can be expressed in terms of speed (kmh for land and sea) or as a descriptive term (light breeze, near gale, etc.). The Beaufort scale (force 7, etc.) is no longer used for weather reporting in New Zealand.

Earthquakes
Although the term is no longer used here, the magnitude of most earthquakes is measured on the Richter scale, invented by Charles F. Richter in 1934. It is calculated from the amplitude of the largest seismic wave recorded.

The measurement is based on a logarithmic scale. For each whole number you go up on the scale, the amplitude of the ground motion recorded by a seismograph goes up 10 times. That is, a magnitude 5 earthquake would result in 10 times the level of ground shaking as a magnitude 4 earthquake – and with 32 times as much energy released.

The scale makes for an enormous difference in power per magnitude number, which needs to be considered in the reporting:
- A magnitude 1 seismic wave releases as much energy as blowing up *six ounces* of TNT.
- A magnitude 8 earthquake releases as much energy as detonating *6 million tonnes* of TNT.

Volcanoes
0. Background surface activity, seismicity, deformation and heat flow at low levels.
   Status: usually dormant, or quiescent state.
1. Departure from typical background surface activity.
   Status: signs of volcanic unrest.
2. Onset of eruptive activity, accompanied by changes to monitored indicators.
   Status: minor eruptive activity.
3. Increased vigour of ongoing activity and monitored indicators. Significant effects on volcano, possible effects beyond.
   Status: significant local eruption in progress.
4. Significant change to ongoing activity and monitored indicators. Effects beyond volcano.
   Status: hazardous local eruption in progress.
5. Hazardous large volcanic eruption in progress.
   Status: large hazardous eruption in progress.

New Zealand scientific organisations

Crown Research Institutes

CRIs are the home of most public science intended to benefit New Zealand by improving productivity and improving the sustainable use of natural resources. Since being set up in 1992, 10 institutes have been whittled down to today's eight:

- AgResearch
- Callaghan Innovation
- Institute of Environmental Science Research (ESR)
- Institute of Geological and Nuclear Science (GNS)
- Landcare Research
- National Institute of Water and Atmospheric Research (NIWA)
- Plant and Food Research
- Scion (Forest Research Institute).

Ministry of Business, Innovation and Employment

In 2012, the Ministry of Science and Innovation became part of the new Ministry of Business, Innovation and Employment (MBIE). MBIE aims to build high-performing science and innovation systems to make New Zealand a more diverse, technologically advanced, smart nation.

Universities

- AUT University
- Lincoln University
- Massey University
- University of Auckland
- University of Canterbury
- University of Otago
- University of Waikato
- Victoria University of Wellington.

Centres of research excellence

Since 2002, some of the best of New Zealand science has been carried out in various centres of research excellence. Crossing organisational boundaries for important and innovative projects, the research ranges from bio-protection to the development of nanotechnology devices. The 10 centres funded through to 2020 are:

- Bio-Protection Research Centre, based at Lincoln University (work on biosecurity and pest management to protect primary industries and ecosystems)
- Brain Research NZ Centre, based at Otago University and Auckland's Centre for Brain Research (work related to the ageing brain)
- Dodd-Walls Centre for Phonetic and Quantum Technology, based at Otago University (researches the physical universe for advanced techonological developments)

- Maurice Wilkins Centre for Molecular Biodiscovery, based at Auckland Univerity (work on biomedicine and biotechnology, targeting human disease)
- The Medical Technologies Centre, based at Auckland University (investigating new technologies benefitting health)
- Ngā Pae o te Māramatanga – New Zealand's Indigenous Centre of Research Excellence, based at Auckland University (research of relevance to Māori communities)
- The MacDiarmid Institute for Advanced Materials and Nanotechnology, based at Victoria University of Wellington (work on nano-engineered materials and devices, and superconducting and other advanced materials)
- Quake Centre, based at Canterbury University (work related to recovery after major earthquakes)
- The Riddet Centre, based at Massey University (food industry-related research)
- Te Pūnaha Matatini Centre, based at Auckland University (developing complex data sets to further national productivity).

About the editor

Associate Professor Grant Hannis teaches journalism at Massey University in Wellington, where he has been a journalism educator for more than 15 years. Prior to joining Massey, he spent 14 years as a senior journalist at *Consumer* magazine. He has also taught journalism in the United States, as a Fulbright Senior Scholar.

Photo: Jacqueline Cumming

About the contributors

Carol Archie

Carol has had a long career in journalism. From the late 1970s, as a television journalist for TVNZ *News* and *Eye Witness*, Carol covered many major Māori events. At Mana Māori Media (1992–2005) she recorded Māori stories for radio and wrote for *Mana* magazine. Her first book, *Māori Sovereignty – The Pākehā Perspective,* was published in 1995 and she wrote *Pou Kōrero: A Journalists' Guide to Māori and Current Affairs* in 2007. Carol recently directed two documentaries, *Skin to Skin* and *Lines in the Sand*, for Māori Television. She was awarded the ONZM in 2000 for services to Māori and journalism.

Professor Ursula Cheer

Ursula graduated from Canterbury Law School, Christchurch, in 1982 and practised as a lawyer for six years. She then moved to Wellington as a speech-writer to the Minister of Justice and later became legal adviser to the Prime Minister. In 1989, Ursula moved to the United Kingdom and completed her Master's degree at Cambridge University, in which her thesis was on censorship. She was then appointed as a senior legal adviser to the Lord Chancellor. She is now Dean of the Law School at the University of Canterbury and a professor specialising in media law. Ursula regularly comments on media law issues and is co-author of *Media Law in New Zealand*.

Associate Professor Margie Comrie

Margie recenty retired as an associate professor in the School of Communication, Journalism and Marketing at Massey University, where she taught journalism studies and communication. Margie spent 15 years in the media working at *The Evening Post*, commercial radio, RNZ and BBC Radio 4, as a journalist and current affairs interviewer and producer. Her research centres on political communication, public journalism, television news and broadcasting policy. She co-edited two books with Professor Judy McGregor on journalism issues in New Zealand.

Colin Espiner

Prior to a move into public relations, Colin had over two decades' journalism experience in New Zealand and Australia, working in print, radio, television and the internet. Colin covered local government in Wellington for *The Evening Post* and was the political editor of *The Press* for eight years. He started the first mainstream media political blog, *On The House*, and wrote on politics for the *Sunday Star-Times*.

Dr James Hollings

James is the journalism discipline leader at Massey University in Wellington, where he teaches investigative journalism. His doctoral thesis was on the decision-making process of reluctant, vulnerable witnesses. Before becoming an academic, he was a reporter and sub-editor. He won the Jubilee Prize for investigative journalism in 1995. He is the editor of *A Moral Truth: 150 Years of Investigative Journalism in New Zealand*.

Jim Kayes

Jim began his journalism career in 1992 after completing the AUT Certificate in Journalism. He worked for the *Waikato Times* and *The Evening Post* until 1997, during which time he won the Duncan Campbell Memorial Award for investigative journalism. He was then appointed deputy sports editor at *The Dominion* newspaper and was sports editor at *The Dominion Post* for two years. He was the senior rugby writer at *The Dominion* and *The Dominion Post* before joining TV3 as a sports reporter in 2009. He was the sports presenter on the *Paul Henry* TV show in 2015–2016. He has covered almost 200 All Blacks tests and five Rugby World Cups. He was named the TP McLean television news sports journalist of the year in 2011. He now works as a freelancer and presenter for Sky, Radio Live, Trackside Radio and a variety of websites and magazines.

Allan Lee

Allan is a senior lecturer in journalism at AUT University. He has worked on business magazines in the United Kingdom and is a former business reporter on *The Dominion*. Allan edited *Business Reporting: A New Zealand Guide to Financial Journalism*.

Jo Malcolm

Jo graduated from the University of Canterbury in 1988 with a Bachelor of Arts and a Diploma in Journalism. She worked on the *Bay of Plenty Times* in Tauranga before becoming an intern at TVNZ in 1989. This was the beginning of a 12-year career in broadcast journalism. Jo worked as a reporter in news and current affairs, and was a foreign correspondent for TVNZ based in Sydney. She now teaches broadcast journalism as part of the University of Canterbury's diploma programme.

Deborah Morris

Deborah is a court reporter for *The Dominion Post* newspaper and prior to that *The Evening Post*. She has been a journalist for nearly 30 years and has covered some of New Zealand's most high-profile criminal trials. Deborah runs training seminars and workshops on court reporting for Stuff.

Danielle Mulrennan

Danielle is a lecturer at AUT University and researcher of journalism studies. She is particularly interested in exploring the theory and practice of using mobile social media to enable student-directed learning. Danni worked for 20 years in television news and production with leading New Zealand networks and production houses.

Charles Riddle

Charles worked as a journalist in Europe and South Africa before coming to New Zealand. He has worked as a travel writer for *Reader's Digest*, a desk editor for an alternative news agency, a UNESCO media trainer and a copywriter. He teaches at the Waikato Institute of Technology (Wintec).

Dr Tara Ross

Tara is head of the journalism programme at the University of Canterbury. She was an award-winning senior reporter for *The Press* and the *Sunday Star-Times* newspapers, and has worked both as a freelance writer and editor as well as for community news publications. Of Pākehā and Tuvaluan descent, her research into Pasifika news media in Aotearoa New Zealand has involved extensive interviews with Pasifika reporters, producers and audiences.

Alan Samson

Alan's 30 years in journalism span *The Press* in Christchurch, NZPA, editor of two London management magazines and journalist at *The Dominion* and *Sunday Times*, most recently reporting science and environment and authoring the "Tomorrow" science column. He reported the tumultuous restructuring of public science and was the only print journalist to cover the Royal Commission on Genetic Modification. Twice a Qantas Media Awards winner and twice science writer of the year, he was also a recipient of the New Zealand Skeptics' critical reporting award.

Jo Scott

Jo graduated from the New Zealand Broadcasting School in 1997 with a Diploma in Journalism, and first worked at Newstalk ZB and RNZ. She became Newstalk ZB's chief reporter and has worked for the ABC in Sydney. On her return she taught at the New Zealand Broadcasting School and the University of Canterbury, before returning to Newstalk ZB as chief reporter/newsreader on the day of the first Christchurch earthquake. Since then she has helped lead the station's coverage of the Canterbury earthquakes and the Pike River mining disaster, helping secure Newstalk ZB a New York Radio Award for its coverage of the devastating February earthquake.

Helen Sissons

Helen is a senior lecturer of journalism at AUT University. She spent 17 years as a journalist in the United States and United Kingdom, working in newspapers and broadcasting. For 10 of those years she was a reporter with the BBC. She wrote the textbook *Practical Journalism: How to Write News*. Her research includes the future of journalism.

Dr Catherine Strong

Cathy is a senior lecturer in journalism at Massey University, having previously taught journalism at universities in the Middle East and the United States. She has been an industry journalism trainer at RNZ and TVNZ. Prior to joining academia she worked as a senior journalist for several decades, spanning newspapers, radio, television and online. She completed her Bachelor's Degree at the University of Washington, Master's at Kent State University and Doctorate at Massey University.

Greg Treadwell

A former newspaper journalist, photographer and editor, Greg is now a senior lecturer in journalism at AUT University. He teaches news photography and photojournalism ethics, news reporting, investigative journalism and production journalism. His research centres on the public right to know and freedom-of-information regimes. Greg has a lifelong passion for current affairs and the pictures that portray them, and has had his photos published in a range of community and national newspapers.

Associate Professor Jim Tully

Jim is an adjunct associate professor in the School of Language, Social and Political Sciences at the University of Canterbury, and senior tutor in the School of Communication, Journalism and Marketing at Massey University. He taught journalism at the University of Canterbury for 25 years, after a career in daily newspapers during which he was editorial manager and assistant editor of the *Auckland Star* and editor of the *8 O'Clock* weekend newspaper. Jim was the inaugural New Zealand Journalist of the Year. He received the Print Industry Award for Outstanding Achievement at the national Canon Media Awards in 2011. He is a frequent media commentator.

Fran Tyler

Fran teaches court and police reporting on the Massey University postgraduate journalism course. She worked as a court reporter for more than 10 years at *The Dominion* and *The Dominion Post*. She was also part of a team of investigative reporters at *The Dominion Post*, focusing on crime reporting. She has a Master of Journalism and is completing a PhD on media reporting on crime and justice in New Zealand.

Richard Walker

Richard was features editor at the *Waikato Times*. He now teaches journalism, including feature writing, at the Waikato Institute of Technology (Wintec).

Vicki Wilkinson-Baker

Vicki graduated from Wellington Polytechnic (now Massey University) with a Diploma in Journalism in 1976. She spent 35 years working in Australia and New Zealand as a broadcast journalist. More recently, as a senior reporter with *One News,* she covered the Bain retrial, the 30-year anniversary of the Erebus disaster, the Christchurch earthquakes and the Pike River disaster. She is a tutor at the New Zealand Broadcasting School in Christchurch and works for *Country Calendar*.

Index